Dear Max,

Ever since third grade, you have been loyal to your friends, helping anyone who needed help. Have a great Bar Mitzvah!

—Quinn

Scoring from Second
Writers on Baseball

Edited and
with an
introduction by
Philip F. Deaver

Foreword by Lee K. Abbott

University of Nebraska Press • Lincoln and London

Acknowledgments for the use of previously published material appear on pp. 325–
27, which constitute an extension of the
copyright page. ❡ © 2007 by the Board of
Regents of the University of Nebraska ❡
All rights reserved ❡ Manufactured in the
United States of America ❡ ♾ ❡ Library
of Congress Cataloging-in-Publication
Data ❡ Scoring from second : writers on
baseball / edited and with an introduction by Philip F. Deaver ; foreword by Lee
K. Abbott.
p. cm.
ISBN-13: 978-0-8032-5991-1 (pbk. : alk.
paper)
ISBN-10: 0-8032-5991-3 (pbk. : alk. paper)
1. Baseball—Anecdotes. I. Deaver,
Philip F. GV873.S36 2007
796.357—dc22   2006027687

Set in Minion and American Typewriter.
❡ Designed by R. W. Boeche.

For my sons Mike and Dan, in fond memory of our baseball days

Contents

Foreword

Lee K. Abbott

Following a game, a storybook little old lady confronts Jon Kruk, then the first baseman for the Phillies, outside the stadium. He's smoking a cigarette.

"Shame on you," she scolds. "You're an athlete. You shouldn't be smoking!"

"Ma'am," the notoriously impolitic Kruk begins, "I ain't an athlete. I'm a ballplayer."

A confession: for almost two decades I hated baseball (well, not exactly *hated*, more like *couldn't care less*). The game—in the Bigs, at least—was virtually unrecognizable to me, what with the "errors" that are astronomical salaries, cookie-cutter stadiums, and free agency. Take, for example, the designated hitter rule: it is, frankly, a sin, venial at a minimum. If you're a ballplayer, friends, then pick up the lumber and go to work with the rest of the fellows in sanitaries. And while you're at it, take George Steinbrenner, the Daddy Warbucks of the sport. How the devil are my Cleveland Indians going to compete against a swashbuckler who's got the keys to Fort Knox? And, please, don't get me started on steroids, HGH, Astroturf, indoor baseball, night games, or the ameliorating properties of flaxseed oil.

Indeed, for those two decades, baseball was either boring or plain exasperating. The same teams won. The rich got richer, the poor got old. Owners blackmailed cities for "better" stadiums and tax deals and lease arrangements and zoning and whatever else greased the wheel on the Bentley. Players became loyal only to their wallets. Strikes and lockouts; lockouts and strikes. Fans paid through the keister for seats and eats, never mind the party favors that pass for souvenirs nowadays. Parking was always in another area code. You couldn't smoke, throw a beverage or two, bang the chairs to "Let's GO, RiCo!" or pull off your shirt and write anything more offensive than "Marry me, Sweet Cheeks" in Marksalot between your nipples. TV broadcasts turned into endless, ear-splitting beer commercials interrupted every seven minutes by a pitch or two. Lordy, the umpires got in shape (remember Augie Donatelli?). Girls—comely, lithe, and too damn wholesome for a game that used to have so much spit in it—took up residence on the foul lines. "Take Me Out to the Ballgame" gave way to "We Are the Champions." The season grew longer—snowfall to snowfall almost. Playoffs expanded. Roseanne Barr butchered the National Anthem (attention, would-be singers: if you're not Rocco Scotti, don't bother). The poobahs from the league's politburo banned Charlie Hustle for, golly, gambling. Mascots became the spawn of Satan. And what's with the Spandex that now passes for a uniform? And put down that stovepipe, Bunky, bats are made of wood, period. And, please, ixnay on T-ball. You're supposed to hit the danged thing in motion, for crying out loud.

Maybe, for the decades in question, I was just grumpy, my own days on the diamond long behind me. I'd played Little League, American Legion, AAU, Pony League—a centerfielder with great speed, great glove, and enough prowess at the plate to impress the current girlfriend; after college, I took up the delights unique to fast-pitch softball—still in center field, still looking over my shoulder for the video camera; a few years into my first job as an assistant professor at Case Western Reserve University in Cleveland, I joined the slow-pitch leagues of the Jewish Community Center (gentiles welcome!) in the eastern suburbs—yeah, again in the outfield but with an attenuated attention span. And then, one dark day in Mudville, I was not playing any form of ball anymore. Worse yet, the Indians couldn't beat a drum, much less a club of grown-ups. Joe Charboneau, our one-season wonder, had disappeared into a bar in Buffalo. And, sadly, yours truly was on his way to Columbus to reckon with the nearly professional sports offered by Ohio State University. I had become John Wayne without a desperado to shoot, Gertrude without Heathcliff, Hekyll without Jekyll—just a guy (think: Nixon, semi-blotto), wandering around talking to the walls and weeping at the sight of his Caesar Cedeno memorabilia (baseball cards and bat: when I have a hero to worship, I worship the dickens out of him [or her: see the pine cone stolen from Emily Dickinson's house; see the pillowcase snatched from the clothesline of Eudora Welty]).

But in the last two years, your humble author has found religion afresh, or the nine-inning version of transcendence. I have, in a phrase, been born again, now as obnoxious a nut on the subject as Rummy is on the subject of the army we "don't" have. I owe my newfound faith to two developments: the publication of Moneyball: The Art of Winning an Unfair Game by Michael Lewis in 2003; and the triumph of the Red Sox over the Moloch of Manhattan, the New York Yankees. Both, in brief, have given me belief that the next time mighty Casey hunkers at the plate, he may whack the potato into the cheap seats above the sign for Ford trucks.

The book is two things, really—a biography/profile of Billy Beane, the scrappy general manager of the Oakland Athletics, and a recipe for success in baseball courtesy of sabermetrics, the analysis of the numbers the game itself produces, from the base on balls to the sacrifice bunt, from the stolen base to hitting into the double play. In effect, the book addresses the following question: How can a team with the second lowest payroll in the game challenge for the world championship? The answer is as surprising as it is daring: you find and field a team composed of players that, gulp, nobody else wants—players, it turns out, who produce the sort of numbers no one in old-time management has the patience or the interest to evaluate: the lard butts and putative slug-a-beds, those with supposedly rubber arms and wandering eyes, the coolie toiling well out of the limelight. What, for example, is the value of a player who just doesn't strike out? How do you capitalize on a player who walks? The book is a doozy of a read, stylish and startling, a story of numbers and people that is as compelling a yarn as the first time David sent chin music upside the head of Goliath.

The Red Sox victory, of course, needs no further description. A four-game sweep of the Bronx Bombers was as sweet an angel full of pie. Sure, as I write, the team as we knew it is already busting apart: Pedro "Who's Your Daddy?" Martinez has, alas, gone over to the dark side; Schilling may start next season on the IR; money's tight, the salary cap even tighter. Still, what remains, for the fan, is hope. If the BoSox can do it, maybe my Tribe can. Or any other roster full of folks, like writers themselves, brave enough to believe that cleverness and anonymity can trump washboard abs and gargantuan payrolls. Indeed, I think writers, innocent-minded and always eager for a happy ending (like Jon Kruk, yes?), have been drawn to baseball because it is most like the work they do between the foul lines that are their margins—timeless and ritualistic, unpredictable and balanced, deliberate and heartening, disappointing and impossible.

Acknowledgments

Here's my thanks to John McNally, who needed to pass on this beautiful project that he'd begun so well and recognized a kindred spirit to pass it to. Deepest thanks to Daniel Mark Deaver for pitch-perfect advice, and professional-level assistance in editing and manuscript preparation—it wouldn't have happened without him. Further, many thanks to the poet Paul Freidinger, friend, fellow writer, and, unaccountably, Cub fan, for baseball advice of all sorts. Of course, many thanks to the unlikely gang of literary renegades and baseball playing has-beens and wannabes who appear in this volume, who calmly provided quick turnarounds on the many requests and patiently awaited the day the book would appear.

During the period of assembling this anthology, I received two Critchfield grants from Rollins College as well as the gift of life itself—blue-sky sabbatical leave for the full academic year, 2004–2005. There is no way to thank Rollins adequately.

Finally, here's a toast of gratitude to Ladette Randolph, of the University of Nebraska Press, and her staff.

Dr. Philip F. Deaver with his son of the same name,
outside old Busch Stadium, April 1963.

Introduction

Philip F. Deaver

In 1971, I had a letter to the editor published in *Time*. It was a comment on the military, and I wrote it while I was an E-5 in Europe. I was one of the very few draftees assigned to Germany in the years after the Tet Offensive, let alone before it. I don't know why I was that lucky. Vietnam would have served me right. Anyway, the full-bird colonel I was working for at the time read that *Time* magazine before I did and spotted my letter. He called me into his big fourth-floor corner office in a modern building near in Frankfurt.

"Specialist, is this you?" he said, tossing the magazine across his desk toward me. I was standing at ease, reached for it, and took a look. What an odd sense of pride I had about it, even though I was in trouble. They printed it! I was twenty-four, and had been writing antiwar letters to the editor since the Gulf of Tonkin, but until then my biggest publication was the Champaign-Urbana News Gazette.

"Yes, sir, that's me," I said. There was no denying it. It was signed "SP/5 Philip F. Deaver, U.S. Army, Frankfurt, Germany."

It was a top secret NATO unit. It was a strack operation, elite even, or as elite as things got in that man's army.

The colonel rebuked me for ten or fifteen minutes, defending the army my *Time* letter had attacked. Then we sat down on his long green couch and had a less "top-down" discussion. He was a warhorse from World War II. He knew the army had its problems, but it was his life. He was proud of his service and committed to it. He knew many men who'd given their lives. With regard to the military, there wasn't a questioning bone in his body. Duty. Honor. Country. The pure thing, that's that.

But with respect to Vietnam, history was on my side, and the colonel was hurting from that. He saw my letter as kicking the army while it was down.

Finally, he said to me, "A soldier with this kind of attitude probably doesn't belong here. Exposure like this, inside the covers of a magazine distributed worldwide, well, it's not good. Furthermore, it's an embarrassment, to me. I could have you shipped out to Vietnam tomorrow," he said. "But we need a shortstop on the softball team."

One of the most compelling themes emerging from this collection of essays is baseball's quiet role in the life of people who aren't professional baseball players. Many of the authors here grew up back in the day, back when we had baseball heroes. Many of them had their first initiations into real life playing ball in their hometowns or adopting nearby professional teams and following their story through many seasons. There's at least a chance that baseball saved my life.

In a recent spring on a sunny Friday morning I sat down at a local coffee shop with Davey Johnson himself. After all my years of watching the game (I attended my first professional game in 1957 at the age of eleven), Davey was the first ballplayer I ever sat down and talked to. I'd been anticipating this interview for a year and had the questions written out in front of me—things to be sure to find out. I wanted the inside dope, from the horse's mouth. Or I *thought* I did.

I'm no longer a kid, but I can still muster awe, and though Davey in his comfortable presence doesn't ask awe of you, he does still inspire it. I set aside my notes, and we talked. Someday I'll write at length about that discussion, one of my favorite episodes ever, but here I just want to say that in a season when baseball was on the carpet in front of Congress because of steroids, and the players were mostly multimillionaires who seemed to be in the game for themselves (a fact that seemed always to be mentioned about baseball in particular), Davey Johnson's interest in the game, his love, drive, and expertise (at least in a discussion with some guy who wanted to interview him), were strictly nuts and bolts.

You know who this guy is, right? He broke into the majors on the Orioles in 1965 and had a thirteen-year playing career followed by notable service as a manager of four Major League teams. He earned two Gold Gloves at second for the Orioles, playing up the middle with Mark Belanger most of the time. One year he hit 43 home runs, tied for the record for second basemen with Rogers Hornsby even now, even after Joe Morgan and Roberto Alomar and a number of contemporary designer second sackers. For a time he played in Japan and came to respect the purity of Japan's version of the game. Among the four teams he managed were the 1986 Mets, who won the World Series. If you don't remember that Series, you probably won't own this book.

I asked Davey if he would return to managing. He said no. He said, "Do you realize the toll it can take, to be on the road six months a year with a baseball team, for thirty-eight years?"

And do you know what? I actually *hadn't* realized that until I heard him say it, his throat slightly squeezed and his eyes flashing. Thirty-eight years. "Once you realize what life's like when you aren't traveling like that, it's very hard to go back. Besides," he said, "they've fired me four times." He laughed. "I think they're trying to tell me something."

I asked whom he made lifelong friendships with in the majors, and he said, "In baseball, you make a lot of not very deep friendships because everybody knows everybody could be traded at any time." I recall that wonderful picture of Yogi Berra and Whitey Ford, in business suits, in their late seventies, Yankees forever. No more. Still Davey did mention he'd attended Keith Hernandez's recent wedding and that he occasionally talked on the phone with Dusty Baker, the former manager of the Cubs. The phone still rang now and then, someone testing the waters to see if Davey wanted to return.

I was sitting at a coffee shop table with a man who'd played on the same infield not only with Mark Belanger but Brooks Robinson and Luis Aparicio. I looked at his hands and arms. Davey was a trim, tanned sixty-two years old, six feet tall he seemed to me, and carried himself still with a ballplayer's happy bowlegged strut. I asked him if he still worked out. He did. Six days a week, aerobics and weights. Running didn't work for him anymore—his ballplayer's back would have none of it. I asked if he still had a ball glove. Yes. I wished I could have held it in my hands.

He told me a few stories that he obviously had told before, but they still worked. And they illustrated his view of the game and had the rhythm and pop of parables. In his first year on the Orioles, making the rounds of the league, he finally was standing out at second base in Yankee Stadium.

And Roger Maris came to bat. Maris was toward the end of his career, but he was Maris—Yankee, home run king, and legend. On the second pitch, he hit a ball at Davey so hard that, on one bounce, it was in Davey's glove before the bat was out of the hitter's hands. Davey said, "It was pretty clear to me that Roger was just gonna take a right turn—you know, head for the dugout. I was a rookie, and Maris was king. I stood out there and held the ball, didn't throw it to first until Roger finally realized what was happening and ran. Then I threw him out." Davey's face was bright-eyed telling that story. After a moment, he sheepishly said, "My teammates got all over me for that one. It's probably the worst thing I ever did."

Another story Davey told bespeaks his notion of the purity of baseball. He was sitting in the dugout midseason before some game, fairly early in his career, and Brooks Robinson, a veteran and an all-time great fielding his position at third, was taking grounders. "It happened day after day," Davey told me. "He'd be out there taking hours of infield, grounder after grounder. I said to him, 'Brooks, you've got six Gold Gloves—how come you're out here taking all this infield all the time?' He says to me, 'That's how you *get* six Gold Gloves.'

"Well, Luis Aparicio was playing short, playing out the end of his career on the Orioles after great years with the White Sox. He was this real little guy, but he had a legendary shotgun for an arm. And he was always out at deep short, firing seeds to first base. Always out there before games, throwing, throwing, throwing. So I said to him, 'Luis, everybody knows you've got a fabulous throwing arm. How come you're always out here throwing balls to first?' And he says, 'That's how you have a good arm. You throw a lot!'"

I loved these stories. I loved the honor and straightforwardness of them. Robinson and Aparicio thought in the same nuts and bolts way about the game that Davey did. No talk of destiny (though any fool could feel destiny quaking in the afternoon sun when Robinson laid himself straight out in the air to pick a Major League line drive down the line), no notion of innate talent (though if anyone had it it was Aparicio at shortstop, darting behind third, backhanding it, planting and zipping the ball to first on a wire). This was what we wanted from baseball, that these men carried their beautiful talent respectfully and called it hard work. And that their fellow legendary brothers on the field honored them for it and passed it down. "Well, after that," Davey said, "I started taking a lot of infield, too."

I was playing back the tape of the interview, and noticed something. I could hear in my voice sometimes that I wanted to start telling Davey *my* stories, from back in the day, down on the block, out on the sandlot. About how maybe the game saved my life when I was in the army, about how baseball figured in the short relationship between me and my father, and the very little literary story of me and Wally Moon. About the effect Davey and others in the majors had on me, us, my friends, my generation. There wasn't a way to get into that with him. Davey was not philosophical, he was not nostalgic, he was not—absolutely was not—literary. For him, baseball was not a metaphor and primal pastoral poem, not a nostalgia trip, a field of dreams, no, no, no. It was a game—a boys' game in which you could learn some lessons, a hard, tough, man's game that could break your back and get you fired, a precision game like golf, with sweet spots and perfect timing, time-honored techniques, exacting mechanics, practice, and discipline. "Too many American power hitters swing up," he said, employing the broader perspective of having seen the game played in Japan. "Too many Major League pitchers are just throwers, or lapse into periods when they're just throwing instead of pitching. You throw with your arm. You pitch with your brain."

"Sometimes," he said, "a team calls me in when things aren't right." What Davey means by things not being right is not that someone's home life is breaking down because of all the travel and the concentration is gone, or some young millionaire ballplayer has become an alcoholic or speed freak, or the "chemistry"—the combination of egos and personalities—on an otherwise talented team has gone haywire and taken them into the basement of their division and it isn't even the All-Star break. For him, things not going right is a second baseman not following through on his throw to first; a pitcher losing the groove—elbow too low, curve ball too flat—or he simply can't get the ball across—all velocity and no location—or your number two hitter isn't getting on base and your numbers three, four, and five aren't batting in runs because they're swinging up. Look. The money's insane. There's a war. There's an ozone hole that's grown bigger than the shrinking continent of Antarctica. At first, I thought this was funny, the lack of introspection Davey had about the game and the big, complex, existential morass contemporary players are trying to play it in. But I was wrong. Davey Johnson was pure baseball. It wasn't his job to teach the life lessons and make the metaphor. It was his job to *be* the metaphor by keeping the game pure for the sake of the game and the purity of it, not for the sake of the metaphor, because it is pure unself-conscious baseball that is the metaphor, and when the game gets self-conscious about its glorious literary relevance, poetic beauty, and epic significance, it just becomes more of the crap.

So Davey was the real thing. And I could hear on the tape of the interview my desire to tell him stuff. For some reason, I would like to have shown him, the only ballplayer I've ever had a chance to talk with, the black-and-white picture of me and my dad, in 1963, going to a ball game in St. Louis. That's old Busch Stadium next to us, formerly known as Sportsman's Park, but it was Busch Stadium that day in April 1963. Why did I want to take Davey's time to show this picture to him? I don't know. It was the same urge you get to talk about your struggle with faith when you realize at a party that you're talking to a minister or a priest. The topic has been steeping inside you, the person you are talking to is the essence of it, and you suddenly want to dump your bucket. On the tape I can hear myself trying to do that, and I can hear Davey sort of flatly going, "Uh huh, uh huh." He'd seen that phenomenon before, you can bet. Gently and with a smile, he gave off every signal that we were short on time, his time. He was most cordial, not abrupt about it at all. But just as he was clear he isn't a metaphor, also he's not my frigging confessor! Nod to Jon Kruk in Lee K. Abbott's gritty foreword to this book: he's a *ballplayer.* Dig it.

A few years ago John McNally pulled together an anthology of short stories—fiction—that had baseball as the theme. The stories weren't "about" baseball—instead they were about people, but the writers knew how, for some, baseball lives in people's lives long after they stop dressing for the game. Those writers put baseball in their short stories as an element of authentic reality like you would include a fictionalized version of home, a girlfriend, a parent, your first car. In some ways, in fact, baseball was all those things to us at once, or a metaphor for them.

Many of the writers who were in McNally's anthology are in this one, only this time they are not writing fiction. Their stories are from their real lives, told true, and here you see how the game took its place among the many grounding features of their experience that made them who they are. Cris Mazza, for instance. Here's the perfect Mazza sentence: "When I had only a vague idea what was involved when girls in the restroom spoke of *making out*—but also had no desire to find out—it was consoling to find out there were at least eight ways for a runner to score from third with less than two outs and that, until his Achilles snapped, Dave Campbell could be counted on for any one of them." In her contribution, Cris tells about her life as a virtual San Diego Padre, her fixation on their 1984 season, and how the Padres figured in her life, as heartbreak and as resilience. Floyd Skloot, recovering from an inflammation of the brain that seriously impaired his memory, writes about a small, almost nondescript moment in a ball game many years ago that was one of the odd tableaus in memory that the infection didn't take, amazing and perplexing all at once. What was it about that play?

Of course, I broadly defined "creative nonfiction" for this book. There is some sports writing in here—had to be, per Davey Johnson, per Jon Kruk, to keep our eye on the ball, on the pure game. So we open with Dan O'Neill's straight piece of sports writing, as he lithely gives us a recap of a Cardinal-Cub clash in midsummer. I was at that game, I had an awful lot of fun, and O'Neill's piece was almost as much fun in the *Post-Dispatch* the next day. Whet your appetite for good writing with that one, right out of the paper. The estimable literary editor and baseball writer Louis D. Rubin Jr. addresses head-on the matter of literature and baseball, and collides with the matter of ghostwriters, about as important to the famous ballplayer of the 1920s as sharpened spikes and a good bat. The renowned essayist Hal Crowther is here, too, pinpointing a quiet historical moment that takes place in the stands instead of on the field. Larry Blakely, too, works the stands, in spring training from Tucson, catching a glimpse of a young fan having a religious moment in the fine green grass of center field.

The great story writer Ron Carlson tries to settle an old score to explain a dropped fly ball. Robert Vivian tells of being haunted by the suicide of a fellow player and all the implications that became clearer looking back. The writer and professor Leslie Epstein happens to be not only a famous writer but the father of Theo, the young GM of the world champion Boston Red Sox. Epstein gives us a high-arching and stately essay on us, the members of the crowd, the occupants of the grandstand, attending the game with our full lives in tow. Read Lee Gutkind's backstage look at a crew of National League umpires as they move from one venue to the next. I love this piece; we almost never hear inside tales of the men in blue. And take a look at the piece by story writer Susan Perabo—are you sitting?—in which she tells how it happens that she's in Major League Baseball's Hall of Fame. Yes, we're talking Cooperstown, baby! As a player! Memoirist Jocelyn Bartkevicius also recalls growing up female and athletic and reveals from her life the recurring images of an old catcher's mitt, cancer, and the sky.

The late, great story writer Andre Dubus had a physical man's appreciation for the athleticism of baseball, and many memories from attending games at Fenway—and this is all recalled by him from his wheelchair affording him, we hope, solace and, we are sure, plenty of pain, phantom and otherwise.

Rick Bass recalls a kid named Jimbo, a bully who beat him up regularly. Somehow the kid ended up on Bass's youth baseball team and, one day, "influenced" young Rick to throw strikes. Turns out Jimbo had a flare for instruction. Jeffrey Higa writes about trading baseball cards and how it all came down to Mike Lum and friendship. The award-winning essayist David Carkeet speaks of continuing to play ball as proof of still being alive, which renders quitting sort of ominous. I once attended a Royals spring training game with William Least Heat-Moon so I had to go find that tiny riff on the fastball and TV from his seminal creative nonfiction book *Blue Highways*—oh, it had to be here.

Christopher Buckley has a hard, detailed recollection of baseball in the 1950s, when there were fewer choices but of course "fewer of us." Like Buckley, Luke Salisbury chronicles how life and baseball got all tangled up. Luke ardently remembers a doctor's receptionist named Cissy, and a baseball season that got foreshortened and the Red Sox, symbol of us all that year, lost the pennant by half a game. Richard Jackson surrounds a poem of his with a recollection of his father's baseball lessons. Recent *Atlantic Monthly* prize winner Kyle Minor is here with a story of many generations of fathers, including himself. Earl S. Braggs gives us the creative nonfiction version of Van Dee Zee's "Negroes Walk to Church in Nebraska on Sunday Morning" through the filter of baseball in the days of his growing up. The year the Red Sox finally won, Tim D. Stone's grandfather, who pulled for them for so many years, wasn't there to see. Stone's own son was there, though, to pass it on through the ages.

Lee Martin recalls his father, a man who lost his hands in a farming accident, and imposes his father's own lesson in geometry on the family narrative. You will never forget this story. Try to keep your eyes dry as the essayist Peter Ives tells the story of accompanying his ill son to Yankee Stadium on the generosity of the Make-A-Wish Foundation. And Michael Steinberg, editor of *Fourth Genre*, and a man who seems to be equal parts creative nonfiction writer and ballplayer, contributes his celebrated memoir.

This book seethes with the generation's longing for heroes. Jeffrey Hammond is here with his great reflection recalling one of baseball's classic clowns, Lefty Gomez, who became a model for Hammond's own survival, in the game and out of it. In fact, there is homage here to many professional players all through the years. At last, Rick Campbell gets to air his lifelong fascination with Roberto Clemente, of course all wrapped with his memories of his father and his grandfather and his lifelong dream, still alive, of playing with the big boys. Rachael Perry imprints on the image of Lance Parrish. Kurt Rheinheimer recalls his fixation on Jackie Brandt, the cool Orioles center fielder, by way of revealing his deep knowledge and love of a city and its baseball team.

Mick Cochrane is here, his easygoing statement of his faith in the ham-and-eggers, learned from the Twins in the 1970s and applied with satisfaction in academe. Sure you could be sent back to the minors, but what's so bad about Toledo? And there is the piece by Michael Chabon, his complex and controversial *New York Times* essay on modern heroism in the shape of none other than Jose Canseco.

The novelist Gary Forrester is here with what may be our oddest contribution: a mournful, primitive tone-poem melding religion with a contemplation on the death of St. Louis Cardinal Darryl Kile and a remembrance of the great Jack Buck. Michael Martone tells the story of someone who played baseball in the army in the era of the Korean War—I mean, that was his occupation in the army, baseball. Well, that and bringing meat to the men. What?

In closing, we have, drawn from Tom Stanton's great book *The Final Season*, an excerpt about attending, with his father, the last game ever played in Detroit's Tiger Stadium.

Well, Davey Johnson couldn't be expected to understand that in this picture of my father and me going to a ball game, me age sixteen, my father forty-three, that my father has one year to live. Though we don't know it in this picture, we are having one of our last father-son days together, and perhaps fifteen minutes after the picture was taken, we were in our seats, bumping elbows over the same armrest, drinking our ballpark cokes, watching the visitors take the last of their bp. We were a little beyond third base, almost at field level, and, once the game started, had a real good view of Ken Boyer, number 14, at third. I'm a fiction writer, but I really want to tell that true story over and over to whoever will hear it, so I understand the impulse common to all the writers in this book. Baseball and the last days of my dad are all braided together in a memory wrapped around me, heart and soul. I wanted to tell it to Davey, but he wasn't philosophical or nostalgic, and anyway the interview was about him, not me, and later, after I thought about it, I was okay with it. The pure, basic, green, beautiful game needs to be kept that way, or it doesn't work in memory. The writers in this book have taken baseball with them into the world. Even for those who are wrestling with its current embattled state, its earthy purity well remembered still works—even now, perhaps *particularly* now, when so little seems to work as expected or intended anymore and not much is still pure *except* in memory.

Scoring from Second

1. The Heat Is On for Cards

Dan O'Neill

Two ships, passing in decidedly different directions, met in the middle of downtown St. Louis on Friday to renew a ritual feud now spiced by post-season implications. They passed and—for one evening at least—continued on their present course; the Cardinals delightfully so, the Chicago Cubs destructively so.

With their largest regular season crowd (49,675) since 1997 looking on, the Cardinals clobbered the Cubs 6–1 to open a three-game set at Busch Stadium. The victory stretched the local nine's winning streak to seven, part of a run that vaulted the Birds on the Bat to the best record in the National League.

They began the sultry evening with a 52-32 mark, the fourth-best start in franchise history. Each of the other three starts of 52-32 or better resulted in pennants.

"We can't lose our edge," said manager Tony La Russa, who lost his seat on the bench when he was ejected in the third inning. "And the way to start doing that is to start enjoying the highlights. We still have a lot of work to do."

The sinking North Siders came propelled by the business end of a broom, freshly swept in three games at Miller Field by the Milwaukee Brewers, hard-pressed to remain pennant solvent as the All-Star break approaches. The series in the House That Beer Built will be their last this season. The caramelizing Cubs (46-39) play the Cards two more times in Chicago on July 19–20.

"We're just going through a period right now where it seems like nothing works," Cubs skipper Dusty Baker said. "There's not a whole lot to say. It's kind of like Groundhog Day. It's like the day before and the day before that."

The game featured a pitching rematch between future Hall of Famer

Greg Maddux (7-7) and Cardinals starter Jason Marquis, who won his career-high ninth game against six losses. The meeting was the third between the two former Atlanta Braves teammates. The Cubs won the previous two, with Maddux getting the decision on May 3.

But this time was a charm for Marquis, who scattered nine hits in eight-plus innings, getting thirteen ground outs and two double plays.

"It seems like he was getting a lot of ground balls and in order to do that, you have to keep the ball down," Maddux said. "He's got a good sinker now. He didn't throw that much in Atlanta. I think he throws it every pitch now. That's a good pitch."

Marquis was given a standing ovation as he departed in the top of the ninth, a kind of appreciation he never knew in Dixie.

"Being here, now I can see why everyone wants to come here and everyone wants to play here," Marquis said. "Before coming here, that never happened to me. It makes you want to go out and pitch like that every time out. It makes you feel like you're part of something and part of a city that really cares."

Marquis also enjoyed loud support from an offense that collected four solo home runs to take an 8–7 edge in the season series with the Cubs. Edgar Renteria, who had a marvelous defensive game, landed the first big blow, pounding a 1-2 pitch into the left-field bullpen for his sixth homer and a 1–0 lead in the first. With one out in the top of the second, Derrek Lee matched, hammering a Marquis pitch for his twelfth homer and tying the score 1–1. The run was the first for the Cubs in sixteen innings and only their third in four games.

After leaving a runner on second in the bottom of the second, the Cardinals flashed "tenacious D" to hold the Baby Bears at bay in the third. Mark Grudzielanek began the session with a single. Catcher Yadier Molinathen gunned down Grudzielanek on the back end of a failed hit and run. Moments later, Renteria skirted to his left and threw across his body to retire Rey Ordoñez.

As the Cardinals began their half of the third, emotions that create the college football atmosphere of a Cards-Cubs game spilled over. Home plate umpire Derryl Cousins abruptly ejected La Russa who, apparently, was voicing some displeasure with some previous strike zone arbitration.

After Cousins chased La Russa, the Cardinals chased home a lead run. Tony Womack singled with one out, then scampered to third on a Renteria single. All-Star first baseman Albert Pujols lifted the next pitch to center, collecting Womack and a 2–1 advantage. Renteria stole second in front of Major League RBI leader Scott Rolen, but the All-Star third baseman struck out.

The Cubs bunched together two singles in the fourth, but Marquis dialed a 4-6-3 extension, getting an inning-ending double play. Molina started the Cardinals' fifth with an opposite-field double, nothing coming of it. But the Cardinals broke out the big guns in the sixth. Pujols led off with a rope to left that got out of the park quicker than Mike Tyson ran out of money. The homer was number 22 for Pujols, the RBI his 59th.

One out later, Jim Edmonds launched his 19th homer—his third in as many games—into the left-field pen and the Cardinals led 4–1. Maddux has allowed twenty home runs this season.

"It's nice," said Edmonds, batting .359 (28 for 78) with 20 RBIs and 15 walks in his last 23 starts. "We're playing well and guys are having a good time. We're doing everything we can to win. We just have to keep going."

One inning later, Womack yanked reliever Jon Leicester's offering into the right-field seats, making it 5–1. The homer was Womack's fourth. He has hit in 8 of his last 10 games, batting .368 (14 for 38) in that span. In the eighth, Rolen doubled and stole third as Edmonds knocked in his second run of the night with a single. Marquis left after allowing a lead-off single in the ninth. Julian Tavarez came on to complete the job, sending the Cardinals 21 games over .500 and 7 ahead of the Cubs.

"Our pitching staff is doing a great job, what can you say," Edmonds said. "People were totally blown out of the water in spring training, saying we couldn't even get close because of our pitching . . . and this and that. They've been the main reason why we're where we're at."

2. The Softball Memo
Ron Carlson

September 5
To: *Greg Sellars, left fielder;*
           bats right, throws right. Avg.: .320

From: *Ron Carlson, center fielder;*
           bats right, throws right. Avg.: .278

RE: "Mine!"

In baseball one of the most respected and time-honored traditions is calling the ball. As we all know, in the ninety-degree quadrant demarked by the foul lines, nine and sometimes ten players share the field, each with the shared intention of putting the batting team out of business. Many times this means that two or sometimes three players may have an opportunity to make a play on a single hit ball: for example, the grounder between third and short, the pop fly behind second upon which three players (center field, shortstop, and second base) may have a legitimate claim, or the deep, high drive between any two of the outfielders.

We had a prime opportunity to witness this last example yesterday during game 2 of our tournament at the ragged edge of Mesa, Arizona, when that batter, who we'd seen do it three or four times before, hit again a high, arching drive into deep left field. Wasn't it a shot? Wasn't it the perfect example of the way a ball is supposed to use the sky, riding the apex of the trajectory like a summer holiday and then descending deliciously, reluctantly, in the inexorable arms of gravity again.

We, of course, were earthbound. I know you could see the ball and I was following its route. The temperature was close to 104 in the outfield and there was only a slight wind coming our way. When the batter hit the long fly ball I'm talking about here, and I moved to my right, immediately locating the white dot in the blue sky, I heard something.

I heard you call, "Mine!"

The reason we call the ball in baseball sometimes seems, to the uninitiated, a courtesy, some ritual out of the ancient scrolls of teamwork, developed in the same way all game chatter evolved, for the general good of the team, to help us bond, feel closer in the limited way men can by calling extraneous information back and forth. Just the cry of those male voices, the wisdom tells us, regardless of the words it may carry, soothes us the way dogs are soothed simply by hearing their masters' voices. Some baseball noise may do this, but not calling the ball.

Calling the ball is a notion that came along well before the warning track, that strip of dirt that lets the outfielder know he's running toward a fixed object, in his case the home run fence that is twelve feet away. And calling the ball serves two purposes. The first is safety, so that when two players both pursue the same fly ball, one can call it and the other will back off and not collide with him and generate harm. The bronze annals of baseball are full of the harm, insult, and injury that are the progeny of not calling the ball or ignoring the call. I have one of my most vivid baseball memories from the year I was nine years old and saw two twelve-year-old teammates, Rod Brown, who was catching, and Garn Ray Woodall, who was playing third, go after the same high pop-up foul by the third base dugout, and when they hit each other running full speed they struck mouths. I have never in all the years since that summer afternoon seen more blood at a baseball game. The other purpose of calling the ball is efficiency, so that a player who sees that he can make the play calls it so that the others may back him up and not get tangled in the process of trying for the out. It can make for cleaner baseball and for fewer extended last-minute negotiations about who is going to pull the ball off the fence and make the throw.

Yesterday, as I'm sure you well remember, we all spent a little time on the warning track. I first had occasion to be leaving my cleat marks in that rare space an inning earlier when the same guy who hit the towering fly ball to left field, the one I left in the air a paragraph above, hit one deep to center, a ball I chased with all of my might. Oh, how I wanted that ball. On the way back toward the fence that time, I thought, you're going to hit the fence, and then I had this exhilarating thought: good, hit the fence, just make the catch. I missed by the width of a glove and had to grovel in the dirt for the ball and throw, still giving the guy third.

That hurt. My tracks there in that moist gravel seemed like the definition of mistake, like some golfer who hasn't raked his fuckup out of a sand trap.

So I was geared up and ready when this guy came to bat again. I was saying my little saying to myself as the pitch went in—and my little saying is simply a kind of insistent chant that urges whoever is up to hit the ball to me, near me, somewhere I can be involved in running or diving after it, getting it and throwing it in. *Hit it to me* is a fair paraphrase, and when that batter swung I thought he had complied.

But.

The ball rose in the hot air, almost disappearing in the midday sky bleached to a blue that is only seen in the eyes of dogs that could kill a man in a minute and the only reason they don't is that nobody they've met is worth the effort.

Then the ball started down. I had already heard you call it.

I started running toward it.

I heard you call it again. "Mine!" you said. I heard that and everyone heard that and even some of the quivering raccoons, consumed by disease and racked by fever, about to be exterminated at the Rabies Control Center a half mile west of our field, heard you say it: "Mine!"

At this point I should have taken my eyes off the ball and watched you. I should have pulled up short, instructed by your call, in case I might have to play my role as backup. But I didn't. I kept the ball right in sight. It fell, a fat white pill toward us. And then a strange thing happened, something that determined my fate. Having heard your call and made none of my own, having heard your call and still keeping my eye on the ball, which by now was a huge thing, a pillow, a sofa falling from space, I locked onto it. I got it on my screen and only your sudden foot on my neck (which I wish to God I had felt as you kicked me to my senses) could have dislodged it. Goddamn it, regardless of the calls and the protocol and common sense and safety and efficiency and the brotherhood of the outfield,

I had the fattest pig of a fly ball on my radar screen and I could not play any role in this drama but first through the door. I saw the ball drop and become full size, its stitching and the blurred printing of the label as it socked into my mitt at the very same millisecond I felt your glove at my forearm. I saw the ball rise again from the leather of my mitt as I turned in the sunlight, which forever now will be slow motion sunlight, and I had one last grab for it, and I touched it again, badly, and it fell to the warning track and that dirt. I do not remember who, you or I, made the throw. It was all over. Two runs had scored and though we would lose by three in ten minutes, everyone knew what play defeated us.

I heard an infielder call, "We all heard Greg call it." And what he meant was, though he'd tried to be oblique, "How in the hell did you get your head up your ass so far that you can't hear something the rest of us heard perfectly?"

And I had no answer; and I have none now.

I heard you call it. I heard each "Mine!" with more clarity than I'd heard anything else that day. And, oh, at this distance, would it were so. I wish it were yours. I wish you'd stepped up, fended me off with a foot or a knee or a straight-arm (a remark would not have done the job), and you would have made it yours.

But. Some atavistic thing in me, some hope to catch that fly, led me to the largest error of the day. And here's the irony. I didn't say a thing. I didn't say, "Mine!" or "I got it!" But now I do. I got it. Believe me. And it is mine. It is mine forever more. I have the sun frozen where it was and the ball wheeling down forever, the contact with my glove forever mine, and the next missed hop, eternally mine. A fly ball on a sunny day. Mine, mine, mine.

3. Reaching Home
Susan Perabo

The afternoon my parents phoned to tell me that I was in the Hall of Fame, my immediate reaction was that any good tidings that might come my way in life from that moment on would simply be gravy. *The Hall of Fame*. There had been no voting of course, no emotional induction ceremony. There is no weathered uniform or bruised home run ball on display. In my life I have played somewhere in the neighborhood of twenty innings of organized baseball, less than most American boys have played by the age of nine, but enough to warrant a plaque at Cooperstown that reads, in part,

> *The 1980's saw women make the rosters and, eventually, the starting lineups of men's college baseball teams. In 1987, Susan Perabo appeared at second base in a handful of games for Webster University, an NCAA Division III School in St. Louis.*

Baseball in America has always been a family affair, passed from generation to generation like a treasured heirloom. Logic tells us, therefore, that as many girls must be "born into" baseball as boys. In many cases, of course, society interferes early on, embracing boys in the brotherhood of the sport and steering girls in other (and often equally worthy) directions. But we all know women who—for a variety of reasons—cannot ignore their baseball heritage, women who live and die on certain pitches with the same intensity as do men. I am one such woman, born with a seemingly genetic disposition for the game. My great-grandfather Hernan saw the first World Series, played in Boston in 1903. As a child I poured over his hundreds of scorecards—mostly Cardinals, some Browns, a few others—dating from the 1910s through the 1950s, every at bat on every scorecard documented with meticulous detail. As a teenager in the 1920s, my grandfather lived down the street from Rogers Hornsby, who roomed in a modest apartment on Louisiana Avenue in St. Louis. On the other side of my family is my great-grandfather Broeder, who, stone deaf to conversation and well into his nineties, would wait through winters for the chance to sit on his sun porch, a cruddy transistor radio in a leather case pressed to his ear, and the joy of another spring with his beloved Cardinals. In 1963, when he was younger than I am now, my father was at Sportsman's Park to see Stan Musial's final game. Indeed, the Cardinals were more than baseball history to me; they were family history.

For most of my childhood it never occurred to me that I would not grow up to be a Major League baseball player. My family connection was part of it, but equally important was the fact that I grew up on a block with several boys my age. I had little interest in Barbie or ballet. Instead, with my friends, on our quiet suburban street, I learned to turn flawless double plays, to wait on pitches, and to hit to the opposite "field" (the Brands' front yard for us righties). My buddies and I perfected the intricacies of hotbox and tossed balls to each other behind our backs like in the "Gas House Gang" videos we had seen at Busch Stadium. We took turns mimicking Dave Parker's perfect throw from right field in the 1979 All Star Game: right field was the O'Neils' driveway; home plate was the front yard of my best friend, Alec Bolton, three houses down. Alec's and my favorite game was to throw each other "divers" into the Kims' yard— balls tossed just enough out of reach that they couldn't possibly be caught without getting a stained shirt and skinned knees in the process. At night, getting ready for bed, I would stand before the bathroom mirror, wiggling my hips, narrowing my eyes, and wagging an imaginary bat in my hands, waiting for the full-count pitch that each night I rocketed into the bleachers to win the World Series. I shared that evening ritual, I know now, with a handful of girls as well as a million boys. It is the truest gift of youth: the unwavering assurance that such a day is inevitable.

When I finally played organized ball, though, it was not baseball. My parents were (and are) wise people; they knew I would have rather been playing hardball, but they also knew the circus it could become were I to try to break into the boys' league, especially at the tender age of ten. And so I played softball. In the early years the other girls in the league seemed perplexed by my habits: first base gardening, a quick spit in the glove when my mother wasn't looking, the tap of the bat against my sneakers before I stepped up to the plate. Eventually, in the less forgiving years of junior high, teammates and opposition alike rolled their eyes when I slammed against the dugout fence going for a pop foul or went in hard at second to break up the double play. These girls didn't know from hotbox, didn't know when to bunt, didn't know to shift the field for a lefty. They didn't understand—and how could they?—that softball was serious business for me, because they didn't realize that I was always headed toward a loftier goal, a greater end. My turn would come eventually, I knew, and I would get the chance to be a Cardinal or a Yankee, like my hero Lou Gehrig.

Around high school, real life caught up with me. At fourteen, I had discovered the danger and sadness of dreams. My grand plan of World Series heroics disintegrated under the harsh scrutiny of adolescence. I remained a loyal Cardinal fan and occasionally played catch with Alec or my father, but I squashed the image I had for so long and so fervently carried: me, emerging from the dark tunnel into the dugout, up the steps onto the turf, the lights in my eyes and the crowd in my ears as I strode to the plate with the game, the season—everything—on the line.

There was no softball team at Webster University, a small liberal arts college in suburban St. Louis I began attending when I was seventeen. Had there been, chances are pretty good I would never have made it to the Hall of Fame. One evening in February I saw a flyer tacked up in the dorms announcing an organizational meeting of the baseball team the following Friday. For the remainder of the week I was perpetually distracted. When I ate that week I tasted how much I wanted to play; when I listened to music I heard how much I wanted to play; everything I laid eyes on told me: *I just wanted to play.* The very possibility made the world seem ripe.

I walked into the organizational meeting on that Friday afternoon and began my baseball career. I was nervous, more than a little embarrassed; my main goal at that point (and throughout the season) was to not cause anyone on the team discomfort. I was not looking for controversy, just the opposite. I sat through the meeting, weathered the curious stares, and afterward spoke to the coach. I told him that if he didn't feel right about having me on the team I wouldn't play, and I meant it. But my coach—Karl Karlskint—was a good man; if he did have misgivings, he did not have the heart to admit it.

And so I became a member of the Webster University Gorloks men's baseball team. The Webster sports program was in its infancy, having become a Division III program just two years earlier. The year I played marked the first year of varsity baseball at Webster; previously it had been a club sport. Tryouts were not necessary; fourteen guys and one girl went to the meeting, and fourteen guys and one girl made the squad.

There was little question that my position would be second base. I had a good arm, for a girl, but a poor arm when compared to the rest of the team. Many women find such statements demeaning and offensive; those who know the game recognize them as reality. There is no shame in admitting that a bullet throw from deep short is the exception for women and not for men. I had the quick hands and feet of a second baseman, and I felt confident that I could field anything hit my way. I also had a good eye at the plate. From the beginning no one—least of all me— had any illusions that I was going to be knocking the ball over the heads of outfielders. But when taking my swings in practice I was fairly adept at stroking a fastball up the middle or dropping a looper over second or short. In scrimmages, I did not have the speed to turn singles into doubles, but I possessed enough arrogance ("balls" the guys would say with a wink) and joy to take advantage of a botched or lazy play.

There is something to be said about playing the game of your heroes. I have come to realize that this—perhaps more than anything else—is what always separated baseball and softball for me, and perhaps what separates it for many other "baseball women." There are other things in favor of baseball—for one, when playing softball I always feel like I'm catching a volleyball in my glove—but I think what made me want so much to play baseball was the connection I felt to the athletes I had always admired, as well as the connection I felt to my father and grandfather and great-grandfather who, although not players themselves, were essential members, in my book, in the brother- and sisterhood of the sport. Baseball is about history, more so than any other game in this country. I respect the women who play serious softball now—the Olympic team is a fine example—women who want to give that sport a history for young women who are just now beginning to play. But I always had that connection with baseball only.

And so, the spring afternoon I was given my first baseball uniform—number 4, Lou Gehrig's number—marked a monumental day for me. After practice I went to my parents' home and put on the uniform, and I stood in front of a mirror I had stood in front of in softball uniforms hundreds of times before. This time it was different; this time *I* was different. And that night, back at the dorm, I hung the uniform on the curtain rod above my bed so that when I woke in the middle of the night, afraid that it was all a dream, I would see it there—the gold and the blue and the number 4—and know that it was real, and that I had to appreciate the chance I had been given.

Later in the season I came face-to-face with my great opportunity. It happened when we were warming up before a game on an away field that sat on the top of a hill. It was a beautiful field, the closest thing to a professional ball field I had ever been on, and as I was warming up I looked down the hill and saw several girls playing softball on a small, unkempt field. I promised myself at that moment that no matter what happened in the season, or in my life, that I would always remember that on a sunny day I had stood on the field of my heroes.

I didn't play in the first several games of the season. I was neither surprised by nor resentful of this fact. Was I good enough to be on the team? Yes, I believed I was. But I also knew that I was certainly no starter. I was perhaps the most amenable benchwarmer ever, happy to have a quick catch with whoever was about to go in, happy to offer encouragement at all times and observation when appropriate.

My first appearance came in the field. Karl put me in to play the last two innings in a game we were leading by a comfortable margin. It was an away game, and I was not surprised to hear a few chuckles from the opposing bench and few fans when I took my position. At some point in the game I made a routine play. I believe I also took a cutoff throw from the outfield. No trumpets blew; no confetti fell from the sky. It was just the way I wanted it. I had contributed, in some small way. And when the game was over I put my gear in a bag like everybody else and went home.

My first at bat was slightly more dramatic. It, too, came at an away game (because of our newness as a program, we had limited home games, just a couple at the field of Webster's junior high school). I was enjoying my role as benchwarmer when Karl barked at me to get on deck. I suspect he thought that the less time I had to think about the at bat the better, but as soon as I picked up my bat and left the dugout whoever was at the plate grounded out and suddenly I was walking to the box putting on my helmet and batting glove and feeling in no small daze. I stepped up to the plate, just a shade more conscious than a sleepwalker.

I don't remember the first two pitches. I'm not sure I even saw them. But they both were called strikes and finally I snapped out of my daze and came to my senses. I called time and stepped out of the box. I reminded myself that I had been waiting approximately eighteen years for this moment and that if I didn't at least take the bat off my shoulder then I should forever be ashamed. So I stepped back in and when the pitch came I swung.

I don't think I ever saw that one either. But when the ump called me out I walked happily back to the dugout, realizing that all my dreams of belting one to the fence in my first at bat had been pure fantasy, that, in fact, striking out was probably the only possibility there had ever been for my first at bat.

As I set down my bat I realized people were cheering. I turned back to the field and saw that a group of young women, fans of our opposition, were on their feet behind the home team's bench, hooting and clapping wildly. I appreciated it. But more than anything, I was just glad I had swung the bat.

I couldn't stay hidden forever. Midway through the season I got calls from a suburban newspaper and the *St. Louis Post-Dispatch*. They wanted stories, pictures. I told them I didn't feel comfortable giving an interview. They kept phoning. They called the Webster Sports Information Office and said I was being "difficult." Finally, one day after practice, I talked to my teammates about it. I told the guys that I did not want to be the focus of the team. We were having a surprisingly strong inaugural season, and I did not want to take the spotlight off the players who were actually contributing. I worried that the team would become a local joke, known only as "that team with the girl." For myself, and for them, I had no interest in being a sideshow.

After I finished my little speech the dugout was quiet. Then, almost in unison, they all said, "Do it." They convinced me it would be good exposure for the team, good for the program. It may have been this same day that, following our media discussion, somebody complained that he couldn't get the stains out of his uniform and needed some laundry advice. Karl thought about this a second and then turned to me. "Maybe Sue has some suggestions," he said. It was times like these that I felt completely part of the team.

It was a strange assortment of guys, linked together only by their passion for baseball. Division III sports is a unique animal, made up of athletes who, rather than receiving incentives to play college sports, have to give things up to play and who by their very nature play for joy. What better reason could there be? The guys on the team came from a variety of backgrounds and experience. They all had different interests and, off the field, had little in common. But on the field they clicked. They all played together, and I learned a lot about baseball watching them—hours and hours of benchwarming gave me the best view possible of this.

We also had fun. A week or so after I had given an interview to the *St. Louis Post-Dispatch*, a photographer showed up in the early innings of one of our home games. He came to the back of the dugout and shouted in to me that he wanted to take my picture. He wanted me to come out of the dugout and pose against the backstop while the game was going on. It was exactly what I had feared: I had become the focus; the team on the field was going to simply be my backdrop. I told him that he would have to wait. I told him that I was a member of the team and my place during the game was in the dugout and not outside posing for pictures. He was irritated, kept badgering me. He had places to be—I understood this— and he didn't have the time to sit through most of a game to wait for me. Finally the photographer gave up and decided he would have to take my picture through the dugout fence. I tried to look as unphotogenic as possible. I was chewing a wad of gum and the photographer said he wanted to get a shot of me blowing a bubble. So I'd blow a bubble and then pop it really fast before he could take the picture.

I paid for this foolishness in the end. The picture that appeared of me in the *Post* the following week was out of focus and the position of my mouth, thanks to the popping bubble, makes me look rather like something from a horror flick. I felt humiliated and a little bit sorry I had not composed myself for a flattering shot.

We had few fans, but we had more fans than the rest of the team knew about. Unbeknownst to my teammates, my parents were following the season with more than a passing interest. Across the street from our home field at Webster High was a church parking lot. During our few home games, the lot was empty save for one car, my mother's. She did not want to embarrass me by coming down to the field and sitting alone in the rickety bleachers—nobody else's parents *ever* came—but she sat up there in the parking lot and watched every inning of every game, regardless of the fact that I almost never played.

The last day of the season, the day I had my first and only start, my father took the afternoon off from work and he and my mother both sat in that car and watched what turned out to be the final game of my baseball career. Later that day my father admitted it had been difficult to remain in the car. One inning I made my best play of the season, fielding a bullet of a ground ball with a backhand stab and easily getting the runner at first. When I made that play, my father said, it was all he could do not to run down onto the field and hug me.

I ended the season with a fielding percentage of 1.000 and a batting average of .000. My final at bat came on that last day of the season. In the late innings I got a sweet pitch, a fastball right over the heart of the plate, and I nailed it. I knew from the feel that it was going hard up the middle, that I would finally have my hit. But in an instant it was over. The opposing pitcher twisted out of the ball's path and flung up his glove; when I heard the thwack of leather on leather my heart sank. I don't think I even had time to drop the bat.

That day marked the end of my baseball career. I played some fall ball the following season, but the team that year was more competitive and I knew in my heart that I was not good enough. So, with some friends, I began a women's softball team, and we competed that year on the club level. And inevitably it happened that one day in April I played softball on that dilapidated field I had looked upon the year before, the one at the bottom of the hill. I would be lying if I said I did not look up several times during the game to the baseball field above me and feel a great sadness.

It took me a long time to get over playing baseball. For several years I dwelt on that pitcher who snagged the hit away from me, and I questioned whether or not I should have tried harder to play another season, whether or not something wonderful could have happened, something could have *clicked*, and maybe I really could have been great. I know there are hundreds of thousands of men in this country who have wondered the same thing, who have waited for that same day. I tortured myself with thoughts of what might have been. I had given up my dream, one more time. Was it really the end?

Well, it was and it wasn't. It was in the sense that I have never played organized baseball since, and I never will again. But baseball is too big to ignore, and of course so is family. A few years ago my father signed the two of us up to be "batboys" of sorts for a Field of Dreams charity event at Busch Stadium. The game pitted local celebrities and a few former ballplayers against some St. Louis businessmen. My dad and I got to sit in the Cardinal dugout and swing bats on the field before the game. At one point during the game I got to run out on the field and hand the warm-up ball to the first base coach: Terry Moore, the great Cardinal outfielder from the 1930s and 1940s. Terry Moore was about eighty years old, and when I held out the ball to him he simply nodded at me. He didn't say, "Thanks, honey" or wink or smile or do anything but nod. It was a ball game, after all. "Here you go, Mr. Moore," I said, and I put the ball in his hand, and I looked up into the lights.

I remain, of course, a die-hard Cardinal fan. And I still go to the batting cages, especially in the spring, and rare is the occasion that some bystander—always a guy—does not shake his head when I walk into one of the "fast baseball" cages, thinking that I have made some mistake. And rare also is the occasion that I can risk sneaking a peak at that guy after hitting most of the pitches. I even still sometimes throw myself "divers" off the back of my house, although now they are the kinder "stretchers"; instead of giving me a dirty shirt, they give me aching stomach muscles.

It's been many years now since my season as a Gorlok, and I'm glad to say that it's not the almost-hit I remember most anymore, nor is it dreams of the illusive might-have-been. It's not a particular game or a particular play, and it is certainly not the label of "pioneer" that some have tried to pin on me. Ultimately, the image that remains most burned in my mind from my short career in baseball comes from the day the reporter from the *Post* interviewed me after a practice at Larson Park. Jim Costello, our first baseman, third baseman Pete Lang, and Coach Karl hung around while I talked to the reporter, and when the interview was over and the reporter had gone, we decided to shag some flies in the waning light of the afternoon. I don't know whose idea it was; Karl just picked up a bat and the three of us ran on out into the outfield grass. There was a little bit of sun left in the sky and we had nowhere better to be. The thing is— the thing I see so clearly now—was that on that cool evening there simply was nowhere better to be, nowhere better than a baseball field, shagging flies in the outfield with my teammates, my friends and I playing simply for the love of it.

When I think of the Hall of Fame, I think of that day.

4. Death of a Shortstop
Robert Vivian

When I heard about the shortstop, an ex-teammate, I saw the gruesome end unfold before me: not the blast itself or the leak of a sob or whimper coming from the car, but the dust creeping after him on a lonely country road where he stopped and took the handgun from the floor. I can see the dust drifting over the car and the back of his head before he angles the gun awkwardly into his mouth and his skull becomes a mist of blood, bone, and brain. The dust must have been everywhere around him then, closing in like a fist without a hand. When I read about him in the paper, I could almost feel the dust following my eyes down the ink of the page like an invisible scroll, and then I was troubled about the purpose of a life gone wrong. We called him Wob, and he had been nice to me, a transfer from Northeastern Oklahoma Junior College, an underclassman, one who was already losing interest in the game, which I would later come to think of as my own peculiar brand of betrayal against my father. Wob alone made me feel welcome.

There was the dust of the infield at Buck Beltzer Stadium at the University of Nebraska where we played and practiced, before I gave up my scholarship as a center fielder; and Wob, prematurely balding, light on his feet at short like a tap dancer, his accountant's spectacles belying his ability to go deep inside the hole, snatch a hard grounder backhanded, pivot and throw a heartbreaking arc back across his body to nip the runner at first. He knew that infield dirt and the ways a ball could come off it as if he had grown up on it all of his life, as of course he had; we all had, in one way or another. It was a kind of birthright for anyone who played the game. That American dust, that heroic and mysterious dirt that stays with you all the days of your life in dragged infields, at least enough to tell someone *I played once and almost made it into the pros.* You go back again and again to those days in summer when your whole life seemed to loom up before you in verdant promise and grandeur.

Who knew then that death's emissaries were already gathering around as Wob swept his toe in the dirt before settling in to his crouch to wait for the next pitch? The day I decided to hang it up for good, I noticed from the left-field fence a sputtering four-seater a few hundred feet off the ground, fading away to the north. Later I learned it crashed and everyone aboard was killed. Was I among the last to see it go? Did they notice me shagging fly balls? Did they wave to anyone, gesture to me, curse their failing instruments, or plead once and forever into the radio? How irrelevant were we to those four passengers falling out of the sky? I stood in the outfield and decided to give up the meal ticket that had gotten me into college in the first place, giving up on my dad's tacit hopes for me to play the game he loved so much at another level. From my vantage point, nothing could have been more peaceful or final in the world: a coasting plane, catching a few last fly balls, realizing I had finally broken away to begin my life in a new direction. I never did see the plane go down, but I saw the black purling smoke lifting to the sky miles away.

But I can still see my dad standing at the fence behind third base, with his sunglasses and cool demeanor; he never missed a game unless he was out of town, and he took in everything with those dark glasses, like a town sheriff whose authority was never questioned, never missing a play or a pitch or an umpire's call. Sometimes he'd call me over between innings, telling me how to play someone: "He pulls everything," or "You're playing too deep for the number five hitter." I'd nod and sprint out to my position in center field. I could turn it on just for him, believe in my heart I could run down any fly ball or cut off any line drive, that the gaps were mine, and that any runner foolish enough to try it would be thrown out at third. I played recklessly, especially if he was there, running into fences and giving up my body. I didn't want him to ever say, "You were dogging it out there." On the few occasions he wasn't around, I just didn't have the same kind of energy and sometimes even wished for rainouts; the game only seemed crucial if he was watching. I could almost hear him speaking through me, talking position and strategy.

I had a quintessential American boy's life in the Midwest, probably like Wob, playing sports all year and goofing off with my friends during the long summer nights. We used to go to tryout camps together, just my dad and me, check into a hotel in Kansas City, and the next day I'd run, field, hit, and throw against other promising kids from all over the Midwest who made the cut in Omaha or Des Moines. I got butterflies in my stomach and couldn't sleep the night before as I listened to the hotel AC rattle and hum until morning, going over in my mind how I'd fare against the competition. My entire identity was wrapped up in running faster than some other kid, or throwing out a runner if he tried to reach for extra bases.

One summer I ran a good time in the sixty and a scout came up to talk to me about signing in the rookie league for the Royals if they had an opening for an outfielder, so here was my chance to play pro ball. I could tell how excited my dad was, even though he is always careful not to show too much emotion. It seemed like a chance for both of us somehow, something we could live out together, the same dazzling dream. But I knew even then it was mostly his vision, and whatever grains I had to offer toward it were already trickling out, my heart and desire beginning to wane at seventeen. My dad talked to me about switch-hitting, or maybe moving to second, because you don't see many 5´8″ center fielders in the Major Leagues; he said this might be a good opportunity, but offers down the road were bound to come if I just worked hard enough and got tougher mentally. But they never did because I quit two years later. I didn't have the killer's instinct, a fatal weakness. I saw it in Wob, too, a gentle soul who loved the game but who never played with that streak of special meanness any sport requires in order to be the very best.

My dad and I drove around Kansas City, talking about the possibilities; Florida was a world away, and looking back now there was no way I could have left my home and future wife to play somewhere in the sticks. I just didn't love it enough, which would become my secret heresy. I loved the love my dad had for my playing, the palpable and sweaty urgency of it, but maybe that's all I really cared about, what we shared together when the game ended. He didn't push me like other dads, but his love for sports quietly pervaded everything our family did and believed until few alternatives had room to grow, let alone be mentioned: competition was the mantra of his life, the reason he could leave his working-class roots on the poor side of a paper mill town in Michigan and make a better life for himself and his family, the one constant, abiding value we ate with our bread each night. There were only winners and losers, the strong and the weak, nothing in between, no mitigating shades of gray. I felt inarticulate and dumb in the face of my own accelerating trajectory, not just at home but everywhere I went because I believed somehow without actually experiencing it firsthand that there were other points of view outside the world of sports and competition, other kinds of values and people whose mere existence would cause a quickening in my blood and later change me, even if I had not yet met them.

What sports gave us more than anything (what it gives us still) is a common language hewn out of the efforts of athletes' bodies and our own on a playing field in the near or long ago, with its own built-in, unshakable grammar, and subjects never veering too far from crude hard arithmetic (the W-L column, who made or didn't make the final shot). With language as simple yet as poetic as this, we could swap souls, move in each other's skin, embellish if we had to, make vivid once again an instance in time when a decision seemed to *matter* even if it was just a game, to define by its very outcome the character of a player and thus, by extension, of ourselves. To never give up, to be honest, to play through pain—what other verities could a man or woman possibly need? And they were all right there, codified by our own experiences and those of an entire nation. We could be passionate without dropping our guard, walking and talking the fine edge between real communication and shooting the shit. But often I have felt the beginning of tears well up in my eyes for no reason when we're talking about the Final Four, or a hitting streak, or the phantom hook of the Ali-Liston fight, and have wondered why.

So often though, even as a kid, I suspected a terrible inadequacy; sometimes I wanted to say, "Some things aren't a game," but I knew enough to keep my mouth shut. I would risk alienation or, worse, bafflement and incomprehension, things I myself didn't understand. Instead I clung to some deep interior limb growing all the time and saw my inchoate belief confirmed everywhere I looked: my father was right, the world is indeed divided between the winners and the losers, but the winning and the losing often happens with a randomness that has little to do with talent or volition. More onerous still was the gnawing notion that it did not necessarily have anything to do with drive or the competitive spirit but blind pig luck, a graze of a ghostly fingertip that could set a life to spiraling or ascending. The game was rigged—or so complex and mysterious it amounted to the same thing. In fact, in the ways that truly mattered, how people really lived their whole lives, winning and losing had nothing to do with it: there was only a deepening context enfolded into incomprehensibility, tendons and tissues so fine you could almost hear them tearing into something else.

I sensed this as the deepest reality I knew, but I didn't have the words. Some kids were crippled at school, and most were not; a girl from Turkey was perpetually picked on because of her scimitar nose, and two huge black boys named Miles and Andre were beloved because they were the tokens of their race in a Catholic school where almost everyone was white and everyone wore uniforms. My older brother Bill's head found the hard, unforgiving surfaces of concrete and stone and other boys' fists until concussions became like a woozy friend to him, seven, eight, nine times—who knows how many—as he would say wiping his bloody nose obsessively like a pint-size drunk, "Don't tell Mom, don't tell Mom." I crawled under some bushes one summer to watch a neighbor clean his pistol on his back porch when he pointed the glistening barrel at me, smiled, and pulled the trigger on an empty chamber. I made haste backward on my shirt front, scuttling out of there. I heard the locusts scream from the top of our house at sundown one hot evening when I was nine and believed it was the end of the world—and it was the end of the world, as it always is the end of the world at such twilit hours when you dread the same sleep that will help you forget the immutable fact of all endings. These ambiguities bled into me like a slow-spreading dye until my blood seethed in it, coursing down the strangely lit corridors of experience to the warping and shifting of shapes: at some point unknown to me I passed an invisible divide and came out the other side, troubled and surprised at the complexity of the world and my own inability to control or predict it. The often crude dichotomy of sports sometimes does not allow room for such ambiguity, and maybe that is why so many love and need them, including me; but they rarely are able to reflect what goes on around and inside us, the mysteries of living and dying that break out of the void like waves, granting dispensation here, catastrophe somewhere else: but where the pattern is, no one can say for sure. There really wasn't anything else to compare this gut feeling to, but I couldn't compare it to sports.

My decision to quit baseball suddenly, inexplicably, for reasons I still do not completely know, continues to haunt me, like the dust I see rising from so many American roads. My dad supported me in my decision, but something quietly died between us, some unspoken and common ground of understanding that we lived out and played. We lived our connection during long innings and doubleheaders, a father-son telepathy running a one-way circuit from his heartbeat to mine: it was a privileged rite of passage, and I turned away from it. For some, it is not a passage at all but a place to live, a destination clearly marked. Go there, it seems to promise, and you never have to grow up. My father and I have never been closer than during that postgame drive, I in my muddy uniform, he commenting with calm and easy sagacity how the game could have gone, or how it did go, or how it could go in the future: "You need to get your hands away from your body a little more at the plate." I miss those Zen-like instructions and the way we shared so much that was coded into our very genes. He was one of the best teachers I ever had, and he knew just what to say, how to praise and instruct at the same time. I lived for his praise, and for the praise of my coaches, for any man older than I who could take the measure of myself and hold it up to me.

I wonder if Wob ever felt that; I wonder if he, like my own father, loved the game so much in his own quiet way that nothing else could measure up; I wonder if part of his suicide had something to do with the loss of playing baseball, of the myriad rituals and easy camaraderie associated with it, if life after it just got to be too monotonous or too real. I don't know, and speculations about the dead simplify and muddle the context of their passing. But I know Wob loved baseball very much, maybe too much for all his meekness, and maybe that would have been reason enough to want to live, if only he could have kept playing. The way he cleaned his spikes with a special screwdriver seemed evidence enough. But he had a faraway look in his eyes even then, looking away toward

some bleak horizon only he could see. Or am I guilty of seeing in retro-
spect small glimpses of his own murderer?

Why did you do it, Wob?
Why did you pull the trigger?

If I could talk to you again, I would ask you about baseball. I would
ask you what you loved about it, if you thought maybe, just maybe,
you could play at the next level. I would ask you in a roundabout way
(neither of us would have a thing to lose) why you sought out the small
pebbles of your home at short, why you inspected them like a fastidious
gardener, collecting them, then casting them away with your glove. I
would ask you about the American Dream and where it began to fail you
and those fireflies that lit up the trees near the train tracks behind left
field, the loud speaker blaring Eric Clapton, the long-legged and heart-
stopping girls who shaded their eyes from the sun. I'd ask you about your
favorite part of the season, and tell you about a second baseman in high
school whose name was Tommy Brown, killed on graduation night by a
drunk driver, his body torn in half. We would converse of dusty things,
Bruce, maybe even pick up a handful of it somewhere. Bye and bye we
might get to the subject of your death, but it would not be the point, just
a bright white marker somewhere down the road. We might even go out
for a beer, though I know neither of us drinks beer. I would try to tell
you why I quit playing ball, how your kindness meant so much to me
at the time, and how you were the one on that new and final team who
seemed truly decent to me, even noble in a way. We would have all the
time in the world to talk about these things, Bruce, and you wouldn't
have to feel alone.

But the death of a shortstop, especially a suicide, is an event far out on
the edge of the American psyche, so strange and almost shameful that I
do not think most people would want to dwell on it; it's a betrayal even
greater than mine, Bruce, I who turned my back on competitive sports
when it was all laid out before me. I need to tell you that, Wob: you need
to know how few of us can understand that kind of fear and despair,
including me. It's like that plane going down; the story hits the paper,
but no one has a clue about what it means. We were spiritual cousins the

moment I quit and disappointed my dad and the moment you decided to end your life; we are tied at the same gnawing root, only I had the blessing to see other roots, other possibilities.

I think I know what winning and losing is now because of your haunting infield memory; I think they are one and the same, a brief veil lifting, the ancient and irretrievable song that sings only of the now before us, and the promise that sometime, somewhere, in some other faraway place, the losers and the quitters will lift the winners from their graves.

5. Opening Ceremonies

Kyle Minor

An astronaut, Buzz Aldrin, the second man on the moon, stood on the pitcher's mound. He gave a speech—I don't remember the details—but I imagine there was talk of Saturn V rockets, and lunar orbiters, and landing modules, and one small step for man. Moon rocks, moondust, craters, scant gravity. Or maybe he wasn't Buzz Aldrin at all. Maybe he was the astronaut who snuck a golf ball and driver into space and hit a half-mile tee shot, or could be farther.

I was standing with my Youth League team near the first base dugout, all of us weary from the ten-block parade, dressed in our green jerseys, clean white pants, green stirrups, new black cleats. I was dreaming of equipment—black catcher's mask, orange shin guards, black chest protector—all the tools of ignorance, the tools of my chosen trade, catcher, mythic strongman crouched behind a swinging bat, waiting to catch a speeding projectile, to stop it with my body if need be, like my father had taught me. I was well trained in the art of falling, of diving, of throwing to second, of blocking home plate with my body, hoping, even, for a base path collision with an oncoming runner, the ball landing in my glove just in time to make the out before the fading of consciousness, and when I came to, I would pull the ball from my glove with my free hand and hold it high in the air, having never dropped it, not even after taking the knockout blow, taking it for the team, taking it like a man.

Space had lost its glory. When my father was a child, the race was on, Soviets versus Americans, good against evil. The president said we'd go to the moon, and Mars couldn't be that far off either. Neighborhood children climbed onto rooftops and watched the procession of the planets in the night sky, and for a few years, a decade or so, they did not seem so far away. Everything was attainable, the thick mist forests of Venus, the retrograde spin of Neptune around its axis, the distant icy ball of Pluto, the epochs star to star. Now space was serviced by shuttles. Space had become routine, a trip to the convenience store for milk and bread, and would stay that way until a few months later, when my fourth grade teacher would pull me aside at the science fair, away from my terrariums full of frogs, and tell me that the shuttle *Challenger*, its payload bearing a schoolteacher, had exploded upon liftoff. For several days, charred remnants would fall from the sky along the Florida coast where we lived.

But for now the men of my father's generation stood at attention, rapt with wonder in the presence of this middle-aged man in a sport coat, and we held back our own worship until two minor league ballplayers, recent spring training castoffs from the Montreal Expos organization, settled onto mound and catcher's box and threw the new season's ceremonial first pitch. We cheered, we cheered, and then one of my teammates, son of a county judge and so by nurture given to seeing through things, leaned across us, got our attention, and said, "Who the hell *are* those guys?"

None of us knew. We knelt and dug up handfuls of the orange red clay with our hands and rubbed it onto our pants so we looked like we had been diving for line drives or sliding into third. Pockets of yellow and purple and black—jerseys of every color—drifted past us and into the backs of station wagons, buses, the beds of pickup trucks. Soon my teammates left, too.

I walked with my father toward the parking lot, to his big white air conditioning repair van. The passenger seat was piled high with blueprints, and he moved them to make room for me.

"I saw those men land on the moon," he said. "On television. That night I went outside and stared up at the moon for a long time. It was white, and full. I thought I saw a black dot somewhere near the middle. I thought, *It might be Neil Armstrong all right. It could be him.*

"The next day, when my father came home from work, he asked if I wanted to play catch. We went out back by the orange trees and warmed up slow. I always wanted my father to ask me to play catch. In some ways it was better than space. Better than men walking on the moon. We threw the ball back and forth for a long time. We didn't talk at all. We threw until it was too dark to see, then we went inside."

His father had worked for the railroad. He worked long hours and came home used up and silent, without much left to give to his wife and sons, and spent his evening hours in his recliner, watching television. Shortly after his retirement he suffered a stroke and lost the ability to speak. He hardly left the chair after that, and I came to know him in the same way my father knew him, sitting silent in the chair, watching television. I never knew him, and neither did my father.

He stared out the window of the air conditioning van for a long time— my father, who threw with me every day, who rose at five o'clock every morning so he could get off work at three-thirty and coach our team.

He stared out the window, and I stared at him, and though I was not a grateful child, I could feel the blisters on my feet from the long parade, and I could see the sunburn on his face, and I knew he must have blisters, too, knew that he did not like parades but that he had enjoyed walking with me as much as he had enjoyed playing catch with his own father, as much as he had enjoyed watching the man on the moon.

Now I am almost as old as my father was the day Buzz Aldrin stood on the pitcher's mound at Camellia Park, and he is almost as old as his father was the day they played catch in front of the orange trees. Our time together is very short, and growing shorter, and in two years, my own son will be old enough to walk outside with me and throw the baseball. We will throw until the sky grows dark and the white face of the moon keeps us gentle company.

Then we will talk, and this is the story I will tell him.

6. Hardball

Jocelyn Bartkevicius

In the beginning, before everyone got cancer, baseball was an old black catcher's mitt tucked in the back of my stepfather's closet next to the rifle he pilfered from enemy troops in Italy. On summer afternoons, Kirdy dug out that glove and an old baseball, and invited me outside to throw the ball around. I learned to lift my glove precisely, catching that small fastball in the web, never in my palm. Only the softball would let you get away with that.

Baseball was also the TV with no volume, the phone ringing, my mother and stepfather taking in bets. The teams didn't matter, just the odds. It was the 1960s, before state lotteries cornered the gambling market, when even policemen stopped by the corner news and smoke shop to play the numbers. Those were the days when my stepfather's burlesque nightclub was still thriving, and when for the occasional "stag" party he transformed the ladies room into a secret enclave for high stakes poker games.

"The phone is for business," my stepfather always said, when he caught me trading gossip with elementary school friends. And so was the TV, which ran those baseball games almost exclusively (except for the occasional old black-and-white movie that seemed to tell the story of their individual lives: soldiers taking a bridge in World War II; a dashing nightclub owner toasting elegant couples as the floor show took the stage; a beautiful younger woman captivating an older man).

My parents gambled for entertainment, so there was never really any trouble. But their old friend Johnny—they called him by an Italian word that meant something so vile my stepfather wouldn't translate it—lost most of one ear to gambling debts. The story was that he'd played the horses in a desperate attempt to recoup money he'd lost on baseball games. He'd sit at the pool behind our nightclub, and I'd stare at the space where his lobe and ear folds should have been. I couldn't fathom risking a body part on the slim chance of getting rich. Another family friend had lost his house—complete with a custom "Sinatra Room"—in a poker game, and that spiraled into the loss of his wife, kids, and business. I went to grammar school with his kids, and the rest of us whispered behind their backs about their father's loss.

Baseball was forbidden, unless you wanted to watch, to cheer a team, or bet the odds. At my mother's and Kirdy's urging, I put money on jai alai and the dogs. The two of them sat enthralled with their drinks and the game (not the playing but the outcome, racing to the window to collect their winnings, or ordering a drink to forget their losses). But watching games bored me. The allure of free money did nothing for a person like me, who anticipated only loss. I handed over five dollars, imagining what I otherwise could have bought with it—lipstick, an album, a book.

Baseball was for boys and softball was for girls, even though George Carlin's shtick made baseball sound prissy and feminine. "Football is played on a *gridiron*," he'd say, his voice deep, that last word coming out like a growl. "Baseball," he'd say, voice high, soft, almost tender, "is played on a *diamond*." The object in football, he'd add, was all about penetrating defenses and other such violating. "In baseball, the object is to go *home*." Diamond. Home. He coyly dragged out the vowels as if the words were quaint.

Softball was also played on a diamond; its object was also to go home. It retained the things girls were supposed to like. "Diamonds are a girl's best friend," my mother always said. In seventh grade the school bus took us across town where the girls studied home economics while the boys took shop. Home was for girls, a place we were supposed to make. Softball was also for us, and during recess, we pitched that fat bumblebee of a ball (fat like the big orange kickball in first grade) underhanded, slowly, nice and gentle over the plate where some girl tried to bash it into the outfield— just like the boys. Fat was for babies, for sissies, for girls.

By sixth grade my glove was broken in from a year of intramural soft-ball. My team took first place. The coach gave me prime spots: shortstop, pitcher. I could hit to right field where, he told me, the weakest player would never expect the ball and never catch it. He taught me to subtly angle my hips, to swing fiercely with follow-through, to savor the satisfying sound of the heavy wooden bat smacking the very center of the ball. Race to first, round the corner to second. Slide. I sprinted down the same base lines the boys ran, tagged the same bags. The same dirt stained my pants.

But nothing in my life back then was closely examined, and none of this occurred to me as I ran the bases. I played softball and the boys played baseball and that was as inevitable as gravity. I no more questioned why the hardball was forbidden than I fretted over the strength of the earth's gravitational force as I ran the bases. The prohibition was as invisible as the particles of asbestos showering over us every day from Rebestos, the brake lining factory across the river.

At my father's house, where I'd spent every Sunday after my parents' divorce when I was a toddler, there was never any baseball. We watched football exclusively—and for fun, not business. We watched his favorite team, the Green Bay Packers, win the Super Bowl year after year. We talked about Bart Starr, the passing, the touchdowns, and that spring the Easter Bunny left me a football instead of a basket of candy. Outside, my father showed me the precise placement of fingers to laces on that regulation pigskin ball with Bart Starr's signature embossed in black. We threw that ball around every weekend, and had pickup games whenever we could.

When I was in fifth grade, recess meant football, not softball. We could opt out, sit in Mrs. Lane's class drawing pictures, but most of the boys joined Mr. Kelly out on the gridiron, along with girls like me, whose tough and boyish visions of ourselves compensated for the humiliating spectacle of our skirts flapping as we ran and our underpants showing when we dove for the ball or got pushed to the ground. I played wide receiver to Mr. Kelly's quarterback: Run out from the line of girls, penetrate the line of boys, turn your head as you run, see tall, lanky Mr. Kelly lifting the football above the boys' heads, see his fingers cradle the ball, right on the strings, see his arm go back, way back, see the ball spin toward you, that point heading directly your way, reach up, jump up, pluck the speeding spinning football out of the air, cradle it like a baby at your side, turn, and race toward the end zone until the boys, hands pressing

your back and other places for the supposed tag, pushed you—hard—
to the ground.

That same year, my father moved out to the country, and every weekend on the way from my mother and stepfather's house on Long Island
Sound to his farm in central Connecticut, we passed the brake lining
factory across the river. Rebestos was monolithic, a conglomerate, a dark
metal lump of connecting buildings. In the shadow of Rebestos, tucked
under the railroad bridge, there was a small bar called the Frog Pond.
I'd say its name whenever we drove by, and my father smiled, getting
my reference to the frog pond on his land, where I'd stand for hours,
Zen-like, until tiny frogs became as used to my presence as the shadow
of a tree, and ceased jumping into the pond even when I bent, reached
out, touched their backs, and lightly probed the delicacy of the ethereal
bones beneath skin so loose it seemed unconnected to the skeletons.

Above the Frog Pond, a billboard advertised tickets for the Rebestos
Brakettes, the company's locally famous women's fast-pitch softball team.
The name sent my mind spiraling the way the bar's name did. "Brakettes"
sounded like "Rockettes," a name I'd heard first, and all I could picture
were those dancing women at Radio City Music Hall, a line of slender
thighs raised in a provocative, but still feminine, pose. The billboard
showed a Brakette in action, a thick-thighed woman rearing back like a
Major League Baseball pitcher ready to throw, front leg raised, like Mickey
Mantle or Ted Williams in drag.

We passed the billboard and drove out into the country, past the army-
green Housatonic River that reeked of chemicals. We headed to my father's
farm where I'd put on a cowboy hat and cowboy boots and ride my
horse as vigorously and wildly as any boy. But the sight of that masculine Brakette somehow appalled me: legs were supposed to be slender
and elegant, part of a look. Legs were for business, and the business of
women, my mother was trying to impress upon me, was to walk straight
and slowly, the energy going into the hips, not bouncing up on your toes
with your whole body rising, and she had me practice in her high heels,
back and forth across the floor.

By the time my half sister, Carolyn, was old enough to take note of, it was clear that she didn't share my tomboyish streak. She took ballet and tap almost as soon as she could walk. She enrolled in gymnastics with her friends from school, and the same select clique made the cheerleading squads in both junior high and high school. They were content to cheer on the boys while they played football, and to show up to clap and do shorter routines for basketball and baseball. When they found a picture of me alongside an article on "being an individual" in an old copy of the high school newspaper, an issue from seven years before when I was their age and a self-proclaimed hippie, they laughed at my remarks about the need for girls to have more access to active sports instead of cheering boys on from the sidelines. Those were the days before Title IX, when schools didn't offer much in the way of athletics for girls. In my school you could be a cheerleader (too girly), a tennis player (too prissy and upper class), or volleyball player (too nerdy). There was no track, no swimming, no softball.

On a whim, Carolyn and her friends joined intramural softball the summer after sixth grade. Their oafish, mild-mannered college student coach couldn't handle a recalcitrant back-talking group of girls more interested in lipstick and *Seventeen* magazine than practicing for games. When he heard that my sixth grade softball team had been the town champions, he asked me to be the assistant coach. My job was to yell at the girls, and his was to buy them ice cream. No matter what we tried to teach them, they threw like girls, struck out, ran slowly, and lost every game. The coach treated them to ice cream anyway, at Carvel, where the Little Leaguers flirted with them. It took me years to figure out that that had been the point all along.

My mother must have been relieved about my sister's inclination to be "girly." Carolyn didn't need boot camp in feminine carriage and demeanor the way I had. From birth she seemed obsessed with babies (hanging around with young mothers, entertaining the kids for free), while I had always been more canine inclined (begging the neighbor to let me walk her mutt, Butch, several times a day).

My tomboy streak must have terrified my mother. "Don't *ever* let anyone change you," she'd said after a basketball game in which our junior high coach yelled to me to get more aggressive. "We've got to *find* you someone," she said in a late night phone call, when I was in graduate school and the news media was proclaiming that women over thirty had about as much chance of marrying as getting struck by lightning. When I took up martial arts instead of hanging around the law or engineering schools ("You can meet *anyone* in a university," my mother always said), she seemed dismayed. By then, my sister had married a local engineer and settled into a three-bath-four-bedroom slice of suburbia to have kids.

I'd planned on transforming myself in college. My mother hoped that meant finding a husband, but I dreamed of cutting my long hair and becoming a scholar athlete. I didn't cut my hair or go out for varsity, but I did talk my unathletic hippie friends into forming a women's intramural softball team. Like my sister's sixth grade team, we lost every game. But for different reasons. While my sister's team played like "girls," my hippie team played like they were stoned. In the game that made me disband the entire team, the batter hit a grounder right to me, at first base. I scooped up the ball, tagged first, threw to second for a double play, and watched in slow motion horror as my throw hit our second baseman— who stood with her head down, looking at something on the ground— on the top of the head.

Around the same time, I took a trip to meet my boyfriend's family, and the highlight of the trip, Pete prefiguratively suggested, would be driving into Philadelphia to see the Phillies. The surprise left me nonplussed, but Pete was such a rabid Phillies fan that he'd crossed out the "Red" on our box of Red Rose tea bags and penned in "Pete." It was the 1970s, pre–gambling scandal, and Pete Rose was baseball's king, but I was still so clueless about Major League ball that I'd never heard of him. I gave my boyfriend a look, figuring he was up to some kind of juvenile punning about erections past.

The week before the game, I offended the host—Pete's father—by refusing to tag around the golf course watching him and his four sons play eighteen holes. The Phillies tickets were already purchased, or perhaps he would have *un*invited me. When he heard me say that I preferred playing sports to watching them, the family patriarch stomped off pouting. By then, I'd watched jai alai played by professionals, and basketball, football, and ice hockey played by college teams. I'd sat through football, basketball, and baseball games on TV. I'd watched the Rangers slap a puck around the ice at Madison Square Garden. But I could never focus on the game. Where my friends got caught up in the unfolding contest—a narrative they'd revisit in the newspaper the next day—I spaced out during much of the game and noticed only odd ritualistic moments. My mind perversely separated out scenes that flowed right past the notice of my friends: outrageously tall basketball players in a contorted ballet beneath the net; outsized football players slapping each other's flat butts; the burn-unit-skin look of the hockey goalies' pads; the crotch adjusting and tobacco spitting of baseball players. I was doomed to be a stranger, outside the dramatic tension of play captivating everyone else.

The Phillies game was played under the lights, the stadium bright against the dark sky. From up in the stands the diamond was beautiful, the players' arms long and lithe, the tableau brilliant as an ice sculpture, the fast-play story of the game absorbing. If there was crotch grabbing or tobacco spitting, I didn't notice. I ate a hotdog, drank a beer, cheered for Pete Rose, and bought myself an ugly red Phillies cap and wore it even outside of the stadium. For the rest of college I watched baseball on TV, even when my boyfriend wasn't around.

By then, our family nightclub was struggling. The year I graduated, my stepfather ran the last floor show for a small, aging audience. It wasn't so much that burlesque was dying out as that the people who paid to see it were. Every time I came home, my stepfather had a new list of the dead, all pruned from his list of gambling and sports buddies: his best friend from lung cancer; this friend from cancer of the esophagus; that one from throat cancer. It always seemed to be cancer, the reasons for their demise always assigned to the usual suspects: smoking and drinking. No one thought for a moment about the asbestos spewing into our lungs from the Rebestos plant, an unindicted coconspirator. And by the time I left for graduate school, this malignant endemic began consuming my stepfather.

Every year I visited home, my stepfather was smaller, grayer, sicker. By the time he figured out it was cancer (that blood coughed up comes from lungs, not a stomach beset with ulcers) he was already doomed. He stopped reminding me that I was no spring chicken and shouldn't jog or play sports. For years he and my mother had grown silent when I talked about tae kwon do (fighting in tournaments, breaking bones, taking kicks to the head). But near the end, my stepfather said that maybe martial arts wasn't so bad, even for a woman. "It's life," he said. "You should live it, live it up." After we watched him die in a hospice and buried him, we sorted through his belongings. The old rifle was still in his closet, but his old black catcher's mitt was nowhere to be found.

The first time I met Chris, who would become my stepson eight years later, he was only five, too young for Little League. The cancer may have already been at work inside him, one or two cells turning against him, hatching silent insurrection. On the surface, though, it was invisible. His gait was all boy, energy exuded from him. His father, Matthew, invited me to the kids' tae kwon do class Chris had been taking all summer. It was 1995 and, under the influence of the Ninja Turtles, every five-year-old wanted to throw on a belt and execute killer spin kicks. I'd moved to Florida the year before for a teaching job, met Matthew in the winter, begun dating him in late spring. It was August and I guessed that after a summer of dating, Matthew was really testing me with his son, not Chris's mastery of tae kwon do.

Matthew was broad shouldered and muscular and walked like a football player. There was something oxymoronic in that big swarthy guy holding hands with the tiny blond five-year-old boy, head peeking out of an oversized uniform with the white belt tied wrong. Chris checked me out, then turned and gave his father a thumbs-up after every kick he delivered to the kicking pad—or the air next to the kicking pad. Matthew looked warily at the mother cradling an infant in front of us, as if a serious relationship meant that whole battle all over again. And it might have, if Chris had stayed well.

By the time Chris joined Little League the following year, Matthew and I had moved in together and attended games as a couple. Chris played right field, where we used to put the deaf girl when I coached my sister's softball team. Out there, a kid gets bored. Chris stared up at the clouds, down at blades of grass, over at his elementary school. He put his hat on sideways, then backward. He threw it up in the air. One afternoon an ice cream truck, bell ringing madly, approached. The opposing batter was up, but instead of standing ready, Chris was waving frantically at us. While the pitcher threw his first pitch, Chris ran toward us, shouting for his father. Matthew stood up.

"Can I have an ice cream?" Chris yelled.

Matthew waved him back into the outfield. The batter hit the ball to the shortstop. Chris resumed staring at grass and bugs.

Chris was seven, and still playing Little League, when his doctors finally figured out that the reason he woke up screaming and sweating every night, walked like a bowlegged old man, and got strep throat twice a month was that he had leukemia. It is a word with a certain beauty, like "wisteria," suggesting something lovely, exotic. But leukemia meant two and a half years of chemotherapy, long hospital stays, projectile vomit, sweat, crying, terror.

The doctors said that Chris had an 85 percent chance of surviving. "Surviving" is one of those Latinate words that mask the harsh reality behind them. What they meant was that Chris could die. Sure, the odds were that Chris would not die. But whenever Matthew and I watched Chris, hobbled and panting, we had to force ourselves to look happy about the odds. Who wouldn't play the numbers or put down all their chips on poker or bet a hundred on the Dodgers with an 85 percent chance that they might win? But at night, when Chris crawled into bed with us, sick from chemo, terrified that he was dying, the odds overwhelmed us.

At first Chris was too weak and nauseous for baseball. But by spring, thin haired and pudgy cheeked, barely stabilized on a new anti-nausea drug, Chris was back out in the Little League diamond at the local elementary school. He ran the bases as if bowlegged, still sore from the deadly cells that packed his bone marrow.

The winter of his second year of chemotherapy, I took Chris outside to throw the football around. By then he'd had burning liquid chemo jammed into his thigh muscle and injected into his spine so it could penetrate the blood-brain barrier. He'd had bone marrow dug out of his hip in a procedure that sounded like the crunching excavation of bone that it was. He'd shed some tears, moaned and complained, but borne it all with more pluck than I could ever imagine being able to muster. But when I threw the football and he missed, and the point jammed him in the shoulder, he fell to the ground and cried.

We switched to baseball, but he cringed when I threw the ball and claimed I'd broken his hand. I remembered my stepfather then, how he'd throw the baseball so hard it would smack my palm, leave it stinging even through the thick glove. I was mystified at how Chris could take all those invasive medical procedures and yet not be able to endure the comparatively minor pain of football and baseball.

Over the next two and a half years, Chris continued chemotherapy and played Little League whenever he was well enough. He watched his favorite video, a children's baseball movie called *The Sandlot*, repeatedly, yelling out his favorite line with the little boy who says it: "You throw like a girl." I thought about objecting, giving a lesson in sensitivity, or just taking him outside to show him how a "girl" really throws. But after he watched me throw a few more times, he gave me his ultimate compliment: "You don't throw like a girl."

About a year into chemotherapy, when Chris had adjusted and felt well enough to play most of his team's games, his mother started stage-managing his baseball teams and publicity around his cancer the way she had stage-managed his early hospital visits (I was not to be there when she was present). Chris showed up in newspaper ads and on a billboard for the American Cancer Society, and was interviewed—along with his mother—on radio and TV. Chris talked about his love of baseball while his mother talked about his love of God and country and described the trials of being the single parent of a little boy on chemo. The local TV news covered one of his games, showing Chris standing up at bat while the voiceover told a barely recognizable story of a boy fighting cancer while managing to remain an all-American boy.

That year, Chris's mother pulled him out of tae kwon do. It was too violent, she said. She didn't want Chris to be a fighting boy. He was going to be gentle and genteel. He was going to be all about baseball, Mom, and apple pie.

In the end, when pancreatic cancer came on so suddenly that she was already dying when she was diagnosed, my mother was in love with base-ball. She'd begun watching it after my stepfather died, and she rooted for the Yankees—the team itself, not the odds. On her deathbed she was still a Yankees fan, shushing us to watch the final inning—Yankees versus Red Sox—on the TV suspended above the bed in her hospital room. The pneumatic pump keeping her immobile legs alive inhaled and exhaled, a robotic presence in the room. My mother lay propped up on pillows to ease the pain from the incision where the doctor tried to unwrap the vine-like tumor from her spine. Her belly protruded like a woman about to give birth.

She's pregnant with tumors, I thought.

Above her, the Yankees played on. She's a *die-hard* Yankees fan, I thought.

Some part of my mind had separated perversely to pun and obsess over language and odd details, like the heads-up penny at the foot of her stretcher in the trauma room. Find a penny, pick it up, and all that day you'll have good luck, I thought. I picked it up. But we were out of luck, and my mother died the next day.

Chris had passed the five-year mark by then: he was off chemotherapy and officially pronounced "cured." He was devastated by my mother's death, in part because he had genuinely grown to love her, but also because he remained traumatized by his own bout with cancer and frantically mourned the cancer deaths he encountered. His leukemia had come on suddenly. He never stopped fearing that it would come back, like a vil-lain in a horror movie, and kill him the second time around. When my mother died, Chris searched frantically for a navy blue turtleneck she'd given him to wear under his baseball uniform on cool evenings.

"I'm so irresponsible," he said, when it couldn't be found.

Chris hadn't played Little League that year. He'd only wanted to pitch, he said, and he couldn't find a coach who would let him. He played less for the sheer love of baseball than to become "a famous Yankee." When years passed and he was still standing in the outfield, he got frustrated.

Instead, Chris returned to tae kwon do. He was still a beginner, a white belt, and he faltered. But when he got his yellow belt, he was hooked. By the time he earned his green belt, we were attending classes together, and when he was thirteen, we planned our first trip together without his father, a tae kwon do encounter on a beach an hour from our house. By then Matthew and I were married, and Chris had asked permission to call me "Mom," an endearment that drove his birth mother crazy.

The week before our trip, Chris's mother signed him up for baseball camp, which would end the day before the tae kwon do encounter began. Chris was nervous about going, having been out of Little League for two years, but convinced that there was a rift he needed to heal—a mother who advocated baseball and a father who objected to it. Matthew had never objected to baseball, only to Chris's lack of commitment, and the day before the baseball camp began, he shopped with Chris for cleats, baseball shirts, and pants—he'd outgrown the ones he'd had in Little League—and took him to camp that first day. Still, Chris couldn't let go of the notion of a battle: the genteel sport of baseball versus the rough and tumble martial arts.

Chris returned from camp mesmerized by the pitches, and chattered endlessly about curve balls, fastballs, change-ups, and sliders. In the car on the way to the tae kwon do encounter, he gripped a baseball, demonstrating the fingering for a curve, a change-up, a fastball. He'd join Little League again, he said, if they'd let him pitch.

By then, girls were no longer banned from Little League, and a few of the teams in his league had had a lone girl in the outfield. But baseball—and the secret knowledge of the pitches—had always been forbidden to me, and so it seemed that what Chris possessed as we headed off for our weekend was a body of knowledge that I would never have. I was mystified, though, by that former prohibition. How could that baseball be more dangerous or manly than a basketball or football, both of which I was allowed to handle in school? How could baseball be more masculine and risky than tae kwon do, where I trained and fought alongside men?

At the encounter Chris, as an intermediate student, was assigned to forms class. "No fair," he said, when he saw my schedule of gun disarming and self-defense with canes and sticks fashioned out of wooden baseball bats. He stared as I entered my classroom, envious of the secret knowledge, the curve balls and knuckle balls of self-defense, that he would someday have. Chris was cured, but to him, the future was far off, abstract. He worried about the future ceaselessly, as if it might never come, as if—should it arrive after all—the ADD and learning disabilities he'd acquired as a result of the chemotherapy would render him lost and incapable of functioning in the greater world.

Our tae kwon do master had been gentle with Chris when he was a beginner, but once he was a green belt, he was starting to push him. On a clear spring night, after we'd practiced self-defense escapes from neck attacks, he wrapped both his hands around Chris's neck and squeezed. "Okay, Chris," he said. "Escape."

Chris panicked, and instead of doing the move we'd practiced all evening he tried to pry the teacher's hands from his neck. The teacher grabbed tighter. Chris was coughing and turning red, but if you can't escape correctly because you panic at the grip of someone you trust, you'll never be able to defend yourself on the street. Chris was supposed to be raising his arms, fast, striking the attacker's elbows, while simultaneously spinning out of reach.

"Your arms, Chris," the teacher said. "Your arms." Finally Chris got a hold of himself, raised his arms, and escaped. On the way home, we were laughing about it, and Chris was reenacting the scene, squeezing his own neck and exaggerating coughs and choke sounds. "Your arms, Chris. Your arms!" he said, mimicking our instructor, and then choked, gagged, and flailed in the passenger seat.

"I could never tell my mom about this," he said. "She'd never think it was funny." He tapped me on the shoulder. "You're different," he said. "You're cool. I tell my friends when you were little you used to be a tomboy." He stared out the window. "Hey," he said. "You're a *tom* mother."

He was silent for a while, and I assumed he was contemplating this discovery. "God," Chris said, suddenly. "I survive leukemia and then get choked to death in tae kwon do."

We both burst out laughing. It was the first joke he'd ever made about cancer. It was the first time he was the one to say that he'd survived. We were quiet then, and a New Age music show began on the radio station we had on. It was slow, haunting jazz with a flute predominating. Chris pointed up at the dramatic heat lightning that crackled and sparked through the night sky. My mother had taken note of the sky just before she'd died, pointing up at the full moon, telling us it was beautiful. Even insects struck her as lovely in the end, and she pointed to huge brown bugs clinging to the screen beneath the porch lights. Beautiful, she'd said. But Chris wasn't dying.

"It's so beautiful," he said. "The music rhymes with the sky."

7. Brothers
Andre Dubus

In the winter of 1974, I met my agent, Philip Spitzer, and his brother, Michel. I had liked Philip for months when he was only a voice on the phone. I had sent him a collection of stories in the summer of 1973, and he wanted to try to sell it; till then, I had not had encouragement from anyone in New York about a book of stories, without a novel. After that, I talked too often on the phone with Philip. He was friendly and patient, but I had no discipline then, and I phoned at least every week to ask if a publisher had taken my book.

Of course if a publisher had taken it, Philip would have called me. But I can be suddenly and powerfully filled with a hope that feels like certainty: *an editor has just called Philip, now is the time, it is happening now*—something like that. In the winter he called to tell me he was going to visit his brother in Exeter, New Hampshire, and they would like to see me on their way north from the airport in Boston.

Philip is a sensitive man; calling me about having a drink together probably gave him some difficulty: he would know that, when I heard his voice, I would expect him to say he had sold my book. That happened later, in the spring. I lived alone in a two-room apartment, up three flights of stairs Philip and Michel climbed one night. I had very little furniture, and one or two of us sat on the bed. Philip and Michel are witty, athletic, good-hearted men who like to tell jokes and stories. That evening, we became friends. It is a deep friendship, though we rarely see one another. I feel like a brother to them; a few summers ago, I went to the wedding of Michel's son, and either Philip or Michel pushed me up a sloping lawn to pose with the Spitzers for the family photograph. Michel's son said, "You're an honorary Spitzer."

In April, after meeting that winter, we went to the Boston Red Sox opening day at Fenway Park. I was a teacher then; I taught five afternoons a week and had never been to opening day. But that year—and for the next twelve years, till I retired, early and burned out—I canceled my classes and went to the game with Philip and Michel and my friend Jim Valhouli, a teacher of literature who twenty-one winters later broke through ice while skating on the Exeter River and drowned. Yet there we were, the four of us, in our thirties, laughing in Michel's car, on a holiday not only from work but from Time and what we perceived as our daily lives, and from what would become of us. That is what a baseball game gives. When Sandy Koufax retired from the Dodgers, he said that baseball was not reality; it entertained people and allowed them to escape for a few hours.

At a baseball game in Fenway Park, I feel like a boy, watching grown men on a playing field, and watching grown men and women in their seats in boxes and the grandstand, and faceless bodies across the field in the bleachers; watching them watch, cheer, eat, talk, drink; watching them go up and down the steps for food, drinks, or the restrooms. The sound of the crowd is steady, the calls of roaming vendors rising higher, as the cries of certain people do, those who yell at umpires, players, managers, and those who call to the players: *Good eye*; *You can do it*, as if they—we; I do it—had been infielders years ago, when the voices of infielders were part of the game, calling to the pitcher: *Come babe, come boy*, we used to say in spirited voices, our bodies poised, our weight on our toes, our gloves ready. During ball games at Fenway Park, strangers talk to one another about the game; people cheer when one catches a foul ball; vendors standing on steps hear an order from someone sitting the middle of the row; the buyer hands money to someone in the next seat, who passes it on; the paper and coins move from hand to hand to the vendor, who places in these hands popcorn, hotdogs, peanuts, beer, soft drinks. Sometimes at mass I think of Fenway Park, for at mass there is the same feeling of goodwill: people are there because they want to be, and I feel among friends who share a passion.

For me, baseball is real in a deeper way than much of what I do. I do not begin a baseball season hoping the Red Sox will win a pennant and the World Series. I enjoy each game. Next day, I wait with excitement for the game on television that night or afternoon. Then I watch what happens and does not happen in a moment. I rarely concentrate on a moment of anything but writing and exercise and receiving communion. Yet watching a game, I do. A batter steps out of the box, looks to his left at the third base coach; the coach moves his hands, touches his arm, his chest, his face, his cap; the batter steps to the plate; the catcher's right fingers signal to the pitcher; the pitcher shakes his head; a runner on second creeps away from the base, glancing at the shortstop and second baseman; the catcher signals again, the pitcher nods, brings up his hands, kicks, throws. I watch the ball, and the batter. The ball is moving ninety-three miles an hour, but there is time for me to focus on it, maybe hold my breath, enough time so that it feels like waiting. Then I am amazed: the batter not only hits the ball but times his swing so well that he pulls it, a line drive right at the third baseman, who somehow has time to dive for it, but he does not touch it; he is lying on the ground, the ball hits the grass a hundred feet behind him as the left fielder sprints toward it to stop it before it bounces and rolls to the fence.

The reality I am watching is moments of grace and skill, gifts received by men who do not turn away from them but work with them for the few years they are granted. One spring, the batter will not be able to hit a fastball, the pitcher will not be able to throw one; the gifts are gone, as if they existed independent of men, staying with one for a time, then moving on to another, a boy in the womb, and when he is in elementary school, you can already see that he has it.

A Zen archer does not try to hit the target. With intense concentration, he draws the bow and waits; the target releases the arrow, and draws it to itself. A few summers ago, during an All-Star game, retired pitcher Steve Carlton visited the television broadcasting booth. One of the announcers asked him if hitters had ever intimidated him. He said he had ignored the hitters and played an advance game of catch with his catcher; it's an elevated form of pitching, he said. I have told this many times to young writers, and have also told them that Wade Boggs watching a pitch come to the plate, starting his stride and swing, probably does not know his own name, for his whole being is concentrating on that moving white ball. I could have said this about any good hitter, or fielder, or pitcher: men whose intense focus on a baseball burns their consciousness of the past and future into ashes blown quickly up and away from the field. This happens over and over in a game, and these moments are so pure, they may be sacred. They are not ephemeral; they seem so, because they exist in Time, but so did my friend Jim Valhouli; a river took his life, but it did not take the life he lived.

After that first opening day, we went to every one for twelve more years, the four of us becoming a crowd of sometimes forty men and women, writers, editors, teachers, publishers, booksellers, husbands, wives, boy-friends, girlfriends. In late fall, when the Red Sox ticket office opened, I would drive to Boston and buy tickets: two for me, ten for the Spitzer brothers, some for my publisher, David Godine, and people who worked for him, and always we had rows of good seats behind third or first base, and everyone sent me checks for their tickets. Cold weather postponed one game, and always we wore coats, hats, gloves, scarves. I wore a Red Sox jacket and cap. There must have been days with warm sun, our coats on our laps. In my memory, I see them all as warm days, weather for throw-ing and hitting and catching a baseball, for sitting and watching a game. The last year we went was 1986, my last spring as a biped, and in the late fall of that year, I was in a hospital bed in my home, my right leg in a full cast that would be on it till June, my left leg amputated above the knee, and none of us bought tickets for opening day.

I was thin and weak and in pain and could do very little for myself. I could eat, but not much; talk, read a book, try to write, but I could not lift my four-year-old daughter, who weighed thirty-five pounds. In March, walking to the bathtub with crutches and an artificial leg, with two strong women, a physical therapist, and a home health aide, I took my first shower since a car hit me in July 1986. I wore loose-fitting gym shorts. When I reached the tub, I slowly turned my back to it and the shower bench I would sit on, and held a grab bar on the wall as the women took the crutches; they squatted, held my leg and the artificial one, gripped my arms at the shoulders; then, as I held my breath, they rose, pulling up my leg and the other one, and eased me onto the bench. Now I could release my breath. They pulled off the leg, and unrolled onto mine a rubber sheath like a condom that covered the cast, and we laughed. I closed the curtain, pulled off my shorts, handed them to a woman whose hand was in the water from the faucet; when it was very warm, she pushed the lever to divert it, and out of the shower nozzle it came, spraying my face, my hair, my chest, hot joy on my body, which for eight months had felt unclean, and I closed my eyes to it, lifted my face to it, then washed my body, my hair, and stayed a long time in the shower, with a window at my right. Out the window were poplars on the steep hill behind my house, a hill I had loved to climb; at its top, near the electrical fences of the dairy farmer whose hill rises from mine till it peaks and descends to the Merrimack River, I had hung two rope hammocks. Sitting on the shower bench, in the blessing of hot water, I believed I would climb that short hill again. It would only take time. Then my right knee would bend, the damaged muscles and nerves would be again and for all my life sound, and, wearing jeans and boots, I would climb that hill, with my golden retriever, and I would lie on a shaded and swinging hammock, and while the dog lay on the grass chewing a fallen branch, I would look up through the poplars at a summer sky. In 1987 I watched opening day on television, sitting on the couch I transferred to from my wheelchair while my wife held the leg I could not lift in its cast.

So the Spitzer brothers and I saw thirteen baseball games, forty hours or so, with twenty or thirty or forty other people, some of whom I saw only on opening day. Jim Valhouli did not go to all the games. He left the college where we taught and moved to Exeter to teach at Phillips Exeter Academy. Probably in the third year, some of us began meeting for lunch before the game at a Japanese restaurant someone discovered on Newbury Street: the chef performed on the grill at our table while some of us drank hot sake. In 1977, eight of us sat at a table, the Spitzers married but without their wives; I was with mine, and our friends George and Tom were with theirs. A year later, the Spitzers and George and Tom and I sat in the same restaurant, smelling and eating shrimp, filet mignon, chicken and vegetables and rice, talking about baseball, checking our watches, timing our pleasure so we could walk to Fenway Park and see the first pitch of the game. George was talking, and then he stopped, chopsticks in hand; he blushed, looking at the rest of us, his mouth open. Then he said, "Last year, we were all married."

We stopped eating, looked at one another: we were all divorced. Then we laughed, not at the dismal pain of divorce, not at the loss of hope, of faith, of love that divorce is; we laughed because it was opening day and during the year since the last one we had each lost, each suffered, some less than others, as our wives had, but then they had moved strongly, it seemed, onto new courses. And here we were, perhaps with invisible limps and aches and longings, eating Japanese food with wooden sticks, sitting as if poised in Time, waiting for the excitement of being with over thirty thousand people and watching a game that does not employ a clock.

I do not remember any of the games, only moments, and the one I remember with most love was in the early 1980s. I had a wife again. The weather was good. Probably we wore jackets, but the sky was blue, the sun warm, and the Red Sox won. I happily left the game, walking with my wife and Philip and Michel, and other friends, slowly with the talking crowd, down the steps and the ramp, to the paler light and coolness beneath the grandstands, the smells of steamed hotdogs, beer, hamburgers, tobacco smoke, a faint scent of urine from the restrooms, and the smells of people, of their clothes, hair, skin, makeup, and that indefinable smell in a crowd, as if you are smelling the fact of being alive. We moved slowly, with thousands of others going to the sidewalks and streets that would be filled with people who, for now, were happy.

We reached an exit and walked into the sun again. About ten yards ahead, I saw eight or so white teenagers beating three black ones who lay on their backs on the ground, their arms covering their bleeding faces. I ran to them, jerked collars, necks, shoulders; pulled and pushed white boys, and grabbed the black ones, pulled them as they stood; I pushed them against a car to protect their backs, then turned to face the white boys. I raised my fists. "Police!" I yelled. I was both afraid and sad. I said to the white boys, "It's opening *day*. It's opening *day*." That is all I said, between cries for police. The white boys edged toward me, their fists ready; the one closest to me lunged, feinted punches, and hissed through his teeth. Not one of these boys was bleeding. "It's opening *day*," I said, waiting for the attack that would hurt. Then I felt a touch on my right shoulder, and then one on my left, and I looked, and Philip stood on one side of me, Michel on the other, their fists raised, and we stood like that, our shoulders touching, with the three bleeding boys behind us, until my wife came with police officers, who dispersed the white boys, then looked at the black boys' cuts, and sent them on their way.

As we went on ours, to drinks and dinner, then to drive to our homes in the night. Jim Valhouli was not with us that day; he would have joined us in front of the boys. Michel would marry again; then, nearly a year after my crippling, Philip would, and a few months after that I would not have a wife. All of it happened in our lives: the love of wives that was good and still is, with the pain of its loss, outside of Time; the baseball games I cannot remember but which still exist not only because they are recorded but because of what men brought to them and received from them, on the field, in the dugouts and bullpens; and what women and children and men brought to them and received in Fenway Park and at home with a television set or a radio; what athletic and passionate Jim Valhouli and his wife and two sons gave and received till the ice broke; and on that April afternoon, lit by the sun, those moments of violence, injustice, fear, and love, when my two friends came to my side and stood with me, waiting.

8. Jimbo

Rick Bass

Everyone loves to be a teacher. Of course, it's easy to see why this love has survived over the generations: it favors the species, certainly. The magic in learning is no stronger than the pleasure of teaching something: giving a part of yourself, and having someone take it.

There was a bully when I was small who used to beat me up regularly. If I rode my bike through his neighborhood, he would chase me down on foot, push me off the bike, and let me have it. Once by massive misfortune we were on the same baseball team. And there was some rule whereby everyone had to pitch. This athletic bully's team, our team, was winning about three thousand to nothing until it got to be my inning to pitch.

They started catching up real fast.

The bully, whose name was Jimbo, shouted at me from third base. Several times he started toward the mound, ignoring the other team's runners, who kept circling the bases faster and faster. Jimbo banged his fist in his glove and told me all the things that were going to happen to me.

You could see the desperation on his face when this did nothing to improve my pitching. It was like the worst dreams: I wasn't getting the ball near the plate, even after his threats. I aimed at the plate, praying that when the batters walloped the ball someone would make a miraculous catch, but my pitches started going behind their backs, over the catcher's head, everywhere. It was as if I had a serious physical disability. The ball was going about halfway between the plate and the dugout, at a forty-degree angle away from where it was supposed to be.

Jimbo stormed over and grabbed the ball and put it in my fist. He showed me a way to grip it that I'd never seen done. Then he took it back from me, and with this tremendously hateful, determined scowl, showed me, without actually releasing the ball, how to throw it. He demonstrated in a slow, barely contained, angry motion the reaching, pulling, aiming.

"Pretend with your free hand like you're pushing someone out of the way," he said. It was easy to see that that was what he was thinking of. His hand concealed the ball until the last moment, then shoving (slowly, for my benefit) the imaginary, offensive person aside—there was a sudden opening where that person and his free, gloved hand were—like spit and hate, Jimbo threw the ball through there, through that clawed gap of air, a strike, and made the catcher yell "Ouch!"

I tried it and threw strikes. He stood there on the mound and watched to make sure I did it right. I was relieved and amazed. I remember his face: he grinned and hid his own amazement. I don't think he had ever taught anyone anything before. I don't think anyone had ever listened.

I threw more strikes. We won the game. The next day Jimbo beat me up. But I knew there was something else in him no one understood: I think I was the first person ever to see it, and I was amazed that even an ogre who drubbed me could feel that sensation. The last I heard of him, he was in jail. He couldn't, or wouldn't, spell or write, and in my most tearful moments, tasting my own blood, I would remind him of this. But he could teach you how to throw a baseball better, I suspect, than it has ever been done. There is a tremendous amount of genius in being able to take someone throwing wildly into the dugout and tell him one sentence and have the ball go precisely over the plate.

If I was angry enough, or desperate enough, could I tell someone how to find oil so well that he or she could go out and do it immediately? Could I do it in one sentence? Not even in my most confident moments do I imagine that I could. I do not know what that sentence is. I think that Jimbo was a genius, and I hope he got out of jail. The closest I can come to that sentence, beyond "Listen to the earth," is that you have to get down under and beyond the mere occupational greed and look into the simplicity, the purity, the sacred part of it—the act, not the results, and yourself—and be aware that it is history, buried.

Jimbo's sentences were so much shorter. He would scowl at what I just said and beat me up.

9. 2004, a Red Sox Odyssey
In a Hundred Years and Four Generations
Tim D. Stone

The Boston Red Sox could have never repeated the sensation of their 2004 World Series victory—even if they had won the World Series a second year in a row. For in the days following Boston's first World Series championship in over eight decades, an odd phenomenon permeated New England. Cemeteries were reportedly dotted with Red Sox–capped males visiting the graves of their forefathers who had not lived to see their team emerge from eighty-six years in the wilderness to enter the land of Canaan. Such an outpouring did not merely rise from the souls of die-hard fans engaged in histrionics. In an age that questions religious tradition, it is not surprising that the achievement of a goal sought for over four generations triggered a broad-based mystical experience.

Take even me, an anti-spectator. The only time I voluntarily watch a baseball game is when the Red Sox are in the World Series, which means four times in my forty-three years. The male interest in professional athletic competition is something I don't understand. My idea of sport is to go for a run with a couple of buddies or play a game of doubles on hard top. Watch baseball? I'd rather read a book. Yet the victory of the Boston Red Sox in the 2004 World Series had a kind of spiritual effect— even on me.

How could this be possible for someone who views spectator sports as his nemesis? First, being raised in New England, I am a socialized baseball fan. Expressions of either organized religion or patriotism were an anathema in our modernist suburban household. But not organized sports. Led in the 1960s by the orthodoxy of my older brother, a precocious Red Sox fan since the age of six, and my cigar-puffing paternal grandfather, whose team had not won the World Series since his senior year in college, I was introduced to the tenets of the game from spring to fall. That meant that from age four to thirteen, our indoctrination into a system of societal myths and beliefs involved not the Father, the Son, and the Holy Ghost, or Moses freeing the Children of Israel from bondage, or Comrade Lenin liberating the workers and peasants from the czarist yoke, but Carl Yastrzemski leading the Boston Red Sox to the 1967 American League pennant.

Before we had gained television privileges, my brother's transistor radio projected the hiss of the crowd and the crack of the bat so consistently that they seemed as much a part of our natural environment as the blue jays chirping in the New England pines. Announcer Ken Coleman's unflappable monotone was as familiar to me as my father's breathless staccato. In our dogmatically enlightened household, while the belief in one God was dismissed as a practice unfitting for the modern age, polytheism was perfectly acceptable: There were nine gods, and they dwelled at Fenway Park. We were permitted graven images, purchased in small blue packs containing several photographs of the man-gods accompanied by two pink rectangles as thin as razor blades. This meant that instead of reciting the Holy Communion before taking the bread of the Eucharist, or chanting the Passover Ha-motzi over the bread of affliction, the most serious ritual in our household was to buy a pack of Topps baseball cards, rifle its contents in search of a Rookie of the Year, and pop into our mouths the accompanying stick of Bazooka bubble gum. Once its waxy consistency melted into a wad that bolstered the finances of dentists across the nation, informal contests ensued with gesticulations and grunts emitted from the mute bubble blower, whose expanding reputation risked deflating into worthlessness should the monstrosity pop and collapse in his face. If, instead, the practitioner disgorged his carbon dioxide blimp and raised it with three fingers, perhaps in implicit homage to the Baseball Hall of Fame, he had achieved the closest equivalent in our subterranean society to a mystical experience.

Despite my disinterest in spectator sports, my stubborn loyalty to the Red Sox stems not only from my childhood but from my grandfather, the smell of whose cigars, nearly twenty years after his death, still evokes both the man and the team more than any photograph or broadcast. Since by college my father had lost his boyhood passion for baseball, the responsibility for legitimizing our already entrenched culture of grand slams, throws to first, and ground-rule doubles fell back a generation to a man whose childhood interest in the sport took shape when Teddy Roosevelt's athletic patriotism led the country, Ty Cobb ruled the batter's box, and Babe Ruth was still playing stickball. Embracing the all-American sport also represented one of the quickest ways to transcend class, religious, and ethnic differences in turn-of-the-century America, especially for someone born into the Yiddish-speaking Eastern European immigrant community of Boston's West End. In an age when Jewish immigrants faced social barriers not unlike Hispanic newcomers did a century later, virtually all males—Irish or Jewish, rich or poor, fresh immigrant or old-line Brahmin—could find common ground in the latest Red Sox battle.

The sport's assimilatory properties particularly suited the ethos of my grandfather, who, like many first-generation Americans from non-English-speaking families, was eager to cover his migratory tracks. Playing baseball was a natural extension of his ancestors' efforts to integrate into their adopted homeland: My great-grandfather's uncle had made the first move by changing the family name from "Sacowitz" to "Stone" upon arrival from eastern Europe in the late nineteenth century. Moses, as he was appropriately named, led a gaggle of prepubescent descendants out of Vilna to spare them servitude in the czar's army, which conscripted Jewish boys to a life of misery.

The next major step toward Americanization came in 1900 when my great-grandfather and his new wife struggled in their mid-twenties to give their firstborn a name that satisfied both themselves and their adoptive country. Initially, they settled on "Sergei." But although this name sounded like one of the boys in czarist Vilna, the name drew attention in a society that did not welcome eastern European immigrants with open arms. Only fours years before, the Supreme Court had upheld the South's segregationist Jim Crow laws that discriminated against African Americans in *Plessy v. Ferguson*. In other words, if Africans were third-class citizens at the turn of the twentieth century, eastern European Jewish immigrants were second-class citizens. Whatever the exact reason, some time between the registration of three-week-old Sergei in the 1900 census and the issuance of his birth certificate a week later, his parents renamed him "Sylvester Robert." It was the first lurch in the Immigrant Shuffle. The free market of sandlots and public school recess soon jettisoned "Sylvester" and condensed "Robert" into "Bob." His parents acquiesced to what was in effect the boy's third name change in a decade, listing him in the 1910 census as "Robert S." To acknowledge his legal name, the young man later concocted a fourth moniker, "S. Robert Stone." By his senior college year in 1918, he possessed an Ivy League degree, an impressive name, a tweed jacket, a striped tie, a Boston Irish accent, and a passion for the Boston Red Sox. When his home team won the World Series that fall, the transformation was complete. Within a generation, the tracks of the Family Sacowitz from Vilna to Boston had been virtually wiped clean.

Since minding the children was not the paternal role in his own youth, Grandpa Bob, as we knew him, did not get down on all fours and romp with his preschool grandchildren. He remained content to let his wife play cards with the toddlers and bake them Schnecken (walnut coffee cake rolled in the shape of a snail, which its Yiddish-German word denotes). It was not until his wife died that he ventured out from behind his cigars. The easiest topic of conversation for a man who did not instinctively relate to young children was the one theme that united all New England males— the walks, wins, and RBIs of the Boston Red Sox. By the mid-1960s, the team's multicultural lineup of Italian, Polish, and Swedish ancestry— Petrocelli, Conigliaro, Yastrzemski, and Lonborg—sounded as quintessentially Bostonian as the African Americans—Scott, Howard, and Foy. Such a motley collection of names must have provided some comfort to a first-generation American who could have just as easily been named "Sergei Sacowitz" instead of "S. Robert Stone."

In contrast to their winning performance when my grandfather began his senior year in college, the Red Sox failed to win the World Series during my own youth or teen years. Nor as a single adult could I witness the feat. I eventually found myself approaching middle age, thousands of miles and decades from Boston, stubbornly loyal to the team of my ancestors, but with no World Series championship to show for it.

Bostonians are not alone. Chicago was doubly cursed: In fact, the Cubs have gone longer than even the Boston Red Sox without achieving the ultimate victory (since 1908). Ditto for the White Sox, who until 2005 had not won the championship in eighty-eight years. The (White) Sox probably would have won in 1919 but were accused of throwing the Series to the Cincinnati Reds in the infamous Black Sox Scandal, an alleged curse only lifted in 2005 with a victory against the Houston Astros. Although this represented a longer World Series drought than Boston's, White Sox fans had not dramatized the same epic yearning as had Boston. Was it the singular focus on a New England team that counted as many as six states under its allegiance and had one of the oldest baseball traditions in the country? Was it the star-studded allure of the Curse of the Great Bambino, since after trading the legendary Babe Ruth to the New York Yankees in 1920 the Red Sox went eighty-six years without a championship? Was it the frustration of playing in the same division as the winningest team in World Series history, the New York Yankees, who won the pennant twenty-six times during a period of more than eight decades when Boston could not deliver once?

Perhaps most of all, it was because the Red Sox had come so agonizingly close so many times to winning the coveted championship. After all, what other professional sports team inspired the creation of a derogatory English word—named after an *error* committed by one of its players, Bill Buckner, who had the misfortune of concluding a string of Red Sox errors by bobbling a simple grounder to lose the 1986 World Series to the New York Mets? Yahoo lists over twenty-five references to the adjective named after the hapless player, as in a mistake of "Bucknerian proportions." (A similar error was committed by the Sox's Tony Graffanino in the 2005 playoffs, resulting in a new term that made the rounds of the sports world—a "Gaffe-anino.") And what other team would adopt the title of a hit Broadway song, "The Impossible Dream" (from *The Man of La Mancha*), consoling itself for coming in *second* place, as the Sox did in 1967? That Boston lost the World Series that year to the St. Louis Cardinals was heartbreaking especially after coming back to tie the Series after being down 3–1. Winning the American League pennant was good enough to celebrate in mythic proportions because the team had finished in nearly last place the previous year and were not expected to be even mild contenders.

Whatever the reason, the older I became, the more I pegged the date of the last time the Red Sox had won the World Series, not to the Gregorian calendar but to my grandfather's age and circumstances, a precocious college senior who began his freshman year at age sixteen and sped through in three years to save money and make room for his siblings. The more time that elapsed after my grandfather's death in 1987, the more I anticipated a Red Sox victory, not only as a commemoration to the first-generation American in my paternal line but as a final communication.

Like my grandfather, my own toddler is at least partially a first-generation American: his mother is European. Even with an American husband in a land favorably disposed to northern Europeans, she sometimes struggles to master our social cues and mores. Since our son's weltanschauung sometimes differs from those of peers with parents born in the United States, I find myself reliving a shadow of the same concerns that my great-grandparents must have harbored a hundred years earlier. Although the all-American sport would seem the ideal antidote for my son, I had long ruled it out. My son's world is divided into two kinds of male toddlers: Ball Kids, who instinctively interact with spheres, and Fantasy Kids, who interact with people, real and imagined. This meant that when my son's athletic peers were shooting hoops at three, kicking soccer balls at four, and swinging tennis rackets at five, he was skewering Captain Hook, rescuing an imaginary victim from a burning Lego set, and sailing the high seas in a laundry basket.

So I was surprised when Aaron announced at age five that he wanted to play Little League T-ball. His best friend was in, his Dad was coach, and we must follow suit. After the first day of practice I realized drastic steps were in order. With no past interest in balls, my son lacked the fundamentals I had assumed T-Ball would teach him. But not in suburban California, where many kids had been throwing balls since age three. And then there was the slow learning curve. While a Ball Kid new to the sport would gauge the velocity of a rubberized ball and try to meet it with his glove, a Fantasy Kid would imagine that same sphere as a spaceship, a meteor, or a cannonball shot from the Jolly Roger. This meant that for my son, the logical reaction to a T-ball thrown toward his face was not to put out his glove and try to stop it but to cover his head and duck.

Theoretically, I opposed raising children with rewards. I had long rejected the hypercompetitive world of my youth, where students were ranked by academic achievement and judged by athletic prowess—a world to which I had insufferably conformed. I regretted that even in mellow California our milk cartons sported pictures of cows running races with medals around their necks. But I was willing to abandon my high-minded values. Not only was I concerned for my son's ego and sense of belonging on the playing field. At this level, it was a question of self-defense.

Somewhere I had read that performing an action two thousand times confirmed a reasonable degree of mastery. I thought of my son's most cherished objects. Play Mobiles. We went to our backyard and worked out a deal. Every time he caught a ball, he earned a dime toward his favorite Play Mobile. Ten catches, one dollar. One hundred catches, ten dollars. Two thousand catches. Bingo. Two hundred dollars' worth of Play Mobiles. My plan was shamelessly materialistic, but I didn't care. While I was his baseball coach, my son was not going to suffer blunt trauma at shortstop. He settled on his first dream object, a skeleton with a dungeon led by horse-drawn carriage. This macabre scene would not have been my personal choice, but barring a request for a plastic Kalashnikov assault rifle or a lifetime supply of Snickers bars, I figured my son should choose his own incentive.

At first, the going was tough.

I explained the need to cock back the arm, step and throw, move the glove toward the ball when attempting to catch. In an intense weekend he snagged the horse-drawn skeleton carriage with two hundred catches and throws. Over the summer, he secured a yard-long pirate ship with enough swords and daggers to pit Bob the Builder against Captain Ahab. My son still eschewed baseball on television. And I was no role model, since I didn't watch it myself. But he had undergone an essential rite of passage of American boyhood.

It didn't surprise me when he decided to forgo T-Ball the next year. But for several days in the fall of 2004, I underwent a metamorphosis that puzzled my son. The Red Sox had entered the World Series. Suddenly Daddy was doing the inconceivable—turning on the television and intently watching baseball. As together we watched the beginning of the decisive game, I struggled in vain to explain to my son the historic meaning of the Red Sox to the Stone family. But we were living in California and there had been no baseball indoctrination from radio or TV or an older brother or grandfather.

Though my father had never said so, the America of beer-drinking, Coke-guzzling, hotdog-gobbling, flag-waving baseball was too gritty and patriotic for someone interested not in reinforcing his American identity but advancing social justice. Starting with the French Revolution, advocating "universal rights" allowed even the most secular people of Jewish ancestry to reinforce their sense of assimilation while tapping into some of the deepest traditions and experiences of their people. For even the most fervent agnostics of Jewish descent heard the words of the Passover tradition ringing somewhere, deep in their souls, that "As our ancestors were once freed from slavery in Egypt, we hope that someday all people will be free."

I couldn't explain to my son that although my father had been an obsessive baseball statistician at fourteen, as he came of age, he could not square his evolving liberal values with his own father's belief that as a self-made man, anyone in America could make it if they worked as hard as he had. I could not explain that although as an adult, my grandfather had followed baseball and played golf, my father had needed to go his own way, abandoning spectator sports altogether and playing tennis. This athletic generation gap, to which I was also a party, complicated my efforts to convey to my son that as New Englanders, Stone men and boys had been awaiting a World Series championship for longer than the life expectancy of the average American male. Nor could I readily explain to him why, as we watched the team of our ancestors try to bring home the elusive victory, I felt compelled to set a photo of my grandfather before the televised baseball diamond, as if he were watching the game with us.

By the middle of the final game, I ruefully put my son to bed. I couldn't force him to endure a personal obsession to which he had not been properly initiated. After the final play, my son appeared from his room rubbing his eyes. What was that loud sound? he asked. I couldn't explain that at the moment when the Boston Red Sox beat the St. Louis Cardinals, I had heard again the tinny paternal calm of announcer Ken Coleman's voice emanating from my brother's room. I had relived the anticipation of new baseball cards. Sniffed the sweet homey smell of white powdered bubble gum. Inhaled again the rank well-being of my grandfather's cigars.

I couldn't explain to my son that after that final play, I was calling to my brothers and cousins in New York and Florida and Chicago. And shouting down the throat of death to tell my grandfather that for the first time since he was in college as the firstborn in an immigrant family, the team that had reinforced his American identity had won the World Series.

Perhaps my Red Sox séance has planted a tiny seed in my son. Or maybe it's his neighborhood playmate, a Ball Kid, who spends hours batting in the park beside our house. This fall, my son has demanded that I pitch him wiffle balls. Now he must decide for himself whether the Chosen People dwell in the city of his birth (San Francisco), the city of his forefathers (Boston), or some unknown city of his dreams. If he is lucky, maybe that team will lose for so long that someday his own yet unborn grandson will be clutching his photograph, communing with his own long-suffering ancestor during a World Series victory, as three generations in the future, his team, too, enters the land of Canaan.

10. My Life in the Big Leagues

Cris Mazza

Using my androgynous name, I got a paper route when I was eleven. Girls weren't allowed to deliver the *San Diego Union* or *Evening Tribune*. But I allowed my younger brother to come along with me on Sunday mornings. He and I both received our first fishing poles and reels the same Christmas. So it wasn't unusual that our baseball mitts were also the same age, his with Maury Wills's signature and mine with Brooks Robinson's. We played catch, both of us pitchers, winging our fastballs in at each other, or one of us would bounce grounders for the other to field then throw a frozen rope to first. But when he suited up for Little League baseball games on the dirt fields behind the junior high, I remained in the bleachers . . . playing my image of a tough guy, legs spread and feet propped up, smacking a fist in my mitt, ruminating on whatever phenomenon might cause the coach to spot me and call me down to the field, to the pitching mound or batter's box, to save the game, to be the first girl to be allowed to play Little League.

Consolation did come, and eventually became solace for much more than being left out of Little League. Became consolation for a range of adolescent angst and even adult frustrations. The San Diego Padres, in their first year as a Major League franchise, may not have acknowledged girls when they held paperboy night at the stadium, but girls could be Junior Padres. In 1969 I was condescendingly invited to join the Junior Padres when my brother's Little League team sent in their 7-Up bottle caps. We each received six free games and a Padres T-shirt—a thin undershirt with a silk-screened logo, which I persistently wore, even after it began to stretch unbecomingly over my developing body.

Of course baseball clubs have reasons for courting kids, *all* kids. While developing future players in the minor leagues, Major League clubs develop future fans with a festival atmosphere and giveaways, trying out everything to see what's going to succeed: the free T-shirts and caps and balls and posters, "the wave" surging through the crowd, the cotton candy and (later) nachos and (even later) sushi, the beach balls batted around overhead . . . or maybe even the players and the game itself. For me, nearly overnight twenty-five men between the ages of twenty and forty playing an intricate, aesthetically symmetrical, mythical sport became more important, even more substantial than any of the beardless faces in the crowd at a junior high party who might (but never did) ask me to dance.

In 1969 the former minor league Padres entered The Show as an expansion team full of rookies nobody wanted and castoffs too used up to play for a contender. Names like Ed Spezio, Ivan Murrell, Chris Cannizzaro, Al Ferrara, Al Santorini, Al McBean, and Billy McCool. They owned Joe Neikro, not at the end of his career but the beginning. And the Padres had another pitcher named Johnny *Podres*. For one season, at the end of his career, it was his team. Between January 1, 1969, and the start of the baseball season, no fewer than ten boy babies were born who would someday become players on the Padres. The boys old enough to play in 1969, and those a little *too* old, won 51 games and lost 110. San Diego was not a young city but an old one, two hundred years in 1969, the year Major League Baseball turned one hundred.

Those who call themselves purists decry baseball in San Diego as being without tradition, without the character born of a long and colorful history dotted with triumphs, controversy, curses, rivalries, and disappointment. But when you follow a team from the time you're eleven, you don't care that it has no history before you—you and the team evolve together. And in many ways, you are each other's history.

In 1970, even though I was unaware that the mayor and several city council members were indicted for corruption, I did know that the Padres manager committed the unforgettable (and unforgotten) crime of pulling his starting pitcher in the eighth inning of a no-hitter he was pitching but that the team was losing 0–1.

By 1972 I was in high school. Although I'd never played a real game of baseball, I was the first girl to play trombone in my high school band. And, finally, in possession of my own transistor radio. I didn't miss a single game broadcast that year. Some of the names were new: Johnny Grubb, Leron Lee, and Enzo Hernandez (shortest player in the league, fewest RBIS for anyone with 500 at bats, and acquired in a trade that sent a future twenty-game-winner to Baltimore). The first time I ever marched with my trombone in San Diego Stadium in front of a football crowd of over 40,000, my thoughts were mainly that I was standing in center field.

I wasn't aware that the Republican National Convention was scheduled to occur in San Diego that summer and at the last minute was moved to Miami to thwart protestors, or that in the public relations fallout the mayor announced a weeklong celebration for San Diego as "America's Finest City," and the name stuck. The catchphrase was used for decades afterward. I assumed the city had won it in a contest. But I was entirely cognizant that Nate Colbert made baseball history when he hit five home runs and batted in thirteen in a doubleheader. I clipped every article and photo in the newspaper after a winning game and pasted them in a hand-made scrapbook. I bought (and actually chewed the gum inside) packs of Topps baseball cards, searching for any of the Padres. For one glorious day I lay on the sand at Torrey Pines beach—while my father and brothers fished, my mother and sisters bodysurfed, I listened as the Padres climbed out of last place for the first time in their Major League history.

When I wasn't marching with my trombone, I spent hours pitching a baseball against a brick wall beside the driveway, counting balls and strikes or fielding the resulting grounder or line drive, keeping track of hits, outs, and runs in my head, until a nine-inning game was over and I, of course, was the winning pitcher. By this time Johnny Podres had retired and a young staff was actually allowing the Padres to lose by scores of 1–0 or 2–1 instead of 8–2 or 15–5. There was a dentist who had a private practice and came two outs from throwing a no-hitter. There was a screwball specialist not even six feet tall. And there was my new idol, Clay "The Kid" Kirby, someone's handsome hometown hero pitching in the Major Leagues, losing twenty games but sustaining an ERA under 3.00. In 1970 and 1971 he'd had no fewer than three near no-hitters—he was the one who earned infamy when his manager pinch-hit for him in the eighth inning of one of them, then he lost two others for lack of run support. It was his pitching motion I memorized and practiced from my pitching rubber (a crack in the front walk); it was his teammate that I fantasized myself becoming—but who would discover me, how would this come about? Would scouts spot me pitching against a backstop at the local elementary school? Would I win a raffle to pitch an inning and prevail so well they couldn't let me go? Or perhaps I would catch the eye of my young hero whose instant ardor would lead him not to ask me to a drive-in movie or grasp my breast but to invite me to train with him.

During a time I didn't know why I wasn't feeling the surging hormones my health class predicted would arise, it was comforting to understand the infield fly rule or how the conditions are right for the hit and run. When I had no idea how my body could ever want another person to penetrate me with a part of himself, it was easier to yearn for Clay Kirby or Steve Arlin to strike out Pete Rose two times in a game. It was preferable to be anxious and apprehensive only because of the batters' consistent impotence to produce runs for these endowed young pitchers, rather than agitate about why boys didn't call me on the phone or what would I do if one ever did. When I had only a vague idea what was involved when girls in the restroom spoke of *making out*—but also had no desire to find out—it was consoling to find out there were at least eight ways for a runner to score from third with less than two outs and that, until his Achilles snapped, Dave Campbell could be counted on for any one of them. And when my high school band boy buddies practiced for dates with their girlfriends by squeezing *my* breasts, I could put off stewing about it alone at home—for at least two hours I was busy listening to Jerry Coleman give personality to each futile ground ball or lonely two-out hit or impudent and costly error; for two hours too consumed with concern about Fred Kendall's alarmingly low percentage throwing out runners attempting to steal to worry about disturbing circumstances at school I'd not only allowed but actually viewed as my social life.

With that going on, how could I have any knowledge about C. Arnhold Smith, the Padres owner. That he'd once been named "Mr. San Diego," that he controlled a taxicab/hotel/tuna fleet/real estate/banking/brokerage empire; that he was an insider crony of Richard Nixon's and laundered hundreds of thousands of dollars in campaign funds for him; that other Nixon insiders shielded him from federal banking regulators; that Nixon's fall spelled the undoing of Smith's fortune and as Nixon's power dissipated, auditors swarmed into C. Arnhold's bank and discovered it had been looted; that despite billions of dollars of deposits, Smith's bank collapsed in the fall of 1973. What I *was* acutely aware of, in January 1974, was that the Padres, after six losing seasons and some nights when only 2,000 people sat in the 60,000-seat stadium, had their moving vans packed and would be leaving in the morning for a new home in Washington DC. Then, mere hours before departure—after I, having just turned eighteen, had finally agitated myself to sleep—McDonald's baron Ray Kroc bought the team from C. Arnhold Smith and ordered the vans unpacked.

During the rest of the 1970s, when first Randy Jones then Gaylord Perry won the Cy Young Award in Padre uniforms, boys in marching band still didn't call me for dates. They were different boys in a different band. They were supposed to be called men. I was in college. Dave Winfield was a college man who went straight to the Major Leagues, not riding the bench or pinch-hitting, but playing regular and hitting, too. Unfortunately Clay Kirby was gone by then, traded away for more hitting, the hitting he had always needed, ironically traded away to get it. Other players came and went during the Dave Winfield era. Even some whose names were familiar from other, better parts of their careers. Willie McCovey, Bobby Tolan, Tito Fuentes, Doug Rader, Willie Davis. A few, like Ozzie Smith, would go elsewhere for greatness. Still, there were the likes of Mike Champion, Tucker Ashford, Rick Sweet, Paul Dade, and a catcher who developed a neurosis about throwing to second base. At times Winfield seemed a powerful Gulliver playing a boys' game with bumbling gnomes.

Around the time *Fear of Flying* was influencing my sensibility not only on future conjugal relationships but on the novels I would someday write, *Ball Four* was the other book I read until the spine disintegrated. Both were held together with rubber bands. When I sat with my trombone at basketball games—surrounded by the strident, urgent, male brass players of the pep band—wondering why I felt such terror and rage when nothing was happening to me, my mind registered and remembered a name repeated over the arena's loud speaker like a mantra: *Assist by Tony Gwynn, assist by Gwynn, field goal Gwynn, another assist for Tony Gwynn.*

In fall of 1978, nearing the end of what should have been Ozzie Smith's

Rookie of the Year first season, I entered the secondary education program for prospective high school teachers. The next baseball season in 1979 started just after I decided I would never be a high school teacher. Still, Gaylord Perry, Randy Jones, Dave Winfield, and Ozzie Smith were promising better than a last-place finish. At the end of the season's first month, and my last month of student teaching, the Padres were 9-14, in fourth place but flirting with third. I finished the term of listless, ineffectual "teaching," and sometimes I think back and calculate where those students would be now. Only four years younger than me, they could be doctors or lawyers or professors or bankers in the upwardly mobile years of their careers. They could be in jail or dead. But they could also be animal trainers or caterers or disc jockeys or wildlife biologists or sculptors or news anchors or musicians or waitresses . . . or baseball players who'd won eight batting titles . . . or were long since washed out.

Following that season the Padres hired Dick Williams to manage, and I was married to a man who had to be taught the difference between a base hit and ground ball. He was a quick and passionate learner. I never asked for nor desired a diamond ring. It was that other diamond that personified our union.

Nineteen eighty-two and 1983 foreshadowed a hodgepodge of what would someday transpire. Instead of worrying that I was feeling no desire to be touched by my new husband, there was some dismay when Tony Gwynn broke his wrist, then came back to hit .348 the last two weeks of the season, but the long time off had done its damage and his average did not rise above .300. It would never happen again. Other glimpses of the future were an eleven-game winning streak and a fourth-place finish instead of sixth, the first cocaine bust and suspension for a swift and cocky second baseman, and a National League consecutive-games-played record for a former Dodger star.

And then, 1984. Ray Kroc, venerated McDonald's mastermind and 1974 savior of the doomed Padres, died in January, and his widow dedicated the season to him. As if the corporate angels had decreed, the Padres were winning.

They'd built the team around a young Tony Gwynn on the cusp of achieving the first of his eight batting titles. Added some tarnished stars from the Yankees and Dodgers—Mr. Clean Steve Garvey cut loose by the Dodgers the year before he set his consecutive game record, and Graig Nettles needing to move on because he authored a Yankee-blasting book called *Balls*. When Goose Gossage likewise abandoned the Yankees and signed with the Padres, someone on the Yankees noted, these days if you don't want to be a Yankee, you have to take a number. There was a short-stop who had once flipped out and flipped off his hometown fans now affectionately dubbed "Smooth Operator," the second baseman with a criminal drug record, the slightly above average outfielder who'd been chosen before Tony Gwynn in the 1981 amateur draft, miscellaneous others found under the heading "Who Are These Guys?" and a pitching staff that included a card-carrying member of the John Birch Society, a near professional bass fisherman, and a left-hander who would in the near future lose his left arm to cancer. These were the 1984 Padres who surprised the world—well, surprised anyone who bothered to notice— by coming back from two games down in a five-game playoff, beating the Cubs three straight to win the National League pennant. There were a few other significant events for me that year, including a national writing award, but it is largely because of the Padres that I look back on 1984 as a heady, happy time, nearly exactly in the middle of my decade of a distressed marriage.

Through the spring and summer there was usually something vital, something invigorating to float on, or concerns more gratifying than intimacy dilemmas to wrestle with: Would Steve Garvey and Graig Nettles be able to shoulder the club's power needs? Would the ten-game suspension of Dick Williams after the multiple mob on-field skirmishes in Atlanta be worth it for the possible incentive, the spark it might provide the August-weary players? Was it possible Terry Kennedy wasn't any better at throwing out base-stealing runners as expansion-draft Fred Kendall and neurotic head case Mike Ivie of the 1970s? Which of these current tender personalities needed to be coddled, which needed a boot in the butt? And talk about head cases, would philosopher, physicist, jazz guitarist, and neo-Nazi Eric Show keep his head on straight for the whole season? As one mind, my husband and I followed the season, studied player statistics, knew weaknesses to avoid or overcome, and eccentricities needing to be understood. Along with the team, we were kindled and rekindled during midseason brawls in Atlanta, crucial series with Los Angeles, and slump-breaking blowouts. We only felt listless or distressed or uneasy if Templeton made an error, Gossage blew a lead, or Tony went 0-4. In giddy 1984 those things didn't happen often.

The Padres lost the first two games in Chicago in the League Championship Series. Lost badly. Looked like the Padres of 1970. The newspapers spoke of the end of some kind of century-old curse we'd never heard of. When the team flew back from Chicago and arrived at the stadium on buses at 2 a.m., we were there with thousands of other people to scream and whoop and whistle and yell and sing "We Are the Champions" and "Let's Get Excited." We cheered and hugged and kissed for each hit, run scored, and key strikeout during the three home games in the League Championship Series, as the Padres came back to eradicate Chicago's belief that its forty-year World Series drought was over. When Garvey hit his incredible home run in the ninth inning to win game 4, we burst out our front door to shriek toward the sky, and we could also hear the clamor and roar of sixty thousand other people screaming at the stadium in Mission Valley a few miles away. We danced in the street again, waved and shouted from an open car window to strangers on the freeway, after the Padres won a frenzied game 5 and had won the pennant. Two weeks later, we sang songs and yelled our throats raw with a crowd of tens of thousands in the stadium—not during a game but at a rally after losing the World Series (while Detroit celebrated their victory by burning overturned cars, breaking windows, and looting). From September through the end of the year, we slept profoundly, side by side.

At first 1985 was more of the same. Until the team began the agonizing process of letting a five-game lead slip away to the Dodgers. One of my show dogs had been lame for two months, over eighty houses burned to the ground in our neighborhood, and we weren't even pretending to have a sex life anymore. I went to a doctor complaining of chest pains, positive the stabbing sensation was because the Padres were blowing their lead, not a symptom of my impaired marriage.

Like many winning teams, the 1984 Padres are characterized and remembered not by superstars but with the cliché of team chemistry—a difficult to reproduce magic potion. It just means everything was working, the parts fit. If the team's pinnacle in 1984 harmonized with the best companionship or partnership my marriage had to offer, then the corrosion of the elements in that team chemistry coincides with our marital dissonance and eventual silence.

It started when Allan Wiggins didn't show up for a game, then missed several games in a row, and they didn't know (or weren't saying) where he was or what had happened, until a reporter broke the story that he was checked into drug rehab. Kroc's philanthropist widow vowed he'd never play for the team again. He was traded before the end of June, just before over sixty canyon-rim houses with views of the stadium in Mission Valley were condensed into piles of ashes in the worst wildfire in city history, a few miles from where I lived. The smoke rising over the treetops looked like a jet crash. On July 13 the Padres were nudged back into second place. On September 2 it was third place. On September 11, Eric Show, as always petulant, sat in moody insolence on the mound after giving up Pete Rose's record-setting hit in Cincinnati, while the ball was presented to Rose and ovations given. On September 15 the team was in fourth place.

In 1985, Ed Whitson, who'd opted for free agency and the hot lights of New York, broke Yankee manager Billy Martin's arm in a bar brawl.

In 1989, Dave Dravecky, by then pitching for the Giants, came back as a starter after cancer treatment, but his left arm snapped while throwing a pitch.

In 1990, Steve Garvey, who'd retired a hero two years before—the first Padre to have his uniform number retired—had to give up his budding political career and admit to fathering two illegitimate children, in addition to the child carried by his supposed fiancée. All over San Diego, vehicles exhibited bumper stickers proclaiming "Steve Garvey Is Not My Padre!"

In 1991, Clay Kirby died in his hometown. Probably a heart attack. And Allan Wiggins died, possibly of AIDS. Dave Dravecky's cancerous pitching arm was amputated. Eric Show, pitching elsewhere, went on the disabled list for an infected thumb from biting his fingernails.

In 1994, Eric Show died of unknown causes at a drug and alcohol treatment center.

My marriage, likewise, died. But besides pumping most of my zeal into training and showing my dogs, into inventing alternate worlds in stories and novels, I learned to find glimmers of the 1984 feeling: Promising rookies, conquests in the free agent marketplace, and of course, always, Tony Gwynn. The late 1980s and 1990s were the heart of Tony's career. Stealing five bases in a single game . . . setting a Major League record when he and two other Padres lead off a game with back-to-back-to-back home runs . . . going 3-4 and 4-5, not just once, and his second league-leading batting average at .370. Breaking up no-hitters in the eighth or ninth. Another season's batting title secured with a 3-4 on the last day of the season to beat the man he was tied with who'd sat out the game, hoping Tony would be oh-for. Five hits in a game for the fourth time in one season. Batting .394 and on a tear, a .400 batting title eminent, when the players union called a strike in 1994. All-Star appearances. A record-tying eighth batting title. A 3,000th hit.

In 1998, fourteen years after the 1984 miracle, the Padres were finally back in the League Championship Series. After scoring decisive victories in the first three games against the Atlanta Braves, the Padres lost the fourth game, then had a lead in the seventh inning of the fifth game. Sitting still in a chair was out of the question. Likewise incapable of standing in one place, I paced a circle through my house muttering *please, please, please, please*, which shifted to *no, no, no, no.* . . . A few walks, a few well-placed hits, and the lead disappeared and I flung myself onto my bed, overcome with strange sobbing. After my listless divorce I never vowed to never marry again. After holding my first dog's face close to mine while a vet injected her with a fatal dose of barbiturates, I did not vow to never form another attachment that would only lead to this desolate grief over its loss. But on my bed in the fall of 1998, I vowed I could not afford to love another team again. I knew I lied.

The Padres did eventually win the National League pennant in the sixth game against the Braves, bringing me and Tony—and, wherever he was, my ex-husband—back to the World Series. Boomeranged back to euphoria, but we were swept in four games, losing a game 1 lead, then losing heart. All except Tony. He was 8-15.

Eighteen years after I played trombone while he played basketball, I got to meet Tony Gwynn at a book signing. His book signing, not mine. I waited in line for over two hours. He was scheduled to sign books for an hour and a half. At the time he was supposed to leave, Tony came out, surveyed the line of people extending outside the bookstore's front door and curled around the food court. The he called out, "Okay, let's do it!" and returned to his table to sign every book, baseball card, and ball. When it was my turn, and I had a fleeting moment to say something to him, I sputtered, "Thank you for staying in San Diego." He handed me my autographed book, smiled, and said, "Thank *you*."

After the player strike in 1994, they said fans would have to forgive the players, would have to be won over again, would have to be seduced. I was an easy conquest.

11. The Bad Case
A 50th Birthday Love Letter
Kurt Rheinheimer

Onset, 1954. There's no more heroic and unattainable image of life than, say, the Babe's film-quickened swing unfurling above those small feet about to begin the trot he taught the world how to do, his eyes uptilted toward the bleachers as he minces toward first. The man, the swing, and the era are as long ago and faraway as a legal spitball. Yet I am, certainly and unashamedly, a part of the same family tree that holds George Herman Ruth—by virtue of the simple conceits and connections of being born in the same town as he and of the same German heritage, of knowing he was an Oriole before he was anything else, of knowing that his father's tavern once sat where Camden Yards' right-center field is now, of having lived the core part of my life within the geography of that line of Baltimore-native greatness that runs from the Babe to Kaline to Ripken. It is a heritage as deep-rooted, as multi-limbed and strongly cherished, as the one I was born into, a love that has broadened and deepened almost invisibly across the decades, building perfect measures of the distantly majestic and the intimately personal.

The blood connection that certifies my branch of the Baltimore baseball tree began with a perfect, pure incarnation: I was eight years old and, in the manner of my peers under the tall, innocent-blue skies of the 1950s, was enlivened by nothing so much as things huge and threatening. Our conversations ran nearly solely in the vein of one mammoth pending concussion and what made it more threatening than the one just previously mentioned. We lived on a tiny peninsula just northeast of the city, and in the little cove behind our house was a sea turtle as big as a Buick, able to eat a high school guy in one bite. The quicksand pits at the end of the peninsula had swallowed up not only any number of cats and dogs, but also at least one escaped convict. The giant seaplane being tested near our spit of land would crash again nearby.

Then one day, in whatever way an eight-year-old becomes aware of such things, all those compellingly monstrous things fell away in favor of something stronger, something more beautiful and even more riveting. The baseball team was coming to town. Something brand-new and brighter than sunshine: the Baltimore Orioles.

Who was I to be so susceptible? There was no explanation that I can recall for the sudden shift—no coaxing, no impetus, no warning. Certainly my father, born in Germany in 1916 and on that April day an intense, intellectual, thirty-eight-year-old man with two jobs and in pursuit of another degree, had no interest and to this day carries nothing but disdain for professional sports. My mother was less adamant but equally oblivious. There was no apparent cause beyond the entity itself: the triumphant arrival of the baseball team. I'd not been aware, until that dawning, of the concept of hometown. Now I had one. That the team was just a few months removed from being the lowly, laughable St. Louis Browns meant nothing, simply because I didn't know it. The business machinations of Baltimore investors and their success had unfolded in perfect sync with the need of a big-eyed boy to take full hold of something, to look upon a space so perfect as a baseball diamond and understand what was occurring there.

In the span of one week, the world opened up. I'd never read the newspaper before that day in April 1954 when the war-type headline announced the coming of the Orioles, but I read it every day thereafter. I'd listened to the radio only for the Saturday Top 40 show, but the line of great Baltimore baseball voices that began with Ernie Harwell and Chuck Thompson became an instant source of comfort, trust, and security, and of deep, joyously one-way friendship. My instant love was virginally pure, tinted orange and black.

Symptom, 1960. My father found no peace with my early adolescent pursuits. He played Bach and Beethoven and Brahms on the big hi-fi and I turned away to Joan Baez and then Bob Dylan. He presented John Steinbeck and Joseph Conrad and I snuck away to *Mad* magazine and

Baseball Digest. He showed me his stamp collections and I showed him cartoons on the backs of baseball cards. He led a daily, impassioned intellectual life and wanted the same for me—a deep understanding and appreciation of the artifact and the great effort behind it.

Neither of us had the capacity, in the spring of 1960, to realize that the habit I began then contained at least the seed of what he wanted of me, even if the focus was far off target. To him I was cutting up a worthless part of the newspaper. What I was doing was collecting every paragraph and photograph I saw pertaining to one compelling if arcane aspect of the vast sea of baseball information that began the flow that has continued over the too many years since.

Hero worship among just-teens has long since gone the way of respectable earned run averages and complete games, but in that spring when the team was six, I was fourteen, and he was twenty-six, one John George Brandt came to town to be the new center fielder for the best team in the whole wide world. People had told me I was quick, and that I turned the right way on a fly ball most of the time, and so I decided I was a going to grow up to be a center fielder as cool as Jackie Brandt. Not only did he glide around without apparent effort in center, he did equally wondrous things off the field. He once convinced half the team to drive over to DC to check out the new thirty-some flavors ice cream store, carefully considered the flavor array, and then ordered a vanilla cone. You could go out to Memorial Stadium early for a Sunday doubleheader to watch him in outfield practice and see him go back to the wall, pretend to watch a long drive go over the fence, and then nonchalantly glove the ball mid-chest.

My scissors habit with Jackie Brandt news continued through 1960 and was still going strong in 1961, when Jim Gentile arrived to help the Orioles challenge for the pennant for the first time. By now I was clipping the *Baltimore Morning Sun* and the *Evening Sun*, and sometimes going to the neighbors' to get the *News Post* and cut it up, too. The huge-format Orioles yearbooks from that era now sit in a box in my attic, with one page carefully sliced out of each, and a gap in other pages here and there, where my man Jack stood with Brooks and Diamond Jim and Gus Triandos, holding their bats out in front of them as if they were divining rods in search of that first championship.

I never thought to show my father my clippings collection, and he'd not have cared to see it if I had. My daily attention to the facts and figures of the box score, to the game dispatch and the opinions of every columnist in three papers was a simple necessity for me, and when noted at all by my father was judged as ongoing, increasingly discouraging evidence of mild wastrelhood. He continued to try to wean me; I continued to read and clip, and take baseball deeper and deeper into my Baltimore blood.

Outbreak, 1966. Even today, you can drive old U.S. 40 northeast of Baltimore—running in nearly perfect parallel to the aorta of the East Coast interstates—and aside from an occasional gasoline price sign or sudden, bright Wendy's box, successfully pretend for stretches of many miles at a time that you are driving through a decade long past, along a road that couldn't possibly still exist. The low-slung taprooms and cabin-style motels look only slightly more worn than they did in the summers of the mid-1960s, when college boys from East Baltimore rode out there to apply for jobs at Bata Shoe or Tasty Freez, or around the Aberdeen Proving Grounds, at any one of hundreds of little buildings wherein tires were repaired, eggs and pancakes were slung, or hamburger buns were baked. The highway was fast and alive and slightly dangerous, touched with a feel of much-farther-south.

My job, that summer and fall of 1966, was as an assembler of windows and screens in a small, hot, square building out on 40, where the rock lots crackled with Mustangs and Camaros, and the weeping willows swept around carelessly in the dusk. In October my fascination with 40 and my love of the Orioles were put to the test. Part of the ethic my parents had instilled was that when you had a job you went to work. Much as I had not realized until after I was out of high school that teachers were actual people who had families and took trips and went out drinking, I had no concept, at age twenty, that there was any choice but to go to work when you were scheduled to. And so it was that on Sunday, October 9, 1966, I was at a hot workbench forcing rubber stripping into a tiny groove that just barely accommodated the rubber and the screen behind it. On one side of me, blowing on me and an older, career screen builder, was a floor-mounted fan the size of a manhole cover; on the other side was a little transistor radio, competing with the noise of the fan and the factory to tell us what was going on with game 4 of the 1966 World Series: Dave McNally and Don Drysdale in a pitching classic, in a series that was 3–0 Orioles and had already featured astounding pitching from Moe Drabowsky, Jim Palmer, and Wally Bunker.

Late that afternoon, when the Orioles prevailed 1–0 on the strength of a Frank Robinson homer and McNally's four-hitter, the old man next to me looked up at me for the only time that I remember and smiled. As I met his glance, I felt my face begin to pull in against itself with the beginnings of tears. With nerve that I didn't know I had, I put down my stripping tool and went out front to watch Route 40 explode with Baltimore joy. I went because I couldn't hear the horns blaring from inside, and because I wanted to wave to all the other people who had come out of the little buildings to wave back to me and celebrate the unbelievable moment that had just occurred. Thirteen years after its birth, the best team there was had at last proved it to the world.

But Route 40 looked exactly as it always did. Cars rolled by in their usual numbers and speed. The world appeared just as it did on any day along the highway. I was not prepared: I jumped and whooped and whistled, working to prime the pump as the seeds of a since-sustained sense of keen injustice were sown in one moment. Just as I had no capacity to understand where everyone was on that October afternoon, so have I none to understand that there are but a few of us who remember that from that day forward for the next thirty years, the Orioles were the true kings of baseball. And even fewer who know that you can go back to those days when Jackie Brandt arrived in 1960 and count all the wins and losses for all the teams all the way until the middle of the last decade of the century, and you will find that the Baltimore Orioles had the most of one and the fewest of the other.

No, it isn't just the very-bad-case fan with his eyes brimming with pride about the Oriole Way or the homegrown Hall of Fame pitchers and infielders; or the triple crown winner in 1966, the string of hundred-win seasons from 1969 through 1971. It is more than that. It is, in the manner of my father relentlessly championing the three bs of classical music or ceaselessly pointing out the grave inconsistencies in American foreign policy, an involuntary addiction to a great truth unknown to the world, creeping farther into used-to-be with every year of the abyss of the ownership of Peter Angelos.

You could look it up: Records of all Major League teams: 1960–96. 1. Baltimore Orioles, 3,194-2,641. 2. New York Yankees, 3,176-2,667. 3. Los Angeles Dodgers, 3,162-2,690. 4. Cincinnati Reds, 3,154-2,690. 5. Pittsburgh Pirates, 3,044-2,795.

Critical, 1979. When I was thirty-three and the Orioles twenty-five, a crisis arose. The franchise had by then left the enlightened, hardworking, nurturing hometown ownership of the National Brewing Company and had come to rest in the hands of powerful Washington lawyer Edward Bennett Williams, who aligned himself quickly with the game's strongest owners in seeking to modernize baseball's marketing of itself. A Williams interview in the *Washington Post* talked about the days of the "ma and pa Orioles" being over. He said Orioles fans were "on trial" for their tepid support, and he flirted openly with DC, which had lost the Senators in 1961 to Minnesota and lost them again in 1972 to Texas.

I felt called upon as I had not been called before or since. The open letter to Edward Bennett Williams ran in the *Baltimore Evening Sun* on August 21, 1979. Their headline writer titled it, "Dear Mr. Williams: A Great Chunk of My Life Rests in Your Hands."

There are times when zealotry is the best policy.

Dear Mr. Williams

I guess I should admit right off that the main reason I'm proud of being born where I was is the fact that in the spring of 1954, in the month that I turned eight, the baseball team came to town. The word Baltimore suddenly had meaning for me; it went alongside the word Orioles, and the sound flowed together nicely, and described a team that played the most wonderful game on earth.

As a third grader I was ripe for heroes, and my earliest were men named Diering and Turley and Hunter. I played my Little League ball with full knowledge and conviction that I was as graceful and talented as the players I saw at the stadium. The shape of my life was framed around the day-to-day fate of the big league team from my hometown. I filled notebook after notebook with clippings from the Sun papers and the old News Post. I covered my walls with photographs. I learned my earliest lessons of fair play and best-team-win and lose-with-grace and try-again-tomorrow from the Baltimore Orioles.

And I guess I should admit, too, that my early addiction has not been cured in the twenty-five years since. I agonized over the leaving of Paul Richards and the coming of Billy Hitchcock. And in 1966, when Hank Bauer brought Frank and Brooks and Boog home against the Dodgers, I was a twenty-year-old eight-year-old boy—filled with a kind of euphoria I've not experienced since.

Since 1966 I've lived in Philadelphia and Omaha and Roanoke, but my soul has been kept in the town where I was born by the knowledge that Baltimore has had the best team in baseball for all the years that I have been man and boy. I have listened to scratchy radio transmissions from a thousand miles away. I have not outgrown my boyhood need for the final score before I go to sleep at night.

Perhaps I should admit, too, that although I have never counted myself a patriot—never flown the flag on the Fourth or marched in a parade—I do have a life as an American, and that life has been formed and defined by my unashamed and unending love for the national pastime as played by the Baltimore Orioles. My pride in being a Marylander and Baltimorean was born out of youthful study of the map to learn where the Orioles would be on their long midsummer road trip.

Implorations for you not to break the flow of city and sports history need to be as strong as the tradition which forms that history. And that tradition cries out for you to do several things: to maintain the most productive farm system in baseball—a system that has spawned a Robinson, a McNally, a Powell, a Palmer, and a Murray, to name but a few; to hire men who will make trades in the tradition of those that brought Frank Robinson and

Luis Aparicio, Mike Cuellar, and Ken Singleton; to seek and sign young men who will develop into fine pitchers and solid defensive players—to continue the string of Cy Young and Gold Glove Award winners that has marked Baltimore's teams.

A great chunk of my life has come to rest in your hands. It is on this day my most fervent wish that those hands possess the proper blend of sensitivity and strength to continue to advance the heritage of the modern Baltimore Orioles Baseball Club— that the hands are cautious enough to cradle their vast inheritance with necessary, mandated care.

Sincerely

It was not long before Edward Bennett Williams was saying things like, "There may come a time when I leave baseball, but baseball will never leave Baltimore."

Rally, 1992. When you drive into downtown Baltimore from out to the northeast of the city where I grew up, you drive Pulaski Highway, the citified name of old U.S. 40 as it heads into urban territory. You drive past smaller, dirtier versions of the buildings out toward Aberdeen—the individual-cottage motels, the taprooms, and the silver-faced diners. You get closer to downtown and things turn darker, closer together, even less cared for. Piles of rusting iron castings fill lots on either side of the poorly paved roadway. Buildings are boarded up here and there, or fully abandoned. Amid broken, trash-strewn residential strips—their only pride being the old marble steps—flash tall, neon-colored billboards touting extra-long menthol cigarettes and tall cans of malt liquor. When I traveled this route as a late teen, I was on my way to one of two places: the civic center to see Earl Monroe, Gus Johnson, and Wes Unseld and the rest of the Baltimore Bullets, or a few blocks east of there to The Block, where we would walk around for hours trying to get up the nerve to walk into one of the two blocks full of bouncer-guarded doors behind which the likes of Busty Russell and a hundred others with even more pointed names reigned as the female denizens of the harbor area. If you walked a block farther south, you'd encounter their male counterparts—the drunks who lived along the wharves.

The first time I went to Oriole Park at Camden Yards I came at it from that same direction, and carried those recollections of that part of my city. I was not prepared to like the new park. The boy who'd gone hundreds of times to Memorial Stadium to watch Brooks and Frank, Eddie and Cal, Palmer and McNally; the boy who had idolized Jackie Brandt; or even the boy who occasionally went to see John Unitas and Lenny Moore and Ray Berry—that boy was still strongly alive in a middle-aged man in 1992, and carried a sort of chin-forward, semi-pugnacious prove-it-if-you-can perspective about the product of the three years of hoopla and hype around the inner harbor.

But unlike a sustained longing for eight teams in each league, a still alive disdain for the designated hitter and an only recently dissolved distaste for wild card teams, my predilection for reactionary traditionalism when it comes to baseball was overcome before I even reached Camden Yards, walking from the east. The darkest, scariest, smelliest part of my city had been transformed. The mammoth B&O Warehouse—there forever but heretofore invisible among other warehouses and shipping detritus—was now striking in its identity as the longest building on the East Coast. It stood clean-bricked and proud, as if in sentinel role for the field behind it and for the whole of the harbor, which was now a place that made you think of Austin or San Francisco way before you considered it to be downtown BalmerMerlin. And it was the ballpark, with its unmarked spot in right-center where once sat the Ruth family's tavern, that was the prime destination amid the bustle of shoppers and diners and sightseers moving around what had so long been the city's dirty big secret.

And if the Orioles—only four years removed from the ignominy of the 0-21 start and the most losses in a season in franchise history—were not the Orioles of the glory days, there were signs of hope. They would win twenty-two more games in their first season at Camden Yards than they had in their last at Memorial Stadium. The attendance of more than 3.5 million would shatter the team's old record by more than a million and earn a spot as the fifth highest in Major League history.

So it was that my visits that first season fit snugly with all the Oriole years that had gone before. Cal was here, after all—his consecutive-game streak now at more than 1,700 and only three seasons from Gehrig—and

Mike Mussina, and a smattering of other homegrown Birds with promise, including Ben McDonald and Gregg Olson. The original Oriole logo popped out all over the place, and Boog Powell had a presence, too, with a mammoth barbeque stand on the promenade out between the right-field seats and the warehouse, near where the Orioles Hall of Fame plaques were mounted.

I looked and strolled and smiled and got shivers at my neck. A grand new home had been built for the team that had found me as a boy and that had held me all my life. I found myself recounting even more than usual the proud history and championship chapters. And then it occurred to me what, amid all this glorious black and orange, was not here. Not on the outfield walls where it is in some parks. Not on its own piece of facade somewhere in deep center. Not on the tall, majestic reach of the warehouse wall beyond the stadium's right-field wall.

Where, oh where was my team's history? Where did it say, for all to see and drink in and recall,

> World Champions: 1966, 1970, 1983
> American League
>   Champions: 1966, 1969, 1970, 1971, 1979, 1983
> American League
>   East Champions: 1969, 1970, 1971, 1973, 1974, 1979, 1983

Not to mention at least a few uniform numbers up there somewhere, too, Hall of Fame numbers:

> 4: The best manager of his era
> 5: The best-fielding third baseman ever
> 20: The man who came from Cincinnati at "an old 30"
>   and transformed the franchise
> 22: Eight 20-win seasons with that big-kick high heater.
> 33: The man who retired the game-winning RBI stat with
>   as consistent a set of seasons as anyone

Yes, the warehouse is clean looking, an attraction in its own right. But somewhere between those stacks of windows, the history needs to be mounted and displayed. Part of moving ahead is knowing every day where you came from.

Terminal, 2000. Your earliest memory of a stadium is the long view, when you walked up toward the big facade out front with a group of buddies in awe of the palace you were about to enter. You were home again, the same way you were when you went to visit your grandmother at Christmas. And you remember being a part of the huge organism that rose up with a majestic roar at certain moments. When Eddie Murray, say, as a twenty-year-old switch hitter barely out of Double A ball, took the low-and-away pitch from his lefty stance and drilled it on a line off the left-field wall to clear the bases. It was all one noise, all one collective rising from the seats, all one town elevated in pride over another homegrown Oriole about to fledge.

You think a little harder and you realize you saw Jim Palmer and Cal Ripken as twenty-year-olds there, too, opening their wings before the world. You saw an infield of Brooks Robinson, Mark Belanger, Davey Johnson, and Boog Powell. A four-man rotation that won twenty games each.

But more keenly than any of that, you remember a hundred lesser guys whose movements on the field are as clear as they were the first time you saw them. Look out on the mound at Dick Hall—all nine feet of him— with legs as long as most men are tall, his Adam's apple protruding like a swallowed acorn, going into the stretch, hawk-necking at the runners and then moving toward the plate.

Here's Paul Blair, skinny and grinny as a high school boy, playing way too shallow in center, turning on a long fly before it leaves the bat—before anyone but Paul Blair knows it's a long fly—flashing toward right-center for a ball he has no chance on. And then easing into a cruise to turn it into a routine catch.

Here's Hoyt Wilhelm, with the big-eyed, smooth-skinned face of a marionette and his head cocked off to one side as if he awakened with the worst crick in the history of bad pillows. He goes into a lazy, loping windup—appearing vulnerable to a wind gust—to deliver an even lazier pitch: the slow, arcing knuckler that spawned the glove nearly as big as a trashcan lid that sent Gus Triandos to a record for passed balls, that is to this day more than forty years later the last pitcher to no-hit the detested, detestable Yankees.

At the plate here's little fat Gene Woodling way late in his career, feet tucked together, knees bent deep and touching, and the bat curled back in the perfect poor-man's-Musial stance. And here's even littler, even fatter Earl Weaver, out of the dugout in full charge at the home plate umpire, his face exploding in full, splendid disbelief before he even reaches this most incompetent man on the planet. Weaver cannot contain in his body the huge offense that's been done him. His arms fly here and there. His legs twitch and jump. His hat is either a weapon or a hindrance he has to throw away. Words cannot come out of his mouth fast enough.

Those movements live in you forever; motions are as intact in the body as images are in the head—a gift from the stadium that held them all.

I was in search of some tangible piece of those memories on a September Saturday in 2000, when I arose before the dawn to make a three-hundred-mile drive to visit her one last time. This was the day for Baltimore baseball fans to take home a seat or a sign or a brick—some remnant of Memorial Stadium before it was laid to rest with a wrecking ball.

The line when I arrived had its head at a hole in the center-field wall, and it curled all the way to the front, where the pretty silver typeface still shone as the stadium's welcome. The line was half a mile long and four to six across—filled with faces I knew as home, but without specific names. People talked and joked and remembered as they waited to be let in—in sets of fifty—to take home a piece of their lives. After walking along the line, I stood near where people were let in and wondered what I should do. A man my age told me—in full Balmer accent—about having driven half an hour for nothing. He couldn't take the three or four hours in line on top of the time it took once he got in. "And besides," he said, "who knows what'll be left by then anyhow?"

I told him I wasn't too sure about the wait either.

Then a man with a megaphone came out of the stadium to walk the line and give people an update. "I think by the time you get in there will still be some chairs," he said in hearing distance of perhaps the first hundred feet of the line. "And bricks. But a lot of the other stuff is pretty well gone. The signs and all." He continued along, walking against the line, changing his news to more and more pessimistic the farther he moved from the center-field opening. I followed him, and between his little speeches he told me I could e-mail the Babe Ruth Museum and reserve a brick.

Back in the car, at 1 p.m., I punched up WBAL on the radio. The Orioles have danced around the Baltimore AM dial in their history, but WBAL is where they belong, with Jim West doing the pregame and Chuck Thompson doing the play-by-play. This day there was a smooth-voiced man named Greg Sher, taking and making calls on the theme of the day—the heart being ripped out of the city.

I drove on out I-70. I heard a woman read a poem—a simply rhyming, mixed-image homage to a grand old lady whose skirt had been ruined by winter. Out past Frederick, I turned onto U.S. 340, listening to more Baltimoreans bemoan their loss.

Back on I-81 and back in Virginia, Greg Sher called Chuck Thompson, who told him a story about Brooks Robinson Day, when Doug DeCinces—the man who replaced the greatest-fielding third baseman ever—was charged with representing his teammates in presenting a gift to Robinson.

"DeCinces came up out of the dugout and walked straight to third base," Chuck Thompson said. He paused then for effect, as only he knows how. You could envision him turning his head gently to one side, as if for pacing, before he spoke again. "He reached down and pulled the bag right out of its moorings and handed it to Brooks." Another, briefer pause. "Not a word was spoken," Chuck Thompson went on. "Just a great gesture from one professional to another. The place went crazy."

I was a third of the way down the Shenandoah Valley and that was the last thing I heard on WBAL. I glanced at the milepost sign and it dawned on me that over the years I had tried scores of times to keep the 'BAL signal with me as I drove toward Virginia, and had always lost it long before now, long before I reached the state line. And this was in the middle of the afternoon.

My brick sits on its own little table there by the window. It's number 22745. Certified by the Babe Ruth Museum.

Closure, 2002. In the deep, fallow period that has overcome the Orioles since soon after the takeover of ownership by Peter Angelos, there has been a need for new ways to sustain one's love of the franchise he has despoiled, for new techniques to revisit its ascent to excellence and its forty-year reign as the game's premier organization. The four-year infancy between 1954 and 1957, when they first won as many as they lost, seemed interminable as it occurred. The mediocrity now maintained since 1998— the six consecutive American League East finishes ahead of only the now onrushing Devil Rays—has been both longer in time and far more deeply injurious, in the manner of an unnecessary death too soon, or of Herb Score falling so suddenly, so sadly. The difference is that this descent is not an accident but a preventable tragedy brought on by a rare combination of shortsightedness, stupidity, and stubbornness.

And so it was that when my father turned eighty-six in the spring of 2002 and told me that his eighty-four-year-old brother had invited him out to Denver for a family reunion, I told him I'd drive him out west. The only condition was that we drive a route through Omaha and plan an overnight stop there. I'd lived in Omaha for five years in the 1970s, hadn't been back since, and had no tie to the city save an Oriole one—a connection I had decided over the previous year or so I needed to invoke.

I found the name in the phone book one morning at the end of June and drove to the address. I cruised it twice to convince myself this modest one-story home with paint cans out front was the one I wanted. The door was answered by a burly man in his sixties who said that the object of my stop was already out at the golf course. The burly man made a phone call to let them know that a guy who used to live in Baltimore was looking to catch up with one of the group teeing off at 10.

Half an hour's drive through a cornfield later, I was directed out to the second tee, where a little greeting party stood at the ready.

"Don't even talk to him," said a thin guy in his seventies.

"We do all we can not to encourage him," said another fit guy well north of sixty-five.

And then there he was: Jackie Brandt. My first and only hero—the object of my greatest Oriole affection—was immediately recognizable: thin, fit-looking, sixty-eight years old and grinning with the attention. He kept grinning while I shook his hand and then asked me what the hell it was I wanted.

What the hell I wanted went back to those seasons of the early 1960s, when my father had been impatient with me for cutting up newspapers as I collected every story, column, and photograph I could about the man who stood before me. Now, forty years later, I had carried a fat manila envelope halfway across the country. I was ready to give something back to an Oriole, in exchange for the joys of every summer since I turned eight. I'd come to realize, over recent years, that the pile of clippings might well mean more to their subject or to his family at this point than they did to me. Even my father, still immune to the Orioles, said I was doing something good and generous.

Jack Brandt, the clown of those about-to-fly Birds of the 1960s, was no less one now. He joked that he wasn't sure he could trust his roommate not to use the old bits of newsprint for toilet paper. He feigned huge offense when he paged through and came across a full-page image of Jim Busby and pretended I'd clipped the page for Busby instead of the full-pager of Brandt on the other side. In the end, the Oriole center fielder of my early teen years accepted my gift and placed it carefully in the back of his golf cart.

As I turned to leave, one of his golfing buddies came over and asked me to stay long enough to watch Jack Brandt tee off, asserting that at nearly seventy, he still drilled the ball on a line every time. As I waited, it occurred to me that the reputation of this man among the Baltimore columnists of my youth was that he might be just as likely to whiff his tee shot on purpose as to put forth his best effort. He'd been good copy: The guy who did his best only when he felt like it.

Jack Brandt's swing came back true and strong, the impact was perfect and the drive was long and tall, right down the middle of the fairway. In his motions was a full respect for the game he was engaged in, as he had always asserted there was when he had played baseball for the Baltimore Orioles, as it had seemed to me when I'd wanted to be who he was.

We had not talked about that team, Jack Brandt and I. He talked about going out to see almost every Omaha Royals game and enjoying Triple A ball just fine. I told him about feeling the same way about the A league team I followed back home. In saying nothing about the current, mediocre Orioles, we had nonetheless spent time deeply colored with black and orange. My journey's goal had been to give away the possession that had been my most cherished as a boy, and to give it to the man who had made it come to be. And as I had made my gift, the old Oriole and the old

Oriole fan shared the pain of the void these days. There are millions of us all over this nation, accommodating ourselves with the local minor league squad, or following individual players who grew up in Maryland, or rooting for a Baltimore prospect pitcher at Frederick or Bowie or Ottawa, all the while hoping vainly for the Angelos family to at last realize its legacy, or to move on. We wait, those of us with the Baltimore Orioles in our blood, for the baseball world to be righted again, these fifty years after its twentieth-century star was born.

12. Billy Gardner's Ground Out
Floyd Skloot

The play was routine. A sharp grounder to the shortstop, who fielded the ball and threw to first for an easy out. It happened at Brooklyn's Ebbets Field on a Sunday afternoon late in the summer of 1955. The batter was a New York Giants utility infielder named Billy Gardner, the Dodgers shortstop was Pee Wee Reese, and the first baseman that day was Jackie Robinson. There was nothing memorable about the play. But for the last forty-seven years, I've never forgotten it.

I was eight years old, sitting with my father in box seats halfway between home plate and first base. He took me to several games every season, so this was neither my first nor last visit to Ebbets Field. It was just another game, with the familiar feel of being in the stands with my father on the only day of the week he didn't work at his live poultry market. As usual, he ate peanuts and put emptied shells back into the bag they'd come from. He spent most of a half inning struggling to open the top of a miniature bottle of Scotch he'd brought in his jacket pocket. He rolled the program into the shape of a megaphone and razzed the nearby Giants first baseman. He lit a cigar.

All of that is background to a perfectly meaningless play. When Billy Gardner hit the ball, I watched him run down the line and never looked away. Though the play wasn't close, he ran hard. He kept his head down, knowing there was little hope that he would be safe, and crossed first base well after the sound of the ball reaching Robinson's mitt. Then he slowed and turned back toward the dugout. I noticed Gardner's fair hair below the black Giants cap. I noticed that as he slowed his head bobbed up and down as though in full agreement with the umpire's call. He was out, all right. I watched his face—what I could see of it beneath the cap's bill—and detected no reaction to having grounded out. Then he simply trotted behind catcher Roy Campanella, who stood out in front of home plate as the Dodgers threw the ball around the infield. Gardner wore uniform number 15, and I kept watching as he entered the dugout, walked toward the end nearest home plate, and sat down.

There is no obvious reason why I should be able to recall this so clearly now, in the autumn of 2002, as I sit in my small round house in the middle of twenty acres of forest in rural western Oregon. But that moment has always been with me, recurring like a tune running through my head.

Forgetting is what makes memory work well. Our brains are set up to discard obsolete or unimportant information; otherwise, we'd quickly find ourselves overloaded with data. That's why we can't remember what we had for dinner last Monday, unless it made us sick or was unique in some way. We forget seldom-used phone numbers and the names of friends of friends to whom we were introduced at a party six months ago. If the circumstances aren't special, we normally forget where we went on the morning of May 17 or what an acquaintance said to us on the street last year. Distracted by more vital matters, we sometimes forget that we have keys in our hand, or even why we went downstairs as we stand in the hallway and wonder what we're doing there.

If it is to be retained, information must be used, or must be embedded in memory through potent circumstances such as trauma, study, or vivid association. As Harvard psychologist Daniel L. Schacter explains it, in *The Seven Sins of Memory*, "emotionally charged incidents are better remembered than nonemotional events. The emotional boost begins at the moment a memory is born, when attention and elaboration strongly influence whether an experience will be subsequently remembered or forgotten."

The less we retrieve it, the less likely a name or phone number or event is to be kept in memory. Faces, the plots of old movies, the combination to a lock no longer in use—such detail fades into the mists beyond memory. We're better off this way, less cluttered, more prepared to keep and utilize what's vital. Or, as Schacter says, "a system that renders information less accessible over time is highly functional."

To persist in long-term memory, then, events must have real significance. Usually, that significance is negative. "The primary territory of persistence," Schacter says, is "disappointment, regret, failure, sadness, and trauma." Memories strongly linked with our emotional lives, what Schacter calls "hot memories," are the kind that typically endure despite our best efforts to forget them. This doesn't mean that positive memories can't endure as well—the first meeting with your wife, the trip to Ireland, the day you ran a marathon in less than three hours or saw a brilliant production of *Hamlet*. Only that tenacity of memory, which is made possible by chemical and biological responses to powerful experience, most commonly occurs when that experience is negative.

But what is strange is when an apparently meaningless event persists in memory. What is it about seeing Billy Gardner ground into a routine infield out that enabled it to remain with me as it has? Perhaps I've overlooked something. Blocked a traumatic or otherwise harrowing memory, or neglected something wonderful that is hiding behind the sight of Gardner's bobbing head, his number 15 disappearing into the dugout. "Persistence serves a healthy function," Schacter says. "Events that we need to confront come to mind" in ways that insist upon attention.

At this point in my life, I'm delighted when memories come to mind at all. In 1988, I contracted a virus that targeted my brain and left me totally disabled. It damaged my memory systems along with my balance, concentration, and abstract reasoning powers; it compromised my immune system and left my autonomic nervous system functioning erratically. Over time it became clear that significant parts of my autobiographical memories have disappeared or fragmented. I struggle to learn and retain new information. Yet that scene at Ebbets Field in 1955 has endured. The more I consider it, the more I wonder if that moment in my life was not as meaningless as I've always believed.

In her book *Context Is Everything: The Nature of Memory*, psychologist Susan Engel says "the process of remembering can only be understood as a kind of chemistry between inner processes and outer settings." To figure out why Billy Gardner's ground out has survived time and all the years of memories that competed for space in my memory, and brain damage and the normal losses of an aging brain, I should reconstruct the context. Sift through the facts, see what I can make of the chemistry at work between my brain and events that turned an unremarkable play into something I cannot forget.

It was September 18, 1955. It had to be, because that was the only game conforming to the conditions I set for Sean Holtz, Webmaster of the Baseball Almanac Family of Sites. I sent Sean an e-mail asking if he could find all games played on a Sunday at Ebbets Field between the Giants and Dodgers in 1954 or 1955 in which Billy Gardner batted and Willie Mays homered, something else I remembered of the day. Sean found two, both from 1955, and sent box scores.

The first game was played on April 24 and was an 11–10 slugfest that lasted four hours. I was confident that this couldn't be the game we attended because it was too full of drama; surely I'd have remembered something more from a game like that, won by a three-run homer in the tenth inning. Also, according to the box score's notes, the game's start was delayed twenty minutes by a downpour. My mother would never have allowed me to leave our Brooklyn apartment for a ball game under threatening skies, and my father would never have waited out a storm with me at the ballpark.

So it was the game of September 18, late in the season, and we were two among 13,491 people to watch the 7–5 Dodgers victory. Mays hit his home run in the sixth inning. Billy Gardner had two hits before being replaced by a pinch hitter, Dusty Rhodes, in the ninth inning. But it is one of Gardner's two outs that I remember.

It would be difficult to overstate my childhood devotion to baseball. I not only collected baseball cards, I read and memorized the information on their backs, kept them banded together by team, took them with me in an old cigar box on Sundays to visit my grandparents or cousins. Wherever I was, I played games of my own invention with the cards, spreading them on long hallway floors or on bedspreads smoothed to resemble the grass of a playing field, arranging them underneath dining tables, even inside bathtubs, devoting hours to these games and the compilation of imaginary statistics. I didn't just dream of being a Major Leaguer, I committed myself to the idea, and it wasn't until I was a nineteen-year-old freshman outfielder on my college team that I realized there was no future for a 5′4″ erratic-fielding bespectacled kid with bursitis in his throwing shoulder who ran fast and had once hit a triple.

When I went to a game at Ebbets Field, I went to concentrate and learn. I went to prepare myself. To find models, so I could go home and practice my swing, practice my batting stance, tug my hat down on my head properly.

But why Billy Gardner? It would make more sense for me to remember vividly seeing Willie Mays, who was in his heyday in 1955. I believed Mays was the greatest player in the game. Despite being a Dodgers fan, loyal to our center fielder, Duke Snider; despite recognizing that the Yankees center fielder, Mickey Mantle, was an astonishing combination of slugger and speedster; I accepted that Mays could do everything. And there I was, seeing "The Say Hey Kid" in person, seeing him hit his forty-eighth home run of the season during that game. I vaguely recall the ball flying out of Ebbets Field, a lean and exuberant Mays rounding first base, the back and sleeves of his flannel uniform top flapping in the breeze as he eased into his home run trot. But it's mostly in shadow; I only see him in that one moment of loping between first and second base and the image only comes back when I think about Billy Gardner and his insignificant out.

He was born William Frederick Gardner in Waterford, Connecticut, on July 19, 1927. Though he was six feet tall and weighed 180 pounds, Gardner seemed slight on the field, a modest performer among players whose talent tended to dwarf his own. They called him "Shotgun," in honor of his strong throwing arm. They also called him "Whitey," after the fairness of his hair.

In 1955, when I saw him play, Gardner was in his second Major League season. A typical good-fielding but light-hitting substitute infielder, he had appeared in sixty-two games for the Giants the year before as an aging rookie who'd spent a decade working his way up through the minor leagues. He'd batted only .213 in his first Major League season, with little power (one home run, seven runs batted in). He was versatile on defense, playing second base, shortstop, and third base, but 1954 had been an unimpressive debut season for Gardner on a team filled with impressive talent, including future Hall of Famers Mays, Monte Irvin, and Hoyt Wilhelm. All but one of the team's starters in Gardner's rookie season were named to an All-Star team at some point in their careers, and his role as a rookie was a limited one. The Giants won the National League pennant in 1954 and swept the World Series from the Cleveland Indians, but Gardner didn't get to play in the Series.

Then in 1955 he appeared in even fewer games. Playing only 59 times, he batted .203, hitting a few more homers (3) and driving in a few more runs (17) while playing the same trio of positions.

There was little in his performance, status on the team, or prospects to have called my attention to Billy Gardner when I accompanied my father to Ebbets Field. Nor was his play memorable in subsequent seasons, so that I would have looked back to remember seeing a budding star. The Giants gave up on Gardner after 1955, selling him for $20,000 to the Baltimore Orioles at the start of the 1956 season and overhauling their entire infield. He played more frequently and slightly better in four seasons as the Orioles regular second baseman, leading the American League in doubles in 1957 and establishing a record for his position with twelve put-outs in a sixteen-inning game. Then he drifted around the league for another four seasons, retiring in 1963 at the age of thirty-six, going on to manage the Minnesota Twins and Kansas City Royals in the 1980s. Gardner's lifetime batting average was a meager .237; over a ten-year playing career he averaged only 4 home runs and 27 runs batted in.

It's as though I remember Gardner's ground out precisely because of his lack of memorability as a player or the absence of emotional display. The very ordinariness of the situation, the banality of the play, seems to be part of the point. What is distinct is the lack of distinction.

I remember being intrigued by marginal players, especially those on the Dodgers and their archrival Giants. Maybe this was an early sign of realism creeping into my career plans. I can more readily recall the names of Gardner and the other Giants utility players from 1955—Joey Amalfitano, Foster Castleman, Bobby Hofman, Wayne Terwilliger— than the names of the starting players, the heroes of that team. The back-up players' images from baseball cards are clearer to me still, and their names are the first that come back when I think of the team. I identified strongly with these guys, perhaps more than with the stars, and I paid attention to them at the ballpark. It's like focusing on Angus MacFadyen instead of Mel Gibson while watching *Braveheart*.

I believe I was acutely impressed by seeing Gardner cope with failure. This moment, with its drama built around public disappointment, seems to have been a moment of enormous emotional power for me, though not for Gardner. He knew he was out from the moment he hit the ball, but he ran hard and he returned to the dugout stoically, undemonstratively. And his failure didn't cause an eruption of criticism. The first base coach didn't harass him; his teammate, Don Mueller, who was walking toward home plate to bat next, didn't frown at him; manager Leo Durocher left him alone in the dugout. By the age of eight, I'd already been trained by my parents to believe that nonperformance and defeat bore serious, often violent consequences. As in many homes of second-generation immigrant families in the 1950s, expectations for the children were high and tolerance was low. Nothing made me more anxious than having made a mistake in front of them—spilling milk, leaving fingerprints on the wall, neglecting to put a toy back in its place, saying the wrong thing, displeasing a teacher—because such disappointment triggered immediate physical fury. It must have been bracing for me to see a Major League player controlling his emotions when faced with failure, and authority figures who didn't berate him for it. To recognize failure as something that needed to be accepted with grace.

From a neurological standpoint, the persistence of this memory is explicable if I'm right in discovering such a hidden source of emotional power: I was deeply moved to see someone, only marginally capable of playing for the 1955 Giants, fail before my eyes and yet deal with the consequences as though it were not a catastrophe. In addition, since my goals in life at that time centered around being a ballplayer, and since I worried about being too small to fulfill my goal, seeing a player like Gardner ground out carried extra emotional significance. As Daniel Schacter explains it, "when we relate a current experience to short- or long-term goals, we engage in a kind of reflection and analysis—elaborative encoding—that promotes subsequent memory for the experience." It's true that I witnessed more than fifty outs during that Sunday ball game, but only Gardner's stuck with me. Maybe it came at a crucial moment in the action, or at the beginning of the game, since he was the visiting team's lead-off batter and would have been the first player to hit on that day. I can't reconstruct the exact moment from a box score. But I know that the moment has lasted for me, intact and intense, filled with emotion and meaning.

From a psychological standpoint, the persistence of this memory can have other implications. Freud, for instance, was very interested in childhood memories, especially the negligible ones. In *The Psychopathology of Everyday Life*, he devotes a full chapter to them, having noticed "the striking fact that a person's earliest childhood memories seem frequently to have preserved what is indifferent and unimportant." That certainly fits with my Billy Gardner moment.

Freud acknowledges that there is a "difference between what attracts the interest of a child and of an adult." This makes me wonder at the innocence, gravity, and solemnity of an eight-year-old boy's fascination with Gardner's failure rather than Mays's success—my focus indicating either remarkable empathy or remarkable anxiety. I don't even recall the home run hit that day by one of my favorite Dodgers, Carl Furillo, whose nickname was Skoonj, which sounded enough like my family's name to make him a relative.

Freud also finds, in regard to these mundane memories, that "an unsuspected wealth of meaning lies concealed behind their apparent innocence." He is particularly intrigued by a phenomenon he calls screen memories. These are insignificant childhood memories which, in classic Freudian terms, "owe their existence to a process of displacement: they are substitutes, in mnemic reproduction, for other impressions which are really significant." In other words, by retaining the memory of Billy Gardner's ground out, I may be using a trivial recollection to conceal something that really matters, to resist the confrontation with other "significant impressions."

After years of analytical experience, Freud came to believe that "the indifferent memories owe their preservation not to their own content but to an associative relation between their content and another which is repressed." I don't feel the need to undergo analysis in order to liberate myself from Billy Gardner, but I am curious about what might be hiding behind him, if indeed this is a screen memory. I've already confessed to associating marginal players like Gardner with my fear of failure and my anxiety about not being good enough to fulfill my ambitions as a Major League player. But maybe something else is going on. Was it seeing my father labor over his miniature bottle of booze? He wasn't an alcoholic, and I had no fear of his response to a drink. But his powerful hands—scarred and bent from years of working as a chicken butcher— seemed stymied by the task. Maybe that's what I was noticing, that he was failing. Failing to open the bottle, failing physically as he aged (he was forty-seven in 1955), revealing a previously unnoticed vulnerability. Or was it seeing him neatly manage the mess of eating peanuts and knowing that I always got in trouble over crumbs and spills? Hearing him holler at the Giants first baseman, Gail Harris, and call him a bum, because I feared my father's raised voice? Oh, God, there's also the cigar to consider.

None of that sounds completely convincing to me. But it's possible that, taken together, they add up to a fraught moment in my childhood perceptions. A flashbulb memory of a single event, laden with associations, in which an anxious, dreamy young boy who fantasized a doubtful future for himself as a ballplayer got to spend a September afternoon at Ebbets Field with his father and noticed, simultaneously, a host of his father's significant gestures alongside a marginal player's failure. And never forgot.

I can't help wondering if something else might have been happening on September 18, 1955, something that could have upset me enough to require repression. Well, according to Google.com, it was the day that the United States issued a Fort Ticonderoga three-cent stamp, but I don't think this was a problem for me. Nor was the announcement by the British Foreign Office that, four years earlier, a pair of their diplomats—Guy Burgess and Donald Maclean—had defected to the Soviet Union, confirming the story of a former KGB spy. It had been a week in which Mitch Miller's "Yellow Rose of Texas" was the number one song on Billboard's Top 40, just ahead of Pat Boone's "Ain't That a Shame," a season in which *The Lawrence Welk Show* debuted on television and *Oklahoma* was in the movie theaters and kids were wearing coonskin hats in honor of Davy Crockett.

It was, in short, a relatively mild time in the outside world that I knew. But as with most eight-year-olds, the outside world was far less vital to me than the inside world. I know that in 1955, my parents were approaching the climax of their lives together in Brooklyn, and our small East Flatbush apartment could barely contain their tension. Always volatile together, as they neared fifty, my parents saw their familiar world crumbling and had few resources between them to maintain stability. My father's business was failing as the retail poultry business changed, and he wasn't prepared for any other kind of work. Supermarkets were coming; there were plans to build the Brooklyn-Queens Expressway, which would sever the easy flow of traffic through the waterfront neighborhood where his market was located; the Mafia was increasing pressure in the meat industry and space costs were rising. At the same time, a new medical center was being built across the street from our apartment building and plans called for it to be turned into a dormitory. So my father would have to sell his market and we would have to move. It was all they talked about, thought about, argued about. Even the Dodgers were rumored to be leaving Brooklyn. Everything around me was threatening to change. And at a baseball game, amid blossoming uncertainty, I failed to register the excitement of an action-filled 7–5 contest filled with star players and noteworthy performances, and focused instead on the calm, steady, reliable failure of a little-known infielder to reach first base while, out of the corner of my eye, keeping tabs on my suddenly vulnerable father.

For fourteen years I've been obsessed with piecing back together my autobiographical narrative from fragments that survived the viral attack in 1988. My father died in 1961, and my mother's memory was ransacked by Alzheimer's disease, so those who knew me most intimately as a child can't help reassemble the story. Photographs are a great resource; so are cousins and friends from the past. I use music, listening to songs from the 1950s when I'm trying to recapture the feel of things; I watch period films, use the Internet and reference books to help stimulate and connect shards of memory. But it's a tricky business to sort out genuine personal memory from images that belong to other people's recollections or to the culture at large. What is truly mine?

Persistent memories are among the most reliable, etched as they are into the brain's chemistry by the aroused conditions under which they were formed. So I have learned to treasure them, and treat the most persistent of my memories as gifts from the wreckage, or perhaps I should say clues to the great scavenger hunt that matters so profoundly to me.

We're always shaping the past as we age, and as we age we inevitably lose so much of our story. What I'm doing is hardly unique, though it may have a greater tinge of urgency because of my brain damage, and is put in perspective by my mother's deteriorating condition. At ninety-two, she now has nothing left of her autobiographical self except fragments, and even those are few and widely scattered. She knows that she knows me, but doesn't know who I am. I say my name and she says, "Floyd? The butcher?" She'll look closely at me and say, "It's my, it's, it's my relative!" She knows a few lyrics and the melody to Stephen Foster's "Old Folks at Home." Almost all the rest is now a kind of dust.

At this moment in my life, I think that having Billy Gardner and his ground out clearly in memory is a kind of triumph. Still being able to form a convincing account of why it has endured feels like a real victory over the illness that threatened to eradicate the integrity of my self. A vital scene from my childhood has cohered around this indifferent memory. As Gardner himself made his way from the small failure of September 18, 1955, to a fair career playing the game of baseball and then managing at the Major League level, I, too, have made my way from childhood and from brain damage to a modest level of wholeness. I have memories, I have resources, and I have been putting my story back together again.

13. The Roar of the Crowd

Leslie Epstein

My son Paul and I watched the fourth game of the 1998 American League Divisional Series from seats between home and first that had been provided by my other son, Theo. At the start of the eighth inning, with the Sox clinging to a 1–0 lead, Jimy Williams decided to replace Derek Lowe, who had already mowed down what seemed to be ten (but were in fact five) little Indians, with his closer, Tom Gordon. On the instant, I was filled with foreboding. True, Gordon had pitched brilliantly all season, mixing a ninety-two-mile-per-hour fastball with a curve that dove over the back part of the plate like a cormorant after a herring; no less true, he had been less than brilliant in nonsave situations or when asked to get more than three outs. Four batters later—out, hit, hit, hit, that last a double into the triangle—and the lead was gone and so, as it happened, was the Red Sox season. Not to mention my self-respect. For to my own amazement, and surely Paul's, I had found myself on my feet, yelling across the dugout, "Who are you pointing at now, Gordon? You jerk! You idiot! Point at yourself! Don't point at God!"

What on earth had possessed me? Even as I was ranting, one part of my brain kept insisting that no one among these tens of thousands felt worse at that moment than Flash Gordon himself; and yet another part was whispering, *Your son is here, he's listening, he's watching*; and a third part, deeper than the rest, well beneath the cortex, was doing its best to remind me of another time, seventeen or eighteen years earlier, when I had also lost all respect for myself at Fenway Park.

On that occasion the boys and I had been sitting on the left side of the diamond, up in the grandstand, when we heard a disturbance in the aisle below. There a young fellow, half (but only half) drunk, was waving his hands in the face of an elderly black man, whose own two hands were clamped around a cardboard tray heaped with hotdogs and plastic cups of Sprite and Coke. "Boogie woogie!" shouted the lout, waggling his thumbs like a minstrel. "Boogie woogie, woogie, woogie!"

People all over the world are pretty much the same, alas. In Thailand, in Germany, on an autobus in the nation of Chad, one in a hundred will step forward to reprimand the bully, another one or two will egg him on, and the rest of us will bury our faces in our newspapers—or our box scores, if we were among the thousands of liberal Bostonians who watched the taunting of one out of the handful of black men who had dared to bring his children or grandchildren to this ballpark. I had my own boys on either side. I knew they were waiting for me to do something. I sat on my hands. And two decades later? *I* was the white man, impervious to the signals semaphored from my better nature, screaming at the black pitcher who had failed me.

The myth, of course, is that fathers and sons bond in baseball parks. When I was a boy my father and uncle took me to Gilmore Field to watch the Triple A Hollywood stars: Zesto, whatever that was, and the Brown Derby in bright paint on the outfield walls; Jim Baxis at third, Chuck Stevens at first, Johnny O'Neil making his patented basket catch at short; and my favorite, the free-swinging Frank Kelleher in left. The battery was Mike Sandlock and Pinky Woods—Sandlot, I thought, as in sand-lot baseball, and Pinky because the big pitcher was missing a toe.

My own boys have their memories, too—being strictly forbidden to put anything on their Fenway franks that might sting the players' eyes or cause one of them, just as he was about to put away a game-ending pop-up, to sneeze. When Theo, the skeptic, questioned this edict, I had only to point to the prominent signs stenciled about the infield: NO PEPPER. And not even he could doubt my assertion that, in addition to the usual chocolate and vanilla, one could purchase Eskimo pies made out of straw: Could he not, with his own ears, hear the vendor's repeated cry, "Hey, ice cream! Hey, ice cream here!"? The point of it all was to be there when Dwight Evans tied the game in the bottom of the ninth or won it in extra innings with a long, looping drive over the left-field wall. It wasn't the victory that mattered but the leap we'd take from our seats, the way we'd hug first each other and then the fans in the seats around us, the roar in our ears, the vanishing of the boundary between ourselves and perfect strangers.

Dissolution of the self, transcendence, the feeling of oneness, wholeness, unity: Who can draw the line between, on the one hand, such innocent joy, the return to childhood in the adult, the jump toward manhood in the boy; and, on the other, the echo of a Nuremberg rally or the image of the crowd in that famous photograph in which young Adolf, his pale face bobbing in a sea of identical corks, wishes to volunteer for an army in which he might lose all that he hates in himself and become part of a larger, more powerful, entirely flawless body? Between, finally, the tolerated commonplace, *Kill the ump*! and the no less sanctioned urge to *Kill the Jews*?

A week after the Red Sox season ended, I went to the Bronx to watch the Yankees and San Diego in the World Series. Theo worked for the Padres, and I had a Swinging Friar on my cap and a large, entwined S and D on my jacket. Halfway through the game, Tino Martinez decided things with a grand slam, and I went down to indulge in what the boys still call a number one. A Coke bottle, half full, crashed at my feet. Someone or something tugged at my arm. Yankee fans! A half dozen of them! It was as if they had known that from childhood I'd loathed their team as much as I had the Republican Party—and for much the same reason. Now these top dogs had me surrounded. They were heckling, jeering, drunk on the power of their team. I was the Jew, the scapegoat, damned because in a fit of stubborn Americanism I had refused to doff my cap. What would they do? If I had a beard, would they shave it? Would I have to shine, with a toothbrush, their shoes? A party member shoved me to the right. A fellow fascist pushed me left. Imagine: They were winning; what would my fate be if they were to lose? Then one of their number inexplicably held out his hand. Even less explicably, I took it. Here was the one in a hundred! "Aw, let him alone," my rescuer said, grinning, gap-toothed. Then he added the words that to this moment fill me with preposterous pleasure: "He's got balls."

Long before Freud wrote on the subject (and the quotes that follow are from *Group Psychology and the Analysis of the Ego* and *Moses and Monotheism*), everyone knew that membership in a crowd was a permit to regress to a more primitive form of the instinctual life. What Freud added was the idea that every crowd, indeed every sort of social organization, be it church or army or the aforementioned Republican Party, carries with it some memory of the primal horde. After the original band of repressed brothers had killed and eaten their father, they then renounced the very urges that had driven them to such a crime, creating both a taboo on incest with the desired mother or sister, and a totem animal—a Tiger, Cub, Oriole, or Blue Jay—that embodied the ambivalent feelings, reverence and dread, toward their murdered sire. Sounds pretty reasonable to me, especially when applied to the national pastime. The rule of exogamy explains the male nature of the game and the vague aura of homoeroticism ("homosexual love," wrote Freud, "is far more compatible with group ties") that links the beloved player and his devoted fan. After totemism came "the humanizing of the worshipped being." Animals were replaced by semi-human figures like Giants, Indians, Rangers, Mariners, yes, even Yankees. Freud points out that each year, "in a solemn repetition of the father-murder," there is a great feast and celebration, a ritual enshrined in the idea of victory, of one team left standing after all the others have been defeated. We may even detect a faint echo of the ripping and tearing apart of the totem animal in the cry of the victors as they fall upon their own pitcher, obliterating him beneath the squirming, orgiastic pile of their bodies.

Now and then, because the group "still wishes to be governed by unrestricted force [and] has an extreme passion for authority," a father figure will emerge. Little wonder that the Yankee fans, chafing under a Steinbrenner (the leader "loves no one but himself, or other people only in so far as they serve his needs"), yet unwilling to forgo the glory he has bestowed upon them, will turn their hostility outward upon the stranger who wears the hat of a rival "Padre." Yet other groups remain leaderless, their totem reduced to nothing more than a pair of old socks. Here the only vestige of the father is the anonymous voice that issues from the loudspeaker, urging ("Please do not enter the field of play") good behavior. In these organizations, drifting and bereft, the original renunciation continues unbroken, and abstinence is complete. Its members, in the words of Freud, "demand illusions and cannot do without them": *Wait 'til next year.*

The next year came this last October. Once again Paul and I took our seats in Fenway Park to watch the Red Sox and Indians play for the divisional title. This time the Sox took it to them, hit after hit, homer after homer, until they had scored a record-breaking twenty-three runs. Everyone was hugging everyone. My palms stung from the high fives. My voice was gone from screaming. A few days later, loaded with lozenges, I returned with Paul to watch what would turn out to be the only Red Sox victory over the hated Yankees. On this occasion, another Martinez, Pedro, would outpitch the turncoat, Clemens, who did not make it through the second. "Where is Roger?" crooned the crowd through the later innings, only to answer itself in a delirium of sweet revenge: "In the shower!" Ah, the sheer fun of it! The innocence. After all, the bath that Roger was taking had nothing to do with the showers that had killed the Jews. Why not give full throat to the cry? The answer came the next day, when Clemens's wife revealed in the papers that she had had to leave the stadium during the chant because her eldest boy had broken into inconsolable tears. Even the gods have sons.

And with that answer came, all unbidden, another one: What had possessed me a year earlier, when I had mocked poor Gordon for his habit of pointing his finger toward the heavens? *Who are you pointing at now? Point at yourself!* My own father had died when I was only thirteen, with many more games to see; and now Julie, his identical twin (are not the Twins a totem too?), stroke-stricken, lay in a near coma after almost fifty years of serving as that father restored. I was, in my grief, my sorrow, screaming at myself. *Don't point at God!* For what I had come to realize was that no matter how great the throng about us, or how deafening its din, we stand upon this earth entirely alone.

14. Trading Off
A Memoir
Michael Steinberg

Only a child expects justice.— Gore Vidal

Jack Kerchman, my old high school baseball coach, was a classic ball-buster, a lot like those Marine D.I.s you see in old World War II movies. A Jew himself, "Mr. K" had a reputation for hazing the Jewish players he thought were too soft. One of them was me.

I started hearing stories about Mr. K in the mid-1950s, when I was in junior high. In three years at the high school, his football teams won Queens (borough) championships, and the baseball team got as far as the city championship semi-finals. People in the Rockaways—neighborhood kids, parents, and local merchants—began to take notice. Winning teams and wars have a way of galvanizing a neighborhood, especially in New York, where everything is measured and articulated in terms of "turf."

According to the buzz on the playgrounds Mr. K was an obsessed man. Max Weinstein, a tight end on the football team, told us about the impassioned locker room speeches. Before each new season, Kerchman would gather the team around him in the boys' shower and reminisce about his old college days at Syracuse, where he was a one-hundred-sixty-pound offensive guard and defensive nose tackle for coach Biggie Munn. He proudly revealed how after the war he'd had a tryout with the New York Giants and had made it to the last cut. He always finished up by saying that he did it all "on a little talent, a big heart, and a whole lot of guts."

A Jew from the roughest part of the Lower East Side, Mr. K believed that young Jewish boys, especially those from my suburban neighborhood, were "candy asses" and quitters. At football tryouts he talked about the time he liberated a concentration camp at the end of World War II and of how important it was for the next generation of Jews to "toughen up." So at the first scrimmage of each new season, he made the Jewish boys play without equipment. And if you were Jewish and you wanted to pitch for the baseball team, you had to show him you could brush hitters back by throwing at their heads. The rumors were enough to convince Ritchie Zeitler and Bobby Brower—the two best athletes in our neighborhood—to transfer to Polly Prep and Woodmere Academy, two local private schools. Given my family's resources, I had no such option. It was either play for Kerchman or don't play at all.

The Kerchman stories frightened yet fascinated me. So much so that I wanted to see him in action. In September of my last year in junior high, I collared Mike Rubin and Barry Aronowsky, two of my summer league baseball buddies, and off we went to the first Saturday home football game. Outside the high school field, the street hawkers sold hotdogs and popcorn, along with Rockaway High pennants, pom-poms, and trinkets. In the bleachers, students and parents chanted, "Let's go Seahorses, Seahorses, let's go!" The cheerleaders bounced up and down in their red and blue sweaters and short, pleated skirts as the football team ran out on the field. Most of the players were only a few years older than me, but in their scarlet helmets and full gear they looked like Roman gladiators.

As I scanned the field, I saw the pitcher's mound to the right of the south goalposts. For a long, slow moment, I floated free of the razz-matazz while I imagined myself standing on that mound in a Rockaway baseball uniform. My parents, kid brother, and friends were all in the stands, and the cheerleaders were chanting my name as I went into my windup and got ready to snap off a sharp, dipping curve ball.

Then I spotted Kerchman standing in front of the team bench. He was in his late thirties, maybe 5′8″, heavyset, wearing a chocolate brown porkpie hat and rumpled, tweed topcoat. You could hear him yelling above the crowd noise. Sometimes he'd hurl his hat to the ground and scream obscenities at a player who screwed up. He reacted to missed blocks, fumbles, broken plays—whatever derailed the game plan he'd engineered in his head. A couple of times I saw him hold offending players by the shoulder pads and shake them back and forth; and once when he was really angry, he grabbed Stuie Schneider, a Jewish kid from my neighborhood, by the jersey and tattooed him with vicious, open-handed helmet slaps. His temper tantrums frightened and fascinated me. There were moments that day when I wondered why anyone, Jewish or not, would want to play for such an animal. Then that image of me on the mound would kick back in.

My two friends had seen enough, so I went back alone to the rest of the football games. When I announced I was going to try out for baseball next year, they told me I was crazy to even think about it. They didn't understand. It wasn't a matter of merely wanting to play: I *had* to play.

My dad, an old semipro infielder, taught me how to play ball when I was eight. After dinner, out in the backyard he'd hit me ground balls and pop flies until the sun dipped below the Union Carbide tank near the bay. On Sundays, he took me to Riis Park to watch him play fast-pitch softball doubleheaders with a bunch of other middle-aged jocks. By the time I turned nine, I wanted to be a ballplayer like him.

As soon as the weather turned mild, I'd scale the schoolyard fence or be out on the street with my friends playing punch ball or stickball. On weekends, we'd trek twenty blocks up to Riis Park for marathon choose-up baseball games on the grass and dirt fields. Even when we went to the beach, first thing we'd do was carve out a patch of sand near the water's edge and get up a diamond ball game.

After school, I'd grab a broomstick and run down to Casey's Lot, a weed-choked, rock-infested vacant field on the corner of 129th Street and Beach Channel Drive. There I'd pretend I was Duke Snider or Willie Mays or Mickey Mantle, and I'd swat stones across the road into Jamaica Bay until my palms sprouted blood blisters. At night, my brother and I would grab a pink Spauldeen high bouncer and play stoop baseball till the streetlights flickered on.

As much as I loved to play I knew I'd never be one of the top jocks. I was what coaches called a "schlepper," a slightly ungraceful athlete who somehow managed to get the job done. Whatever the sport, I would work hard at it, no matter what the costs—and there was always a cost. At thirteen, I was cut from the local Police Athletic League (PAL) squad.

Coach Bluetrich told me that I didn't have the quick reflexes needed to play shortstop. Not playing was unthinkable, so I made up a lie. I told Bluetrich I could pitch. There isn't a coach in his right mind that wouldn't take on an extra batting practice pitcher. The next day, he gave me an old torn uniform, two sizes too big, and told me to concentrate on throwing strikes to the hitters.

That summer I taught myself how to pitch. I cut a twelve-inch hole in a bedsheet, and at night in my backyard I threw hundreds of rubber-covered baseballs at the target. I got the balls by trading my Topps bubble-gum cards with a friend who worked at the local batting range. Under the pretense of teaching my kid brother how to bat, I pitched shaved tennis balls to him for hours. By shaving the fuzz, you could make the ball curve and dip crazily.

I didn't throw hard enough to have what coaches call a "live arm." In fact, my ex–high school teammate, Andy Makrides, still likes to rib me. "You had three speeds, Mike," Andy says, "slow, slower, slowest. And your sinker was just a dying quail. You were lucky that the pitcher's mound was sixty feet, six inches, because if someone ever moved it back a half a foot, all your pitches would bounce before they got to the plate."

To compensate, I read how-to books on pitching and studied the strengths and weaknesses of professional hitters on TV. All summer I taught myself how to throw curve balls, sliders, knuckle balls, and sinkers. I kept working on my control, and by mid-July, I could throw four out of every five pitches through the bedsheet hole.

My improvement took Bluetrich by surprise. At the end of the summer, I won three games in a row and was the team's second starter. In the borough championship game, Bluetrich surprised us all by starting me ahead of Lee Adnepos. Lee was my best friend and team captain. He couldn't have weighed more than a hundred pounds and was even shorter than I was. But he was a lefty and he could throw harder than anyone else in the league. He never missed practice and never complained about anything. Nobody, including me, was more dedicated than Lee was. Up until Bluetrich chose me to start, Lee had been the team's number one pitcher. But in the first round of the championships, his control was off just enough for the Jamaica PAL team to beat us by a run.

We lost the championship game 3–2, but I took some consolation in the fact that in the pressure game I'd pitched well. Not surprisingly though, Lee was so upset that he didn't speak to me for two months. He was angry with me for losing, but he also believed that he'd earned the chance to pitch that game. So by age thirteen, I could already sense where all this was headed. Character and hard work didn't have a whole lot to do with who played and who sat. It was a simple trade-off: coaches used you if they thought you could help them win games, and you put up with them because you wanted to play.

Knowing this gave me even more incentive. I improved so much that next summer, I convinced myself that if I kept getting better I had a chance to make the high school baseball team. A lot of others had the same illusion, though. Three hundred dreamers came out for football and another two hundred for baseball. With a student body of over three thousand, Rockaway was the only high school in the entire district. Mr. K had his pick of all the best jocks on the Rockaway peninsula.

As tryouts approached I knew I needed an "in." My dad, a traveling salesman, always preached to us, "It's not what you know, but who you know." Well, I knew Gail Sloane, my parents' friend from across the street. Her daughter Susan and I grew up playing together.

Gail was a slender, attractive redhead who worked part time in the central office at Cardozzo Junior High, where Kerchman taught hygiene and guidance. All the guys on the block were smitten with her. Those who went to Cardozzo swore in secret that Kerchman was hot for Gail, and that she was not exactly indifferent to him. I never did verify those rumors, but the summer before I started high school, I asked Gail to put in a good word for me.

It was early September, my first day of high school. Baseball tryouts were in February, so I figured I had plenty of time before I had to worry about Kerchman. In first period homeroom, though, Mrs. Klinger handed me a note: "Be at my office 3 o'clock sharp." It was signed by Mr. K. The rest of the day was a blur. I couldn't hold a conversation, I picked at my lunch, and every time I opened a book, my thoughts drifted. By three, my stomach was in knots.

Kerchman's "office" was across from the boiler room, deep in the bowels of the ancient brick building. To get there, you had to walk past the showers and through the boys' locker room. As I opened the stairwell door, I inhaled the steam from the shower, and above the hum and buzz of locker room banter and casual small talk, I heard the clackety-clack-clack of aluminum cleats hitting the cement floor. An entire bank of lockers was reserved for Angelo Labrizzi, Mickey Imbrianni, and Leon Cholakis, the veterans I'd been watching for the past year. I'd seen them around school and at the State Diner jock table, but here in their domain they had an undeniable aura. As far back as grade school, this was a prestigious, exclusive club I'd dreamed of belonging to.

Though football would never be my sport, playing varsity baseball offered many of the same privileges. I'd already witnessed it for myself: Adults—your own parents, and your friends, actually paid money to watch *you* play; cheerleaders chanted your name ("Steinberg, Steinberg, he's our man, if he can't do it no one can"), and they kicked their bare legs so high you could see their red silk panties. After school, you sat at the jock table in the State Diner; you got to wear a tan leather jacket with a big blue and red "R" across the left breast; and your girlfriend wore your letter sweater to school. Maybe the biggest ego trip of all was when everybody watched with envy when you left sixth period Econ to go on "road trips."

I tried to push those thoughts out of my mind as I timidly knocked on Kerchman's door. "It's open," he rasped in a deep, gravely voice. The room was a ten-foot-square box, a glorified cubbyhole, smelling of wintergreen, menthol, and stale sweat sox. The brown cement floor was coated with dust and rotted-out orange peels; and on all four sides were makeshift two-by-four equipment bays, which overflowed with old scuffed helmets, broken shoulder pads, torn jerseys and pants, muddy cleats, and deflated footballs, all randomly piled on top of one another. Mr. K stood under a bare lightbulb wearing a baseball hat, white socks, and a jockstrap. He was holding his sweatpants and chewing a plug of tobacco. "You're Steinberg, right?" He said my name, "Stein-berg," slowly, enunciating and stretching out both syllables.

"I don't beat around the bush, Stein-berg. You're here for one reason and one reason only. Because Gail Sloane told me you were a reliable kid. What I'm looking for, Stein-berg, is an assistant football manager. I'm willing to take a chance on you."

I wanted to run out of the room and find a place to cry. Assistant football managers were glorified water boys; they did all the "shit work," everything from being stretcher bearers to toting the equipment.

He sensed my disappointment and waited a beat while I composed myself.

"Gail also tells me you're a pitcher," he muttered, as he slipped into his sweatpants.

Another tense beat. Finally, he said, "In February, you'll get your chance to show me what you've got."

To make certain there was no misunderstanding between us, he added, "Just like everyone else."

Then he said, "So what's it going to be, Stein-berg?"

It had all happened too fast. I couldn't think straight. In a trembling, uncertain voice, I told him I'd think about it and let him know tomorrow.

My parents told me to make up my own mind. Anticipating his own embarrassment my brother advised me to tell the coach to "shove it." That night I lay awake, endlessly debating. "Let's say I took the offer. Does it diminish me in Kerchman's eyes? Will he write me off as a pitcher? Suppose I take this job and don't complain? Will it give me an edge at baseball tryouts?"

The next day in sixth period math, I convinced myself I had to take it. Later, when I told Kerchman the news, his only comment was "Good, we've got that settled." "Report to Krause, the head manager, right away," he barked. "Get some sweats and cleats, and as soon as practice ends, clean up this room. Get everything stacked up in the right bins, mop the floor, and get this place shaped up."

On his way out the door, he said, "And make sure we've got enough Merthiolate, cotton swabs, gauze, and tape. First game's in a week and when we step out on that field, I want us looking sharp and ready. We set the example, Stein-berg. If we do our job, the players will do theirs. You understand me, son?"

Before I could open my mouth, he said, "Let us hope, Stein-berg, that you're not one of those candy-ass Jewish quitters."

My brother was right. I wanted so badly to tell him to take the job and shove it. But I held my anger back. Just hang in there, I told myself. He's testing you, trying to see how much you can take.

Along with doing the coach's dirty work, I had to put up with a lot of crap from the other student managers and star players. Moose Imbrianni sent me on a fool's errand for a bucket of steam; I searched for a rabbit's foot for Leon Cholakis; and came up with a pair lucky dice for Angelo Labrizzi. Before games, I taped ankles, treated minor injuries and sprains, and inflated the footballs. At halftime, I cut the lemons and oranges. During games, I'd scrape mud off cleats, carry the water buckets and equipment, and help injured players off the field. After the games ended, I had to stay and clean out the locker room.

The worst jobs, though, were water boy and stretcher bearer. It was bad enough that I had to run out there in front of thousands of people during the time-outs. But it was humiliating to have to listen to the taunts and jeers of my friends. Whenever I heard, "Hey water boy, I'm thirsty, bring the bucket over here" or "Man down on the fifty, medic; get the stretcher," I wanted to sprint off the field and just keep going.

Away from practice, I avoided my friends. As often as I could, I took the public bus to school, and I stayed away from dances and neighborhood parties. I thought constantly about quitting, but I was already in too deep. If I quit now, I could kiss my baseball dreams good-bye.

Much as I hated those menial jobs, watching Kerchman in action still intrigued me. In his pregame pep talks, he invoked the names of past Far Rockaway football heroes, and gave impassioned sermons on the value of courage, character, loyalty, and team play. His practice scrimmages were grueling tests of stamina and fortitude. If players didn't execute according to his expectations, he'd single them out for public ridicule. His favorite victim, it seemed, was poor Stuie Schneider.

One midseason practice it was getting late and everyone was whipped. On a drop-back pass play, Stuie brush-blocked Harold Zimmerman, the oncoming defensive tackle. Harold and Stuie were friends and neither one wanted to hurt the other, especially in a meaningless scrimmage. But as soon as Kerchman spotted it, he stopped the scrimmage and gave them his "chickenshit Jew" routine. Then without warning, it turned into a scene right out of *High Noon*.

"Let's see what you're made of, Schneider," he said. Without pads or a helmet, the coach took a three-point stance on the defensive line and came charging right at Stuie. As scared as he was to hit the coach, Stuie knew what the stakes were, so he knocked Kerchman right on his butt. Everyone looked down at the ground and pawed the dirt with their cleats, waiting to see what the coach would do. Just as Harold shot Stuie an "oh shit" look, Mr. K got up and brushed himself off. Then he clapped Stuie warmly on his shoulder pads, stuck out his jaw, and spat out a wad of brown tobacco juice. "That's the right way to hit," he said to the rest of the squad. "This is football, not cheerleading practice. You make the man pay."

It didn't take long to understand what Kerchman was trying to teach us, especially the Jewish players. In an early season game against St. Francis Prep, Stevie Berman, our star quarterback, was picking the St. Francis secondary apart with his passing game. When we lined up offensively, their guys tried to unnerve Stevie, calling him "dirty Jew" and "kike," and reciting the old familiar mantra "the Jews killed Christ." We'd heard it all before—from Kerchman—at our own practices. All it did was make our linemen block harder.

By the end of the first quarter, we were ahead by three touchdowns, and everyone could sense a fight coming. On the next offensive series, their nose tackle deliberately broke Stevie's leg as he lay pinned at the bottom of a pileup. It's a dirty play, but an easy maneuver: you just grab a guy's leg and twist. As we carried Stevie off on a stretcher, Mr. K grabbed his hand and said, "Don't you worry pal, they'll pay for this." As if that was going to help Stevie's leg heal.

Leon Cholakis, our 275-pound, All-City tackle, lived for moments like this. All game he'd been waiting for Coach K to turn him loose. Sure enough, on the next offensive series, Cholakis hurled himself full force on their prone quarterback and fractured the guy's collarbone. Even on the sidelines you could hear the bone snap. I had to turn my head away. I felt dizzy and nauseous. At the same time I was grateful to Kerchman— and to Cholakis—for sticking up for all of us.

The retaliation was so overt that the refs had no choice but to eject Leon. As the game went on, the crowd, of course, became more angry and abusive. We knew there'd be a rumble after the game, so as soon as it ended, Kerchman snuck us all out through the stadium boiler room.

At the season-ending awards banquet, Kerchman surprised me again by giving me a varsity letter. When I stepped up to the podium, he shook my hand and said, "Nice job, son, see you in the spring." I'd never have the nerve to wear a football letter; still, the gesture flattered me, and my hopes shot up.

On February 15, over two hundred jittery hopefuls gathered for baseball tryouts in the high school gym. Kerchman announced that he had only ten spots to fill. Four of them would be pitchers. Then he began the tryouts. Standing twenty yards away, he swatted rubber-covered baseballs at the would-be fielders. When he ripped a hard grounder at a player, the rubber ball would skip off the basketball court's wood surface and spun crazily across the floor. If the fielder missed it, the ball would rocket into the gymnasium's brick wall with a loud "thwack," then ricochet back. The terrified rookies watched from the oval running track above the gym while the veterans who'd survived this ritual stood behind the coach horsing around and heckling the newcomers.

The last to try out were the new pitchers. To make this ordeal even more unsettling, Kerchman placed seven or eight pitchers in a line across the width of the basketball floor. We each had our own catcher, and one hitter to pitch to. No nets or batting cages. Kerchman stood up on the running track and when he blew his whistle, all the pitchers threw to the hitters. It was rough enough trying to concentrate on throwing strikes to varsity hitters, but as soon as you let go with a pitch, line drives and ground balls went whizzing past you. It was a scene right out of a Keystone Kops movie.

We did this drill for three consecutive days before I was able to screen out all the distractions and dangers. By the last day, my arm ached every time I threw a pitch. I was sure I would never make the cut. Two days later, Kerchman posted the final squad list. One spot was sure to go to Mike Saperstein, a cocky Jewish left-hander from my neighborhood. I disliked him, yet envied his arrogance. A rich kid with a chip on his shoulder, Sap was handsome, a good athlete, a ladies' man, and an honor student. He kissed no one's ass. Like Kerchman, you either came to him on his terms or Sap simply ignored you.

As I scanned the alphabetically listed names, right below "Saperstein" was "Steinberg." At first I thought there must be another Steinberg, but when I read my first name, I was so intoxicated I immediately wanted to telephone everyone I knew. But my elation dissipated when I went to the equipment cage to pick up my uniform. The student manager informed me that "batting practice pitchers don't get uniforms." Nor, as he told me with a mocking smirk, did they travel to road games with the rest of the team. Then came the kicker. "At home games," he said, "your job is to stand at the home plate entrance and retrieve the foul balls that are hit out of the park."

My gut burned; I wanted to march right into Kerchman's office and ask him why. But I already knew the answer. He'd cut at least three or four pitchers who were more talented than I was. Putting me on the team was his way of paying me back for doing all those seedy football jobs. The rest was up to me.

Later when I calmed down, I remembered my old PAL initiation, and how surprised coach Bluetrich was by my progress. I hated the thought that I was starting at the bottom again. But maybe that was part of Mr. K's strategy. This was another test. If I worked hard enough and kept improving, I bet he'd give me a chance to pitch.

When I began throwing batting practice, Kerchman was observant enough to see that I could throw strikes. But I was cannon fodder, just what Mr. K and the hitters wanted. In the beginning, most of the veterans teased me because I couldn't throw very hard. "Hey water boy, toss that watermelon up here," Imbrianni kidded. This time the hazing didn't bother me. Two years of summer league had taught me that big, free-swinging sluggers—like Imbrianni and our catcher, Mike Hausig—were usually too impatient. They wanted to crank everything out of the park. When I threw off-speed sliders and curves, most of the time the big hitters overswung and popped the ball up. I got a real kick out of that. I also enjoyed it when I got to pitch a few intrasquad game innings with the varsity fielders behind me. I had a good sinker and when it was working, the best a batter could do was to hit a hard grounder, a piece of cake for a good infielder.

I wasn't doing too badly for a flunkie, but when I looked to Mr. K for some kind of acknowledgment, he'd say things to the hitters like "What's with you guys? If you let a little pissant like Steinberg here make you look like a monkey, what's gonna happen when you face a really good pitcher?"

Then there were days where I'd have to stay late to pitch batting practice to the scrubs. The worst times were those Saturday mornings in March when the stiff ocean breezes blew winter's last flurries across the frozen diamond, and the rest of the team sat huddled in parkas while Henry Koslan, another scrubbie, and I threw batting practice. The other painful indignity was having to listen to the varsity players complain about how hard Mr. K was driving them. Those guys didn't know how good they had it.

By midseason I was feeling so down that I had to do a pysch job on myself just to get to practice. The team was good, I rationalized. They're on the way to winning the league championship. Imbrianni was leading the city in hitting. Stevie Berman and Jack Gartner, both still juniors, were two of the best pitchers in New York. Even Mr. K's protégé, Mike Saperstein, only got to pitch the last few innings of a blowout. It's my first year, I kept reminding myself. I just have to wait my turn.

The only thing I couldn't handle, though, was chasing those damn foul balls while my friends in the stands ragged on me. It was too reminiscent of the humiliation I'd felt as a football manager.

By season's end I was just putting in time. We won our last five games and cruised into the playoffs. Just when it seemed that we might go all the way Berman had his only off game of the season, and we were eliminated in the borough finals. Saperstein told me later that on the gloomy bus ride home, Kerchman cursed at everyone. Told them they played like girls. It was one time I was happy not to be there.

The long season ended, as always, with the traditional awards banquet. The local media, school bigwigs, and our families all attended. I got a minor letter, as expected, and enviously watched each member of the "big team," Saperstein included, receive a varsity letter. It came as no surprise that Imbrianni won the John Kelly Award, the gold medal that traditionally went to the team's inspirational leader and its most valuable player. Next year, though, it would be my turn: I'd prove to that S.O.B. I could pitch for him.

Over the summer I grew a couple of inches and put on twenty pounds. I worked in a factory lifting heavy boxes, ran two miles a day, and worked out with weights. On nights when we didn't play a summer league game, I went over to Al Seidman's to work on new pitches and strategies. Al was a friend of my dad's and he used to be a minor league pitcher. Three nights a week in his backyard, he made me concentrate on pitching to specific spots. Al also showed me how to throw the curve ball at three different speeds, and in post-workout conversations he doped out strategies for out-thinking hitters. When I went to the Dodger games on Saturday, I sat behind home plate and kept detailed notes: I charted the good hitters' tendencies, and scrutinized the best pitchers' mechanics.

That fall I wasn't planning on being an assistant football manager again. On the first day of practice, though, Mr. K cornered me in the boys' john and told me this year I'd be the liaison between the football players and the head manager. "Look at this as a promotion, Steinberg," he said, while I stood at the latrine fumbling with my zipper. It later occurred to me that this was the first time Kerchman had ever sought me out for anything. There was no way I could turn him down.

That season I had a much easier time of it. Mostly I worked with Krause, delegating my old chores to the junior managers. On game days I stood behind the bench and kept the stats. And after the games, I wrote up the results for the newspapers. It was actually kind of fun. At the banquet, I got another varsity letter that I couldn't wear. The one I wanted, I would earn this spring. I'd already begun working on it. By early January, I was throwing indoors with Bob Milner, the team's second-string catcher.

This time at tryouts, I practiced with the veterans, made the cut, and got a uniform. I knew I had to wait my turn behind Berman, Gartner, and Saperstein, but I hadn't counted on Andy Makrides and Steve Coan. Both were a year younger than me, and both were big and strong and threw hard. I sensed I was being passed over, but I pitched batting practice and took studious notes on opposing hitters. It was hard but I kept my mouth shut and waited my turn. Just as I was ready to confront Kerchman, he gave me three innings in the last preseason game. Give him credit; the man knew just how far he could go with me.

I knew if I didn't show him something special right then, I might never get another chance. I started out tight; my concentration was off. I walked the first man, got the next on a force play, then gave up a hard-hit double, and walked another man. I remembered Al Seidman's advice, "keep the ball low and change your speeds," and I got through that inning and the next two without giving up a run. Even doing less than my best convinced me I could pitch at this level. What mattered was that Kerchman believed it; and I knew I'd have to wait to find that out.

I got my answer when the league season began. We had another strong team. Berman and Gartner pitched the important games; Saperstein got an occasional start and was first man out of the bullpen. In the blowouts, Makrides and Coan always got to finish. I never even got a call to warm up. During the bus trips home and in the locker room, everyone partied. I felt invisible. To avoid having to deal with teammates, I'd linger in the shower and wait for the cliques to leave. Then I'd dress alone and take the bus home by myself. The few times I hung out at the State Diner with the rest of the team, I had to watch the guys preen for the cheerleaders and hold court for the crowd. And when I read the write-ups in the newspapers about our great team, I was sure I missing out on something special, something that might never happen again. What if we won the city championship and I never got to play?

I didn't sleep, couldn't concentrate on school, and refused to face my friends. During the games I found myself silently rooting against my own team. I sat on the bench or in the bullpen and prayed that we'd get blown out, just so he'd give me a few innings. At night I dreamed up scenarios where Mr. K would be up at bat and I'd hit him in the head with a pitch. Or, I'd be at bat and I'd rip a line drive right at his nuts. There were so many days when I was mad enough to walk into his office and confront him. But I was sure that he'd order me to turn in my uniform. If I quit, I wanted it to be on my terms. With three games left, the team clinched the Queens championship. Everyone, of course, got crazy on the bus ride home; and when we arrived back at school, the cheerleaders and a crowd of screaming boosters greeted us. I slipped away as fast as I could.

Some guys can handle sitting on the bench, wearing a uniform, and boasting to envious friends that they're on a winning team. Henry Koslan, the other batting practice pitcher, had that kind of disposition. He went to practice every day, never got in a game, and never complained. The Koslans of the world are blessed: somehow they've learned to accept their destiny without questioning it.

Not me, though. Every time I sat and watched, I ached to participate, to contribute; I needed to be acknowledged, especially by this coach, this hard-nosed Jewish street fighter, this man whose ethic puzzled and repulsed me. I wanted Kerchman's respect and naively I believed that if I did what Mr. K asked of me and didn't complain or quit, eventually I'd earn his approval. Too absorbed in self-pity, I'd forgotten what I'd learned from Joe Bluetrich three years ago. Hard work didn't matter, character didn't matter, and respect and approval didn't matter. In coaches' minds, the only thing that counts is winning games. But you couldn't win games if you didn't pitch. There was still enough time to earn the letter. Surely Kerchman owed me that much, didn't he?

The next game was at home and we were playing Richmond Hill, a weak team. It was a perfect opportunity for him to make it all up to me. But in front of the home crowd, in front of my friends and family, Kerchman started Henry Koslan. I was stunned, but I figured I'd get my innings later on. Before he even got an out, Koslan gave up six runs. I kept waiting for Kerchman to tell me to head for the bullpen and warm up. Instead he brought in Saperstein, then Coan, then Makrides. How could he pass me up? What was he thinking?

I sat on the bench and brooded, counting the put-outs until the game would end. In the last inning we were two runs down when he told me to warm up. I wanted to scream, "What took you so fucking long?" Instead, I threw listlessly, waiting for the end. But with two outs, we loaded the bases. A single would tie the game. Suddenly, I saw myself out there pitching with the game on the line. That got my adrenaline going and I started throwing harder. I prayed for a banjo hit, a blooper, a dying quail, a nubber with eyes; anything to get me in there. But Hausig's fly ball ended the game and my dream. Next thing I knew I was standing in Kerchman's office, screaming wildly at him, tears running down my face.

He stood there in his jockstrap and undershirt and didn't say a word. When I wound down, he shook his head and said, "Not bad. I didn't think you had the balls for this." Then he let me have it.

He began to lecture me about the importance of momentum to a winning team, and about morale and confidence, and how the team couldn't afford a losing streak right before the playoff. I wanted to say, "What about my goddamn morale, how about my confidence?" But in a voice I didn't recognize, I blurted out, "You don't even have to pitch me, coach. Put me in the outfield, let me bat just one time. I just want my letter." As soon as I got the words out, I knew I'd said the wrong thing.

"I decide who plays and who doesn't," he snapped. And then, as if he knew he'd gone too far, he backed off. "Your day in the sun will come." His eyes narrowed, and he spat out, "And you better be good and goddamn ready when it does."

I walked home in a daze. I thought about how life would be without Kerchman. No more five-hour practices and sitting on the bench; no more getting home at nine o'clock too tired to even do my homework or to hang out at Irv's candy store with the guys. Now was the perfect time to tell him to take the uniform and stick it up his ass. But, I waffled, there's only one more week to get through. Don't give him the satisfaction. Stick it out until the end of the season, then put it all behind you.

I went to the last two games pretending not to care what happened. But Kerchman had one wrinkle left. He called me in to pitch the last two innings of a tune-up game. We were winning by six runs, so there was nothing at stake. I was too surprised to be nervous. I packed two seasons of frustration and rage into those innings. I bore down and concentrated like it was the last game of the World Series. I threw curve balls and sinkers, I changed speeds and mixed locations. I got all six hitters in a row, easy outs. It felt so exhilarating to be out there that I wanted those two innings to last forever. When it was over, I was so high I wanted the varsity letter more than ever. Once I got it, I could walk away from the whole thing. Clean break, nothing more to prove to him—or to myself.

As it turned out we were eliminated again in the borough finals, by the same team and same pitcher that beat us last year. For the first time since I'd known him, he didn't yell at us on the trip home or make a locker room speech. He just went into his office and shut the door. I was so relieved and elated that this painful season was over, I couldn't wait to turn in my uniform and get the hell out of there. But when I passed by his office, Mr. K was still sitting in his uniform staring at the wall. It was more than just a playoff loss to him. He was losing two All-City pitchers and two All-Queens seniors from a squad that had won three straight borough championships. Next year, he'd be starting from scratch. My first impulse was to feel sorry for *him*.

At the banquet the mood was subdued. Still, it was a prestigious event. Kerchman had invited the past years' Kelly Award winners to make the customary inspirational speeches. When I listened to them deliver the old rah-rah, I remembered how good it felt to pitch those last few innings. Stevie Berman and Jack Gartner shared the Kelly Award, and Mike Hausig won the *Long Island Press* MVP trophy. Next year, those guys would be gone. No matter, I'd made up mind to pack it in.

Then Koslan received his varsity letter. That sealed it. I knew I was next. When Kerchman shook my hand and handed me a minor letter my stomach turned over and I had to bite my lower lip hard to keep from crying. My knees were so wobbly I don't know how I made it back to my seat. I don't recall a single detail from the rest of the evening. I didn't even wait for my dad or brother to take me home. For hours I wandered around the neighborhood, playing the same tape over and over in my head.

"How could I have let him do this to me?" "Why didn't I quit when I had the chance?" "Why didn't I throw the letter back in his face?"

When I came out of it, I was wandering barefoot on the beach, my suit pants rolled up to my knees. I took the letter out of my jacket and scaled it like a seashell out to sea. I felt some relief when it disappeared into the black water, but that night and for three nights after that, I didn't sleep for more than a few hours at a time.

The last week of school I sat in the back of my classes behind a book, ducked into corridors when I saw teammates and friends coming, ate lunch alone in an empty classroom, and cut out as soon as the three o'clock bell rang. When school ended, there was no question that I was through with Kerchman. His message was clear. I'd have to have my head examined to go back for more.

With the pressure off, that summer I pitched better than I ever did. Beat Makrides for the league championship and was a starter on an American Legion team that went all the way to the state finals. Yet every time I thought about Kerchman and the baseball banquet, the sting was still there.

The first week of school I was chosen to be sports editor of the paper, and given my own monthly column—head shot, byline, the whole works. The *New York Times* and *Herald Tribune* sports desks assigned me to write up the high school football games for them. Who needed baseball? Who needed to put up with Kerchman's horseshit?

A week after football practice started, I was working late at the paper when Kerchman phoned. "Where the goddamned hell have you been?" he rasped. "You're my head football manager, get your ass down there." What chutzpah the man had. In his scheme of things there was no reason why I shouldn't have been honored to take this job.

I stammered that I'd made other commitments this year and I wouldn't be coming back, then I braced myself for the fallout. All he said was, "I see," and hung up. Instead of feeling vindicated, relieved, I felt guilty, like somehow I'd undermined *him*. It was all I could do to fight off the impulse to call him back.

Two days later, Andy Makrides called and dropped the news on me that Henry Koslan had died of leukemia. Kerchman, it seems, had known about Koslan's condition for almost a year. But he'd promised the family he wouldn't tell anybody. Makrides said that the baseball team would be attending a memorial service the next day and Kerchman wanted me there.

Mr. K's backhanded gesture didn't compensate for what he'd done to me for two years, but it did explain a few things. After the service, I told him I'd take the job, but only if I got time off to write my column. I deliberately made no mention of baseball. He jumped on the offer, of course, and walked away thinking, I'm sure, that he'd gotten everything he wanted.

The next day Mr. K held a special squad meeting. "If any of you gives Steinberg any flak," he told the troops, "you'll answer to me." It was the first time he'd pronounced my name with the right emphasis. Momentarily I was flattered. He'd never said anything like that about Krause or any of the other student managers. Still, I decided to reserve my judgment until much later.

As his second in command, I delegated all the menial jobs to the new assistants.

During the season, I became a kind of silent confidante to this obsessed coach. As the other managers scurried around servicing the players, I stood next to him taking notes on a clipboard while he muttered complicated strategies to me. Though I felt a secret pride at being taken into his confidence, I was angry with myself for feeling so beholden to him.

In the early practice sessions, I noticed a change in Mr. K. He still threw temper tantrums when we lost games we should have won, and he still inflicted public punishments on players who screwed up. But I never heard him make one cruel or derogatory remark about Jews being quitters or candy asses. With so many of his veterans graduated, Kerchman had resigned himself to rebuilding the team. Several times that season in fact, Kerchman caught me off guard by sending me to counsel some of the more troubled players. I wondered what he had up his sleeve.

At the banquet he gave me the customary "See you in a few months" line, as he handed me my third useless letter. This time I wasn't going to get my hopes up. I wasn't even sure I'd try out for baseball.

Two weeks before tryouts, I was working late on my sports column when I came across an article in the *Long Island Press* sports section. It quoted Kerchman as saying that "the mainstays of my pitching staff in this rebuilding season will be my two seniors, Mike Saperstein and Mike Steinberg. Juniors Andy Makrides and Steve Coan will be the number two and three starters." About Mike Steinberg, he went on to say that "the right-hander will be the first man out of the bullpen, as well as an occasional starter. He has excellent control and an effective sinker, both important weapons for a relief pitcher." I read the interview over again before it finally sunk in. Two more articles spotlighting Saperstein and me soon appeared, one of them in the school paper, written by my own sports reporter. It was just too seductive. How could I pass it up? I had to at least call his hand on this one. Didn't I?

From minute one, practices were like a day at the beach. Because I was part of Kerchman's inner sanctum, all of the new players looked up to me; strangers in my classes—even some of my teachers—treated me with a respect I'd never experienced. When I sat at the State Diner jock table, girls fawned all over us. A part of me was waiting for the other shoe to drop.

In the preseason games, Mr. K made sure I got to throw a few innings in every game. By the time we opened our league season, I couldn't wait to get out there and show him what I could do. In the first home game, against Wilson Vocational, Kerchman brought me in to relieve Saperstein. It was the last inning of a scoreless game, and Mike had pitched beautifully. Everyone on the bench saw he was getting tired, but when Mr. K came out to the mound, Sap did something I'd never seen before. In front of the team, fans, and school officials, he screamed, "I'm throwing a shutout here. The scouts came to see me pitch, not Steinberg." Normally, Mr. K would can a player's ass for a lot less than that. But Sap was our best pitcher, and Kerchman needed him. Bringing me in was his only way of keeping his hotheaded ace in line.

Maybe it was because Sap's outburst had shaken me up, or because my parents, brother, and girlfriend were watching—maybe I was tight because this was my first league game. Whatever the reasons, I froze up. I threw my warm-ups in a daze. My first pitch to Fletcher Thompson, Wilson's best hitter, was a gut shot, a letter-high fastball that he jacked out of the park. As I watched the ball disappear, I was sure Saperstein would come charging out to the mound and strangle me. That is if Kerchman didn't beat him to it.

My cheeks burned and my shirt was soaked with flop sweat. How could I have thrown him a fastball? I don't even have a fastball. Thinking about it tightened me up even more, and I walked the next two men on eight pitches. I looked to the bench then to the bullpen for help. Nobody was throwing. Kerchman was going to leave me in to take a beating or to pitch my way through it. Just knowing that somehow settled me down and I started concentrating on what I knew how to do best. Keeping the ball low and mixing my pitches, I got the next three outs.

In the bottom half of the inning our first baseman, Dickie Webb, hit a home run off Thompson. The game ended in a tie, called on account of darkness. I should have been relieved that I got off the hook so easily, but it ate away at me that I'd almost blown the game. The hardest part was knowing that if I didn't get another chance to redeem myself, I'd carry my failure and shame for the rest of the season—and for who knows how much longer after that.

The next game was away, at Jamaica High, and I sulked quietly at the back of the bus. Right away we got off to a five-run lead. But Makrides lasted only four innings before they tied it up. I looked over at Kerchman, but he'd already signaled for Coan to warm up. No surprise there; still, it felt like a razor nick. We went ahead again, but Coan couldn't hold the lead. It's a terrible thing to have to root against your own teammate, but when Jamaica got within a run of us, I began to feel a flicker of hope. In the Jamaica half of the fifth, with the score tied and the bases loaded, Kerchman motioned at me to warm up. Just before he put me in he said, "Show me you've got the guts I think you have." Then he handed me the ball. It was all I needed to hear.

Right from the start, I held my concentration and made sure I kept the ball down and away. By forcing them to hit ground balls, I got my three outs without giving up a run. We scored four more times and won the game, 10–6. When it was over, I'd pitched three scoreless, hitless innings. The full impact didn't register until the bus ride home, where for the first time I joined in as we yelled and whistled and hooted out the window at the girls on the street. We loudly sang along as Dion and the Belmonts harmonized "I Wonder Why" from the bus's radio. Everyone on the team—except Saperstein—signed the winning game ball for me. That night as I walked home in the dark, it began to rain. I slid the baseball under my jacket pocket and clutched it to my chest. When I got to my block, I was soaking wet, crying hysterically, and singing "I Wonder Why" at the top of my voice. Three years of taking Kerchman's crap, and now everything was finally breaking right for me.

Like most coaches who find a winning combination, Kerchman went with the same formula almost every game. He'd start Saperstein, Makrides, or Coan, and in the fifth or sixth inning of close games, he'd come in with me. Usually I got my outs, but the one time I blew a lead, I couldn't study or sleep until I pitched again.

All spring it felt strange to read my name in the newspaper write-ups, sign autographs for neighborhood kids, and listen to the cheerleaders chant "Steinberg, Steinberg, he's our man, if he can't do it no one can." My new problem of course was Mike Saperstein. He hated sharing the lime-light, especially with a former scrubbie. Every time I came in to relieve him, Sap took it as a personal insult. "You better not blow my game, peck-erhead," he said one time. And on another occasion, "Keep it low, jerk-off. I don't want my ERA getting screwed up because you can't keep the fuckin' ball in the park." But after two years of Mr. K's hazing, Mike couldn't rattle me. I was pitching well and I knew it.

With a week left, our ragtag team was in a four-way tie for first place. The whole season came down to consecutive road games against the three other leaders. In the rematch against Wilson Vocational, Saperstein threw eleven innings of one-hit ball before he walked two men and gave up a sacrifice bunt. At that point, Kerchman brought me in. We had a 1–0 lead and they had the tying run on third, the winning run on second. With everything on the line, I had to pitch to Fletcher Thompson again. What if the son of a bitch did it to me again? From the bench, Saperstein screamed, "Walk him, asshole." This time, Sap was right. With first base open, it was the obvious strategy. But Mr. K didn't agree. He walked out to the mound and ordered me to pitch to him.

I knew Thompson would be salivating to get another crack at me. Tease him, I told myself. Keep the ball low and away, out of his kitch-en. Walk him if you have to, but don't give him anything fat to hit. On a 2-1 slider that was deliberately low and outside, he reached out and upper-cut a soft fly ball to left field. Ira Heid dove and caught it on his shoe tops. When the runner at third tagged and headed home, Ira bounced up and threw him out at the plate. Bang, bang play. The game was over, we were still alive. When I got to the bench, Saperstein was livid; and to tell you the truth, I didn't blame him. He'd pitched an almost perfect game for twelve innings; I threw just four pitches and got the game ball—and the next day's headline. Welcome to the club, Sap.

Against Andrew Jackson High, Kerchman put me in again in the last inning of a 5–4 game. Coan was pitching with a one-run lead and they had the bases loaded and no outs. At bat was Otto Agostinelli, a 6′4″ free swinger who led the league in home runs and strikeouts. My favorite kind of hitter. For reasons I'll never understand, Kerchman waited until Coan went all the way down to 3-0 on Agostinelli before he yanked him and brought me in. It was an impossible situation.

"You've got a run to give, but that's all." He spat a plug of tobacco juice and slapped the ball into my glove. "Get me out of this with a tie. I just want one more at bat."

I was sure that with a 3-0 count, even Otto would be under orders to take the first two pitches. So I threw him two strikes, both gut shots with nothing on them. I saw him grimace on the second one. He wanted that pitch back. With the count full, I had a chance. He'd seen my first two pitches and he'd be looking for another cripple right down the middle. On the 3-2 pitch, I gambled and jammed him with a sinker that should have been ball four. He swung, thank God, and tapped a weak ground ball to me. Easy force play at home plate. One gone.

A kind of seesaw psych game goes on between a pitcher and opposing hitters. At first you've got to prove yourself to them; they're all over you, yelling stuff like "Come on, cream puff, show me what you got." But once you get that first out, the pressure shifts, and the hitters start to tighten up. And that's just what happened. The last two outs were almost too easy. A soft line drive to second base, a grounder to third, and that was the game.

On the bus trip home I wanted to sink back in my seat and enjoy what I just accomplished, but I didn't have that luxury. We still had to beat Van Buren. Their pitcher, Joe Sabbaritto, was the top prospect in the city; and their three and four hitters, Bill McNab and Al Schumacher, were leading the borough in hitting. For the first three innings, Sabbaritto was throwing over ninety miles an hour. But he couldn't find the plate; and when he did, his catcher couldn't hold onto the ball. Kerchman knew that when this guy got his rhythm back, we'd never hit the ball in fair territory again. So we scratched out five runs on walks, passed balls, bunts, errors, and stolen bases. In the third inning, Sabbaritto found the groove and then he shut us down. Struck out eight of nine hitters in a row. He was throwing so hard his fastball looked like an aspirin tablet as it buzzed past your chin.

Meanwhile, they kept pecking away at the lead, and when I relieved Makrides in the sixth inning we were ahead 5–4. With two out and two men on, McNab hit a hard single to tie the game. I knew we were in trouble. For the next five innings Sabbaritto got even stronger, striking out batter after batter. I was tired and my control was off. Van Buren had men on base each inning, but somehow I managed to stagger through it without giving up the winning run.

From the sixth inning on, there was a strange sense of inevitability about this game. We all felt it. There was no chatter on the bench. Even Mr. K was subdued, almost as if he, too, was hypnotized by what Sabbaritto was doing out there. We were in a tie game with the league title on the line, yet it felt like our team was ten runs down. It was weird going out there every inning and knowing that unless Sabbaritto had another sudden wild streak, we wouldn't score again. It didn't look like that was going to happen, so I decided to take it one batter at a time. I created my own private little game-within-a-game just to see how long I could make the real game last.

I got through six more scoreless innings, mainly on adrenaline and fear. But in the bottom of the thirteenth, McNab got to third on a misplayed fly ball, and on a 2-2 count, Schumacher punched a weak-ass sinker past the shortstop for the winning hit. For the last six innings, I'd known it had to end this way—we all did. Still, I was in a daze. Five years of dreams and struggle, and just like that it was over. On the bus ride home no one said a word. One minute I was empty and sad because I'd lost the season's biggest game; the next minute I was elated because I'd pitched the seven best innings of my life.

A few days later I realized that we'd gone way beyond even Kerchman's expectations. He knew it, too. So much so that at the banquet, he gave *everyone* a varsity letter. While I was chewing on that injustice, Mr. K began to recite the customary platitudes before giving out the Kelly Award. I'd heard the speech so many times that I tuned most of it out. Besides, Louie Stroller, the student manager, had leaked it to several of us that the Kelly already had Saperstein's name engraved on it. Mike was a jerk, but he'd had a great season. We all knew he deserved the award.

I looked over at Sap, and I could read his mind: with one hand he was slipping the medal around some pretty cheerleader's neck; with his free hand he was reaching down her blouse to cop a feel. So when Kerchman announced my name and said to that roomful of people, "Mike Steinberg is a kid who'd made the most out of a little bit of talent, a big heart, and a whole lot of guts," I was too stunned to move. Before I could even stand up, Sap yelled, "I don't fucking believe this!" and he stormed out of the restaurant, kicking over tables and chairs as he went. I hated Sap for upstaging me again, but I admired his chutzpah. A year ago in that same room, I'd wanted to stand up and tell Kerchman to stick it. Instead I let him sweet-talk me into playing. And now this.

I can't recall how I got to the dais, but I remember standing next to him—my thoughts scrambled, my throat so dry I couldn't swallow. Kerchman had his arm draped around my shoulder, flashbulbs were popping all around me, and everyone was standing and applauding. I squinted through tears, frantically searching the crowd for a glimpse of my dad and brother.

Last year, while rummaging through an old trunk, I found the Kelly Award and a memoir my brother had written about his own high school baseball days. "In his locker room speeches," Alan wrote, "Mr. K talked about this little Jewish relief pitcher whose uniform didn't fit and who didn't have a whole lot of talent. But the boy, he said, always seemed to be at his best under extreme pressure. In fact he'd bring this kid into impossible situations, tie game, bases loaded no outs, that kind of thing, and he'd say to him, 'Son, I want you to get me two ground balls and a pop fly.' And that pitcher, my brother Mike, would somehow figure out a way to get the other team to hit two ground balls and a pop fly."

As I scanned the passage my first response was, "A typical Kerchman speech; the old psych job for the benefit of the rookies." But I was also moved by what I'd read. Some part of me knew that in his own perverse way Mr. K had given me what I had been asking for all along: a nod of acceptance from one kind of Jew to another.

15. Begotten, Not Made

Gary Forrester

Begotten, Not Made

1. Emptied Out Before You

> *Then you shall be radiant at what you see,*
> *your heart shall throb and overflow*
> *for the riches of the sea shall be emptied out before you,*
> *the wealth of nations shall be brought to you.*
> *Caravans of camels shall fill you,*
> *dromedaries from Midian and Ephah;*
> *all from Sheba shall come*
> *bearing gold and frankincense,*
> *and proclaiming the praises of the Lord.*
>
> Isaiah 60:4–6
> (The Feast of the Epiphany, 2003)

Ole Jack Buck, he be dyin.
No bobble-head doll fer he!
Heh heh.
Heh heh heh heh heh.

Son Joe slip inter de hospital, ter say:
"Dad, DK pitched the Redbirds into first place in the National League
    Central."

& Ole Jack Buck grit he toofs & say: "I am well pleased."
Den Jack Buck *cross ober de Jordan*!

He *pass troo de curtain*!
He *gib up de ghost*!

But.
Darryl Kile, he die *too*, one week later of all ting!
Eben befo he next *start*.
Dead in *hotel room* at de age er 33.
D-E-A-D.
"It looked like he was sleeping," newspaper say.
Sleep ferebber.

& dose Cardinals *sail long* in 1st place
Fer de rest er de regular season in dat year of our Lard 2002.
Chosen Ones
(Til Tony LaRussa, de *Cap'n Ahab* er de postseason,
Toss it all 'way by leabin he right-hand hurler Mr. Matt Morris in too
        long.
Sigh.)

(Ahab sell he hair, buy *watch chain* fer he lubber-boy,
He sell de *watch* ter buy new *hair comb*.
Ahab gwine ter *die* paintin he masterpiece,
Winter leaf on de sick girl *window*.)

Well suh,
Jack Buck be *ole* & *bound* ter die.
He hab de *lung cancer* & de *Parkinson*
& de *diabetes* & de *catarack* & de *pacemaker*.
Wo!
Dat be 'nuff disease ter kill *Brer Moose*!

But.
DK in he *prime*, mon.
DK be de blue-collar *warrior*, what *nebber* miss he turn in no rotation.
He hab de beauteous wife name *Flynn*, of all ting, & de beauteous
        chilluns.

Den DK sleep, alone in dat hotel bed,
& *nebber wake up.*

Houston, Colorado, St. Louis, dey *mourn* fer DK—
Dey stitch he number 57 ter dey *hats* & dey *sleebes* & dey *britches.*
& me, de Damage Boy, me mourn too.
Heh heh.
Heh heh heh heh heh.

Me saw he pitch once, versus dose *Astro* er Houston, nigh de end er
      2001,
Just befo Ahab dispense de October *Kool-Aid* ter de po Red Birds,
& ruin me life again ha ha.
Darryl *lose* dat day ter dose Astro,
But.
He be fun ter watch, yes *suh*!
He just keep *workin*, *workin* he tail clean off, all de lib-long day.
Nebber mine how many *hits* dose Astro get, nebber mine what be de
      score.
When he get *clobbered* in de middle er de 5th,
& Ahab *pull de plug* & motion ter de bullpen.
DK just *lower he head* & lumber inter de 1st-base dugout wif de *dignity.*
Finish fer de day.

But.
DK *always* be back ter take he turn in de *rotation.*
Even if he got de *whimsies,*
Even if de *odds* stack plumb agin he,
DK conduck heself wif de *quality.*
DK.

& de Damage Boy watch he on de *color t.v.,*
& one time DK get hit smack in he *face*
By de *line-dribe* back up de middle!
Wo!

Somehow, Mr. Kile *pounce* offa dat mound,
Like de *bobcat* scroungin atter squiryels,
& he *fetch* dat baseball atter it bounce offa he *mouf,*
& he trow de *bullet* ter 1st base ter *nab* dat speedy runner!
& *den*, DK tuck he glub unner he left arm, & he *spit* inter he hands,
& he keep on a-*hurlin* fer a *whole nudder innin*—
Eben wif he *top lip* a-puffin up ter *twice* it natchel size.
Dat DK *tuff*, mon.

But.
Dat tuff mon hab de big *heart*, just as big as de *hebbens*!
'Cause when de *rookie* pitcher, Mr. Rick Ankiel (de *wunderkine*, heh
        heh)
Go teetotally *crazy* atter all he *wile pitches* in de 2000 postseason,
DK takes dis young feller unner de *wing* er he mighty right arm.
& dose 2 pitchers *confab* fer hours out dar in de bullpen,
Er lallygaggin 'bout in de clubhouse,
& de *stinkin bref* er *Brudder Def* be close ter dat young Mr. Ankiel.
(Closer eben dan ter *DK*!)

Well suh,
By & by, Rick Ankiel whisper de *magic word* ter Mr. Kile: "I believe."
"I believe," say Rick Ankiel, heh heh.
"Help my unbelief."
Heh heh.
Heh heh heh heh heh.

& when DK *die*,
Me canna get he outta me *mine*.
Me keep wantin ter lib de *sinless* day!
Ebery mornin, me wake up & say ter me young wife (in de *Brer Rabbit*
        talk):
"Me no wanter be far from God terday, heh heh."
& she *rolls* she young eyeball & looks *exasperate* inter de bedroom
        ceilin,

& she replies ter de Damage Boy:
"*Please* don't talk in that *stupid* accent."

So.
Darryl Kile keep on *truckin* only in me *mine*,
Wif de *obsession* inside dar,
& de sinless day roll on fer 2-3 whole *week*—
Til DK slip from me memory like de *yalligater* slippin troo de *swamp*,
& me (fool) *beliebe* Ahab (Master er de Regular Season, Master er
    Disguise),
What say dat de Cardinal gwine ter win it *all* fer DK,
In de year of our Lard 2002!

In de mumpf er August er '02, atter DK & Jack Buck be *D-E-A-D*,
Me dribe ter St. Louis fer de night game versus de Mets,
Wif me friend de *Florida Writer Mon*
(What win *bofe* de Flannery O'Connor & de O. Henry prizes, bless
    gracious)

Befo de game, me stand at *detention* dar, wif de *Florida Writer Mon*,
In de *drizzle* outside dat Busch Stadium—
Befo de home-made shrines dar, ter dese *dead mons*, unnerneaf de
    will-call box:
& *one* er de shrine be ter honor Darryl Kile,
& de udder shrine be fer Mr. Jack Buck.

Well suh,
Dar be de 1998 DK *baseball card* a-restin in one er dose shrines,
& me want it *bad*.
(But no.
Be bad luck ter rob de dead.)

No mas, Cardinals lose anyway.
Andy Benes pitch great on de mound fer de Cards,
& Eduardo Perez make 2 *spectacular* catches in right.

But.
De Mets' Mr. Al Leiter be too tuff dat day.

& a few week later, Darryl little boy (what be name *Kannon* of all ting)
He pose in de Cardinals' postseason *dugout*,
Like de good luck charm nailt ter de *whalin ship*,
& me go troo a few mo day wif no sin.

But.
Ahab *out-smart* he self & he team (like he always do),
& Matt Morris drop de final game out in San Francisco (de *City by de*
     Bay).
(What in de name er goodness be Ahab *tink*,
Ter leabe Morris in ter bat fer he po *self*,
Wif Tino Martinez wastin 'way on de *bench*?
Whuffo?)

Dat's it, life be back ter normal,
& me settle back ter de happy life er *sin*.
Sigh.

But.
Darryl dinna *completely* vanish from me fool head,
No.
Whensoebber he *spirit* descend, me muddle troo *anudder* sinless spurt.

Me tink 'bout Darryl now,
As me write dis,
And me feel de *pura vida*, mon, de *pure life*.

Well suh,
DK be same age as *Jesus* when he die.
& me wonder: Why God make he only son be *kilt* in such a way,
Naked dead mon wif de nails what pierce he hand & he feet,
Open wound in he side,

He head bleedin from de crown er torn.

Why *Jesus* dinna die alone in he *sleep*, in de hotel room, like Darryl
　　Kile?

(DK wonder de same ting in de minor leagues,

Starin troo de bus window fer hours,

Or alone in de cheap hotel.

Did God *murder* he own son?

Did God pick up where *Abraham* leabe off, wif dat po boy *Isaac*?

Was de def er God's son ter make up fer de *banishment* & *def* & *sufferin*

Er *all* he little chilluns, just because dey wanter hab de *sexes*?

Who be redeem? wonder Darryl Kile.

Who sin Jesus die fer, ours er he fodder in hebben's?

Dis fodder try ter make tings right at last?

Dis fodder *learn* from he own *mistakes*,

He own *cruelties*,

He own *pettiness* & *manipulation*?

& gentermons!

& dis *agony* in de garden, dis *crucifiction*,

Dis de price God pay in he own *twiss mine*?

De *cross* be de 2nd def er *innocence*?

What come next? *Mo* misery & sin? *Mo* drinkin er de blood?

At lease Darryl hab de wife & de kids.

DK know ter stain he hand wif *human waste*,

Ter load de *dishwasher*,

Ter lose de *argument*,

Ter keep he *mouf shut* fer he fambly sake.

DK reckon dat udder folk be *right* sometime, & sometime he be *wrong*.

What if *Jesus* hab de kids er *he* own,

& hab ter saunter inter some dam *baseball game* in de bottom er de 8th,

Wif 45 tousand folk a-*screamin* inter he ear fer mo dan *loabes & fishes*?

& what if he *blow* dat save 'cause he be *distrack*,
Wif he little daughter home wif de *flu*?
What if he grow ole & *paunchy*?
Gnarlt & *past he prime*?
Heh heh.
Dese be better dan *Satan* measly tests.)

Well suh,
When me meet up wif Darryl on de road ter *Damascus*,
Me hear he *teammates* whisper,
"So what do you say, Darryl?"
Dey say dis ter *test* he.
DK bend down in de *on-deck* circle & write on de *ground* wif he finger.
But.
Dey *keep* axin he de same ting,
So.
He straighten up & say: "I'm ready."

Agin he bend down & write on de ground,
& dey walk ter de *dugout*, one by one.
& DK be left *alone*.
& Ahab (Master er Disguise) come & stand befo he.
Darryl straighten up & say ter he:
"Tony, where are they going? Is there no one to back you up?"
Ahab say: "No one, Darryl."

Darryl say: "I'll take the mound. We'll see what happens."

Darryl grab he *baseball glub* & stroll ter de *pitchin rubber*,
& he finger de *seam* on de ball.
He be 33 *year old*.
Only *Mike Matheny* join he on de field, behime home plate.

When he reach de mound, Darryl turn & look inter de dugout.
He teammates all stand dar in a row, facin de mound,
Dey fingers grippin de iron rail er de dugout.

Darryl take he warm-up tosses:
A couple er *lollipops*, a few breakin balls.
Den he trow he *heat*,
Nuthin what oberpower,
But.
It set up he bread-&-butter, dat *curb ball* where de bottom fall out.

Darryl chuckle ter he self.
"None of this matters," he tink. "Why do I care?"

A woman run onter de field from de stands,
& she *trow* she self at he spikes.
Darryl look 'round, embarrass, but he dinna stop she.
She roll up he pant legs & rub she *long dark hair* all ober he calves.
Darryl laff.
De rest er dose Cardinals *whoop* & *whistle*.

When she finish, Darryl take she by she shoulder.
She cry.
He lift she face ter he own.
"This day," he say, "you will be with me in paradise."
De Cardinals lob baseballs from de dugout ter de mound.
Darryl shield she wif he body, & *escort* she back ter de stands, unhurt.

He turn ter go back ter de mound,
& *anudder* woman reach out & touch he on he jersey.
He feel de power er he pitchin arm *leabe* he fer a moment,
& he turn & say: "Who has touched me?"
But.
No one speak.

DK gaze inter de faces er de *vendors*,
Dose black men & white men wif dey *hotdog* & *peanut* & *beer*.
He gaze inter de *Sea er Cardinal Red*.
He gaze inter de face er de *chilluns* wif dey little bats & glubs,
Dey eyes transfix in *glory*.

Agin de open sky east er Busch Stadium he see de tip er de *Arch*.
A few block from where he stand, he see *Roger Taney*, de Chief Justice
    Mon,
What say dat *Dred Scott* be de piece er *property*
(Not a mon, just de master's *black slabe*.)
DK see de *grabe* where *Chief Pontiac* be bury, what be de leader er de
    Iroquois,
Bury dar beneaf a *parkin garage*!

He circle de stadium, he see dose statue er *Gibby* & *Stan* & *Lou* & *Enos*,
& de *eternal light* on de statue er Ole *Jack Buck* (de broadcast mon).
He dribe he car ober de bridge inter Illinois, & back agin,
He enter ole Sportsmon Park wif it short right-field screen,
Where *Stan de Man* slam de double fer 20 year.
He see *Wally Post*, de Cincinnati Red, hammer one so hard it hit de
    neon eagle in left.

He rememmer Gibby wif de *broken leg*, see he fall from de mound in
    pain.
He see Curtis Raymond *Flood*, de artist-mon in center field,
Curt Flood what *hain't* gwine ter be sold like no piece er *property*,
Like de *black slabe*!
No!
Orlando Cepeda & Bill White & Wally Moon & Red Schoendienst &
    Rogers Hornsby & Bob Forsch & Kenny Boyer & Dick Groat &
    Julian Javier & George Crowe (de great pinch hitter mon).
& de McDaniel boys, Von & Lindy, & Dizzy & Paul Dean, & Keith
    Hernandez, & Ozzie, & Tim McCarber, & Joe Garagiola, &
    Vinegar Ben.
& he see *Grober Clebeland Alexander*, "Ole Pete" what drink de
    whiskey,
& he see *Sunny Jim Bottomley*, de Nokomis boy what set de record fer
    de RBI.

So *many* er dey, dey face come ter he now so fast dat DK canna name dey,

He dinna *wanter* name dey,
Dey become *one* face, *one* child, *one* innocent ting, *one* def.

He sleep in Chicago & *nebber* wake up,
But.
It be only he *body*,
De *temple* er DK,
De temple er he *soul*.
Dat be what fail & turn foul and decay.
DK.

He *see* eberyting still, he *know* eberyting still.
He hear *Pavarotti*, de *Nessun Dorma*,
He see *Jackson Pollack*, de *Blue Poles*, a-crumblin from de wall
In de Australian National Gallery.
He be *Dersu Uzala*, stackin *kindlin* in de Siberian hut
Fer de lost trabbelers he nebber meet.
He be *Bobby Kennedy*, a-lying in de pool er he own blood,
Clutchin de black rosary on de kitchen flo.
He be *Steve Biko*, he head bangin senseless in de back er de truck
Rollin troo de South African night.

He be de *fodder* ter de *Florida Writer Mon*,
Crashin he car on de country road in Illinois,
He last 3 word what no one ebber gwine ter hear: "I love you."
He be *Moshe Dayan*,
He be *Truman Capote*, he baffrobe open at de door ter he New York
        apartment.
He be *Atticus Finch*, he gun pointin at de rabid dog.

& he be *mo*.
He be *clone*.
He be *legion*.
He be *unchain*.
"Tell no one about this," he say.

But.
Dey tell anyway,
From *Galilee* ter *Mozambique* ter *Eau Claire, Wisconsin.*
Dey feed 5 *tousand* wif de *loabe* & de *fish,*
Gentile & Jew,
Slabe & free,
Male & female.

Dey cross ober de Jordan,
Dey in Canaan's Land.
"Farther along," he sing, "we'll know all about it."
DK sing: "Farther along, we'll understand why."

(& de Damage Boy wonder why grampa be *deaf,*
Why God take 'way he *hearin,* of all ting?
Dis *little* man, dis *music* man, *whuffo* God do such ting?
What de *matter* wif God?
De Damage Boy *rememmer* dis grampa in he wee black Chevrolet
Fill wif de pencil & de matchbook & de calendar wif de naked lady,
Rememmer he blowin de notes from de *trombone,* de notes what he
       nebber hear.)

"All who are thirsty, come to the water," say Darryl Kile,
He left toe *massage* de pitchin rubber.
He toughts hain't be *you* toughts.
He ways hain't be *you* ways.
"My word shall not return to me void, but shall do my will," he say.

"Give us Barabbas," dey cry,
& Ahab turn 'way, washin he hand.
Darryl carry he *cross,*
He stumble, he be hept by de *stranger.*
He teammates abandon he,
Dey fear what dey canna unnerstand.

Only de *women* remain at de foot er dat cross
(De mudder, de ho.)
De cock crow.
(Darkness at de break er noon,
Handmade toy, chile's balloon.)
Dey gib he de *vinegar.*
Water *pour* from he side.
"It is finished," he say.
But.
He be *dead wrong.*

'Cause here come ole Ahab (Master er Disguise),
Arguin dat in de absence er confusion,
Human folk hab no dialogue 'tall!
Ahab & Joseph er Arimathea *bury* de body.

Ahab (dis *Pharisee,* dis *teacher* er Israel),
Come ter he *befo,* in de night,
& Darryl say *dis* ter Ahab:
"The wind blows where it wills,
And you can hear the sound it makes,
But you do not know where it comes from or where it goes;
So it is with everyone who is born of the spirit."

Mary Magdelene cradle de head er Darryl Kile: "Quid est tetigit,
    nisi creditit?"

What is touch, Darryl, 'cept beliebe?

Quid est tetigit, Darryl, nisi creditit?

2. The Road to Emmaus

> *And behold, two of them went that same day to a village called*
> *Emmaus, which was from Jerusalem about threescore furlongs.*

And they talked together of all things which had happened.
And it came to pass that, while they communed together and
reasoned, Jesus himself drew near, and went with them. But their
eyes were holden that they should not know him.

Luke 24:13–16

Well suh,
De last night dat DK walk on dis earf be de *Friday* night,
When he tote he cross up ter Golgotha's 11th flo.

He *'spose* ter start versus de Cubs on de Sunday atternoon,
So.
He settle inter he cornder suite at de Westin Hotel ter *relax.*
(He be restin at de Westin!
Befo he twix-start *routine!*)

But.
Saturday mornin come, & DK *nebber make it* ter no Wrigley Field.
No.
& when DK *still* no-show at de ballpark at 11 a.m.,
De Cardinal fellers phone ter he hotel room,
But.
Dar be no answer dar.
No suh.

Den dey hab de hotel *security mon* knock on Golgotha's door.
Tock tock tock.
Still no answer.
De "Do Not Disturb" sign be a-danglin from de doorknob!
& de *safety latch* be drawn on de *inside* (shhhhh)!
(Wo.)

So.
De security mon *whack down* de door!

& *dar he be.*
DK.
D-E-A-D in he bed,
Still stretcht out dar,
Whilst he teammates be takin der *battin* practice a few block away.

Well suh,
By & by, de word *spread* ter de playin field,
Twix dose line er chalk at Wrigley,
& Ahab (Master er Disguise) *gedder* he players inter de visitor
     clubhouse.
& he *pernounce* ter dey dis message:
"They found DK dead."

& Mike Matheny
(De catcher in de *rye*),
He axe all he teammates ter bow dey head.
& he lead dey in de tearful prayer.
Dey pray fer DK, & dey pray fer he fambly.
Dey pray fer us *all.*

De game twix de Cardinal & de Cub be set ter start at 2, mon,
But.
Dose Cub, *dey* gedder in front er *dey* dugout on de 3rd base line
Wif Ahab (Master er de Regular Season, Master er Disguise) by dey
     side.
& de Cub catcher Joe Girardi,
He speak inter de microphone ter de Wrigley crowd:
"Due to a tragedy in the Cardinals' family, today's game has been
     canceled."
(Dat be de *direck quote.*)

& oh my!
Dat Wrigley crowd start ter *boo* & ter *hiss,*
But.

Dey see Joe Girardi wif de broken face.
& dey fall silent.

& Ahab, he walk de *slow* walk 'cross de diamond, back ter de Cardinal
    dugout.
Here be what Ahab say ter de press:

    Our club is just totally staggered. I mean, devastated.
    You need someone smarter than me to explain it,
    because I don't understand it.

& 8 day later, befo de Montreal *Expo* play *der* next game at de
    Olympic Stadium,
Versus dose Indians what be from O-hi-o,
De *ghost* er DK *enter* de Expo clubhouse!
Eben wif de *door* lock!
Wo!
& dat ghost *stand* dar, 'mongst dose Expo.
& de Expo 3rd baseman, what be name Fernando Tatis of all ting,
He say:

    In my mind, I can see Darryl Kile right next to me.
    We always joked together. I can't believe he's dead.
    I have to see it to believe it.

So.
DK say unter Fernando Tatis: "Fernando. Put your finger here and
    see my hands,
Stretch out your hand and put it in my side."

& Fernando Tatis say:

    We have to realize that
    he's dead, but in my mind, he's alive,
    because he was one of the greatest.

& DK say unter he: "You believe because you see me.
Happy are they who have not seen and yet believe."

& us folk what *dinna* see,
We can check de *stats*!

Here be de *stats* er Mr. Darryl Kile:
He be only de 30th-round draft choice in de year of our Lard 1987,
Fer dose *Astro* what be from Houston.
& 4 year later, in de year of our Lard 1991, he be *called up* ter dose Astro,
& go 7-11 as de *rookie*.

He stay dar in Houston fer 7 *whole year* (out dar in de *wilderness*),
& in he *best* season dar, he go 19-7 wif de 2.57 ERA!
Wo.
Dat be *some pitchin*!

Den he get traded ter Colorado,
De home er de *Rockies* & de home er de *long ball*,
Where *all* de pitcher mons get belted *all ober creation*!
(Colorado be de hitter *paradise*, mon, & de pitcher *hell*.)
& DK lead de league in *losses* in de year of our Lard 1998, wif 17.
Crikey!

Den he get traded ter dose Cardinal from St. Louis,
& DK hab de best year er he *whole life*, dar in de *Promise Land*,
In de year of our Lard 2000
(Dat *millennium* year, Y2K).
DK be 20-9!

But.
Dat *next* season, 2001, be de *last* full season befo DK die.
He trow fer 227 & $^1/_3$ innins dat year.
He go 16-11, wif de ERA er 3.09.

& at de end er 2001, DK hab de surgery on he mighty right shoulder.

Well suh,
2002 be de end er de road.
DK hab only 'nuff time in he life fer 14 measly game.
He be 5-4 wif de ERA er 3.72.
But.
He win 3 er he last 4 start!

Atter de final game, what put dose Cardinal inter 1st place in de NL
    Central,
DK say: "Once you take the ball, you've got a job to do."

DK.

DK.

16. That's Why We're Here

Peter Ives

On Thursday morning, May 4, 2000, my eleven-year-old son, David, stood before our living room window waiting for the stretch limo that was to take us to the airport. He had never been in a stretch limo, and this was a very big deal because we don't do limousines in our family. At the time, we did a 1983 Toyota Corolla with 179,000 miles, a broken air-conditioning unit, and a passenger-side window that wouldn't roll down. We did a late model Honda Civic with a dent in the front passenger door and a huge stain on the backseat carpet where, a month after bringing the car home from the dealer, I spilled the better part of a quart of motor oil. Luxury rides were for the rich and famous, and we were definitely not in that league.

We had the bags, all four of them, stacked in a pile near the front door. Too many bags for a four-day trip, even if it was the Big Apple. Next to the suitcases were some miscellaneous items: my camera bag, some snacks for the flight, and David's knapsack in which he had deposited his baseball card collection, a ball glove, an autograph diary, pens, Magic Markers, a GameBoy, and two glossy soft-cover photo books about the New York Yankees. We'd spent the evening before going over the pictures and making sure that we could attach names to all the faces. The big names would be no problem—Jeter, O'Neil, Williams, Torre—but we wanted to be prepared for anything because in a little more than twenty-four hours David was going to meet baseball's world champions.

The trip was, in the argot of Las Vegas, comped: the limos, the flights, the room at the Marriott Financial Center, meals, game tickets—even cab fare and spending money. I was along for the ride; a guardian keeping watch by night and day while an early adolescent had his day in the sun. David had earned this trip by staying alive, beating the leukemia that he was diagnosed with three and a half years earlier.

I was in the kitchen drinking coffee when I heard David yell, "Oh my God! It's bigger than a house!"

I went to have a look, but he was already out the door and at the curb, standing next to a gleaming white Lincoln Continental stretch limo so huge that I had to question whether it could have any real locomotive utility. A veritable Moby Dick of the open road with a hood that could have come in at a par five. When the driver's door opened, a big, barrel-chested man in a dark suit stepped out. He was completely bald and tanned and wore wrap-around sunglasses, and for a split moment I wondered why Governor Jesse Ventura had to moonlight as a chauffeur in Orlando, Florida.

"You must be David Ives," he said, looking down at David who was looking up with his mouth opened wide. "I'm Hank, and I'll be taking you to the airport." He stuck out his right hand, and David awkwardly reached up with his left hand to shake it.

"Hey, Dad!" he yelled, turning to see me coming down the drive. "The limo's here!"

"Hmmm doggie," I said, affecting a Jed Clampitt accent. "She sure is purdy. Swimming pools. Movie stars."

The Make-A-Wish Foundation had contacted us about two years into David's treatment protocol. Initially, I begged away from dealing with them, leaving the negotiations to my ex-wife, Diana, from whom I had been separated since David's infancy. I just couldn't deal with the thought that my son warranted their services; it seemed like a bad omen, as if by accepting their generosity I would somehow hex David's chances for survival. I had read about Make-A-Wish, had been heart-torn by the stories and images I'd seen in print and on television about the terminally ill kids who get that one last dream fulfilled—meeting Madonna, cutting a CD in a *real* professional studio, spending a week at Disney World, or getting balcony, VIP seating at a movie opening, mingling with the superstar cast at the post-screening party. These kids were dying, and I couldn't think about assigning my son to that noble yet sad beneficence.

He was just shy of his eighth birthday when he was first diagnosed with acute lymphocytic leukemia (ALL), and after the first frantic weeks of treatment—surgery, steroids, chemo, and a battery of painful and invasive tests—went into remission. Of the types of leukemia he could have contracted, ALL has the best overall recovery rate, about 80 percent. Still, I often found myself focusing on the lower number, like a father sending a son off at the airport, being told by the ticket agent not to worry because eight out of ten times the plane doesn't crash.

In mid-April, about a year after his last chemo treatment, David told me that he had had a meeting at his mom's the night before with two women from the Make-A-Wish Foundation. I was surprised. He'd been free of symptoms for three and a half years. Although those associated with the treatment of leukemia will tell you that a "cure" means being in remission a full five years, I felt, we all felt, that he was well on his way, and as a result there seemed to be something innocently ill intended about granting David a wish.

"So, did you make a wish?"

"Yes."

"What was it?" I asked, ready for something sufficiently extravagant.

"I told them I wanted to go with you to see a Yankee game at Yankee Stadium."

I laughed, actually laughed, and David laughed, too. He could have asked for anything—computers, video games and hardware, trips anywhere in the United States, amusement parks, ANYTHING.

"Well, Dave, why the Yankees?"

"Because." He seemed hurt that I was not equally ecstatic.

"Hey, don't get me wrong," I said, reaching across the table to squeeze his shoulder. "It's just. . . . What did your mom say?"

"She wanted a trip to Hawaii, but I said no. I want the Yankees."

"You can't blame her for that."

"I know."

"All right, then. It's the Yankees!"

I knew that David loved the Yankees and baseball. He had no choice. I grew up in a household where the Yankees constituted an aspect of the Holy Trinity, which, in declining order of hierarchy, went like this: God, Jesus, and the Yankees—with the Yankees moving into first place during postseason play. To not love the Yankees would have been a sacrilege and, even worse, an open act of defiance against my father.

I don't follow sports the way I used to, but when April comes around, part of my daily routine is to check the standings every morning in the *New York Times*, go over the statistics columns, and read out loud to David any articles even remotely related to the Yankees. And I had done this for years. The Yankees are something that tie not just David and me together but my whole family—brothers, sisters, nieces, and nephews, one of whom carries "Yankee" as a middle name on his birth certificate.

And David played Little League ball, although for a couple of years it was a hit-or-miss thing, depending on where he was in his recovery. Also, he had a port under the skin on his right side, at a point about a third of the way down on his rib cage. This port, a small plastic diaphragm where all the chemo had been administered, was a vulnerable spot, especially as David is a right-handed batter and the small bulge under his skin seemed like a magnet for wild pitches.

Like his father, David was more enthusiastic than talented. Hitting posed some problems, and although he had a strong arm, his throws from third base had a good chance of landing in the dugout. And although I tried to coach David, my knowledge of nuts and bolts fundamentals was very limited. Still, David loved to play—the normality of it—and looked forward to his games and practices, never getting discouraged by the bench or the muffed pop flies or the consecutive strikeouts at the plate.

After landing at LaGuardia on early Thursday afternoon, we were met in the baggage claim area by a chauffeur holding a sign that read "Welcome David Ives—Make-A-Wish-Foundation" and driven to the Marriott in lower Manhattan. The game, Yankees versus Baltimore, was the next evening and we spent the rest of the day getting settled and exploring parts of the city. I took David down to the World Trade Center, just a couple of blocks away.

"God, Dad, how did they build something so big?"

"One floor at a time, I guess," I said, watching him from behind a camera lens, snapping photos as he gawked at the impossible skyline.

We took a cab up to Times Square and walked up and down Broadway, past Disney's *Lion King*, the MTV studios where a crowd of screaming fans had gathered below a second-floor plate glass window to watch the Back

Street Boys being interviewed. We dropped by a couple of tourist shops and bought an additional Yankee T-shirt, a Yankee pinstripe game jersey, and a satin New York Yankee warm-up jacket. We walked up to Columbus circle and watched a Latin street band. I gave David some dollar bills and photographed him while he danced and tossed money into the donation box. We had a late dinner of hotdogs and pretzels from sidewalk vendors and walked down Seventh Avenue as far south as Chelsea, where I hailed a cab and spent the rest of the evening watching TV and looking out the window at the lights moving up and down the Hudson.

The next morning, we rose early. Arrangements had already been made for a limo to pick us up at around 3:30 for the trip to Yankee Stadium. After breakfast we strolled back down to the Twin Towers and waited in line for the elevator to the top, a carnival of history and kitsch and gift shops. I have photos from that morning: David standing in front of a northside window, Manhattan spread out like a movie backdrop in the hazy light of a warm spring morning. He's smiling and excited and has already fed at least five dollars into the coin-operated telescope next to him.

We still had a few hours to kill before the limo ride, so we grabbed another cab and headed uptown toward Central Park. At 51st Street the cabbie cut across town and we drove past Saint Patrick's Cathedral. A block-long line of people had queued out front and police barricades were in place. The cabbie looked back at us. "For Cardinal O'Connor."

I nodded.

"What?" asked David, straightening up and looking out the window.

"They're getting ready for his funeral."

"Whose funeral?"

"Cardinal O'Connor's," the cabbie said, giving us an incredulous glance over his shoulder.

David turned to me. "What he die of?"

"Cancer."

"What kind?"

"Not your kind."

"How do you know?" He sat back in his seat and stared straight ahead.

"Because if he'd had your kind of cancer he probably wouldn't have died."

"I could have died," he said. "That's why we're here."

I could see the cabbie watching us through the rearview mirror.

"We're not here because you could have died." I reached over and pulled him close. "We're here because you're the boy who kicked cancer's ass."

David laughed, and so did the cabbie. David likes it whenever I use an off-color phrase or word, and he likes it even more whenever I put his battle with leukemia in heroic terms.

About five minutes into our limo ride to Yankee Stadium, this time in a jet black Lincoln with leather interior and all the expected accoutrements, David stopped trying to tune in the small color TV built into the seat behind the driver and announced that he had to go to the bathroom.

"Jesus. How bad?"

He twisted up his face. "Bad."

The driver had told me that the drive would take, at the most, forty-five minutes. "You should have gone before we left," I said. "You'll have to hold it till we get there."

"I'll try."

It didn't take long to hit the first traffic jam. It seemed that everyone in lower Manhattan wanted an early jump for what was predicted to be a beautiful summer-like weekend. The driver left the West Side Highway, and we moved in a stop-and-go zigzag pattern up Manhattan. Two hours later I was contemplating letting David use one of the cut glass whiskey decanters for a urinal when the stadium came into view. The driver pulled up to the press entrance, and we were met immediately by Jason, a representative of the Yankees public relations department, and Juan, a volunteer with the local Make-A-Wish Foundation. Jason appeared to be in his early thirties, tall and thin with close-shaved hair, and he carried a walkie-talkie in his left hand. Juan, in his mid-twenties, was already behind his camera snapping pictures.

After introductions, Jason looked at his watch and shrugged his shoulders. "I apologize. We should have anticipated the traffic."

"That's okay," I said. "I wasn't behind the wheel."

He then leaned down to talk to David. "There are some people I'd like you to meet. Are you ready?"

"Sure. Great!" David said. "But I've gotta pee really bad."

Even if there were no such thing as baseball, God would still have invented Yankee Stadium. I had been there at least a couple of dozen times over the years, starting back in the summer of 1968 when my father and mother took me and eight of my brothers and sisters to see the Yankees play, coincidently, Baltimore. I was thinking about this as Jason led us up a passageway that fed into the lower level behind the Yankees' dugout. David was a couple of steps ahead of me. He had never been in a stadium, let alone the House That Ruth Built, and I wanted to see his reaction, and his reaction was everything I imagined it would be.

After funneling up a dingy and ill-lit concrete passageway, there is an almost explosive flowering of perception when you step into a stadium: it is as if the universe suddenly opens up, becomes transparent. In essence, you are walking through the looking glass.

David stopped at the top step and made a slow three-hundred-sixty-degree turn. Below us on the field the Yankees were taking batting and fielding practice. Emptied of fans, the stadium seemed bigger to me. The sounds of play—balls slapping against leather, the loud crack of the bats as the players took turns in the batting cage—were almost preternatural in their clarity. The outfield, vivid and surreal; the perfect geometry of the infield diamond with the grass cut diagonally to yield a corrugated, undulating appearance; the Jumbotron, black and blank; the scoreboard already turned on, waiting for that evening's numbers; even the advertisement billboards—Hitachi, Budweiser, Fleet Bank, Burger King, Hess oil—contained an incongruous aesthetic as they lined the stadium's perimeter behind the outfield; and above all were the flags, spread out at equal intervals and waving above the stadium's rim.

I took out my camera and started snapping pictures. Jason led us down to the barricade along the right side of the infield. About twenty yards in front of us, Paul O'Neil, the Yankee right fielder, warmed up for his turn in the batting cage. Don Zimmer, the assistant coach, sauntered by, projecting a curiously atavistic image as he dragged a cudgel-like bat behind him and growled at someone in the dugout. Joe Torre, the head coach, stood behind the batting cage, holding court in front of a camera crew. In the batting cage Jorge Posada knocked balls into the outfield.

Jason stepped through a gate and walked out to whisper something to O'Neil. David pulled his ball glove out of his bag and leaned over the barricade.

"Do you recognize anyone?" I asked.

"Him," David said, pointing to O'Neil, and just as he said this O'Neil dropped the bat to his side and turned toward David.

"Hey, kid. Hey, kid!"

David took a step back.

"Yeah, you. Jason says you want to meet me."

O'Neil cradled the bat under an arm and walked toward David, pulling his batting gloves off as he approached. When he got to the fence, he stuck out his hand.

"Do you know who I am?"

David nodded.

"Well, who am I?" he asked, still holding out his hand.

I was afraid for David, that the shock of Olympus might have induced a lapse of memory. I was going to walk down and make the introduction when David stepped forward, took O'Neil's hand, and said, "You're Paul O'Neil, and you play right field."

Everyone, including David and O'Neil, laughed and any lingering awkwardness immediately subsided.

"So, what's your name?"

I imagine that these meet-and-greet opportunities are pretty much boilerplate for professional athletes: Where're you from? How do you like the stadium? Do you play ball? What position? What grade are you in? Who's your favorite team? Do you have any brothers and sisters? Have you ever been to a Yankee game? But it all seemed spontaneous and original to David.

Joe Torre was next. He picked up a practice ball from the field and already had it autographed by the time he got to the barricade.

"So you're the boy who wants to meet the Yankees."

The questions were the same, and so were David's responses. Torre leaned over the barricade and put both arms around David while Juan and I continued snapping pictures.

"Say 'Yankees,'" I said, focusing for the shot, and Torre said, "No. Say 'Yankees WIN,'" and David punched the air and shouted, "YEAH."

In the midst of Torre's good-bye, I heard a voice to my right, "Hey, kid. Do you want a bat?"

It was Jorge Posada, the Yankee catcher. He had finished his batting practice and was in the dugout. In his hand was a massive bat, pine tar running halfway up the shaft.

"Here," he said, passing it over a chain link divider to David, who had walked over.

David held the bat, staring at it and running his hands over the pine tar when Derek Jeter, the Yankee shortstop, walked over. The same questions, responses, handshakes, shoulder pats, and autographs. Behind Jeter, I could see Bernie Williams, the center fielder, walking our way. He wore a batting helmet, and he was laughing at something. When Jeter said good-bye and turned, Williams trotted the last few steps and vaulted over the barricade, landing in the first row, mildly startling David, who was standing only a couple of feet away. He squatted down and put a hand on David's shoulder. The questions were pretty much the same, but his manner seemed more intimate and comfortable. David had his ball glove out, and Williams asked to look at it. He put it on (a tight fit) and smacked it a couple of times in the pocket.

"This is a great glove," he pronounced, handing it back to David. "You can play some serious baseball with a glove like that," and David agreed and started telling him about his Little League team.

Of all the pictures I took, it is the picture of David and Bernie that I love the most. Bernie is crouching down, his arm around David, who is smiling as he leans back into Bernie's embrace.

During all of this, I was more of a photographer than a father. I just snapped pictures, holding the camera in front of my face because if I had put it down, I think I would have cried. If any of the Yankees remember their meeting with David, I'm peripheral to that recollection, the stocky, balding man behind a Nikon who kept saying, *Thank you. This is wonderful. Thank you so much. Thank you! Thank you! Thank you*!

When David was sick, I used to hover near him in the treatment rooms as I watched the biopsies and the MRIs, the injections of drugs and chemicals into his side and spine. I used to hold his hand and sleep in a chair or a fold-up cot next to his hospital bed on the long nights immediately after a regimen of chemo when he would retch and heave for hours on end into an emesis basin. I—all of us—would comfort him as best we could when the drugs threw the large muscles of his legs into spasms or when the sores in his mouth made it impossible for him to eat or when he lost most of his hair and was sometimes so exhausted he had to be carried to the car for a quick trip to the doctor's office or the emergency room.

The Yankees' come-from-behind victory over the Atlanta Braves in the 1996 World Series coincided with David's going into remission, and we watched two of the games while he was in the hospital having chemotherapy pumped into him intravenously. It was something to cheer about during the first days and weeks after his diagnosis, and I unconsciously extrapolated from their victory a parallel ascendancy for David's battle with leukemia. I remember holding out a hand to balance him as he stood on his hospital bed and cheered, the tubes and monitoring cables running from his port and chest and fingers to the machines next to his bed. And I knew that no matter how much I might have ministered to him, the pain and the fear and the danger were always his alone. We, all of us who loved David, had our own terror: the possibility of a life without him. But David was the one who had to fight that bull, and in those terrible months and days I never dared to hope that someday I could stand back and watch him be honored for his suffering and recovery— let alone by the New York Yankees.

Our seats for that evening's game were midway up the second level along the third base line, and the next day's newspapers would report that we were joined by 42,241 additional screaming fans. David immediately made friends with two guys seated directly behind us. They were Baltimore fans by way of Boston, which made them exponentially hostile to the Yankees' fortunes. Nevertheless, we kept a good-natured rivalry going throughout the game, making small side bets as the innings progressed.

The National Anthem was followed by a moment of silence for the late Cardinal O'Connor. Orlando Hernandez, the Yankees starting pitcher, had dedicated his start to O'Connor's memory, and when the Yankees jumped to a 3–0 lead in the first inning (Jeter, O'Neil, and Williams each crossing the plate), it seemed as though a cosmic fix was in the works.

But the Orioles bounced back, and by the end of the third inning the score was tied at 3–3.

Just before the fifth inning began, I took out my camera and told David to pose for a picture in front of me, the Jumbotron visible over his right shoulder. Jason had told me to keep an eye on the Jumbotron before the fifth began, and I had just raised the camera when the two-story-tall salutation flashed on the screen: THE NEW YORK YANKEES WELCOME DAVID IVES. I snapped a couple of shots and told David to turn around.

"What?" he asked.

"Look," I said, snapping a picture with one hand and pointing with the other.

"Oh, my God! It's me."

He went a bit manic, laughing and pointing and dancing. "Look!" he said to Juan and the two Oriole fans behind us. "That's me! I'm David Ives."

The fans around us heard him, and they erupted into a localized wave of high fives, cheering, and applause.

The carnival atmosphere was raised an additional notch or two a few seconds later when eight people, enraged by the recent arrest of protestors on Vieques Island near Puerto Rico, jumped onto the field waving banners and the Puerto Rican flag, darting in between and around the bemused Yankee fielders while being chased down by a posse of security guards. One by one they were gang tackled, handcuffed, and dragged kicking from the field, all to a standing ovation from the crowd.

The lead changed hands a couple more times, and when the Yankees came to bat at the bottom of the ninth, they were down 10–8. Paul O'Neil was first up, and after fouling off several pitches nailed one over the right-field fence.

"Uh-oh," shouted one of the Baltimore fans behind us.

David turned around and raised a hand for a high five. "You're going down!" he said, and I think they believed him.

Bernie Williams was up next. He shot one to right field for a single and was followed by Tino Martinez, who drew a walk.

When Jorge Posada walked from the batting circle to the plate, I knew how the game was going to end—it had been that kind of day. David was standing on his seat screaming, "Jorge! Jorge! Jorge!" with 40,000 other near hysterical voices when Posada stepped into the batting box, took a couple of warm-up swings, settled back in his stance, and nailed the first pitch into the left-field stands.

I have a picture of David taken immediately after that home run. He's wearing his Yankee cap, jug-eared and laughing, his face sweaty and flushed as he holds his glove and dances in the aisle.

David, Juan, and I stood outside the press entrance for about an hour after the game. Juan was on the phone, talking to our next limousine driver who was lost or stuck in traffic somewhere around the vast asphalt domain of the stadium complex. It was cooler than inside the stadium and the night clear, with the stars visible against the competing urban luminescence. David was exhausted in the way that David gets exhausted, which is a sort of manic nonstop soliloquy that I most often respond to by repetitively nodding my head and saying "yes" until I find out I've agreed to his request for a hunting rifle or a birthday party at Hooters.

"Thanks, Dad," he said.

I stopped listening to Juan giving the limo driver directions in Spanish and looked down at David.

"What did I just agree to?"

"The Yankees. Tomorrow."

We still had two days in New York, and the Yankees had two games remaining in the series, one each on Saturday and Sunday. I wondered if the box office might still be open and was about to walk in that direction when I realized it would be too soon. That it would be a mistake. David had been the guest of the New York Yankees, had met and talked with the men who earned that night's victory, but the magnitude of his experience had yet to take root. If we went back on Saturday or Sunday David would have been just another young fan sitting anonymously in the stands watching just another game. Which, in the future, would be more than okay. But I didn't want that right then.

"Can I think about this?"

He nodded.

But what I was thinking about, what I wanted to do right then, was to go back to the hotel, order something from room service, prop the pillows up against the headboard, put my arm around David, and watch the highlights from the game on ESPN. And the next morning, before going to the zoo or a Broadway show or the Metropolitan Museum of Art, I planned to wake up early, grab some copies of the *New York Times* and the *Daily News*, and, like every other day in our wonderful and fortunate and ordinary lives, read the sports pages slowly out loud to my son.

17. Fielder's Choice

Lee Martin

The first baseball glove I owned was a fielder's mitt that my mother bought at Piper's Sundries in Sumner, a speck of a town in southeastern Illinois. We lived on a farm, then, ten miles south down a blacktop road and a few miles west over gravel and dirt. Saturday evenings, we drove up the blacktop to Sumner to do our shopping. "Let's go to town," my father said, "and do the trading."

It was 1960, and I was five years old, the only child of older parents. My mother was fifty; my father was forty-seven. Earlier that summer, my mother had lost her teaching job. Too soft with discipline, the school board had decided, and I imagine there was some element of truth to their claim since my mother was a meek, good-hearted woman, easily liked and easily taken advantage of by anyone, including me, looking to get away with something. She was soft-spoken and patient and shy. My father, on the other hand, was quick-tempered and gruff. They had to keep a close eye on money that summer, and though I don't know what the baseball glove cost, I'm certain it was a sum hard-earned and saved.

My father couldn't help but be angry, then, when he realized that my mother had made a mistake.

"That's for a lefty," he said when he saw the glove. "Jesus Christ. You bought a southpaw's glove."

It took a while for my mother to realize her error. She kept looking at the glove. "Isn't he right-handed?" she said, still trying to puzzle out where she had gone wrong.

"Hell, yes, he's right-handed."

"Well, this glove goes on the right hand." It finally came to her, the fact that a righty would wear his glove on his left hand so he could throw with his right one, and she pressed her lips together and frowned. This was the look I would grow to know so well from her, that frown she wore whenever she was disappointed with me or frustrated because she couldn't do something well. "I'm a dimwit," she finally said.

"You could take it back."

"Oh, no. No, Roy. I couldn't do that."

I suppose my father knew how much it would shame my mother to walk back into Piper's Sundries and admit what a ninny she had been. We kept the glove. I never complained. I learned how to throw with my left hand, and sometimes I wore the glove assbackward on that hand and threw with my right. I threw a rubber ball high into the air or up onto the roof and caught it when it came down. I threw it against a wall inside our house.

My father couldn't play catch with me because he had no hands. He had lost them in a farming accident when I was barely a year old. He tried to clear corn from a picker's shucking box without first shutting down the power takeoff, and the spinning rollers grabbed onto his hand and pulled it in. When he tried to free it with his other hand, the rollers caught it, too. I have no memory, then, of my father with hands, only prostheses, the steel-pronged pincers ("hooks," he called them) that he opened and closed by contracting or relaxing muscles in his shoulders.

He was a baseball fan. Like most people in our part of southern Illinois, he rooted for the St. Louis Cardinals. Evenings, when he came in from the fields, he turned on the radio and listened to Harry Caray and Jack Buck broadcasting from Busch Stadium in St. Louis or from somewhere on the road—Cincinnati, Pittsburgh, Milwaukee. I still have three letters that he wrote to my mother when he was in Barnes Hospital in St. Louis learning to use his prostheses. In one of them, he tells of going to a Cardinals game with one of the other "amputees": "Me and my buddy went to the ball game last nite, but the Cards lost in the 10th inning. Redlegs hit three home runs and the Cards none." At the time he wrote this letter—3:30 on a Wednesday afternoon toward the end of April 1957— he was listening to the Cardinals game on the radio: "Score is tied now, 7 and 7. Braves and Cards at Milwaukee."

I like to think that my father, at the time of his loss—this year when his life and the way he'd always known himself was changing—was still able to take pleasure in a baseball game. Its familiar pattern must have been a comfort to him: the constancy of three outs to an inning, the geometry of the diamond, the flux of time (as long as men can hit safely or draw walks or force the other team into making errors, the game will go on and on; the end will never come).

Baseball is a game that dares to hold time at bay, to blind us to our common failing: our inability to suspend ourselves in a world outside time's measure—a world that forgives us for being human.

That must have pleased my father—that illusion of grace. After all, it is an illusion. Sooner or later, a team registers twenty-seven outs—or more if the outcome requires extra innings—and the game comes to an end. Finally, one team vanquishes the other.

How many times over the years did my father dream himself back to that cornfield, to the moment just before he reached into the shucking box? How many times did he see himself doing what he should have done that day—shut down the power takeoff, stop those rollers from spinning? Maybe he forgave my mother for buying me a southpaw's glove because he knew better than most how our living can corner us, can show us exactly how stupid we are with our trying. I like to think that even though my mother's mistake irritated him, he also loved her for it, as I did—loved her for her kind spirit, for being fifty years old and having in her heart the need and reason to buy that glove, no matter what hand it fit.

I imagine her that day in Piper's Sundries, unfolding wrinkled bills, counting out coins, pushing the money across the counter, and when I do, I smell the glove's leather, see the rawhide strings that stitched the fingers together, the strap that buckled across the wrist, the webbing between the thumb and forefinger (which was between little finger and ring finger when I wore the glove on my left hand), the padding of the pocket. It was a glorious glove because it was my first, and I forgave it for ending up with a boy for whom it had never been meant.

I suspect that my father was also embarrassed because he hadn't been the one in Piper's Sundries buying his son his first baseball glove. Sometime later that summer, he went there and bought me a bat—a Roger Maris autograph model, a Louisville Slugger made of ash. I loved the feel of the varnished wood and the pattern the grain made. I loved the bat's perfect weight, and how I could swing the barrel around to meet the balls my mother tossed to me. I could hit fly balls, grounders, line drives. I don't remember anyone teaching me how to hit. I watched the Saturday *Game of the Week* on television and imitated what I saw.

My father must have regretted that he couldn't pitch to me or, like my mother did sometimes, take up the bat and hit pop-ups or grounders that I caught with my wrong-handed glove. One evening, a father's friend hit fly balls to his son and me, and my father stood by and watched, the pincers of his hooks clasped just below his breast bone, a submissive pose that announced how inadequate he was for this task. He could only watch as my friend's father, young and athletic, tossed the ball up and cracked fly ball after fly ball high into the air.

The next evening, when my father came in from the field, I asked him whether he could hit a baseball. I remembered how my friend's father had complimented my sure catches, my strong throws. "Atta boy," he had said. "That's using the old wing." I had wanted to please him, to earn his admiration. We had shared something that night through his hitting and my catching and throwing, the ball rising from his bat to my glove and then arcing back to him. That arc connected us. Its line carried an intimacy between athletes—their mutual skills working in concert—and this is what I wanted to know with my father.

To my surprise, he responded to my challenge. "Well, let's see," he said.

I held my bat out to him—my beloved Louisville Slugger—and he opened his hooks and gripped the handle. He took a batter's stance, and from a few feet away, I lobbed the ball to him underhanded, and he swung.

Even now, in my memory, I can hear the sound of the bat against the ball, can see the arc of the ball's flight, a pop-up I settled under and caught. "Do it again," I said, and my father obliged.

I pitched and he hit until it was too dark to see the ball. I'm not sure whether I've ever been happier than I was that night.

Finally, I took the bat from him, and I felt the rough wood, splintered from where his hooks had gouged it.

"I'm sorry," he said. "I guess we just didn't think."

I can still feel the scraped wood of that bat, the slivers of ash. I can see us standing in the deepening dusk, my father gently tapping the bat's knob with the smooth curve of his hook, trying to find something else to say, something wise and compassionate like a father on one of the television sitcoms would have said to make his son feel better about what had happened—something about life never turning out the way we expect it and the lesson to be learned. But the only sounds around us were the swallows winging through the darkening sky, flying to roost in the rafters of our barn, and somewhere far back in our pasture, a cow bell faintly clanging as one of the jerseys lowered her head to a salt block or went down on her belly to sleep. All we could do, finally, was turn to the house where my mother, when she saw what my father had done to the bat, wrapped the handle with black electrician's tape. "There," she said in her kind voice. "As good as new."

There would be other bats (a Mickey Mantle model, a Nellie Fox), and there would be other gloves (a Tito Francona, a Brooks Robinson), but none of them is as vivid in my memory as that southpaw's glove, which my mother wrongly bought, and that Roger Maris Louisville Slugger that my father scarred with his hooks.

Only four years had passed since his accident—since he came home from the hospital in a rage. ("Out of his head," my aunt told me years later. "His nerves. Oh how he'd rant and rave.") He took phenobarbital tablets, a tranquilizer to calm him, to ease the pain in his stumps and the sensation of still having hands—those phantom hands that haunted him. We were trying hard to find the rhythm of a regular life, but there were mistakes at every turn—that glove, that bat.

When I think of the people we were in those days, I fall in love with our common need and how desperate we were to pretend we could reclaim all that we had lost. We wanted to believe that we could travel back in time and be who we were before my father's accident. I think now of the scene in *Field of Dreams* when the dead baseball players come out of the cornfield and step onto the baseball diamond that Kevin Costner's character has built. Shoeless Joe Jackson, banned from baseball after the 1919 Black Sox Scandal when he and seven teammates agreed to throw the World Series, becomes overwhelmed with this redemption—this chance to again play the game he loves. He asks in a reverent voice, "Is this Heaven?"

Imagine a baseball field when there's no one on it, when the stands are empty, when it's merely landscape: the outfield grass, lush and green and clipped short; the infield dirt, a rich, brown powder, smoothly raked; the baselines and the batter's box, freshly chalked; the bases, whiter than any white you can imagine. Draw a baseball field with your own hand and you'll feel its beauty—the symmetry of its lines and angles and arcs.

My father, as a young man, loved plane geometry—the logic of its theorems and proofs. Later, when I was in high school and struggling with that course, he would try his best to explain a postulate such as "any two lines contain at most one common point." We were to accept this statement as valid. It was our job, he said, to develop as many true statements from this postulate as we could by using logical reasoning. We would then provide proof of these theorems by offering detailed descriptions of the reasoning we used to deduce them. That's geometry, he said. Thinking about why something's true. "It either flies or it doesn't," he told me, "and if you use your noodle you can figure out which."

"What if the lines are parallel?" I said. "They'll never intersect. How in the heck can they have one common point?"

We were sitting at our kitchen table, under the glow of the fluorescent light ring. It hummed above us. My mother, who always deferred to my father when I needed help with anything mathematical, was in the living room reading a novel—Jane Austin's *Pride and Prejudice* ("It is a truth universally acknowledged . . .")—that she had chosen from a box of books she had bought at a senior class fund-raising auction. My father tapped his hook on my geometry text. "Look at the postulate again, Einstein."

I read it. *Any two lines. One common point.*

"Impossible," I said.

"It doesn't say at *least* one common point." My father raised his voice, getting impatient. "Holy cow," he said, the way Harry Caray did when he was broadcasting a Cardinals game, and he was amazed by a spectacular play or a bonehead error. "It says at *most*. At *most*. Now think about it."

Finally, I saw what he meant. The postulate wasn't claiming that any two lines would share a common point—only lines that didn't run parallel to each other. At most one common point, and that would be the point of intersection before the lines stretched on into infinity, each following its own trajectory, never to meet again.

"Oh," I said, feeling sheepish.

"Use your noggin," my father told me. "Pay attention so you'll never be a dope."

But what about this, I might say to him now if he were still among the living? What about two threads of narrative?

> 1. *A man tries to clear corn from a picker's clogged shucking box, and the spinning rollers take in his hands. He stands there, the rollers mangling his hands until another farmer driving past the field hears his shouts for help.*
>
> 2. *A man shuts down the tractor's power takeoff before he clears the corn from the picker's shucking box. He wipes the corn dust from his hands, job done. He comes in from the field, and later that night he holds his infant son in his arms and rocks him to sleep.*

Two lines through time, each up to a particular instant as possible as the other. Two parallel lines that never meet. Find the common point.

Of course, if my father were still alive, I'd never say this to him because the answer is the moment when he has to choose whether to shut down that power takeoff. It's the moment when he proved himself to be careless. He knows the picker is clogged. He brakes the tractor and throws it into neutral. Here both narratives are possible. Here the lines through time occupy a common point. If he'll only reach for that lever that disengages the power takeoff, everything in our lives will be different.

But he doesn't, and we're left forever with the specter of what might have been, our phantom lives streaking by us into infinity. From time to time, we glimpse their light. My mother, full of delight, buys my first baseball glove; my father swings my bat and lifts a pitched ball into the air.

Let it stay there forever, a white spot in the dusk, a little boy, his arms up, the fielder's mitt on his right hand, open and waiting, no matter that his mother made a mistake, bought a southpaw's glove. The ball hangs in the sky. The boy waits. There is no chance of error.

18. A Fan Letter to Lefty Gomez
Jeffrey Hammond

Lefty Gomez, Hall of Fame pitcher for the 1930s Yankees, died in Greenbrae, California, on February 17, 1989. I surely would have mourned his passing had I known about it, but I was living on the other side of the country and had stopped following baseball many years before. If I had been reminded of Lefty Gomez, even in an obituary, I might not have taken my career worries so seriously. Then in my late thirties, I was depressed about my teaching job at a state university in Virginia. After a decade of facing large classes and finding myself stuck, not unfairly, with the label of English department malcontent, I wasn't having much fun at work.

Thirty years earlier, the old Yankee fastballer had taught me not to take myself too seriously. When I was a fat, left-handed eight-year-old who adored everything about baseball, the message had proven supremely useful. Babe Ruth, who served as John the Baptist in this lesson, prepared the way for the minor redemption that Lefty Gomez extended to an unathletic boy in a small Ohio town where baseball was serious business. I had the wrong physique and half the skill necessary to play the game decently, an intolerable situation were it not for the fact that Babe Ruth was also fat and left-handed. This was the late 1950s, when all-day Saturday kid shows at the Royal Theater were still running grainy old newsreels of the Babe, then ten years dead, rounding the bases in that mincing, top-heavy home run trot. Plenty of people said that Babe Ruth was the greatest ballplayer of all time. My early forays into baseball history convinced me that Ty Cobb deserved that honor more, but no matter. Babe Ruth was important not because he was great but because he was fat, left-handed, and great. Convinced that I resembled him, I mimicked his baby-step trot in our neighborhood games.

If Babe Ruth brought self-esteem, Lefty Gomez offered salvation. Ruth's teammate in the Babe's later years, Gomez gave southpaw eccentricity a decidedly comic turn, a godsend to a kid who played baseball poorly but liked having fun. In a Depression-era game filled with tough street kids and snarly hillbillies, the talkative Gomez had been gloriously different. Famous for his off-beat antics and quick wit, he had earned, in addition to "Lefty," a nickname that I considered the best in baseball: "El Goofy." The first Gomez story I ever heard, I think, was how he held up a World Series game by stopping to watch an airplane fly overhead. It was also Gomez who famously proclaimed, "I'd rather be lucky than good." For an eight-year-old who knew he never *would* be good, those words resonated deeply. When my father told me Gomez's line about inventing a "revolving bowl for tired goldfish," I knew that this was the ballplayer for me.

A deliberately funny ballplayer was both strikingly novel and strangely familiar to a fat boy who routinely told jokes on himself before someone else did, hoping to compensate for so-so skills by making other kids laugh. Words, especially funny ones, proved especially useful for avoiding fights, always a risk given the humorless intensity of the neighborhood Ty Cobbs. Lefty Gomez and I seemed to share a secret—Hey, guys, it's only a game—and the funny left-hander soon replaced the fat left-hander as my baseball hero. Gomez proved that being left-handed was special, and in a manner in which I *could* be special. It wasn't the jump to first base that the momentum of my swing gave me, or the advantage, when I pitched, of throwing the ball from a place where it shouldn't be. It was the Lefty Gomez lesson that a left-hander could counter the high seriousness of his friends with an easygoing, chatty style of play. I started reading everything I could find about him, and when I learned that in his playing days he was 6'2" and weighed 175 pounds, I had no idea how those numbers translated into an adult build. I went to the public library and found a picture from the 1930s, and was surprised to discover that Lefty Gomez was skinny. I also learned that several managers had tried to make him gain weight, which made being skinny *his* version of my being fat. How did Gomez answer cracks about his weight? "You can't fatten up a greyhound." This seemed useful: maybe his skinny defiance could be inverted into a fat kid's pride.

When Vernon Louis Gomez came up to the Yankees from the San Francisco

Seals of the Pacific Coast League in 1930, his money pitch was a virtually untouchable fastball delivered with a high kick. Over the next ten years he and right-hander Red Ruffing led the Yankees to five pennants and five World Series championships. Gomez once claimed that "the secret to my success is clean living and a fast outfield," but that was simply untrue. A pitcher with 189 wins, 102 losses, and a career ERA of 3.34 barely *needs* an outfield, let alone a fast one. If a pitcher can hold opposing hitters to a .242 average over a fourteen-year career, there won't be many balls for that outfield to run down. Gomez appeared in a total of five All-Star games and won three, including the first one ever played. His perfect record in World Series play—six wins and no losses in 1932 and in 1936 through 1939—still stands.

Gomez had four seasons of twenty or more victories, and in 1934 and 1937 led the league in wins, strikeouts, and ERA. The AL strikeout leader four times in the 1930s, he struck out more batters in the decade than any other pitcher. After arm trouble and a poor season in 1940, he came back the following year with a new curve ball and won fifteen games. But the end was near. When he won only six games in 1942, the Yankees sold him to the Boston Braves, who released him four months later. After pitching five innings in a loss for the Washington Senators, Gomez retired in 1943, seven years before I was born. With 320 starts, 173 complete games, and 28 shutouts, he remains third in victories on the all-time Yankee list behind Ruffing and Whitey Ford, and fourth in strikeouts behind Ruffing, Ford, and Ron Guidry.

Lefty Gomez entered the Hall of Fame with characteristic humility in 1972, when he was sixty-four. At his induction he said, "I want to thank my teammates who scored so many runs and Joe DiMaggio, who ran down my mistakes." The quip concealed the fact that the Yankee Clipper owed far more to Lefty Gomez than vice versa. When DiMaggio followed Gomez's path from San Francisco to New York, El Goofy took it upon himself to keep the broody rookie loose, coaxing him out of his frequent funks with funny talk. Although Gomez once called himself "the guy that made Joe DiMaggio famous," referring to the long outs that the speedy center fielder had chased down, his comment contained a deeper and unintended significance. If Gomez had not played the baseball clown, his intense young roommate might have fretted his way straight back to Fisherman's Wharf. One time when Gomez was pitching and DiMaggio decided to imitate outfield legend Tris Speaker by playing shallow, Gomez waved him back. "Don't worry," DiMaggio breezily replied, "I'm going to make them forget Tris Speaker." When the Tigers Hank Greenberg hit a triple over DiMaggio's head, Gomez told his outfielder, "Roomie, you keep playing Greenberg shallow and you're going to make them forget Lefty Gomez."

I was no Joe DiMaggio, nor was meant to be—but Lefty Gomez performed the same office for me. He was that rarest of creatures: a player who delivered the goods with the humility of a player who could not. None of the athletic boys I knew, towel snappers in gym class and scornful mockers of the fat and the slow, seemed likely, when they grew up, to choose license plates that read "GOOF." Nor would they be so philosophical if they saw themselves heading for career batting averages of .147, as Gomez did, no matter how sharp their fastballs were. Although the boys I played with would have been grimly hitting fungoes under streetlights until two in the morning, Lefty Gomez faced failure in a whole other way: by embracing it. "They throw, I swing. Every once in a while they're throwing where I'm swinging and I get a hit." The carefree Gomez philosophy extended off the field as well. Not for him the sober persistence of Ty Cobb or the Cardinals Rogers Hornsby, who refused to watch movies because he thought they would dull his vision. "I never had a bad night in my life," Gomez once remarked, "but I've had a few bad mornings." After the 1931 season he took to the stage for a twelve-week engagement in which he performed a baseball soliloquy. "I lasted three weeks," he said after the show closed, "but the audience didn't." Two years later he married June O'Dea, a musical comedy performer—the perfect wife, I thought, for a ballplayer who knew how to have fun.

Lefty Gomez offered a better baseball life than those locker-room thugs, especially for a kid who didn't have a realistic choice about it. Most of all, he offered a novel approach to fear, balm for a fat left-hander's terror of screwing up. "I was never nervous when I had the ball," Gomez once claimed, "but when I let it go I was scared to death." Especially reassuring was his take on Jimmie Foxx, power-hitting infielder for the Philadelphia

Athletics. Foxx, he confessed, "could hit me at midnight with the lights out." Gomez cracked that his nemesis had "muscles in his hair": Foxx "wasn't scouted, he was trapped." One time when Foxx was at the plate, catcher Bill Dickey came out to the mound and asked Gomez what he wanted to throw. "I don't want to throw him nothing," he replied. "Maybe he'll just get tired of waiting and leave."

I felt that way about some of the tougher kids in our neighborhood. If Lefty Gomez could face the great Jimmie Foxx and joke about it, maybe I didn't have to be so afraid. Or if I *was* afraid, maybe I could exorcise the fear with words, conceding the obvious—yes, they *could* beat me up— and thus gaining some control over it. With Gomez as my model, I made funny talk my constant on-field companion. If I was catching and a tough guy was poised on third, I'd cut the tension by telling *him* what he was surely thinking about *me*. "Hey, Stevie! If you steal home I'm gonna kick your ass!" Naturally, Stevie would laugh at the absurdity of such a threat from a chubby catcher who was a foot shorter than he was. This brought an extremely practical benefit: a laughing Stevie would slide home with less mayhem in his heart.

After over forty years it's hard to remember which came first: the funny talk or the funny play. I can't recall a time when I was unaware of the inherent comedy of a kid shaped like me putting himself through the standard baseball moves: bending to scoop up a grounder, stretching off a bag to take a throw, and—most of all—running like grim death to beat out a ground ball. There was, in addition, a certain comic inevitability in a left-hander's style of play. When I was at shortstop, stagy acrobatics were inevitable whenever I went to my right for a ground ball and made the mandated whirl-around to throw to first. I knew I looked funny, but the example of Lefty Gomez allowed me to *enjoy* looking funny. By being left-handed in the Gomez manner, I could make a virtue out of a necessity.

I began cultivating a style of play that enhanced what I saw as my lefty distinctiveness. While the other kids honed the mechanics of fielding a ground ball to cool efficiencies and minimal movements, I developed an elaborate dance—a studied flamboyance—in which I timed my throw to arrive at the bag at the last possible moment. Things were

more fun that way. I also relished the inversion of the norm prompted by my coming to bat. As soon as someone yelled, "Heads up! Lefty!"
everyone would assume a version of Cleveland manager Lou Boudreau's
famous "shift," devised in 1946 against Ted Williams. If Williams, who
batted left, pulled every hit and was too stubborn to bunt, fielders had
no choice but to accommodate his whims. To watch the fielders theat-
rically reposition themselves felt like a vindication. Those right-handed
desks at school were murder, but here, on the ball field, the world had to
adjust to my left-handed quirks. A Lefty Gomez type of kid might want to
take the unexpected even further: wouldn't it be cooler if I went against
a norm that was *already* against the norm? I got pretty good at swinging
late and pushing the ball into that vacant left field.

Most of all, Lefty Gomez lent dignity to my conviction that I was less
likely to get punched by a bigger kid if I made him laugh. If a tough kid
threatened to kick me in the nuts, I'd remove my glasses, hold them in
front of my crotch, and announce, "Nu-huh, glasses!" Sometimes I'd
make a self-deprecatory crack, like "Go ahead and pound me! I'll bleed
on your shirt and your Mom'll kick your ass!" Other times I'd start chat-
tering about something wildly unrelated to the dispute at hand, like the
length of an adult brontosaurus or something that Jack Benny said on TV
that week, and the tough kid would forget what he was mad about. The
Ty Cobbs of the neighborhood often got into fights over disputed calls
and rough plays—but they rarely fought me. A true southpaw—a Lefty
Gomez type of kid—could almost always talk his way out of a tight spot.
Fighting was a lot like pitching, and as my hero said, "If you don't throw
it, they can't hit it." Blessed are the funny, for they shall keep their teeth.
More important, they will stay in the game. Even more important, they
will *enjoy* staying in the game, even though by rights they shouldn't be
enjoying it at all because they aren't very good.

As we got older, my limitations as a player became more obvious. I
was too shy of pitched balls to be much of a hitter, and unlike my hero, I
lacked the arm strength to pitch. But I was good with the glove. In fact,
funny talk and good hands were my only baseball gifts. I had no range,
but if I managed to haul myself anywhere near a pop fly or a grounder,
it was a sure out. I was also a frequent catcher despite being left-hand-

ed, mainly because I owned a genuine catcher's mitt, a mammoth disk of padded leather that my father had used in the 1930s. I had to wear it backward, of course, which made me look like a boy with two left hands, a lefty squared.

A left-hander's true turf, however, lies along the right-field line—at first base or, on bad days, in right field. First base seemed to have my name on it: a first baseman doesn't have to run very often, but he needs good hands for put-out throws and the occasional ground ball. A left-handed first baseman can throw easily and efficiently anywhere in the infield. Most of all, first base is the one position where a mediocre athlete can feel as if he's in the thick of things. It was Nirvana for a kid who liked to make base runners laugh between pitches, the ideal perch for a baseball clown, and a great spot for waging my furtive war against high serious-ness. Plus, a laughing base runner was unlikely to steal second. Right field was definitely a fallback position, tolerable if first base had already been claimed or, as was more often the case, I had hogged it too long. Isolated from talk and action, I played right field as a kind of penance for the joys of playing first. Although right field offered fewer chances to talk like Lefty Gomez, I was consoled by the fact that playing it was itself a kind of joke. The very idea of a right fielder, all dressed up with little to do, was pretty funny. Years later, when I read Eliot in college and heard J. Alfred Prufrock describe himself as a Polonius type of guy, a man fit to "swell a scene or two," I knew exactly what that meant. Prufrock would have made a good right fielder, resigned to his lesser lot.

When I was twelve, my role as a baseball clown received two serious blows. The first happened during a pickup game at Blanchard Field, one of the town's Little League parks. I had been playing first base all afternoon when a car pulled up and out stepped Wayne Carter, the older brother of my friend Gary, and one of his high school buddies. We were all scared of Wayne's crowd because they smoked and drank and fought, and when the high school guys decided to join our game, the field got noticeably quieter. When it came time for my side to take the field, I trotted out to my spot at first base and started throwing the ball around the infield. I didn't notice Wayne standing behind me on the bag until I heard his drawl: "Yer playin' outfield now." I protested that I had dibs on first, but he just said, "Git!"

Everybody stopped to watch the drama that was beginning to unfold at first base. I glanced at Gary, who was at second—this was *his* brother: what should I do?—but Gary just stared at the ground looking miserable. I stayed put, secure in the belief that Wayne wouldn't beat up a kid half his size in front of so many onlookers. It seemed that Wayne Carter was going to be my Jimmie Foxx. Gomez once claimed that when he polished his glasses and saw Foxx approaching the plate, "The sight of him terrified me so much that I haven't been able to wear glasses since." I tried to come up with a Lefty Gomez type of quip but couldn't think fast enough, and the only response I could manage was deadly—and stupidly—earnest: "I'm not moving!"

The next thing I knew, Blanchard Field tipped on its side, and the crisp line between green grass and blue sky went vertical. Without another word, Wayne had picked me up like a sack of potatoes and was carrying me, kicking and screaming, on a slow, bouncing journey into deep right field. I completely lost my lefty cool. The instant he dumped me in the grass and started walking away, I sprung up and kicked him so hard in his high, blue-jeaned backside that I lost my footing and fell backward. Immediately the field erupted in excited shouts of "Fight! Fight!"—but there was no fight. Wayne turned around, bent down close, and made a fist inches from my face. I decided to shut up and play right field.

The second time my lefty facade cracked was at Little League tryouts. Having witnessed the grim intensity of Little League games, I didn't try out until my final year of eligibility. About fifty nervous kids gathered one Saturday at Blanchard Field, scene of the transportable first baseman, for some serious business and an afternoon devoid of chatter. When it was over, I had made the first cut and was assigned to the Kodak Processing Plant Pirates, who practiced near the clay pits south of town. I arrived for the Pirates tryout the following Saturday, and we newcomers were told to play catch behind the backstop. When I finally got a chance to bat, about an hour later, my confidence rose at the familiar call—"Heads up! Lefty!"—and the sudden shift of fielders. I stared at the right fielder as if to warn him not to impale himself on the fence as he backpedaled in pursuit of my pending blast. In our neighborhood games, this kind of bravado went a long way.

The pitcher was a tall, skinny kid who looked as if he were already shaving—the kind of kid you'd see smoking at recess or leering at the girls in the higher grades. Definitely a towel snapper, he was already a man, with a mean hillbilly face glowering from beneath his cap. After chatting with forced casualness with the catcher, a kid I knew from school, I settled into the box and waited. The next thing I remember is the collective "ooooh" that came from the onlookers. As for that first pitch coming straight for my head, I have only a vague memory of spinning away from the plate and almost falling down, flushed and dizzy. When the umpire called a strike and I gave him a puzzled look, he said that the ball had broken in over the plate. That bullet wasn't even the kid's fastball—it was his curve!

I had never seen a real curve ball before, but that was the least of my worries. What if this kid had a particular dislike for pudgy boys who talked a lot? Worse, what if he *envied* them? I could imagine his father saying, "I don't love yew, son, because yore too skinny and yew don't talk funny." As I choked up on the bat and stepped back into the box, this time a little farther from the plate, the pitcher was grinning as if he had just told a dirty joke. Hoping to compensate for his speed, I was already into my swing when he wound up, but this time the ball floated in like a balloon. I checked my swing and staggered so far onto the plate that the ball nearly hit me. By this time the coach was yelling, "It's a goddamn tryout, Billy! Just give him something to hit!"

Several weak swings and misses followed, and when the coach finally blew his whistle for a change in batters, I wanted to disappear. It was a Lefty Gomez kind of thought. "A lot of things run through your head when you're going in to relieve in a troubled spot," Gomez once confessed; one of those thoughts was "Should I spike myself?" As I walked away staring at my bat as if it had betrayed me, I understood the Gomez impulse to wish a Jimmie Foxx away—but the notion didn't cheer me up. Good chatter could take a guy only so far if he couldn't deliver the goods. Lefty Gomez was funny, but he could also really play. During the bike ride home I could find nothing funny about those pitches.

When I was in graduate school fifteen years later, we fielded an English Department softball team made up of pale grad students of both sexes and two or three something-to-prove male assistant professors. We needed a good-hands, no-run guy at first base, and it felt like a homecoming to occupy the position—*my* position—in a fear-free adult environment. After all, nobody was about to pick up a 220-pound first baseman and carry him into right field. We lost most of our games, but that was no shame in a league that included a Phys Ed team and a History Department team that boasted an immense blond guy who had recently tried out for the Chicago Bears. That his best game was football didn't matter whenever he came barreling into first while I was catching put-out throws. In one of his at bats, when an errant throw from the shortstop pulled me into the base path, the almost-Bear slammed into me so hard that my glasses popped several feet into the air. Frozen in an effort not to throw up or pass out, I managed to hold onto the ball. The guy was as quick as he was strong, and somehow he kept me from slumping into the dirt. Propping me up until my head cleared, he asked, "You okay, man?" When I finally nodded, he whispered, "Don't get in my way again, or you'll get hurt."

A fat kid's vulnerability, long dormant, came back in a muddled flash. I broke free, retrieved my glasses, and mustered all the eloquence of an advanced student of literature: "Fuck you, asshole!" It stung me to encounter, on this day of fun, the old lesson of Wayne Carter and that Kodak Pirate pitcher. Baseball can indeed accommodate people of every size and shape, but sooner or later you'll face a terrifying truth: some guys are bigger and stronger than you, and there will be plays when such differences matter a great deal. I always knew this, of course. From the start, hadn't my southpaw breeziness been a response to this dark truth about what's sure to happen whenever tough guys and not-so-tough guys play together?

While my team was at bat, I grew ashamed of having lost my baseball identity. Lefty Gomez would surely have come up with a better retort than mine, and as I replayed the quavering, hurt-kid sound of my curse I knew that I had lapsed into the high seriousness of the gifted but stupid ballplayer. That footballer had a perfect right to mow down whatever strayed onto the base path. Didn't he keep me from falling, and didn't he warn me under his breath? It was a clean hit and he hadn't shown me up. Besides, he was only stating the obvious. If I got in his way again, I damn well *would* get hurt. When I approached him during the change of innings as he trotted in from the outfield, he gave me the wary look of a lion that was about to be forced to kill something. "Hey," I said, extending my hand, "I'm sorry I lost my cool." We shook hands and agreed that it was only a game. By now I was my old self, and maybe my oldest self: "Next time you get a hit," I said, "I'll toss my glasses and lie down. It'll save us both some trouble."

If you hammer a graduate student of literature, the odds are good that he will intellectualize the experience. I may even have brooded about Bergson's definition of humor as the unexpected juxtaposition of rigidity (an almost–Chicago Bear running full bore) with fluidity (the awkward dance of an overweight first baseman). Another, simpler lesson was more immediate: if you're going to collide with someone, make sure it's somebody who *knows* he's strong and therefore has nothing to prove. A Ty Cobb type of guy will do what he must in order to reach that base, but there's no real malice in the hurt he'll lay on you. You may lose your glasses and see comic-book stars, and you might even discover a massive bruise on your rib cage when you go to bed that night—but that's just baseball's version of the old saw that beneath all comedy there is pain. Whether you laugh or cry will sometimes feel like an arbitrary choice.

Lefty Gomez made his choice and stuck with it. Professional ballplayers often describe the end of their playing days as a kind of death. Many become bitter or nostalgic, and some resort to desperate exercise regimens and miracle operations. Gomez, as always, took a different way. When asked how long he intended to stay in the game, he said he'd keep pitching for as long as his top reliever's arm held out. What was causing his waning effectiveness? "I'm throwing as hard as I ever did. The ball's just not getting there as fast." It was only a game, even when it was over. "My manager spent ten years trying to teach me a change of pace," Gomez said after he retired. "At the end of my career that's all I had."

When he was filling out an employment questionnaire, he answered the question "Why did you leave your last job?" by writing "I couldn't get anybody out."

   The professional "death" of a ballplayer is, of course, only a metaphor. How does a Lefty Gomez type of man confront the real thing? A baseball clown—perhaps *especially* a baseball clown—knows that every game ends with the Great Pickoff. The terror of such knowledge ultimately informs all comedy, and why should baseball comedy be any different? When Lou Gehrig got too sick to play and finally benched himself, it was Gomez who tapped this deeper vein in the human condition. "Hell, Lou, it took fifteen years to get you out of the game," he told Gehrig. "Sometimes I'm out in fifteen minutes." Two months later, when the frail Gehrig made his last appearance in Yankee Stadium and told the crowd that he considered himself "the luckiest man on the face of the earth," I would bet that he drew considerable courage from his old teammate, the one who would rather be lucky than good. When Gomez survived triple bypass heart surgery nearly forty years after Gehrig's death, he had not forgotten how to embrace the mysteries of luck: he dubbed the operation the "first triple I ever had." He was lucky afterward, too. When a seventy-one-year-old undergoes open-heart surgery, ten more years of life is not a bad outcome. Even at the very end, the southpaw perspective was still there. When his doctor asked him to imagine himself pitching and to rate his pain on a scale of one to ten, Gomez requested an indispensable piece of information: "Who's hitting, doc?"

Lefty Gomez died at the age of eighty-one and was buried in Mount Tamalpais Cemetery in San Rafael. June O'Dea died three years later and was buried beside him. I've seen a picture of their stone, which features a photograph of the two of them, probably from the early 1940s. June, smiling from beneath a wide-brimmed hat trimmed with flowers, looks radiant. Lefty is facing her, grinning broadly from beneath a Yankees cap. It's obvious that they're crazy in love.

   When Lefty Gomez died, I was at the nadir of my job situation and had forgotten all about him. I didn't remember that he had experienced job troubles, too, like the time when he had a bad season and the Yankees wanted to decrease his salary from $20,000 to $7,500—a 63 percent pay cut. A career crisis like that would depress most people beyond all humor, but not Gomez. "You keep the salary," he told Yankees owner Jake Ruppert, "I'll take the cut." We don't always recognize the voices that we're hearing, and the unacknowledged ghost of Lefty Gomez may have been giving me a gentle nudge, like one of his chats with the young DiMaggio, to stop whining about my lot and do something about it. That ghost was surely guiding me a year later, when I talked my way into a visiting position at a small college and got a new lease on my professional life. When friends and colleagues asked how I could leave a tenured position at a large university, I cited the usual reasons: salary, working conditions, institutional mismatch. I didn't yet realize what they all boiled down to: I couldn't get anyone out anymore. When my new job became permanent two years later, I was convinced that it really *is* better to be lucky than good.

At the time I did not remember the source of that wisdom, but my connection with first things has gotten a lot stronger in the years since. How could it not, now that I've reached the age that Lefty Gomez was when I discovered him? When you turn fifty and start looking less like Babe Ruth than that balding right fielder J. Alfred Prufrock, you'll want to find a way out of right field. You'll want to stay in the game. You may even find yourself wanting to repay old debts. When I recently looked up Lefty Gomez on the Web, I found the predictable relics of a ballplayer's career. Two balls, one autographed by Gomez and the other by Giants pitcher Carl Hubbell, were on sale as a single lot for nearly $500. Other signed Gomez balls could be had for $120, $175, $275, and $299. An autographed 8x10 was for sale for $65, and a 1941 Gomez Playball card in "VG" condition was priced at $125. A check endorsed by Gomez cost $175, and the signature page from one of his Yankee contracts sold for $185. A memorabilia collection featured one of his famous "GOOF" tags, a 1956 Connecticut plate. When homage is due, it can be hard—even for a left-hander—to know whether to laugh or to cry. Sometimes both feel right.

Every year the American Baseball Coaches Association gives a Lefty Gomez Award for contributions to amateur baseball, but the poignancy of awards and vanity plates and autographed baseballs obscures a deeper truth: the human comedy will continue for as long as someone has the perspective to *see* it as a comedy. Baseball has a rich tradition of cognitive lefties, laughing philosophers like Rube Waddell, Casey Stengel, Bill Lee, Tug McGraw, and John Lowenstein, the Indians/Orioles out-fielder who threw right but batted and thought left. Some of these cognitive lefties have even been righties—Dizzy Dean, Jimmy Piersall, Rocky Bridges, Jim Bouton, Mark Fydrich—and often they are catchers: Yogi Berra, Joe Garagiola, Bob Uecker. I hope that somewhere there's an unath-letic kid who has discovered "Mr. Baseball" just as I discovered Lefty Gomez. Bob Uecker is surely an honorary lefty, a man devoted to keep-ing the southpaw sensibility alive. Uecker once summed up his career in a Lefty Gomez sort of way—a way that could also describe my baseball life. "Anybody with ability can play in the big leagues," he claimed. "But to be able to trick people year in and year out, the way I did—I think that was a much greater feat." Uecker is right-handed, but he embodies the first principle of a left-handed sensibility: there's more than one way to stay in the game.

A left-handed sensibility once kept *me* in the game, and it still pushes me to resist unhappy endings. Lefty Gomez made my baseball life feel essentially comic even though it should have been one sad story. His spirit was certainly in attendance at our final game in that grad school league. When the opposing team failed to show up, we chose sides and played an all–English Department game. Given the diminished intensity and diluted talent, all concern with winning or losing dissolved into base-ball—or at least softball—as I always dreamed it could be. I played first base, naturally, but I also caught when we were batting, blocking the plate and tagging our guys as impartially and gleefully as I tagged theirs. An absurd parade of hitters kept coming to the plate: a young man writing a dissertation on Jack London who held the bat cross-handed, a weight-lifting Jungian who kept overswinging and topping the ball, a Virginia Woolf scholar who couldn't manage a level swing but always got on base because she proved to be a superb bunter, a bearded faculty member try-ing gamely to act as young as we were, a pot-smoking Wordsworthian who hit the ball a mile but trucked the bases so casually that he never got more than a single.

It was a left-handed kind of game, a perfect game for the full flowering of a baseball clown. Among this field of literary types the chatter was deep and funny—and not just mine. There was physical comedy, too: errant throws, outfielders tripping over their own feet, runners frozen in confusion between bases. At one point I ripped my pants sliding into second, with indecent results. Someone produced safety pins, and after some strategic repairs I played the rest of the game with a big, flapping pant leg. A few innings later I pulled a muscle in my thigh and was reduced to a lame-horse lope. Although the pain was considerable, I now had full license to run as slowly as I wanted to.

On such a day, even a baseball clown can deliver the goods. One pitch came in chest high and fast enough to work against, and I timed my swing perfectly. Ballplayers are telling the truth about the ball that is perfectly tagged, the transfer of energy so efficient that your hands don't feel a thing. I wish I *had* felt that hit, but all I remember is watching the ball sail over the chicken-wire fence in right-center and hearing unlikely cheers for a chunky twenty-eight-year-old in flapping pants, loping around the bases like *Gunsmoke*'s Chester in a Michelin Man suit. For the rest of the game and far into the beers that night, a faculty member on the other team kept calling me "Home Run Hammond," the irony of which I chose to ignore. Yes, I had been lucky—but doesn't luck govern most things?

The spirit of Lefty Gomez was surely there, though not yet his ghost. At the time he was recovering from his heart surgery and had ten more years to live, though I had no idea how old he was or what he was going through. We leave a lot of important things behind as we slip into our adult lives, including former passions and longstanding debts, but when you reach a certain age, these forgotten stories and abandoned obsessions start floating to the surface. By then, of course, you've lived long enough to know that it's the things you *don't* do—those nagging sins of omission— that bring the deepest regret. I'm sorry that I never sent Lefty Gomez a fan letter, especially after that operation. I know that it would have been lost among the hundreds he must have received, and it's absurd to think that an old Hall of Famer could possibly miss a letter that was never written from someone he never knew. A Lefty Gomez type of man, however, will feel compelled to seek a bright edge even here. He may even decide that a belated fan letter is better than no letter at all.

19. In April, Anything Could Happen
Mick Cochrane

On April 7, 1970, I conned my mother into letting me stay home from school in order to watch my beloved Minnesota Twins play the first game of the new season against the Chicago White Sox. The Twins won, and a journeyman outfielder named Brant Alyea, newly acquired from the Washington Senators, collected four hits, including two home runs, for a total of seven runs batted in.

My imagination was fired by Brant Alyea. It was not just his name, exotic though it was, or his powerful right-handed batting stance, or even his stylish sideburns, but the sense of possibility he embodied, the potential for heroic accomplishment. At this rate, I calculated, he would finish the season with over three hundred home runs, a thousand RBIs, a slugging percentage to rival the gross national product of Bolivia. I had discovered opening day.

As a Twins fan in the early 1970s, I'd scan the opening day rosters optimistically, always expecting great things from Calvin Griffith's latest collections of imposters: Rick Renick, who had the potential to be the next Harmon Killebrew, who hit a home run in his first big league at bat and managed only nineteen more the rest of his career; Eric Soderholm, an intense third baseman with tinted glasses who underwent hypnosis, hit the ball well for a few months, then suffered a bizarre injury (he fell down a manhole—really, he did, who could make something like that up?) and never wore a Twins uniform again; Bob Gorinski, who had the potential to be the next Rick Renick; Tom Tischinski, a reserve catcher, damned with faint praise even by the local broadcasters, who assured us that Tom excelled at blocking the plate; Paul Ray Powell, who *sounded* fast and looked like a batting champion but never hit his weight; Mark Funderburk, the next Bob Gorinski.

And then there were the pitchers—ah, the pitchers!—a litany of losers, an epic roll call of hapless heroes whose very names evoke years of futility, scores of wild pitches and gopher balls and blown leads: Albury, Singer, Decker, Bane, Luebber, Pazik, Hands, Fife, Serum, mighty Thormodsgard.

I believed in them all, the washed-out veterans, the castoff utility men, those with warning track power, with no wheels, who couldn't hit the breaking ball, who could throw but not field, run but not get on base. I saw in them the glimmer of their greatness, the promise of their best selves. I felt in them the confidence they'd left behind in high school and the Sally League, in Cedar Rapids and Elizabethton.

They disappointed, of course—don't we all?—but in April, anything could happen. Win the opener and you're in first place; get just one hit, and you're batting a thousand. In June and July, though, it was a different story. The law of averages exerted its iron will, and the Twins swooned. The hitters endured their strikeouts and feeble ground outs with grim patience. The pitchers fooled nobody, looked genuinely relieved when they handed the ball over, and didn't even bother to kick the rubber. My favorites were sent to Toledo, dispatched on waivers, released outright. By midsummer 1970, Brant Alyea was playing once again like the ham-and-egger that everyone but me seemed to know all along that he was.

Now, thirty years later, a tenured professor, careful of facts, respectful of documentation, I study Brant Alyea's modest lifetime record in a thick baseball reference book. I discover that his finest year came not in Minnesota but in Buffalo, New York, my new home, where my AAA Bisons play ball in a lovely outdoor park—on real grass—where Buster Bison throws Frisbees into the stands between innings and autographs my kids' gloves.

I am in my forties now, ancient for a ballplayer but just midcareer in academe. I am a steady if unspectacular teacher, a .285 husband and father, a writer who nibbles at the corners. And because I want to believe that my best years are still ahead of me, my career year just around the corner, I still need opening day. Older, but no wiser, I choose to put a twelve-year-old's lunatic faith in possibility, yearning still for the chance to put last year's errors and humiliations behind me, to begin again and be made new, to fulfill my potential at last.

20. What We Remember When We Remember What We Loved

Earl S. Braggs

To imagine an audience for whom these sentiments are tailored is an honest task which I did not consider. Instead, I considered only what Richard Hugo said: "Certain places seem to exist because someone has written about them."

It occurs to me now that before I left Hampstead, North Carolina, at age sixteen, I did not know that some things continue to go missing long after they are discovered and I didn't realize that physics explains every ounce of racial tension in America. But this is not about the explained or the unexplained, not about the cause or the effect; this is about love.

My grandmama Ruth loved three things alone: turnip greens any day of the week, a dip of navy snuff first thing in the morning, and a good radio station late at night. The way she smiled, I knew Grandmama's greatest love was radio love. A transistor on the bedside, too many nights to count, I fell asleep before the ninth-inning Yankee Stadium lights went out. Oh, how I cried every time Roger Maris died at the plate with the go-ahead run swinging, still in the batter's box. The next morning sun would patiently remind me, but I refused to believe Bobby Richardson never crossed the plate.

As a kid I loved baseball as much as I loved Elizabeth Taylor on the cover of *Look* magazine, circa 1964. Even then I paid attention to the way she moved. Richard and Elizabeth, both royal in name. She was way prettier than any photographer could take. He was suave, debonair, and brutally handsome. Antony and Cleopatra, they were perfectly in love. In the years I am talking about, America was number one in the world. Ford and Chevrolet were the duke and duchess of Auto-mo-bile and Chrysler was the sacred king of everything else. Motown was in Detroit then. Berry

Gordy was pressing more 45s than Cincinnati, Nashville, or L.A.—America was beautiful on at least two fronts: the steps and the porch.

In the years I am talking about, I lived on the steps and the porch of an all-white town. My brothers and I never figured we figured much into the population count. We were white for all practical purposes and, therefore, Negro for all other purposes. All the churches were white and all the cemeteries and all the manicured lawns were mowed by a dark-skinned man named Simon. Simon was crazy, no question about that. Niomi, his wife, was half Iroquois and half wind and half thunderstorm. The only thing Simon knew how to count was money and he counted a lot of one-dollar bills during those summer months in Hampstead, North Carolina.

Those were the days when I loved Sunday morning funny papers and comic book clowns. I loved Richie Rich and Sad Sack. The Phantom was a better man than the Lone Ranger and I would be Zorro, any day. I loved Tonto and I loved his horse. Mr. Freddie had a horse that he would some-times let me ride, but I didn't like that horse and that horse didn't like me. Though there is nothing wrong with being tall in the saddle, I knew I could never be John Wayne. From Whitetown to Negrotown we walked to church every Sunday morning. Some Sundays we'd stay late and wait for Frank Brown to give us one of his famous bad haircuts. Somebody named this Negrotown, Browntown, located exactly one thousand miles away on a hot day. Grandmama would grease us up with lard lotion that made us shine and we walked until we passed out beneath a pear tree or a wild grape arbor full of wild grapes.

"Watch out for snakes," she used to say.

"Snakes don't eat no grapes," I can still hear myself say. Grandmama would always smile her famous smile, knowing things would always be all right. My best friend was Bobby Joe Midget. I loved Bobby Joe and Bobby Joe, he loved me. He was the only white boy in Whitetown brave enough to call a Negro his best friend. Bobby Joe and I were everything we said we would be, running through the wild winter woods, playing soldier, sprinting across yards, diving like kites, playing tackle football without pads. No one ever mentioned a helmet. Then, suddenly, came baseball and long summer days. We were the baseball boys of 1964. Bobby

Joe pitched change-ups and curves. I was center field. I have never wanted to be anything so much as I wanted to be a New York Yankee. Call
me a dreamer. Many others have shared this dream. Perhaps I loved the
Yankees because my mother left for New York City one hot, humid Saturday
night only to return ten years later on a cold winter morning. She had to
get away from it all. New York City was a pretty city in my mind. Every
letter stamped by the New York City Postal Service was a pretty letter.
At Christmas time the packages were pretty and we were pretty on any
given Easter Sunday morning. Five Negro boys in New York City cheap
suits and Grandmama with a hat walking along Highway 17. We must've
been a photograph for Van Dee Zee's camera, circa 1928, Negroes Walk to
Church in Nebraska on Sunday Morning. Sometimes Daddy would visit and he would walk to church with us. I loved my Daddy—he was my
hero. I loved baseball cards and I had two shoe boxes stacked plum full,
Willie Davis, Willie Stargell, Willie McCovey, and Willie Davenport. The
envy of any neighborhood kid is what I should never mention, but I was
and I am. Kids everywhere stood in ball fields everywhere looking in the
direction of me. Card traders and ballplayers, waiting for summer with
thirty-two-ounce Louisvilles slung across their shoulders, waiting for
that one curve ball that would carry outta Candlestick, outta Comiskey
Park, outta Wrigley Field, outta Chicago on a windy day. Billy Williams
and Ernie Banks were always hitting long fly balls, deep. And I caught
every one of them in stride.

Bobby Joe and me, we knew the name of every player, every position played, every ERA, every lifetime batting average, and every pitcher's
strikeout rate. We were the baseball boys of 1964. I wanted to be a New
York Yankee. Bobby Joe wanted to be a Pittsburgh Pirate. We longed for
long summer afternoons in grass-covered fields. We knew the names of
every player: Bill Mazeroski, Tony Conigliaro, Rocky Colavito, Roberto
Clemente, Paul Casanova (the lover), and we loved. We loved the sound
of the names: Henry Louis Aaron, Edward Charles "Whitey" Ford, Willie
Mays and Maury Wills, and Stanley Frank Musial.

"That ball is outta here," but I already knew before the announcer said
so. From the earliest age I could tell a foul ball from a home run by the
way a bat cracks on the radio. Call it radio late night love, call it what you
want. I loved the things I could not see.

We lived across Factory Road, a lane-and-a-half highway, from Bobby Joe. Our house was down a narrow dirt road with ruts for infrequent automobiles. Seventy-five yards separated, I measured it every day of my youth. Bobby Joe lived up on the road in a "Dollar Down" house with dirty white curtains. He had a room full of sisters and two brothers, both younger. Hampstead was a fishing community with two fish houses. Every Tuesday night and Saturday morning, fish trucks would pull out leaking fish juice until they reached the edge of town. The smell was wonderful if you like the way fish juice smells in July or frozen December fish juice in a can. Hampstead had a Baptist Church, a Methodist Church, and a Presbyterian Church. Each church had a baseball team, but I never asked to play. Perhaps I knew way back then that if water could be segregated, someone would figure out a way to do it.

Lee Anthony, Earl Sherman, Tyrone Romell, and the Twins as we called them, Alphonso and Alonza—five Negro boys growing up in a white town full of white girls never scared me until much later. Maybe it was because I was too busy figuring batting averages and tallying win-loss columns or maybe it was because I loved Hermia Smith and Cathy Smith equally.

"Snakes don't eat no grapes" and "color ain't nothing but an adjective" is what I must've figured outside the baseball columns. *A Hero Ain't Nothing But a Sandwich* is the only book I ever stole from Mr. Kyle Howard's grocery store, but honey buns, now that's a different story altogether and in and of itself. Harmon Killebrew used to kill baseballs up in Minnesota and we would sit in front of Bobby Joe's afternoon television set and laugh till we were dizzy as Dizzy Dean and Dizzy Trout still dizzy in their retirement years. Saturday afternoons was a dizzy place to be in Bobby Joe's house during the summer of 1964. Margie Mae going out, Linda Ann coming in, Brenda Sue cooking, Janice Marie upstairs putting on makeup, all the boys lined up on the couch. Mudcat Grant was throwing pitches so fast, it made us even more dizzy and Catfish Hunter was throwing pure white lightning. Bubba "Jack" Morton and Bubba "Boy" Phillips were waiting in on-deck circles everywhere in America. Roger Maris hit sixty-one home runs in 1961, that first year of Kennedy. Two years later, I know exactly where we were. We were in the backyard listening to the afternoon on the radio. It was a sunny day in November on the southern coast of North Carolina, 1963. That was the year I fell in love with Roger Maris. I loved his eyes. He had home run eyes. I can see him up there now, shifting in that batter's box, adjusting and readjusting his feet, waiting for that one fastball that would sail outta any stadium. But a lot of pitchers caught Roger swinging and I felt the pain. I ached every time he struck out. And yes, I cried when John Kennedy died.

Eight Men Out was an American tragedy. One I did not enjoy hearing about in Mr. McGee's history class. "Say it ain't so, Shoeless Joe. Say it ain't so." Mr. McGee taught the seventh grade and drove the pencil yellow bus that picked us up every school year morning, taking five Negro boys to the Negro school that seemed a thousand miles in the other direction on a hot day. Miss Ann Snyder, I recall so fondly, a young blonde from Boone, North Carolina, came to be the first white teacher at my Negro school. I was in eighth grade. Miss Ann Snyder loved me because I paid attention to the signs of change. I loved Miss Ann Snyder because she was brave, because she was a woman. At the end of my last Negro school year, she honored me with a Certificate for Highest Academics. She was only to last that one year. I honor her for that one year of love.

Two years later and two years deep into the attendance policy of my white hometown neighborhood school, I loved Mrs. Hart, a plumb Irish woman. She pushed me out into the open. My complexion never caught her horn-rimmed sight; instead, she saw whatever she saw and told me, thus I became an Irish writer for one year. At sixteen, as I said, I left my Grandmama, my brothers, and my best friend. Bobby Joe was the only one that cried. We'd moved so completely away from our baseball years. I left Hampstead walking, and I walked until I got a ride. I hitchhiked until I came upon a city. My city life was living in the projects with Aunt Frances. My city life was breaking into somebody's Sporting Goods Store and stealing enough balls and gloves for a whole team. My city life was selling sporting equipment that first summer on concrete streets. My city life was none too quick to tell me what I already knew, "Grandmama didn't raise me that way."

In eleventh grade, Mrs. Davis, a white grandmother who looked exactly like an eleventh grade English teacher, became my grandmother every day at fifth period. Some people said she was mean, but I loved Mrs. Davis because she taught me to love the language, to love Whitman. In spite of the things I loved, my city school life was a race war. I remember the day the Japanese bombed Pearl Harbor, the day Floyd McCoy's brother knocked out a white boy, then he started combing his hair like he was Muhammad Ali, talking about how pretty he was, but Floyd McCoy's brother wasn't pretty at all. Nineteen seventy-one was an ugly time to be a high school student in Wilmington, North Carolina. The Wilmington Police Department patrolled the hallways with ugly narrow black baseball bats, the Army National Guard patrolled the alleyways and planted ugly rats, and NBC, ABC, and CBS controlled what everyone thought. The Southern Christian Leadership Conference rented an ugly painted bus from an ugly Greyhound station and took all the ugly black kids who wanted to go to an ugly yelling and screaming showdown at the 6th Street Baptist Church where we learned the meaning of the word "revolution." Every day was downtown standing on the steps of city hall, listening to Brother Benjamin and the Wilmington 10. Microphones and loudspeakers blaring, sirens screaming, fire trucks racing; every night the city burned. Every other day was a chair flying across the cafeteria, a tray sliding upside another ugly white boy's head, another ugly classroom window broken. Mrs. Davis never moved, never strayed from the fifth period English lesson plan. I honor her for that.

In 1972 I received a letter from Richard Milhous Nixon requesting my presence at the local draft board. I went. I did not ask questions. A cotton field in Alabama was no more southern than I. I wanted to be a soldier. I wanted to be a soldier because I loved my country, but my country did not love me. Later I realized that my country does love me, but it's a "sad" love, a sad, incomplete love.

On foreign soil in a foreign city I turned twenty-one, Clark Air Force Base, Angeles City, the Republic of the Philippines. My first birthday party was a surprise, so I was surprised when I arrived at Sergeant Winston R. Forgey's home and all my friends were there. We all met his wife and cut the cake. I was happy. It was my birthday, I was a man, I was twenty-one with a gun.

Those were the years when the girls said I looked good in air force blue, the years when I loved the sound of music more than I loved the games they played on Mr. McGee's transistor radio out behind the Negro school in the October of my early years.

"Good in air force blue" is how I tried to look. I was in love with the smell of shrimp fried rice and dirt downtown streets. American music on every Philco, and I played them all for two years in the Republic of the Philippines, Angeles City, the city of angels and crime. I played the Beatles, the Who, James Brown, and Marvin Gaye, but mostly I played the Rolling Stones in those years when I could not write. Piano days as some call them, days when one has to learn to play in the dark with his eyes closed. I lived for a while in a haze of strong scented smoke. Piano days, the time when I loved things I never intended to love. I married my high school sweetheart. I loved a girl named Dorothy and a girl named Dorothy loved me. One daughter, Kamilah, an even image of our love, was conceived in the Philippines and born in Wichita, Kansas. Love carried us through a lot of years. In the end the sides were happy, but the middle simply became confused and fell.

Seams without a middle hold no purpose in this life. I moved on, on into evenings of remembering. By adhering to the things which seem to me decisive, I accentuated the hidden and the manifest, all in an effort to conclude that the things we cherish are born of an intimate light. It is a love of baseball cards and the sheer pleasure of tracking down a deep fly ball that speak to each of us, sacred as church. This I believe. Lately, I've been wondering, wondering what happened to all the baseball cards I scattered across my childhood, wondering what happened to the fish houses of Hampstead, North Carolina, what happened to the spot where I played shallow center field, and whatever happened to all the boys of summer Bobby Joe struck out that last summer we played for the same team, 1964. Nineteen sixty-four, the year Bobby Joe won the Cy Young Award and I hit more home runs than Mickey "Big Stick" Mantle and Maury Wills, the Saturday Afternoon Blur, stole more bases than anyone. Whatever happened to 1964? A few years back, again, I started to collect baseball cards under the pretense of saving them for my younger daughter, Anya, but she just says, "Oh, Dad." Even now, some days, I am nine years old at a flea market, flipping through names, flipping through my life. I see the women who made me, my Grandmama, Miss Ann Snyder, Mrs. Hart, and Mrs. Davis, and I hear, lightly, my voice opening a pack of baseball cards. For a moment I chew the stale, hard gum, then toss it away as I call out the names I love: Rico Petrocelli, Jose Santiago, Louis Aparicio, Bill Mazeroski, Dizzy Dean and Dizzy Trout, Roberto Clemente, and Tony Conigliaro.

21. Willie Rooks's Shirt

Lee Gutkind

Upon arrival in Chicago, umpire Doug Harvey was notified that he and his crew of Harry Wendelstedt, Nick Colosi, and Art Williams would be required to measure the dimensions of the field and bullpen pitching mounds at Wrigley Field—a task umpires must perform in each ballpark twice a year.

Umpires confirm that the pitching mound is comprised of a circle eighteen feet in diameter, the center of which measures fifty-nine feet from the back of home plate; that the front edge of the rubber is eighteen inches behind the center of the mound, thus establishing a distance of sixty feet, six inches, from the front edge of the rubber (pitchers plant their spikes and push off against the rubber) where the pitcher begins his motion, to the point where the catcher receives the ball at the back of home plate. But the most difficult and time-consuming part of the process is the confirmation of the pitcher's slope: this includes the height above home plate at which the pitcher is permitted to throw, as well as the length and uniformity of the slope of the mound.

To check this, umpires hammer one stake into the ground at a point six inches in front of the rubber and a second stake six feet in front of the rubber both in line with home plate. They tie strings to the bottom and top of the stakes and stretch both strings from one stake to another across the mound. Finally they step back and survey the mound to see if it is uniformly sloped from one inch to ten inches within a five-foot-by-six-inch distance. They measure this many different times and in many different ways before granting approval.

Doug Harvey explains, "Actually, we're pretty sure no one is going to tamper with the field mound; it's going to equally affect both the home and visiting pitchers. We don't even have to be too concerned with the mound in the home team bullpen, but you better believe we're especially careful when we examine the mound in the visiting team's bullpen. The home team has been known to raise or lower or otherwise tamper with the height or uniformity of the slope just to ruin the rhythm of the pitchers warming up. The funny thing is, when we do find something wrong, you can't believe how the goddamn coaches and players argue. They actually believe that we should ignore it, not make waves. They expect us to compromise our principles—even jeopardize our jobs on their behalf!"

Aside from officiating each game and measuring pitching mounds, umpires are obliged to follow up each ejection of a player, coach, or manager with a personal phone call to league president Chub Feeney within twelve hours after the game and, subsequently, with a written report of the ejection outlining the reasons for such drastic action. Such a system eliminates the possibility of an umpire's being vindictive to a player or a team, while league officials are informed immediately in case a game is protested in response to the ejection.

Players, managers, and coaches are ejected for many good reasons—for unnecessarily delaying a game by doggedly and uselessly disputing a call or for yelling at an umpire mercilessly and ruining his game concentration. Colosi had ejected a groundskeeper earlier that year for incessantly rapping with a hammer on a Plexiglas screen. "I warned him ten times," explained Colosi. "You have to try to warn the players, tell them they're gone if they don't stop doing what they're doing. Most of the time, they listen. Sometimes they don't, and then you've got to give them the thumb. You can't let people step on you in this game or you won't be up in the big time for long."

"More often than not," says veteran Tom Gorman, "you're throwing people out because they're using vulgar language. Any man who calls me something I wouldn't call him is going to be in trouble. This is not to say that we all don't swear once in a while, but sometimes there's reason, and sometimes they do it just to be nasty. For example, if anybody comes down on my mother, they get the thumb. Right away. Instantly. I can't stand looking at them; they're no damn good. Get out of here. On the other hand, some guys can't seem to put together a sentence without swearing. You take Gene Mauch, manager of the Montreal Expos.

Every other word he says is fuck. 'Fuck this, fuck that.' He probably says fuck when he goes to church and makes his confession. If I threw him out for every time he swore in a week, he'd spend the rest of his life in the locker room."

What happens if you throw a man out and he won't leave? Or if, after throwing him out one day, he cusses you out the next? What happens if, no matter how often you try, you can't seem to discipline the player, manager, or coach successfully?

"Well," says Gorman, "the league is supposed to take it from there. They have the option of suspending a man or fining him after they talk to you and read your report. The problem is, the league is hesitant about taking positive action. The president doesn't want to get the owners mad at him. After all, the owners pay his salary and if he suspends a player or a manager, he's not going to have so many friends come reappointment time." Gorman, a thick-necked man with a scarlet Irish face and heavy, sagging jowls, hesitated for a moment, then smiled.

"One time, right before Chub Feeney took over for Warren Giles as president of the National League, I was having trouble with Johnny Logan, shortstop for what used to be the Milwaukee Braves. I threw him out one day for swearing at me. Next day, he swore at me again and I threw him out again. That night I called up Warren Giles and told him I needed some help with Logan, couldn't control the son of a bitch."

"'I'll see what I can do,' Giles said. I got the distinct impression he didn't care one hoot about my problem.

"Next day I saw Logan on the street and I told him he better watch his mouth or he was gonna end up fined or suspended. 'I ain't gonna let you play another ball game,' I warned.

"'Yeah, sure,' Logan says. "Don't bother me.'

"Next night, Logan cussed me out, called me every name in the book and I ejected him. Later, I called up Giles and Giles was as disinterested as ever.

"'Ok, ok,' he says, 'so Logan swore at you a little. Doesn't mean I need to take drastic action. Give the guy a break. So what if he called you a few bad names?'

"'Called me bad names?' I said to Giles. 'It's you he says is *horseshit*.'

"'What did he call me?' Giles all of a sudden went crazy. I thought he was going to have a heart attack.

"'He called you *horseshit*,' I said.

The next day, Logan was fined $250.

"In 1963, when the league changed the rule on the balk, and the sportswriters were taking potshots at us for calling the balk on pitchers so often, I tried to get Giles to back us up, to defend us, to tell the writers and the fans that we were just doing our job. You think he would? Hell, no! He made the balk rule, but he wanted us to enforce it without him getting involved. He wasn't interested in backing us up by saying one word.

"One day I got really fed up. I called my crew into the umpires' room and told them I was going home, quitting. I'll tell ya, that was the longest plane ride I ever took, but I had my satisfaction. Giles called me at home every day for two weeks, but I refused to talk to him on the phone; I was so pissed off. He wouldn't give us any support on a rule he made up himself. He didn't have the guts to point out to the writers and fans that the umpires don't make the rules, they only enforce them.

"Warren Giles," says Gorman again, shaking his head and staring at the ground. "Warren Giles was the nearest thing to nothing I've ever seen."

Abandoning the umpire's shirt and cap he usually wore during the workday week, Willie Rooks went to church early that Sunday morning, wearing his new, gray tweed sports jacket, a red shirt, charcoal pants, white tie, and brown and white shoes. At 11:30 a.m., after services, he drove to the Pick Congress Hotel to meet the umpires, load their baggage, and transport them to the ballpark in time for the two o'clock game. At Wrigley, the police permitted Rooks to pull right up on the sidewalk to unload the umpires' suitcases and store them safely in the ticket office. After parking, Rooks joined Nick Colosi, Harry Wendelstedt, Art Williams, and Doug Harvey in the umpires' room, talking, laughing, and sipping cups of black coffee until the game started. Then he selected a place to watch the game from any vacant seat in the house. And there were plenty of them, as cold as it was this spring. Near the end of the game, Rooks reloaded his taxi and waited on the sidewalk, engine running, for the umpires to emerge from the ticket office, carrying bottles of Budweiser in brown paper sacks. Rooks would have the umpires at the airport within forty-five minutes.

Wendelstedt leaned forward over the front seat and lifted the lapel of Willie Rooks's jacket. "You know, Willie, I've seen that red shirt you got on before."

"That a very popular style," said Rooks.

"It's got a funny kind of weave in it, something like linen. Looks nice with your white tie. I used to have a shirt just like that. I bought it in New York, three, four years ago, sometime after I got married." Wendelstedt, still leaning forward, lifted some of the slack material of the shirt and ran his thumb and forefinger up and down its surface. "That even feels familiar, goddamn it. What the hell did I do with that shirt?" he turned to Harvey.

"You think I'm your valet? I'm a crew chief."

In the back, Colosi covered his mouth with his palm, and Williams turned to smile out the window. Rooks gritted his teeth, attempting to concentrate on the road.

"You remember the shirt I'm talking about, Nick?"

"I got my own wardrobe to worry about," Colosi said.

Wendelstedt leaned back in his seat, locked his eyes in a half-shut position, then meditated for thirty seconds. Suddenly he jumped forward, grabbed Rooks, and lifted the collar of the fancy red shirt. "Goddamn it, Willie, that's my laundry mark! Since when is your name *Wendelstedt*?"

Wendelstedt folded his arms, shook his head, and then looked around at his friends for any sign of interest or recognition, but Harvey was reading a newspaper, Colosi was studying his fingernails, and Williams was staring at a particularly nice-looking statue of a Civil War hero to his right out the window. "Can you imagine the nerve?" Wendelstedt mumbled to no one in particular. "My crew turning against me, stealing my favorite shirt and giving it to a lying goddamn black bastard cab driver. That's really something. All I ever get is abuse around here."

Wendelstedt leaned back, lifted an amber bottle, and took a deep swallow of beer. His big, blunt face seemed to light up when he drank beer. He always liked two or three bottles after a tiring game, and he disposed of them fast, like water. After studying the traffic for a while and concentrating on receding passersby, he said, "Remember that time the mafia was after you, Willie?"

"I sure do." Rooks shook his head.

"This was two years ago when I was traveling with umpire Lee Weyer," said Wendelstedt. "And you know Weyer; he'll do anything for a practical joke. Anyway, I go with Weyer into this novelty store and we buy a string of firecrackers and some of those decals you put on the rear window of your car that make it look like you've been sprayed with machine-gun fire. Then we go back to the hotel and I call up Willie and tell him to come early to pick us up before the game, I want to buy him a cup of coffee before the other guys get there."

"That's all you got to tell Willie. He'll do anything as long as somebody else will pay for it," said Harvey. "Of course, he didn't charge us anything for wearing your shirt."

"Except the shirt," said Williams.

"Yeah, we had to promise to give him the shirt."

Wendelstedt sneered and continued: "Weyer waits in the lobby till he sees Willie pull up and walk into the coffee shop. Then he sneaks out, pastes the decals on Willie's rear window and walks, cool as a cucumber, back into the lobby.

"Meanwhile, there was this gang war going on in Chicago at the time, spread all across the front pages of the newspaper, and everyone was discussing it—and Willie and I were sitting and talking, and I'm giving old Willie all the gory details about the five people killed so far. Really laying it on, telling about how their skin was all shredded by machine-gun bullets and how police had to search whole city blocks to find the remains of the victims. Willie, you know, he's not much for reading the newspapers, so he's just listening to all this stuff open-mouthed. Keeps saying to me, 'Is that right? Right here in Chicago? Well, goddamn! Hot dog!'

"Then Weyer sits down, orders a cup of coffee, and joins in the conversation. I'll tell ya, Weyer's really slick, calm and quiet, although you know he's just bustin' up inside, thinkin' about what he's going to do to poor old Willie.

"'The funny thing about these shootings,' Weyer says, 'that each and every one of these murders took place in a cab.'

"'No shit,' Willie says. Already you can see his whole face turnin' purple.

"'That's what this cop told me. The victims were all killed in cabs between the hours of noon and one o'clock.' 'What time is it?' I say to Weyer.

"'Quarter to twelve.'

"'Goddamn!' said Willie. Man, that was the first time I ever saw a black man go completely flush.

"After a few minutes talking, we tell Willie we want to go for a ride," Wendelstedt continued. "It was really pretty that day; the flowers were blooming in all the parks."

"That's one of the main reasons I like this town," said Harvey. "The parks are spread out along the banks of the lake and there are flowers of a hundred different colors. In other cities the downtown area is dreary, but in Chicago it's sweet all the way from the hotel to the ballpark."

"So we get into Willie's cab," Wendelstedt continued, raising his voice momentarily to regain the floor, "and Weyer starts telling Willie where to go. Turn here, turn there, you know. In the course of the ride, Weyer also mentions that every one of these killings happened on Washington Boulevard. He just sort of throws that out casually. Meanwhile, I could see old Willie up there in the front seat sweating; his hands are shaking and he's puffing on his cigar so hard it looks like a volcano.

"Just then Weyer says, 'Turn here!' And before Willie knows what's happening or thinks about resisting, we're driving down Washington Boulevard."

"Goddamn," said Williams, laughing, "old Willie musta shrunk three feet down in his seat."

"What I don't understand," said Harvey, "is why Willie didn't see the decals on the back of his cab."

"Shit, you ever know Willie to look in his rearview mirror?"

"Too many things happening in front of me," said Rooks, "to worry about what going on behind."

"Anyway, here we are driving down Washington Boulevard between noon and one o'clock in a taxi, and you can sure guess what Weyer did next. What I am tellin' you is the absolute truth.

"Weyer waits for a time when we're going real slow and there's not much traffic around, then he takes out his string of firecrackers, rolls down the window, lights the crackers, and throws them outta the car. It sounded so real, I thought I could hear the ricochet of the bullets.

"Well, Willie pulls to the side of the road, slams on his brakes, and turns around. What's he see? There's me and Weyer slumped on the seat, our eyes all bugged out, and we're looking so fucking dead, it is sickening. And there's poor old Willie Rooks, who has turned almost albino by this time. Willie looks down at me. My tongue is hanging out. He looks at Weyer; he's got his mouth closed and his eyes all contorted up. Then he sees the machine-gun bullet holes through the rear window. 'Mutha fuck,' he said. Real long and drawn out, 'Mutha fuck.' The next second, he was gone. In my whole life, I never saw an old man jump so high or run so fast. We caught him cowering behind a building nearly two blocks away. Worst thing I ever done to anybody in my whole life," said Wendelstedt.

"I don't know about that," said Rooks. "You got me that time good, but you got me worst before."

"Hey Willie," said Wendelstedt, smiling broadly. "You remember when Pete Roselle called you?"

Late one night while transferring planes in Chicago for a game on the West Coast, Wendelstedt and Weyer wanted to phone Rooks from the airport. When they looked up his number, they discovered that Willie had taken a full-page ad in the Yellow Pages for Rooks Cab Company. "Go anywhere, anytime." It was two in the morning when they woke him up.

"This is Pete Roselle, commissioner of the National Football League, calling," Weyer had said. "I'd like to speak to Mr. Rooks personally."

"This is Mr. Rooks," Willie had said, groggily.

"Mr. Rooks, I've got thirty National Football League officials at the airport, and I want to get them downtown to a hotel, and there are no taxis out here right now. We've got a convention to go to tomorrow and I want them to get some sleep. Now can you send some of your men out here to pick them up?"

"My men? What do you mean, 'Some of my men?'"

"Some of your drivers."

"I ain't got but one man," Rooks had said, "and that's me. And I'm sleepin'."

"You only have one taxi?"

"How many taxis one man need?'

"Then what the hell you got a full-page ad in the goddamn Yellow Pages for?" Weyer had replied in a furious tone of voice.

"Cause ads is cheaper than automobiles," Willie had answered firmly.

A few minutes after Wendelstedt had finished his story, Rooks pulled into O'Hare Airport and chugged up the drive, passing each terminal slowly until he stopped at the blue and white American Airlines sign. Each man shook hands with Rooks somberly, then picked up their cases and walked inside. In seconds they were gone, blurred first by the thick glass of the sliding doors that lead into the terminal, then swallowed by clusters of scurrying travelers.

Rooks folded the money they had given him into a much larger wad of ones and fives that he pulled from his pocket, and then climbed slowly into the green and white Checker. He looked at his watch and mumbled. If he hurried, he could make it back home in time for a cold beer before dinner. Before pulling out into the traffic, he looked up into the mirror and straightened his tie. "I sure love this shirt," he said.

22. Death in the Afternoon
Hal Crowther

Clearwater, Florida—Edd Roush died at the ballpark Monday, a few minutes before the National Anthem, while the pitchers were still running in the outfield and the regulars were autographing baseballs on the dugout steps. I was enjoying the same rituals on the same flawless west Florida afternoon, with an outfield full of seagulls and a stiff breeze off the Gulf. Unfortunately, we were in different ballparks, with Tampa Bay and half the peninsula between us.

Otherwise, I'd be shooting for a Pulitzer here. Imagine the scene. I guess some beardless press box fledgling, some uncomprehending eyewitness, has already attempted to record it. I hope the kid did his homework. I hope he wasn't one of those New Age sportswriters who thinks it's all style and impressions, with no scholarship required. I hope he didn't think that one ancient ballplayer is pretty much the same as another. I hope he talked to old ballplayers, and that he'd seen someone die before. I bet he used too many violins.

I didn't deserve Edd Roush, because frankly I thought he'd been dead for years—an error shared, I imagine by all but Grapefruit League insiders and a few of the most diligent historians of the game. *My Baseball Encyclopedia*, published in 1982, gave no date for his death, but I took that for an oversight or assumed that he'd died a very old man at some point since. When Smoky Joe Wood died a couple of years ago, I consciously closed the book on the generation of great ballplayers who matured before World War I. But it was Roush who was truly the last. He would have been ninety-five on May 8. His father must have given him his first glove when William McKinley was president. He put on his first Major League uniform, a Chicago White Sox uniform, in 1913, when my grandfather was a law student and my late father was a year short of a birthday. Extreme longevity, with its historical perspectives, has always fascinated me. Most of us who've worked in the press box and the locker rooms would never ask for autographs—it's an unwritten code—but if Edd Roush had turned up in the next box I'd have pressed him for the favor. It would be like getting Disraeli's autograph, or Richard Wagner's.

It's wonderful irony that Roush, alone of all baseball's great players, should die in Florida at a spring training game. He hardly ever played in one.

"Spring training was the worst," he told Lawrence Ritter in *The Glory of Their Times*.

"Some of those parks they'd want you to play exhibition games in had outfields like sand dunes, and others were hard as a cement sidewalk. The hell with that! I wouldn't go to spring training, that's all.

"I used to hold out every year until the week before the season opened. That's the only time they ever had any trouble with me, contract time. Why should I go down there and fuss around in spring training? Twist an ankle or break a leg. I did my own spring training, hunting quail and rabbits around Oakland City [Indiana]."

Roush would sign his contract the first week of April, show up on opening day without benefit of Florida, and proceed to hit .350. His employers were left without much of a case for the value of conditioning. Management didn't win many arguments with Edd Roush. This spring as usual the papers were full of indignant stories about the insolent millionaire ingrates who play the game today—about Dave Winfield's new book disparaging his boss, Darryl Strawberry's *Esquire* interview disparaging his teammates, George Bell refusing to work as a designated hitter, everyone holding out for more money. The press loves the myth of the old-timers who were so happy just to play the game that they'd run through brick walls for the rich brewers and robber barons who held them in semi-slavery for $200 a week. They don't write about Edd Roush.

Old-timers remember Ty Cobb for his ferocity and Babe Ruth for failures of discipline that bordered on depravity, but Edd Roush was the stubborn, shrewd, virtually intractable Hoosier who set the standards for every difficult athlete to follow. No sportswriter ever gave him a cute nickname and no manager ever managed him any way but by leaving him alone. At seventeen he quit his hometown team in a salary dispute—

some older players got $5 a game and he didn't—and signed up with its archrival twelve miles down the road. Some of his neighbors never forgave him, he said, and it set the pattern for his whole career. Roush was only twenty when he jumped the White Sox organization for the outlaw Federal League. It didn't faze him that Federal League rebels had been threatened with lifetime banishment from organized baseball. You don't let anyone threaten you out of $225 a month. The New York Giants were happy to take him when the Federal League folded. But he couldn't bear to play for the legendary John McGraw, who had the temerity to use sarcasm on a twenty-two-year-old outfielder.

Roush swore that he felt real loyalty to the Cincinnati Reds. But he held out for more money almost every year, sometimes well into the regular season. In his prime, he spent long stretches of the 1921 and 1922 baseball seasons hunting rabbits in Oakland City.

His long holdout in 1922 almost certainly cost Cincinnati the National League pennant. It isn't certain what his teammates or the city of Cincinnati felt on that occasion, but it's certain that Edd Roush didn't care. Traded back to New York toward the end of his career, he refused to report and boasted that he kept imperious John McGraw waiting four-and-a-half hours before he stung McGraw for a three-year, $70,000 contract. When that contract expired, Roush went AWOL again and sat out the entire 1930 season.

He was ambidextrous, too, the result of a shortage of left-hand gloves in Oakland City. There was never anyone like Edd Roush. They threw away the mold. He was usually identified as the oldest living member of the Hall of Fame, or as the last living participant in the rigged World Series of 1919, that mother lode of myth and literature that still casts a long shadow over professional baseball. (He always insisted that Cincinnati could have beaten the Black Sox without help from the gamblers. It's worth noting that Roush, Cincinnati's star, hit .214 in the Series while Shoeless Joe Jackson, the Chicago star banned for life as a conspirator, hit .375.) But Roush was the last of a lot of things. He was the last of the great dead ball hitters, who made their reputations before 1921 hitting soft baseballs that often, as Roush told it, stayed in play for several innings mashed flat on one side. When you consider that pitchers of the dead ball era were allowed to scuff and tear the ball and spit tobacco juice on it, you marvel even more that hitters like Cobb and Roush could swing at a blackened, lopsided scumball and hit it safely better than once in three tries.

Roush was also the last of the great place hitters, a dead ball subspecialty in the tradition of Wee Willie Keeler. He used a forty-eight-ounce bat with a handle almost as thick as its barrel, and shifted his feet to guide the ball with a pool shooter's precision to places the fielders couldn't reach. They say he almost wept with envy when he saw the Ted Williams Shift, with a shortstop placed on the right-field side of second base to thwart that classic pull hitter.

"What would you have hit against an infield like that, Edd?" they asked him.

"I'd have hit 1.000, for certain."

He was the last important hitter who had faced Walter Johnson and Grover Cleveland Alexander, the greatest pitchers of all, when they were in their youth and prime (his first Major League hit was off Johnson); the last man who could have described the effect of Johnson's fastball, the break on Christy Mathewson's fadeaway, the impression Babe Ruth made when he arrived in the big leagues as a nineteen-year-old half-housebroken left-handed pitcher. He was the last man who could have attempted to describe the character of his old teammate Hal Chase, the gifted and notorious first baseman who was rumored to have thrown hundreds of baseball games for gamblers between 1910 and 1920, and who bragged that he made $40,000 on the 1919 World Series; the last man who had played in the outfield alongside Olympian Jim Thorpe, and who could describe the incomparable Indian's almost superhuman long strides.

He took all of that with him. From now on everything we read about it will be secondhand. I hope his friends in Bradenton listened carefully and maybe ran a few tapes on him, but it isn't the same. I'd be more convincing, mourning the loss of such a priceless resource, if I had known that it was still around.

This wasn't a sentimental man, this old, old man who finally felt the cold hand on his shoulder at Bradenton's McKechnie Field (named after Bill McKechnie, Roush's teammate from 1914 to 1917), or a man who was the beneficiary of much sentiment. It wouldn't do to put a lot of sentiment into his obituary. I wasn't there; I can't describe the scene. But I can describe the kind of day it was if you were sitting in the box seats just behind home plate, in the warm March sun that doesn't burn, with the flag standing out straight from the flagpole, a cloudless rainwashed sky, the Phillies' ace ballpark organist playing everything from Duke Ellington to "Amazing Grace." I was thinking that if I died in a state of grace they'd let me stay right there, watching an extra-inning game that would never grow boring and drinking celestial beer that would never intoxicate or dehydrate the drinker. We shouldn't make too much of the fact that Edd Roush, the man who hated spring training, took his leave at one of the exhibition games he used to despise. He was a baseball man. On a day like that one, where else could he possibly be?

23. Meat
Michael Martone

Because I could play baseball, I never went to Korea.

I was standing on the dock in San Francisco with my entire company. We all wore helmets, parade rest, and were loaded down with winter and summer gear. We were ready to embark. My name was called. I remember saying "Excuse me" to the men in rank as I tried to get by with my equipment. Then I sat on my duffle and watched them file aboard, bumping up the side of the ship, the cables flexing. There was rust in the bilge. I could hear the water below me. Sailors laughed way over my head. It only took a few hours. There were some people there to wave good-bye though not for the soldiers since our shipping out was something secret.

Nothing was ever said. I was transferred to another unit where all the troops were baseball players. I played second base on the Third Army team. I batted seventh and bunted a lot. We traveled by train from one base to another in Texas, Georgia, and on up into New Jersey for the summer. We had a few cars to ourselves, including a parlor with an open platform. The rest of the train was made up of reefers full of frozen meat. The train was aluminum and streamlined. We could stand in the vestibules or in the open doorway of the baggage car where we kept the bags of bats and balls and the pinstriped uniforms hung on rods and look out over the pink, flat deserts. There wouldn't be a cinder from the engine, its wheels a blur. You would see it up ahead on the slow curves, the white smoke of the whistle trailing back over the silver boxcars of meat and then the whistle. Some cars still had to be iced so we'd stop in sad little towns, play catch and pepper while the blocks melted in the sun and the sawdust turned dark and clotty on the platform. We'd hit long fly balls to the local kids who'd hang around. We left them broken bats to nail and tape.

The meat was our duty. It was what we said we did even though everyone knew we played baseball. The army wanted us to use frozen meat instead of fresh. We ran the tests in messes to see if the men could tell the difference. We stood by the garbage cans and took the plates to scrape and separate the scraps of meat to weigh for waste. A red plate meant the meat was fresh. The bone, the chewed gristle, the fat. I picked it out of the cold peas and potatoes. Sometimes whole pieces would come back, gray and hard. The gravy had to be wiped off before it went on the scale. Those halls were huge, with thousands of men hunched over the long tables eating. We stood by watching, waiting to do our job. It made no difference, fresh or frozen, to the men. This pleased the army. Things were changing. Surplus from the war was being given to the UN for the action in Korea. There were new kinds of boots and rifles. Then every camp still had walk-in lockers. The sides of meat hung on racks. The cold blew through you. Blue inspection stamps bled into the yellow fat of the carcasses. All gone now. That's what I did in the service.

But the baseball didn't change. The ball still found my glove. There were the old rituals at home. I rubbed my hands in the dirt then wiped them on my pants, took the bat and rapped it on the plate. The pitch that followed always took me by surprise—hard and high, breaking away. The pitcher spun the ball like a dial on a safe. And trains still sound the same when they run through this town. At night, one will shake our house (we live near an overpass) and I can't go back to sleep. I'll count the men who walked up that gangway to the ship. The train wheels squeal and sing. It might as well be hauling the cargo of my dreams.

24. From *Blue Highways*

William Least Heat-Moon

I drove up the valley of the Red River of the North (which empties into Hudson Bay) and crossed into Oslo, Minnesota. Near Viking, tall stalks from the sunflower crop of a year earlier rattled in the warm wind. For miles I had been seeing a change in the face of the Northland brought about because Americans find it easier to clean house paint out of brushes with water than with turpentine. This area once grew much of the flax that linseed oil comes from, but with the advent of water-based paint, the demand for flax decreased; in its stead, of all things, came the sunflower, and now it was becoming the big cash crop of the Dakotas and Minnesota—with more acreage going each year to new hybrids developed from Russian seeds—because "flower" is a row crop that farmers can economically reap by combine after the grain harvest.

Thief River Falls, another town of Nordic cleanliness, reportedly got its name through an odd mingling of history and language. A group of Dakota Sioux lived on the rich hunting grounds here for some years. Although bellicose Chippewa controlled the wooded territory, the Dakotas managed to conceal a remote settlement by building an earthen wall around it and disappearing inside whenever the enemy came near. They even hunted with bows and arrows rather than risk the noise of guns. But the Chippewa finally found them out and annihilated them. Because the mounds hid a portion of the river, the Chippewa referred to it as "Secret Earth River." Through some error, early white traders called it "Stealing Earth River"; through additional misunderstanding, it came to be "Thief River." As for Crookston downstream, it took its name from a railroad man.

South of Thief River Falls, on U.S. 59, I crossed the Clearwater River; but this one, unlike a dozen others of that name I'd seen in the past weeks, was true to its description. It drained a country that became increasingly heavy with aspen, birch, pine, and spruce. I had come to the western edge of the North Woods. The prairie was gone. On the Clearwater River and upstream from Clearwater Lake and down the highway from the hamlet of Clearbrook was the seat of Clearwater County: Bagley, a village with pines and a blue lake, a village where the names on the buildings were Lukkasson, Olson, Peterson, Lundmark. I stopped for the night and went to the Viking House Cafe for a Viking omelet (cheese, ham, green peppers, onions) and a chocolate milkshake. To the waitress in long flaxen braids I said, "Who's the most famous native son of Bagley, Minnesota?"

"Oh, my golly! I'll ask the cook." When she returned with dinner, she said, "That would be Richard Davids, author of *How to Talk to Birds.*"

Two old men, spectacles like dusty windows, sat slurping broth and arguing about Indian net fishing on the Lake of the Woods Reservation in the Northwest Angle, the northernmost part of the lower forty-eight.

"I never cut an Indian net," one said, "but I never discouraged a fishing partner from cutting. No redskin should have to buy a license to fish reservation land, but he ought to fish fair."

The words came slowly, with long pauses; in the silences, the soft clacking of dentures. "Indians got first rights," the other said. "They fish for a living. You fish for fun."

"Law's law or it ain't law."

The waitress said, "You boys on the fishing rights again?"

They had trouble hearing her, although she spoke louder than either of them. Maybe, after so many years, they didn't need to hear each other.

Louder, she asked, "Who won the argument tonight?"

"I did," they said.

"It's a good friendship where everyone's a winner."

"What's that, honey?" they said.

I walked down to the bakery, the one with flour sacks for sale in the front window and bowling trophies above the apple turnovers. The people of the northern midlands—the Swedes and Norgies and Danes—apparently hadn't heard about the demise of independent, small-town bakeries; most of their towns had at least one.

With a bag of blueberry tarts, I went up Main to a tin-sided, false-front tavern called Michel's, just down the street from the Cease Funeral Home. The interior was log siding and yellowed knotty pine. In the backroom the

Junior Chamber of Commerce talked about potatoes, pulpwood, dairy products, and somebody's broken fishing rod. I sat at the bar. Behind me a pronghorn antelope head hung on the wall, and beside it a televised baseball game cast a cool light like a phosphorescent fungus.

"Hear that?" a dwindled man asked. He was from the time when boys drew "Kilroy-Was-Here" faces on alley fences. "Did you hear the announcer?"

"I wasn't listening."

"He said 'velocity.'"

"Velocity?"

"He's talking about a fastball. A minute ago he said a runner had 'good acceleration.' This is a baseball game, not a NASA shot. And another thing: I haven't heard anybody mention a 'Texas leaguer' in years."

"It's a 'bloop double' now, I think."

"And the 'banjo hitter'—where's he? And what happened to the 'slow ball'?"

"It's a 'change-up.'"

The man got me interested in the game. We watched and drank Grain Belt. He had taught high school civics in Minneapolis for thirty-two years, but his dream had been to become a sports announcer.

"They put a radar gun on the kid's fastball a few minutes ago," he said. "Ninety-three point four miles per hour. That's how they tell you speed now. They don't try to show it to you: 'smoke,' 'hummer,' 'the high hard one.' I miss the old clichés. They had life. Who wants to hit a fastball with a decimal point when he can tie into somebody's 'heat'? And that's another thing: nobody 'tattoos' or 'blisters' the ball anymore. These TV boys are ruining a good game because they think if you can see it they're free to sit back and psychoanalyze the team. Ask and I'll tell you what I think of it."

"What do you think of it?"

"Beans. And that's another thing, too."

"Beans?"

"Names. Used to be players named Butterbean and Big Potato, Little Potato. Big Poison, Little Poison. Dizzy and Daffy. Icehouse, Shoeless Joe, Suitcase, The Lip. Now we've got the likes of Rickie and Richie and Reggie.

With names like that, I think I'm watching a third grade scrub team."

The announcer said the pitcher had "good location."

"Great God in hemlock! He means 'nibble the corners.' But which of these throwing clowns nibbles corners? They're obsessed with speed. Satchel Paige—there's a name for you—old Satch could fire the pill a hundred and five miles an hour. He didn't throw it that fast very often because he couldn't make the ball cut up at that speed. And, sure as spitting, his pitching arm lasted just about his whole life."

The man took a long smacking pull on his Grain Belt. "Damn shame," he said. "There's a word for what television's turned this game into."

"What's the word?"

"Beans," he said. "Nothing but beans and hot air."

25. A Dispatch from Tucson
Larry Blakely

I worry about baseball's future in much the same way I—a man who recently conceded the reflection in the morning mirror appears suspiciously middle-aged—fret about cancer taking me down in life's late innings or my retirement funds running out before I do. It's not an immediate concern like making the mortgage or waiting for that lingering low back pain to disappear, but a vaguer, more shadowy kind of worry that surfaces every now and again, like when I recently heard someone's fatalistic comment about professional football's preeminent popularity: *Well, at least baseball was number one for most of the last century.*

In the new millennium, I wonder if what is still billed as our national pastime might indeed slip to true second-class sports status in twenty-first-century America. Perhaps this game I've loved my entire life will wind up with sparse crowds populated mainly by creakers and codgers unable to entice their children or grandchildren to come out to the ol' ball game. Baseball will, without a doubt, survive, but whether it will flourish is open to debate, speculation, worry.

And so I arrive in Tucson for Cactus League spring training, ostensibly to report on a handful of Major League prospects who call Oregon home, but if the truth be known, I'm more interested in gauging the early mood of this year's crop of fans. I am anxious to gather some sense of how baseball is doing, to check the fans' collective pulse.

Nearly two hours before today's first pitch will be thrown, I wheel my rental car into a parking lot already half full at Hi Corbett Field, home to the Colorado Rockies for the months of February and March. Arizona automobiles cover the largest share of the striped asphalt, of course, but I'd estimate a good third of the cars have arrived from other states and several Canadian provinces.

As always, fans' vehicles represent every socioeconomic strata, except perhaps the very rich, who have no time for games, and the very poor, who have no money for games. A relic from the 1960s, a Chevy Impala, dented rust the predominant color, sits within spitting distance of a Lexus sedan, its clearcoated black paint glimmering in the morning sunlight. A motor home the size of a Greyhound bus, a full-size van with a tricked-out matching paint job in tow, dwarfs its neighbor, an ancient Volkswagen whose duct tape is showing. I recall a trusty Bug (excellent ride, bad heater) my last year of college, the year a graying Willie Mays became a Met, the year Reggie Jackson's A's defeated the Big Red Machine in seven, the year Roberto Clemente's plane, on a mission of mercy, went down.

Inside the park, I forgo the press box, elect instead to wander the stands and mingle with the early bird fans. After another soggy Pacific Northwest winter, the Grand Canyon State's sunshine is all the more refreshing despite the fact my SPF 30 remains stuffed inside a suitcase back at the motel, ensuring my exposed hide will be a pleasant lobster-like hue within hours. The outfield grass—real grass in a state where most of the lawns sport cacti as their sole form of greenery—perfectly mowed in that familiar crosshatch pattern, remains a springtime feast for the eyeballs.

Hi Corbett Field, like the other Major League playgrounds of spring, is minor league–sized and the signs, even those of major corporate sponsors, are modest by big league standards. The ballpark, reflecting the green and purple motif of Coors Field in Denver, holds smallish crowds, less than 10,000 fans whom I've always found are knowledgeable and certainly more well behaved than, say, your typical Bronx bunch.

Today's visiting team, San Francisco's resurgent Giants, is taking batting practice. Plenty of seats behind home plate, most expensive in the house at ten bucks, are not yet occupied, so I tuck my press pass inside my polo shirt, plop down, and strike up a conversation with the nearest fan.

Clovis, eighty-four but doesn't look it, makes a point of watching all the teams, but wears a faded blue cap advertising his loyalty to one. His hearing is on the wane, but otherwise this Chicago native seems to be on top of his game. He is a snowbird now, wintering in Arizona for four months, waiting for baseball to spring to life. Clovis worked in a number of middling steakhouses for decades, moving up from dishwasher to cook; he tells me one Saturday night Al Capone showed up for dinner with some pals, got a good table right away although Scarface didn't have a reservation. When I ask Clovis if he's yanking my chain on that last part, he gives me a smile in lieu of a straight answer. At any rate, Clovis can recall every detail of the prime rib, end cut, a baked potato with the works, devoured by the man who made Elliott Ness famous.

"Should have been here yesterday," he says.

"Is that right? What happened?" I ask.

"Cubs played." Clovis is a Northsider, so open hostility toward Chicago's White Sox is a given. It goes with his portion of the territory in the Windy City.

"How'd they do?" I know the answer but figure it's a good way to keep the conversation moving along.

"Don't recall." I surmise Clovis did not garner any oratory awards before dropping out of school in the ninth grade.

"You didn't stay for the end?" A real fan, of course, always stays until the final out is recorded, no matter what. Turns out Clovis is not only a true blue fan, he's playing me just a little.

"Oh, I stayed all right. But I was mostly watching one of the coaches."

"Who's that?"

Clovis straightens in the molded green plastic seat, his wrinkled dark face alive with the memory of yesterday, about to prove me wrong on the oration issue.

"Billy Williams. Damn, what a player he was. Ernie Banks got more attention, but Billy, he was the workingman's hero. Day in, day out, Billy got it done. Not flashy. End of the season, you could count on Billy to be right up there. Don't get me wrong, Ernie Banks was a crackerjack player. But me and the boys in the bleachers was always pulling for Mr. Billy Williams. Still looks good in a uniform, too."

Clovis leans forward, his eyes narrow, as if to fix the exact spot where a sixty-year-old Alabama native hit infield twenty-four hours earlier, jump-starting an aging fan's memories of an outfielder roaming Wrigley Field for sixteen seasons, 1959–74, piling up the numbers—a .290 lifetime batting average, 1,475 RBIs, 426 taters planted over National League fences.

Over eight decades a Chicagoan and this is what Clovis remembers most: a gangster sinking his teeth into red meat and Billy Williams quietly going about his business, getting the job done.

"Dusty!"

Behind the metal fence and high netting which protects the fans from foul balls and the players from the fans, a stout man who looks to be about fifty shouts at San Francisco's manager positioned behind the batting cage with a pair of coaches, watching some prospects take their cuts. Dusty Baker's back remains toward the fan. Managers are usually not chatty types during pregame warm-ups and Mr. Baker is no exception.

"Hey, Dusty, over here!" Both hands gripping the fence now, if he doesn't lower the volume, he might well receive a visit from one of the ushers—much more tolerant than their regular season counterparts but not without limits. Most fans know the best time to gather a manager's autograph is after the game.

Fans here can even jaw with Don Baylor Lite, albeit usually through a locked steel gate, about an hour after most contests. Baylor, the Rockies' skipper, is a demanding manager and I have never seen him crack a smile—not once—during a game. A patient fan at Hi Corbett Field will be treated to a soft-spoken, friendly Texan after spring training games, a man far removed from the scowling version of Baylor inside the dugout who can dampen a rookie's armpits with a single sidelong squint.

Today there's something out of the ordinary about this persistent fan behind the cage. For one thing, he doesn't hold a baseball or pennant or scrap of paper, seeking ink from the famous or nearly so. For another, he is what we would have cruelly called, in that less kind and gentle time during which I grew up, a retard. Now he is differently abled or mentally challenged or whatever euphemism du jour applies today. This much is clear: he wants Dusty Baker's attention. Now.

When batting practice ends, Baker starts down the third base line but not without sneaking a peek at The Fan.

"Hey, Dusty, it's me, George."

Baker takes a couple more steps toward the dugout, stops, turns, peers over his ever-present prescription sunglasses. "I know you, don't I?"

George shoots an *I told you so* look over his shoulder toward lesser fans in the stands, then points at Baker and hollers, "I know *you*!"

Baker strolls over. On the field, he is another manager more known for his intensity than his humor, but he gives George a warm grin.

"Help me out," Baker says. "You're from San Francisco?"

"Berkeley, remember?" George says, apparently not offended by Baker's memory lapse.

"Of course." Fans are starting to converge, a fact not lost on Baker. "Listen, I've got to get going, George. You want a ball or something?"

"Nah, I just wanted to say hi. Hi, Dusty!" The man-child beams at his own joke, then heads up toward one of the smallish concession stands, stopping to slap high fives with an elderly usher. I follow.

Turns out this is George's first trip to spring training. He lives in a group home, holds down an assembly job, has a girlfriend named Amy, loves the game, adores the Giants in general and Dusty Baker in particular. In fact, George knows more Giants' history than any except the most anally challenged fan. God forbid they should ever move the franchise. A decidedly unquiet George would likely be marching in the streets of the City by the Bay.

No doubt when George returns home he will tell all his friends he talked to Dusty Baker. Not the other way around.

George is the kind of fan we should all wish to be and, on our best and luckiest of days, are.

This is a weekday and thus a school day but there are plenty of kids roaming the park. When I ask three boys, all locals, all under ten, all looking like mischief about to explode, if they are playing hooky, the smallest responds slyly, "It's okay. We got permission."

The remote possibility this might actually be true is quickly dispelled when one of his fellow pucksters slaps him in the shoulder and all three burst into laughter. I suppose just in case the boys think this stranger asking too many questions might be a truant officer, they vanish toward right field where only a low railing by the bullpen separates players from autograph-seeking fans.

Lenny and his daughter Christine, eleven with bright dark eyes and gold hoop earrings, have driven down from New Mexico, which according to their state's license plates is the Land of Enchantment. This is the first of two days they're spending at the park before heading home. Lenny overheard my conversation with the three boys. Christine, he informs me with no small measure of fatherly pride, is the oldest of his three daughters and an honor student.

"Good for you, keep it up," I say. "Do you play?"

"Yeah, last year was my first year in Little League." She sweeps a long wisp of jet black hair behind her ear, trying for nonchalance, but the exuberance possessed by kids of a certain age who have worn the uniform for the first time cannot be suppressed, percolates to the surface.

"She got her team's first hit of the year," Lenny adds. He says he played a little baseball growing up in Texas, but claims he wasn't that good. Christine looks ready to dispute the last point but instead, with a gentle prod from her dad, relates the details of her first hit last spring, a memory as fresh as if it happened an hour ago and will hopefully remain that way fifty years from now when, with good fortune, Christine will help teach her children's children to play the game.

Lenny holds a Colorado replica jersey, white with purple pinstripes, already signed by a few not-quite-famous Rockies. "So, who's your favorite player?" I ask Christine, a small test of a small fan's emerging baseball knowledge.

"Vinny Castilla!" she exclaims before the last word leaves my lips. Besides ethnic pride, I suspect a preteen crush may influence her choice of Colorado's popular, easygoing third baseman, but I, father to two teenaged daughters, know better than to pry. Christine eyes the press credential on an elastic string that has slipped outside my shirt and asks breathlessly, "Can you help us get his autograph?" I cannot—ballpark media rules are universally specific on the subject and I mostly try to play within the lines—and her bright face goes dull for just an instant when I tell her this.

I wish I could. She does her enchanting state proud.

According to the media guide, thirty-two-year-old Rockies right-handed pitcher Kevin Ritz was born in Eatontown, New Jersey, is 6'4" tall, and tips the scales at 220 pounds. Two pint-sized reporters interviewing him just outside the home team dugout are well prepared, making plenty of eye contact while still managing to jot details in their notebooks. Every so often, one diminutive reporter zips the other a wide-eyed hint of a smile, as in *Can you believe we're doing this*? Otherwise, they are all business. Each reporter is about two feet shorter and two decades younger than Ritz.

"What's your best pitch?"

"What are your goals for this season?"

"Who was your favorite player when you were a kid?"

"What's Don Baylor like as a manager?"

The pitcher removes his designer shades, folds his arms, bends toward the reporters, and gives them careful, considered responses, except for passing on that Baylor bit. Ritz, nobody's dummy, is not about to let something slip that might make its way back to his manager. Besides, big leaguers know the media cannot be trusted. And make no mistake, these two are media types.

Vanessa, whose cap features her school's bear mascot, and Addie, whose long, light brown hair keeps getting in her way, are the pride of Dee James's combined fourth-fifth grade class at Tucson's Cragin Elementary. In order to do pregame player interviews on the field today, they won a school newspaper writing contest. The entire class is here, stationed in metal bench seats in the left-field bleachers that offer a decent closeup view of the action. I'd guess more than a few envious eyes are fixed on two young reporters doing their job.

Shortly before the game starts and they rejoin their classmates, the girls display their journalistic mettle by making an impromptu stop at the visitors' dugout. They corner a young nonroster outfielder who seems delighted with the media attention, although the circulation of *Bear Facts* is presumably rather limited. A batboy tries to horn in on the action, but is brushed back by reporters wise to his real motives. One leveling look from a pro named Vanessa, in particular, sends an unmistakable message: *Hey, bub, we're trying to do an interview here.*

A few minutes later, free to be kids again, the girls are surrounded by their effusive peers in the silver bleachers, now fielding questions instead of posing them. Seven springs from now, when these youngsters are teetering on the threshold of adulthood, they probably won't recall a whole lot about Ms. James's classroom lessons (though anyone who knows the value of a day at the park is an outstanding teacher in my book), but I would wager everyone—every single one—will remember this afternoon in the sun, in the bleachers, at the ballpark.

Especially a couple of budding sportswriters named Vanessa and Addie.

After the game, after wrapping up clubhouse interviews and double-checking my notes, I make my way up to the compact press box, vacant except for one fellow hack. We exchange information about cheap places for chow. My per diem, as my daughters would so delicately put it, sucks, so I'm particularly grateful when this cholesterol-fearless member of the print media says she's discovered an inexpensive diner not far away that features real shakes, real fries, and low botulism rates. I'm just one stop away from heading back to the parking lot, now almost empty.

Training rooms are technically off limits to the press, but the rule is sporadically enforced and, anyway, I carry a fail-safe card of entry, a plastic baggie of empty film canisters for trainers to use when rationing out pills to players (please remain calm, these are typically aspirin from quart-sized bottles, not steroids or Percs). The canisters are always welcome but I, like the visiting team's hormonal batboy, harbor an ulterior motive: I want to locate an obscure longtime minor leaguer who has disappeared from my baseball radar screen, and I happen to know a Rockies assistant trainer is a good friend of his. After learning the missing player is in Taiwan earning some healthy bucks during the twilight of his career, I exit from the unmarked exterior door of the training facility and glance toward the field.

I spot the kid out of the corner of my eye.

He's slinking along the forest green outfield fence with the stealth of a cougar pursuing a rabbit entree, a skinny, dark-haired boy about twelve in baggy blue shorts and a white T-shirt sporting the logo of an Oregon sneaker company. How did he manage to remain at the park? Even during spring training, field security is tight. Maybe he's mastered one of my own boyhood tricks, standing on a toilet seat inside a restroom stall, biding his time.

He stops, casting cat burglar eyes to the left and right. I think he's going to swipe a chunk of turf. Big mistake—groundskeepers are known to become downright unpleasant if anyone not wearing a professional uniform so much as steps inside the foul lines. Instead, this young rogue slips a few yards onto center field—the sacred ground of DiMaggio, Mays, Mantle—drops to his knees and rolls back, spread-eagled in the grass, head resting against the earth, eyes closed to the pink desert sky. I try to imagine what he might be thinking at this precise moment. I can't.

But I think, come tomorrow, I just might corner Vinny Castilla in the clubhouse and get him to sign a ball for a dark-eyed girl who swings a mean bat.

26. Playing Shallow

Richard Jackson

My father looked so small standing on the slight slope of the backyard and hitting me fly balls over the white plank fence out into the field that was made treacherous by vines, rubble, and sandpits. The field was enclosed by a triangle of streets, ours being Jefferson Street in South Lawrence, Massachusetts. It was early spring, after any number of suppers, the dark already settling down around me like an oversized uniform. The black third baseman's glove was a hand-me-down from an uncle, not really appropriate for the outfielder I wanted to be. My father was using my favorite bat—a Mickey Mantle model—I would use later for a few years before breaking it one hot afternoon. But Little League tryouts were fast approaching now. My father kept waving me closer, wanting me to play shallow. "Good outfielders play shallow," he said, something that came in handy when I once made a diving catch in right-field foul territory and my sister Sherry jumped up in the stands shouting, "That was my brother, Ricky!" And playing shallow allowed me to cut down a huge number of players when I would position myself in my favorite spot—center field.

Backpedaling, that was the key, as I finally learned. To be able to do that fast, and to be able to move backward effortlessly while gauging the ball's arc as soon as it hit the bat, judging by the angle of the swing and where the ball hit the bat! How many things would go through my mind that I was hardly conscious of in that instant—and then the endless wait for the ball to arrive. It's during that wait that part of your mind's field, at that age, is stormed by your friends and family in the stands even as you try to evict them from your thoughts and concentrate. Or I might worry about the field: Where exactly was that depression? Where was that rough spot? Or I might even, in that moment where one concentrates on the ball so much that other images climb up the fence of consciousness, think of something more important: the lost friends who would seem to disappear into some space beyond the ball, including my father, who would succumb to something vaguely resembling Alzheimer's but was more likely brought on, as it was for his coworkers, from working around deadly chemicals. Struggling against a fly ball meant less, I thought, after that. But I still hadn't learned. Look at Yastrzemski, he'd say just before he got sick: he makes the play, puts his head down, and goes back to work. When I made a good play there were no congratulations: the lesson was that you did your job, you contributed, and you didn't get any special mention other than a momentary slap on the back or nod. "What you do on the field stays with you," he'd say in one way or another, "but what others say about it means little."

Because of his sickness, he wasn't able to understand the following poem when it was written, but every fly ball that was ever hit to me carried with it an image of him, now grown so much larger, waving me in on that vacant lot, "Play shallow." And anytime I still occasionally take up a glove for a faculty-student pickup game, the same image comes tearing at me. All of which is to say he's the person silently and privately addressed in the poem, and if he could have understood then, I suppose this is what I would have said to him.

Center Field

> I don't think it will ever come down,
> It flew so quickly beyond the small hollow
> The field lights make in the approaching dusk,
> And I begin to realize how uneven the outfield is—
> The small holes that test your ankles, the slight pitch
> Toward deep center that makes backpedaling so risky
> But keeps pulling you as if further into your past.
>
> It must be falling out of another world,
> "lint from the stars" we used to say on a sandlot
> in Lawrence, Mass.—and I have so much time
> to imagine what you will say between innings
> about what we try to steal from our darkening pasts,

how age means knowing how many steps we have lost,
remembering that too many friends have died,
and how love is the most important thing,
if only we knew who to love, and when.

The ball is just becoming visible again
And I am trying to remember anyone I have loved,
And it turns out it was usually too late, that we stood
Like embarrassed batters caught looking at a third strike.
Yet somehow in this long moment I have slid
Past the outstretched arms of twenty years,
And I can see Joey Gile crouched at third base
Waiting, as it happened, for the bullet of some sniper
To snap like a line drive into his chest,
For John Kearns to swing and miss everything
From a tree in his backyard and not be found
For two days, for Joe Daly, whom I hardly knew
And who hardly had time to steal away
When the tractor slipped gear and tagged him to a tree,
for Gene Coskren who never understood baseball
and was fooled by a hit and run in Syracuse, N.Y.,
and somehow I am going to tell them all.

And my mother's sister who loved this game
And who complained for years about her stomach,
The family joke, until the cancer struck
And she went down faster than any of them.
And her own aunt, "I don't want to die," she said, and slid
Her head to the pillow not out of fear
But embarrassment, stranded, she thought,
With no one to bring her home, no one to love.

But in the meantime, look, this is a poem
That could go on being about either death or love,
And we have only the uncertain hang time

> *Of a fly ball to decide how to position ourselves,*
> *To find the right words for our love,*
> *To turn toward home as the night falls, as the ball,*
> *As the loves, the deaths we grab for our own.*

I was never one to believe the coaches telling us how this or that sport was about life, about the life lessons we had to learn. To articulate that seemed to reduce it to a slogan. But I also knew that baseball seemed to engage a part of me deeper and more serious than the sandlot games, the stickball street games, or the Little League and later the Babe Ruth League games. A trip to Fenway Park was more than just a trip to a ball game: it was part of a larger way of engaging the world, like later seeing Ted Williams hit his last home run in Fenway, which made everyone feel somehow able to transcend the everyday lives they had to live. Or worrying with everyone else what would happen to Jimmy Piersal, who would sometimes find the game as impossible as his life and stake out a spot between the center-field flagpole and the wall. Or reading the game statistics, which was a way of anchoring all these intangibles to something concrete, of making the whole mythic world part of our own. And when you imagined the game played from those numbers you made an entire world for yourself.

Making that world was something we all did, for in many ways it was one, shared world, not many individual worlds. A myth. Something to substitute for the losses and setbacks in our lives. All those friends and relatives who seemed to disappear as effortlessly and quickly as a fly ball into the lights, they, too, still seem to haunt every game I played, and play.

Years later, when I wrote that poem, I was playing softball every Sunday in Chattanooga, Tennessee, the outfield, as usual, and teaching. And my outfield buddy, we called him "Sky," died then, too, an unexpected suicide. One Sunday he just wasn't there, wasn't to be found, and a few weeks later they pulled his body from the Tennessee River. It started to appear that the game had even more meaning than I even imagined. I started to see it even more importantly as creating some sense of order, of holding onto something against loss. I even started to use baseball as a metaphor for writing in my classes. One year, students made up

a set of cocktail napkins that quipped "Poetry is like baseball." I started to think of the art of it, the beauty of the arc as it goes from bat to
glove, something that transcended the mechanics and the score. On the
other hand, there's also the craziness of it—I mean how can a simple game
come to mean so much to anyone? Ridiculous, my friend Bill Matthews
and I would joke, while we sat around over wine and made outrageous
analogies. Sometimes we'd invent teams made up of writers. Frost? He'd
never want to bunt. Shakespeare? Think of the ground he'd cover at center, or short. Who's up to handling the hot topics at third? It was just "too
serious to take seriously," he'd say.

Like playing shallow. You challenge the hitter who inevitably tries to
put it over your head instead of hitting naturally. You learn to backpedal
sometimes even during the windup. You don't play deep to protect yourself and let someone on with a cheap hit, was the point. It comes down
to playing the game right. It comes down, really, to an act of love, which
is why Joey Gile would take the time to try to teach me, while Bill and I
could joke about it, why my father would spend those endless, and what
must have been for him frustrating, evenings, hitting out those fly balls
across the fence. He seems so huge now. They all do. It comes down to
letting it all come right at you. It comes down to backpedaling and grabbing it for your own. We just have to decide how to position ourselves.

27. Hard to Love as the Red Sox
Luke Salisbury

Can baseball save you? That is the question. Don't tell me I root because the Red Sox might win the pennant and World Series. This isn't the night before Christmas. Jewel in "As I Lay Dying" says, "If there's a God, what the hell is He for?" What the hell is baseball for?

It's there when we need it.

It wasn't once.

One cold, lost opening day.

The April Cissy St. Claire left me. Nineteen seventy-two. The heart in last place. Not one day at a time, but one minute. One minute. One minute. How can you stop thinking about her? About him? When will you sleep? A world comes to an end—an act, a self, victory—closed, inadequate, lost.

Names: Bowie Kuhn, Marvin Miller. Red Sox, Tigers, Red Sox. Cissy St. Claire.

It was the year everything got messed up.

Young men are good at pissing on themselves.

Cissy and I lived on Valentine Avenue in the Bronx. Poe Park was at the end of the street. A wretched little piece of dirty city green, ragged trees, grass worn down like a bad infield, and the cottage where Poe lived with his tragic bride. The cottage was so small one wondered how anyone could have lived in it. I told Cissy the model for Annabelle Lee might have succumbed to claustrophobia. She laughed. Cissy had a fine sense of humor. It didn't occur to me our relationship would die of claustrophobia. Poe's cottage was moved from another part of the Bronx, so our short, hot, unhappy time did not occur on the same block as Poe's, but I felt the connection.

We were an unlikely pair to be in the Bronx. I was born into the *New*

York Social Register to a family long on pretension and short on cash. My mother cared about the *Social Register*; my father said if there were a revolution, we'd be shot first. I took great pleasure in putting my Bronx address in the NYSR. I was a poor relative in WASPdom, an outlier who wanted that world and knew it wasn't worth wanting. The world of manners, privilege, and limited imagination gave my father a great yawn. He came from nearer its center, so his opinion carries more weight.

Cissy was an archetypal prep school girl—long, straight, light brown hair, 5′7″, hazel eyes, a nonaffected, eastern way of speaking, and manners. Yes. Manners are part of the story and Cissy had manners—I didn't say morals. She was the girl with perfect manners. That's what my friend Jake George called her. I don't usually find irony erotic, but irony was part of my attraction to Cissy. She kept a distance—a neat, mannerly distance. Always. It made me want her so badly. She was hard to know, hard to love, like the Boston Red Sox, which is the way, if not the reason, I loved her so hopelessly, so completely. The season would end badly.

I came from Long Island and Cissy from New Jersey. Oyster Bay and Summit. Not Long Guyland or Joisy. But not Manhattan either. Her family was richer, mine better connected. Our mothers were similar. Tolstoy says Ivan Ilych's house "was just what is usually seen in the houses of people of moderate means who want to appear rich, and therefore succeed only in resembling others like themselves." We were both raised thinking ladies had thin ankles and are never rude by accident, life is 80 percent table manners, told the word "aunt" should be pronounced the New England way unless your relative crawls, and, courtesy of my father, "a tomato is something you whistle at, a tomotto something you eat."

Had this been 1952 or 1962, we would have gotten married. It was 1972. I was twenty-four, Cissy twenty-one—both caught in the freedom that careened out of the 1960s after John Kennedy's brains were splattered over a limousine and the Beatles stepped off a Pan Am jet. We came of age when hair got longer and skirts shorter and you didn't have to be married to live together. Smoke this, snort that, follow the Tambourine man. You were on your own and it was hard to remain graceful.

Baseball lost its balance, too. The Yankees, as dependable as U.S. Steel, had their swan song in 1964. God, how I wanted the Orioles to catch them. I remember an August game when both clubs started rookies who didn't have twenty big league innings between them: Dave Vinyard and Mel Stottlemyre. Wouldn't you know the Yankees bring up an unknown and it's Mel Stottlemyre. Dave Vinyard's existence is confirmed by the *Macmillan Encyclopedia*.

Nineteen sixty-four was a summer of rookies. Tony Oliva and Tony Conigliaro. Two rookies. Two Tonies. One a Cuban who escaped on his brother's passport and won the batting title; the other a nineteen-year-old Massachusetts townie who hit the most home runs by a teenager and did it for the Red Sox. Talent and flash, a new world.

I was a rookie, too. I fell in love. It wasn't Cissy but a girl of the summer by Lake Ontario, where Arcturus hangs over the lake in August, and I had to stay close to Jack Lunman or some local with hair like Elvis would kick my ass because a Beatle haircut was regarded as an aphrodisiac.

It lasted two weeks. Two weeks before I headed back to prep school. All those high school years that weren't high school—no dates, only guys around, vertigo at the presence of girls—exploded in the minutes and hours behind sand dunes, under our raft, in Jack's car—it was doomed and I knew it—shelter, love, telling everything about myself—it was like discovering baseball—showing yourself, your real self, and being loved. She said I was different, said I could fuck her, took off her clothes—we didn't—but she meant it. I was loved. I was a goner. She went back to high school.

The next summer the magic, shelter, and sinful Eden were gone. She found someone else. If falling in love is religion based on a fallible god, I followed that lost August too long. Not that self-pity wasn't useful. I felt I had a 007 license to be a son of a bitch.

Nineteen sixty-five was bad for love but good for a Yankee hater. By the All-Star break, they were fading. Not just the pennant race, the dynasty. Mantle was hurt—old before his time—old because of his time—a man who whored and beaver shot and drank and courted the night like Babe Ruth himself—not because the boy was locked up and every night was a jailbreak—but because Mickey's father died young. Mutt Mantle died after Mickey's first year with the Yankees. Died after working in the tin mines, after giving up a minor league career for World War II, like a generation of guys—after naming his son for Mickey Cochran, and teaching the kid to switch hit, spending the daylight after work throwing tennis balls at him so Mickey wouldn't fear the ball. Mutt who, when Mickey wanted to quit baseball, said sure, come home and work ten hours a day in the mines with me. Mutt died and Mickey got drunk and cried for his dad and chased women with Billy Martin and acted the drunken hick— no dad but big league pussy, as Don Hoak once put it in a speech to a Triple A club. Big league pussy and big league whiskey, a triple crown, three MVPs, always in the World Series. Mickey Mantle, white god of the 1950s. A god when America had gods. When the enemy was communism and tooth decay—not racism, poverty, and ourselves. Elvis. Big cars. Big tits. Marilyn Monroe. Mickey Mantle. White trash done good—something they don't understand in New York but instinctively respect.

Why am I going on about Mickey Mantle? I hated Mickey Mantle. I hated the New York Yankees. They represented privilege, advantage— like having the right parents, going to Groton or Yale. I understood with a child's prescience that life was rigged, stacked in favor of WASPs (I, like, Mickey Mantle was one, but we were at different ends of the tribe), but baseball, baseball was different. With a child's understanding I knew football belonged to the strongest and most powerful—just like the biggest houses and biggest cars in Oyster Bay belonged to the richest. I couldn't compete. My family couldn't compete. No matter how snooty my mother was about neighbors who went to Paris for Christmas (they had four children; she hinted they might be Catholic), I knew she wanted Paris and couldn't have it. I didn't want it.

I wanted baseball. I fell in love with baseball the first time I batted because I knew no matter how ill equipped physically (I was skinny— looked like I'd just got down from the cross) or scared—I *was* scared— scared of everything: fastballs, Elvis, girls, fighting, dancing—but the batter's box was yours. If you swung, you might hit it. You! No big guy shoved you, no fat guy held you down, nobody took the ball away. Your chance. Scary. Magic.

The equal of anybody.

I fell in love with the Boston Red Sox.

Why?

Ted Williams.

He'd been in a war, two actually, though only one in combat. My father had been in Normandy and the Huertgen Forest, Grandpa lost a finger in Belgium, his father was shot through the ankle at Antietam and his boot rested on a bookcase in Scarsdale with a pencil through the path the minié ball took through Moreau Salisbury's ankle. I knew with the prescience of a lonely child I wanted baseball, not war. When I saw Williams's statistics, I was transfixed. Those numbers were from the solitary, egalitarian, god-chance of the batter's box. No one was better. No one playing in 1957. When I read his biography and learned of the two last-day-of-the-season pennant losses, the inability to beat the Yankees, the French salute for the Fenway press box, I knew—prescient again—this was me.

Ted Williams. Never getting what you want. Never getting what the world says you want. Alone, against history, against numbers.

Perfect.

I learned to love. I learned to love alone.

I was no more prepared for Cissy St. Claire than for Ted Williams—no more able to fend off an obsession with this representative of a world I tried to escape, thought I had, and then found myself hooked, lined, and sunk. I met her in prep school, at a dance I was chaperoning. My first reaction was Cissy was pretty—heavy top and hip, which I liked—thinness in women and patriotism are the most overrated commodities in America—she lied about her age, which was charming—and so began a long-distance courtship that would slip and slide, wane, ebb, but not go away. Cissy was the kind of girl I was supposed to marry, which was exactly what I wasn't looking for. It was 1965 and I was off to New College in Sarasota, off to a college without rules—a place completely in step with the times. No more prep school, no more mooning and dreaming and imagining sex. No more early 1960s. If you wanted to remake yourself, this was the time and place. Everyone at college was an intellectual or trying to be. I, Red Sox fan and contrarian, proclaimed my allegiance to baseball, *The Great Gatsby*, and Buddy Holly. I liked Dave Van Ronk and Dylan, too (must have played "Mr. Tambourine Man" a thousand times and the Palm Court, a square of royal palms at the intersection of the three I. M. Pei–designed dorms, remains the incarnation of evening's empire and those smoky ruins of time—part of me, part of everyone who went there, is still following the Tambourine man), but marijuana and LSD weren't Koufax, Marichal, or Frank Robinson.

In that little, licentious world, I experienced my best friend sleeping with my girlfriend, stayed in a relationship for the purpose of revenge, reduced a troubled girl to a wrist-slashing dropout, abandoned any pretense of relationships, went through a period of white Levis, starched shirts, and rabid promiscuity. Then the full bore of what we call "the sixties"—kicked out of college, draft physical, back in college, went to Europe, taught third grade in the Bronx for a draft deferment. From 1963 to 1972—Dallas to Watergate—my life ran with the energy of the times. Everyone's did.

I held onto baseball. I thought about Cissy.

My parents separated. The year of teaching in the Bronx was, as I liked to say about another endeavor, "No action but a million laughs." I learned a lot. The students provided endless commentary from the verbal epicenter of the streets. "You know how I can tell you're a white Spanish fool? By the hair." "They sued a teacher where I live. They even took his desk." "My cousin picked up a frog in Puerto Rico. He thought it was a sandwich." Call: "David, kiss my you-know-what." Response: "You don't got a clean one to kiss." I borrowed a television and one afternoon we watched the Mets finish the improbable 1960s with their improbable world championship. It was a time anything could happen.

Cissy happened.

The first time I saw Cissy after prep school was in Florida in 1966. She snuck out of her grandmother's condo on Delray Beach and informed me I hadn't brushed my teeth. She was wearing a nightgown and second base never was so lovely. We didn't see each other again until a rainy November weekend in New York in the hard year of 1968. I thought I was sophisticated, had seen enough lust and hurt and been taking care of myself long enough to handle anything. Cissy said she wasn't a virgin and I said, "Great," adding some bullshit like, "You don't want to be first and you don't want to be last."

I would be neither.

I thought the height of sophistication was taking Cissy to a dirty movie in Times Square. She was amused. This wasn't *Taxi Driver*. She had no qualms about sleeping with me and that made me nervous. Something I'd thought about for years was suddenly here but it wasn't love and I knew it and thought I'd be the last person to care about that but I did. I couldn't transcend the guarded, cynical casualness I hid behind—I suppose brittle cool was less cynical than proclaiming love and peace. Cissy was a sophomore at Vassar involved with a musician. (He had Cissy and her roommate the same day—it was Cissy's first time. She had pain but her pain hurt me—I didn't know what to do.) Then we were in bed. It was too easy. I played not to lose. Ted's moments of perfection—sanctuary, grail—were gone and I was lonelier than ever.

It wasn't bad. It wasn't good. It wasn't love. I tried to be the big stud, which meant doing it longer than anyone ever had. (Is that what I knew? Is it?) If I could have said how scared I was—scared because I liked her too much, thought about her too much, dreamed too much, rooted too much. If I'd told her she was beautiful naked, comforted her, understood, understood anything. Jesus Christ, she was lonely, too.

Cissy left on Sunday—everything wrong, nothing said. I talked the whole weekend. Put on my show: charming, funny, irresistible, irreplaceable (I probably talked longer than anyone), but hadn't said what I felt. Couldn't. I was sure I'd never see her again.

I wasn't a Red Sox fan for nothing. I nursed and replayed and relished the hurt. The Red Sox never won in New York when it counted either. Pain was as close to self-knowledge as I could manage. Never learned anything, never forgot anything. Who doesn't love his pain provided there isn't too much?

That we'd had sex made it sadder.

Two years went by. I taught, the Mets won, the lottery eliminated the draft. The Orioles were the AL power now. I spent a summer writing about teaching in the Bronx and a winter in Princeton, house-sitting for Cynthia Gooding, the folksinger. It was strange being back in Princeton, where I'd gone to prep school and met Cissy. Strange walking down snowy

Nassau Street no longer answerable to anyone—free, writing, and lonely—and then one Sunday afternoon, Cissy called, and said, "Cissy from a long time ago." It didn't feel like a long time. She said she could come for a few days and was going to California, where not one but two men from her Vassar days resided.

The weekend was powerful. I was still posing and talking, showing off, but something else happened, including Cissy's second orgasm (the first was in California accompanied by a rape fantasy). I couldn't believe the way I felt. It was the way you were supposed to feel—not words, not lust, not power. The night before Cissy left, she said, "Don't look at me like that." I was thrilled because no matter how stupid and puppy-dog I looked, I had shown it.

Cissy left and I saw the symmetry of the weekend in New York and the kindness now. That she came and went I took for the unavoidable order of things. I was, after all, a Red Sox fan. You can't have what you want but get close in a way no understands. Unhappy. Proud. It went extra innings.

Then Daisy Buchanan came back. Her grandmother gave her money and instead of returning to California and rape fantasies, Cissy came back to Princeton. I met her at the train. It was snowing. We lay on the couch and watched Errol Flynn in *Robin Hood* and Cissy fell asleep. Take from the rich. I didn't think life could be that good.

That night was my 1967. I dislike the epithet Impossible Dream because 1967 was no cliché. The American League had ten teams, and no matter the Red Sox were the weakest of four contenders, came in ninth the year before, had starters like Lee Stange and Darrell Brandon, survived the Dealey Plaza beaning of Tony Conigliaro, needed Dalton Jones and Gary Waslewski, got a preposterous throw from Jose Tartabull, a triple from Jim Landis, found Superman in left in September. It happened. They won. No divisions. No playoffs. It was 162 games and the last club standing went to the World Series. This was the penultimate year of baseball played for the long hunt and grind of the season, not for ratings in October with wild cards and 83-79 fools making the World Series. This was baseball like Ty Cobb and Nap Lajoie and Ed Walsh fighting it out in the wild four-team

1908 race, the Giant–Dodger death march in 1951, Red Sox and Yankees in 1949. This was a pennant race. This was baseball.

This was love. Or as close to love as I could get. I wrote in the morning, screwed in the afternoon, watched TV at night. It couldn't last—not because life can't be that good but because I had the princess in the tower—I was the only Red Sox fan again—studying Ted Williams's numbers alone in Oyster Bay. Who knows why we construct towers? Need, fear, fun, the Holy Ghost? How long do we live in them?

Cynthia Gooding came off the road and Cissy and I went to my father's house in Delray—not on the site of silky second base but a cinder-block house and studio next to a beach umbrella rental business on the wrong side of the Intracoastal. Dad was alone and without saying anything gave us his bedroom and slept on a door in his studio. I was finishing the book, living in fantasy, my personal 1967, but nothing is as perishable as paradise and the wolf was at the door. The wolf was jealousy. Cissy maintained contact with at least three old boyfriends, didn't hide it, said there was nothing to hide, but the past was there like ghosts, Scorpio was rising, Cissy wouldn't say she loved me, said she loved me as much as she could, and even a fool could see that wasn't enough. My father, in his diffident way, said Cissy would be trouble because she had nothing to do. Didn't have a career. I enlisted her to type and Cissy said all she was doing was fucking, typing, and cooking. Fantasy finds reality.

We moved to New York and I got a job working for the local school board in the district where I taught, got the apartment on Valentine, and tried to reestablish the tower. I had the princess all the way up in the Bronx. I had a good job, sent out the manuscript, started another book, studied *Who's Who in Baseball* like the Torah, and watched myself destroy the relationship. It was awful. Like the Phillies self-immolating in 1964. The Cubs bending over in 1969. Everything reminded me of her old boyfriends, including their phone calls, everything reminded me I hadn't taken her virginity. Everything reminded me I didn't have her. Where was the future? Where was I?

I didn't think of marrying her, her life, children.

Couldn't. Didn't. I tortured myself and tortured her. Why did I ask about that shit in the first place? It's not honesty; it's the wolf. I must have wanted the wolf because I invited him in. Invented him. In *The Natural* Robert Redford says, "I didn't see it coming." I saw it coming—everywhere, all the time. Cissy said it was a self-fulfilling prophesy. I remember a terrible fight in the cafeteria of the Museum of Modern Art. She got up and shouldn't have come back. What was it? The invisible. Me.

I had two models for disaster: *Lolita* and the Kennedy assassination. Perfect plots. Nabokov said all literature is fairy tale: hero, heroine, villain. Me, Cissy, me. After Humbert tells Lolita her mother is dead, he says, "You see, she had absolutely nowhere else to go." That's what I wanted— the doomed trip, the motels, sin, possession, the Bronx. Where were we going?

I told Cissy love was an open car ride through Dallas. Sit in the limousine, show your woman to the world. Then there's the Book Depository, Elm Street, and the Grassy Knoll.

No beautiful woman has no place to go. I knew she would leave. I didn't understand. Everyone else did.

Cissy got a job as a doctor's receptionist. He was thirty-four and married and I knew Claire Quilty had come for Lolita. Cissy told me the doctor had come on to the last receptionist. She said that ruined him for her, but I knew the wolf was here. When Cissy said how tongue-tied the doctor got when she corrected his grammar, I knew the UR-WASP had the little shit in tow.

I tried to bury us in the Bronx. I worshiped the past and the religion failed. I couldn't blame her. I believed in sex, I believed in looks, I believed in ghosts. I told her she'd never find anyone better looking, more interesting, more sexually suited to her body. Jake said, "She'll leave for someone worse."

Maybe he wasn't worse. He told Cissy he'd worked so hard and for what? His wife didn't appreciate him, excite him, the good husband and good son was old before his time and for what? I knew for what. What else would a nervous, little guy who wore undershirts and operated on people's feet work so hard for? His mother? So what if he had two kids and a wife who said, "I'm not really crying, it only looks like it," as he slipped away.

One night I saw his car parked two blocks from our apartment. They were talking—leaning into each other. I knew it was over. He had her attention. He had money. He wasn't crazy.

I confronted her and Cissy admitted there was "something," and now I tried, really tried, to fight a rearguard action. What I feared was here, it was midnight, my nose hit the mirror but instead of going wild or making threats or being the usual pain in the ass I said, "I'm going to Boston. I want to see opening day."

It was the first week of April. Cold in New York. Cold in my heart. Jake was in Boston. He was funny and a Red Sox fan and never slept, so for four days and four nights I talked and Jake listened. Jake had lost a girlfriend in November—he was obsessed and helpless, saw betrayal as inevitable and the inevitable as comic. We talked about Cissy, the Red Sox, and the Major League Players Association, which was threatening a strike. It didn't seem possible. No baseball was like no Easter—how could it not be there when I needed it so much?—but Marvin Miller was about to impact the game like Babe Ruth.

We walked up Marlboro Street through the Back Bay to Fenway Park on a misty afternoon hoping somehow the strike would be called off—how could they not have opening day?—and stood alone in front of the locked ticket offices.

Jake said my only chance was to forgive her and start over. He didn't believe it but he said it. What are friends for? I went back to the Bronx.

I said the right thing. I told Cissy I understood whatever she did she had to do, that I would go to a psychiatrist, church, anything to stop being jealous—anything, anything, anything, if she wouldn't leave.

She left the next day.

Baseball started. The commissioner decided the schedule would be played from the day the games started. No adjustment. The Red Sox played one game fewer than the Tigers.

They lost the division by half a game.

28. The Roberto Clemente Fictions

Rick Campbell

This is the first thing I say I remember about my life: I am standing in the backyard of our row house, age three or four, hitting stones toward the railroad tracks that parallel the Ohio River and Conway Yards, the huge corral of coal cars and tankers that rumbled and clanked all night while Baden was trying to sleep. My mother told me that my grandfather, a player in his day, saw me trying to hit my stones with a stick and went to the store to buy me a little bat. If this is true, then my baseball life started in 1955 or 1956, about the same time Roberto Clemente hit the Major Leagues and started making legends.

Roberto Clemente is at the center of everything I love about baseball, but my grandfather invented baseball for me (and maybe fiction, too). The facts of my grandfather's life are all fuzzy, often woven loosely around things and events that when explored turn out to be false. To be kind, my grandfather wasn't always sure about his facts; that's probably the family reckoning of his story. In actuality, some cold finality that might be this essay, he lied a lot about his life. He embellished it, made it better and more heroic; he denied and forgot the messy, failed, and cruel things. The problem was that he had no license to change or disguise his life. He didn't write stories whose lack of accuracy could be forgiven because of elapsed time and the accumulation of data. In town the old men knew Charlie Campbell as a bullshitter, but it didn't seem to hurt his reputation or him. Who really cared what he did and didn't do? He was just a street corner, bar stool bullshitter, and in our valley, he was far from the only one. But to his family it mattered more—his lack of accuracy in facing up to what he'd done as a father and a husband. These things filtered down the family grapevine, for us, a tangled and gnarled thing, a dark vineyard so poorly tended that there are no stories directly handed down, no truths, no promises, no trust. So I say these things about my grandfather—that he was cruel to my father, violent and arbitrary in his discipline, and that he resented my grandmother's whining, clinging, dominance of his life.

Something, maybe love, made him come to live in my grandmother's hometown, made him leave a job in East Liverpool and spend his life trying to find satisfying work in the Beaver Valley mills. He drank too much and sometimes became violent with his wife, a slap, a punch maybe, and that drove his daughters away from him. He squandered the money his second son sent home from his time in the military. He spent a few too many hours on those bar stools. He didn't live up to his family's expectations, and he probably never lived up to his own either.

By the time I came to know my grandfather none of his children respected him and wanted anything to do with him. I loved him. It's true that I saw him drunk once or twice, sprawled on a stoop when my father had to go get him, but it didn't hurt me. He wasn't my father and I didn't have a reputation and ego that would be damaged by a stoop-sprawling father. And, mostly, he stopped drinking before I came to spend a lot of time with him. So though he was a sad and broken man long before he was an old sad and broken man, I didn't know him that way.

I knew him as the one who played checkers with me, who sat on a blanket-covered cedar chest and told me stories as he watched long coal barges work the river. He was still working at Valvoline Oil when I used to wait for him to come home; I'd look out the smaller, side window of their bedroom, the one my grandmother sat at when both windows were being used, and watch him get off the four o'clock bus, cross State Street by the drugstore, walk up the sidewalk, black lunch box in hand. When he disappeared from my sight I would go out into the hall of their building and wait at the landing as he slowly climbed the stairs.

For most of the 1960s—he retired in 1963—they both sat at their windows when the weather was cold and watched State Street's meager activities. Grandpa looked out at the doctor's office and the theater; Grandma could see the drugstore and Overholt's grocery. They spent a whole decade watching a slow town's life; our town only had three thousand people, but it was enough, it seems, to satisfy them. They were especially interested in who visited Dr. Coffey, especially as their friends got old enough to both see the doctor frequently and lose their battles with age. Grandpa had a better shot of the river and the mill so his vision was sometimes broader. He was often lost in the longer story, the silent rhythms of the river, the fires burning in the mill, the smoke rising from its stacks. He kept a small pair of binoculars on his sill so that he could see the numbers of a barge or get a better look at a train running to or from Conway Yards. He was content, after he retired, to spend hour upon hour at that window; Grandma would leave to tend to her housework, but Grandpa had nothing else to do. He didn't drive and he only walked to the barber for a haircut. For years he wasn't allowed out alone because he would stop at a bar. Their only change of venue was when they sat in the carport during warm summer nights; their constant companion then was Bob Prince and Pirate baseball games.

It was so normal to see them sitting in their windows that still, on my once-every-five-years trip down State Street, I look up at the windows ready to wave at them, expecting to see faces that, I think now, must have been sadly waiting for something to happen.

This grandfather that I loved and listened to so intently when I was a small child turned out to be quite a liar, an embellisher of the truth. My father told me that Grandpa didn't arrest dangerous crooks when he was the town constable—I'm not even sure now that he was the town constable—and that he didn't lead labor strikes at the oil plant. He claimed to have done these things and more, but as I grew older I began to listen more closely; I realized that the stories often contradicted each other. One time the Shoops lived on Bryan Avenue, next time they're up on Dippold. By the time I was a teenager he was telling conflicting stories all of the time. By the time he'd reached his eighties the conflicts came fast and furious; each day at dinner brought almost the same story. He didn't remember what he'd said the day earlier and unfortunately his new version wasn't any more interesting than the old one. But by then his stories seemed so inconsequential and boring that I never bothered to correct him; my father, however, seemed to have lost what little patience he'd had and would slam his fork down on the table and tell us exactly which Pfeiffer boy married which Shoop girl and then everyone would eat in silence for a few moments. By this time maybe I was too old to hear the baseball stories, or since I was the only one who had ever listened to them, and I had not been around or been listening for many years, Grandpa seemed to have dropped them from his repertoire. Now, I see that only his baseball stories matter to me; they are my sense of him, my stories of my childhood, and a part of the story of myself.

If my grandfather lied about most things, which he seemed to do, how do I know that he really was a baseball player? I have my reasons. Most importantly, I need him to have been a baseball player, and that need alone might be enough reason to believe. But I believe he was for many reasons. He never claimed to be better than he could have been. He claimed that he was a good sandlot, semipro ballplayer who got a pro offer from the Cleveland Indians. I don't know when the offer came, and I don't know if I ever knew, but I assume it was before he married my grandmother in 1921. He claimed that the Indians made a lukewarm offer and that he was making more money playing ball in the mill leagues and working in the mill during the week. Certainly at that time this part of his story could be true; he didn't claim to turn down a big bonus and even the stars didn't make much money then. Mill teams were quite common in Ohio and Pennsylvania; there's no reason to suppose that he didn't play a little semipro ball. How good was he, that's the real question. I don't know. He was a wiry man who looked, for most of his life, as though he was in good enough shape to play a doubleheader. He had a different body than my father, brother, and I did; we are all rather round and fat like my grandmother. No one that I know or knew saw him play in those mill leagues, so I have only this to go on.

Once when I was about twelve—it was soon after my grandfather had retired in 1963—we were playing ball at the Little League field and he was taking one of his "walks down street." He came up to the field to see if anyone was there; he was Baden's first Little League coach and he felt a sense of propriety about the field, even though the field we were on that day was nothing but woods where he hunted rabbits in his coaching days. He watched us for a while and since we were just fooling around, playing Indian ball or something less than a real game, he asked if he could hit some. The other kids didn't think this old man was going to hit anything worth catching, but they indulged him because he was my grandfather and because in those days in Baden, Pennsylvania, kids were still polite to their elders. He grabbed a bat, surely too small and light for him, and someone started lobbing him some meatball pitches. After a couple of rusty cuts, a miss, a slow grounder, the kids in the outfield started rolling their eyes. Then he got his timing and ripped one into left field. Things changed. He hit some good long flies that we ran down and then hit a couple over the fence. He apologized because he was only trying to hit us flies we could catch, not make us climb the fence and shag balls in the weeds, but he couldn't keep them in, balls kept going over the left-field fence, so he switched and started hitting lefty. After the first couple of grounders, balls started flying over the right-field fence. That was even more of a problem since the woods were thick there and the hill fell away sharply into deeper woods and brambles. After we lost three balls and there were more of us outside the fence looking for balls than inside fielding, he finally quit.

I never saw him hit again, but I still see him with a swing that's graceful and seemingly effortless, popping balls over the fence, and I think that if he could hit like that forty years after his prime, maybe he had been good, good enough. I know it's hardly infallible and that there's a whole lot of distance between a good sandlot swing and the pros, but because he hit like that, because a home run is a home run and because I have always wanted to believe his baseball stories, I have kept these stories true.

He had two types of baseball stories: those that he witnessed or heard and those that he participated in—call them fan's stories and player's stories. Though he was the hero of the latter, it was really the stories of the Major League games that were most important. Whether we are playing or watching, there is an intimacy in baseball, a handed-down sense of myth, a universal language of emotion and experience. Those who tell baseball stories, and, more important, those who listen to them, live for the moment of the story in a world defined only by baseball—a forgiving world, a world of suspended disbelief and shared experience. The baseball storyteller is taken out of the stands, out of that one game that only he saw or heard, and is placed in the context of baseball games and base-

ball stories. The awe, the exultant qualities of the story and its characters are such that they are romantic and heroic, but believable and intimate as our family stories, our life stories. Maybe baseball stories even
substitute for our life stories; for my grandfather and me they did, but I
suspect that this is true for far more people than just us.

My grandfather floated above his stories like the Goodyear blimp; the
camera and the mike dropped down to the field of play capturing scenes
and lines, facial gestures and sighs that no camera, no mike, could have seen
or heard. Just as new journalism gave its subjects the status of characters,
allowed them to think thoughts, recorded dialogue no journalist heard,
and rendered the inner consciousness reserved for fiction, my grandfather's baseball stories and the other good baseball stories I have heard
have this aura of infallible plausibility. If what was seen didn't really happen, it could have. If what was said wasn't really heard (or said), it should
have been. It was right for the story, the players, the game. Perhaps that's
the metanarrative of baseball working: the thing that allows baseball
stories to be, like myth, believed, remembered, revered, and that's what
makes them useful to us as a people.

So I understand that my grandfather's baseball stories of his exploits
are probably exaggerated, and that everything he claims to have seen he
may have only heard about or read in the papers, but I need to believe that
in essence, at their core, his stories are true. I extend the same courtesy
to myself, sort of; I know that everything I claim to have seen Roberto
Clemente do I could not have witnessed with my eyes, but I have no
doubt that Clemente, and sometimes some other Pirate—Billy Virdon,
Bill Mazeroski, Dick Stuart, Smoky Burgess—did what I claim that they
have done. The stories are true; the perspective of the narrator may be
off. I need my grandfather's baseball stories, and I need my own stories
because I want to believe I'm not lying and I want to believe that I am a
part of the legends I live in and through.

His stories about the games he saw in Cleveland or Pittsburgh, or the
games he heard, almost always involved players long before my time. I
heard more Nap Lajoie stories than any kid my age. Like most of us, the
stories from his younger years carried more weight with him and were

told more often and better. Though he had lived for forty years twenty miles down river from Pittsburgh and Forbes Field, almost all of his stories took place in Cleveland and involved the Indians, the team of his Ohio youth. So though I was, and am, a Pirate fan only, I grew up on Cleveland Indian and American League stories. When I bought baseball cards I had a special affinity for Rocky Colavito, Bob Lemon, and Herb Score, and could pick them up cheap in trade since none of my friends paid attention to the Indians or the American League—except Mickey Mantle; everyone paid attention to Mantle.

For most stories my grandfather rarely said who was calling the game, rarely made it clear whether he was on the family farm around Salem or in the stands at Municipal Stadium. So for the terrible story of Herb Score being smashed by a line drive up the middle, I'm there because my grandfather told his story as though he was there, as though he could see every pitch and smell the peanuts. But really neither of us is there because it's 1959 and I know where both of us were—Beaver Valley.

My favorite spectator story and maybe his, too, if the number of times I heard it is any indication of affection, is the Walter "Big Train" Johnson story. In this tale Johnson strikes a batter out without throwing the ball. It's as vivid and true a story to me as other kids' *Little Engine That Could* or Mother Goose. In the Big Train story Walter Johnson is on the mound. I've forgotten who was catching or hitting. The setting is important; *it's the ninth inning of a game that's gone late into the afternoon. The sun had dropped behind the stadium facade and home plate is deep in shadow.* It's not a time when a batter wants to hit a 98 MPH fastball and apparently not a time when an umpire can really see one either. Maybe whoever was batting was the variable that changed with each telling: who struck out on a ball not thrown is irrelevant; who threw the ball not thrown is important. *It's getting dark; two outs, the ump's ready to go home. Johnson throws his first pitch, a pitch so fast the batter barely sees it and doesn't swing. Strike one, says the plate ump. The poor batter just mumbles something, steps out of the box, and slowly steps back in.* There are no signals for this. *Strike two smacks into the catcher's mitt as the batter edges away from the plate.* It's clear that no fastball is going to be hit this afternoon. *The catcher calls time and walks to the mound, says something quickly and walks back. He settles behind the plate and the batter steps in.* Anyone ought to be afraid of Big Train Johnson's fastball that, in this twilight, you can hear but not see, and this guy is, but he's a Major League ballplayer, a hitter, and he can't admit it. *Johnson goes into a bigger and slower than ever wind-up. Big kick, in the dark everything is faraway, distorted, exaggerated, and then the ball explodes into the mitt. When the batter looks back and down, there's the ball, knee high, outside corner. He turns slowly to the ump and says, "Jesus, I didn't even see it." "Neither did I," says the ump, as he walks away, mask in hand, already slipping off his chest protector.*

As many times as I heard that story, I don't recall it prefaced by a year, a season, even a locale. I don't know if Johnson was at home or on the road. I don't know if it happened in Cleveland, though I think it didn't. It doesn't matter, except to the statistician, to those among us, or that place inside us, which lacks faith. For them, for us, some fact will give us a crowbar of doubt, something to tear the story down and turn it into the misery of daily lives where we think every fact is true and necessary, where a fact is a speeding car running a red light and we're the pedestrian who just stepped off the curb forgetting to look both ways.

Perhaps the crucial story in my baseball fiction life is one in which my grandfather is playing center field for a mill team against a barnstorming team of black ballplayers led by Satchel Paige and Josh Gibson. Most of the stories that feature my grandfather as a player take place in eastern Ohio, around East Liverpool, Zanesville, or Youngstown. The Gibson story takes place in Youngstown at Idora Park, an amusement park known to my generation for its wicked roller-coaster. As a kid I made a couple of trips there for American Bridge or Jones and Laughlin's company picnics, and I looked for the ballpark, though I can't remember if I ever found it. It's possible that it was already torn down as other ball fields were built and semipro ball lost its wide appeal.

This story, before it reaches the magical climax, has a touch, however small, that lends weight to the tale's believability. Grandpa always claimed to have faced Paige only once in this game and to have struck out.

Most liars would have at least made contact—lined out, a deep fly. Those addicted to the lie and the glory would have claimed to have ripped a hit off Paige, especially if the story was being told to a child. My grandfather struck out; no long foul balls, just went down swinging. His Gibson story went like this: *It's getting dark, the Idora Park roller-coaster is casting strange, giant shadows over the field. It's the ninth inning.* There are, as in all myths and folktales, a set of constructs that are more or less common in each tale, no matter the subject. The setting of the ninth inning (or last inning), two outs, is probably the most common expression of time in a baseball tale. Before the era of lights and night games, dusk or near darkness was a time when strange events could occur. The ball is harder to see; it plays tricks on the eyes. The players and umpires are tired and sometimes want the game to end. Both of these constructs play an integral part in this tale. Ninth inning, two outs, maybe runners on base, maybe not. It doesn't matter because the score doesn't matter, winning or losing isn't being measured here. The white boys of the mill team had little chance of winning this game and they knew it; they probably had their butts kicked. They'd spent the day striking out against Paige and running down doubles and triples. They would have watched helplessly as Cool Papa Bell stretched every single into a double and then streaked home on the next base hit. They played because they loved to play. So though we never know the score, it has to be the top of the ninth since the barnstormers would be winning and the mill boys are the home team. Gibson steps to the plate. Deep in center field where the shadows arch across summer-brown grass, my grandfather stands waiting.

The base umpire, a mill hunk like most of the guys, is hot and tired and ready to go home. He's worked hard for a few bucks; it's almost over and he's not about to hustle anywhere. That's when Gibson cranks a shot deep into left-center; it's rising through the shadows like a bird in flight, rising still as it goes over my grandfather's head. He knows he'll never get it but he turns and races into the dusk; the farther he runs the farther he gets from the tired ump who is still standing behind second base looking up into the sky. My grandfather, by his own admission, could run like a deer, but no deer, no cheetah even, is going to catch this one so here's where the magic twist comes in. My grandfather has a ball in his hip pocket, Lord knows why. As he runs deeper and deeper into the shadows he reaches back, grabs the ball and flips it into the air, hardly missing a stride, and then he leaps high and backhands this ball as it comes down. He flashes a white blur in his web as he runs back toward the ump and the tired, maybe now confused man, calls Gibson out. Gibson is stunned; he's already trotted around second. The game and the story just sort of fade away here. I've never heard if there was an ensuing argument, if anyone ever discovered the ruse. Maybe it didn't matter, maybe the barnstormers were so far ahead no one really cared whether Gibson had been robbed. More likely, the black players knew not to put up a fight with a bunch of white guys, white umps, and white fans in a white ballpark. They probably just picked up their stuff and went back to their bus. I'd like to think that Gibson had some small respect for the trick that had been played on him, but that's not part of the story. Grandpa's climax is on the catch. For me, the ball is still flying over Youngstown's dirty skyline.

I have my own baseball stories. Some of them might be completely true, but none of them is a lie. I sort of know how these things work now. My spectator stories usually involve Roberto Clemente, call them the Roberto Clemente Fictions, because they can't all be completely true.

Clemente is like my fish in the apocryphal fishing tale—his exploits get bigger and bigger while I claim to have seen more and more of them. It's probably true that they happened, that he did the things in the stories. In a sense, the narrator is unreliable; the narrator, me, doesn't know for sure what he saw and what he only heard. Most of the Clemente stories are hearsay gathered from my grandfather, radio, newspaper, and poorly remembered TV games. I was more of a Clemente anthropologist than a liar or a writer. I gathered the tales and carried them with me to lands far from Pittsburgh where the audience had not grown up watching Clemente play right field. The farther I went in space and time, the more the tales became my own telling, the more the original tellers dropped from my narrative. After a few years had gone by, no one in my audience was likely to have seen Forbes Field, heard Bob Prince, or even, in this new millennium, seen or heard of Roberto Clemente.

So the Clemente fictions become more and more mine. There is less reason to slow the tale with disclaimers, to throw out historical oddities about Bob Prince, to explain when Forbes Field was torn down (unless I want to show off and say that my wife saw the last game there and her father has a brick from the wall). None of these things is necessary to the narrative and each telling assumes more power told in the first person with the narrator present, watching the action. And as I move more and more into the first person, as I become present at each event, it makes my life richer and makes me seem more interesting. I try not to embellish the tale with too much setting, try not to say that I'm on the right-field line, just a few rows from the screen, or that I can see the wind ruffling the ivy on the left-field wall and swaying the trees in Schenley Park. That's fiction. I don't even know for sure that I am there, so I just say that *Clemente goes back to the wall near the 375 sign in right-center, picks up the ball, whirls, and throws a strike, knee high, on a line, home.* The runner is not only out, but he stops two-thirds of the way down the line and stands in a stunned silence, looking out to right, trying to figure out what just happened. Smoky Burgess (I use Smoky because I like the name) walks down the line and tags him gently. Smoky also isn't sure if what just happened was real and he holds the ball as if it might be a holy icon from the arm of Roberto.

For Clemente it is his arm that is most miraculous. Ruth had a home run swing; power is the word of his stories. For Clemente his arm is superhuman; his hitting, fielding, base running, all of these were performed at superstar level, but his arm is the stuff of myth. Most of the stories, then, involve a throw. Another goes like this—again he is at the base of the right-field wall where he unleashes a throw home. It doesn't look like a throw because it keeps rising and rising, more like a rocket than a throw, more like a ball hit into the gap than thrown from it. It's flying home. The catcher doesn't leap, just turns like an outfielder to watch the ball go into the stands, maybe ten or twenty rows up. The ball, they figure, goes maybe 425 feet. Nowadays it would be a tape measure home run that we would see for a week on ESPN. Then it was an error and a miracle.

In one Clemente story I always leave the original narrator, announcer Jim Woods, in my tale. I need him because the theme of this story is how Clemente excites even those who see him every day to a state sometimes beyond words. Woods was Bob Prince's sidekick, a good play-by-play man, one whose calm, quiet style was always overshadowed by the flashy Prince. On this day, an ordinary game, the Pirates are playing, let's say, the Dodgers. It's after the Dodgers have moved to California, and before ESPN resurrects West Coast baseball, so no one outside of Brooklyn really cares about the Dodgers anymore. The game is officially dull. There's a runner on first and someone singles to right, not a line drive at Clemente but something he has to cut off; the third base coach thinks that his runner ought to be able to get to third. Almost any runner ought to be able to get to third on a hit like this. Woods takes over: *the runner's trying for third* (a note of disbelief has crept into Woods's voice; someone is running on Clemente), *here comes the throw* (his voice is rising, excited, he sees more than he can say; he means here comes this thing across the infield, stretched like a five-foot-high rope from right field, whistling as it flies). The third baseman is squaring up, readying himself for a play that he cannot believe he'll have. The runner sees the third baseman and knows it's not a decoy; the coach's eyes say get down before the words come out and the runner hears the ball coming. Woods knows this, sees this, but doesn't have time to say it, so his voice rises in intensity with each word: *Here comes the throw, it's going to be close. He's out. Oh, what a throw, what a throw. O Lord, what a throw. They should never, never, never, run on Roberto Clemente.* Woods is shouting, almost crying. He can't stop himself. It's not the World Series, not even a pennant race. This throw doesn't even win the game. It's just Roberto Clemente reaffirming his place in legend. Everyone is delirious that the runner took a chance and ran on Clemente, ran on a ball that no other outfielder alive could have possibly thrown him out on. I hear Woods still. I know that he's just seen a miracle, as if the Virgin of Guadalupe had appeared on second base. Woods was in awe, scared of what he'd just seen and what it did to him. He's scared of being driven into rapture by a throw to third in a game that doesn't matter.

There's only one story of Clemente as batter that I tell. He was a great hitter, as everyone knows. He was exciting even when he swung and missed because he would swing so hard he twisted around and sometimes fell to the ground, as if he was supplicating himself, throwing himself to the earth in front of the baseball gods, begging for another pitch, another try. This story also takes place in Forbes Field; Forbes Field is as much a character in these stories as are Clemente, Mazeroski, Dick Stuart, Billy Virdon, and Willie Stargell. Forbes Field was 465 feet to dead center field; it was so far out there that the Pirates stored the batting cage on the field and had a statue of Honus Wagner at the inside base of the wall. Balls were rarely hit 465 feet by anyone. In my story, Clemente swings and is fooled by the pitch; his left hand flies off the bat and he follows through with only his right. The ball flies off the bat, a low line drive, eight or nine feet high, straight out to center field. But it never comes down or slows down and clears the fence, 465 feet away, on the same line.

Center field is the heart of the game. Center field is the place where the magical realism of baseball emanates. It has no foul lines, no boundaries, no place where it ends and right or left field begins. On my sandlot fields in Pennsylvania we often had no fences and center field could go on into infinity. I remember once playing on a field in the hills above our town—in the Borough of Economy, where everything was only a few years removed from farms and pasture—that had no fences. Beyond the grass of center field the earth fell into a field of cattails and tall weeds; someone hit a ball deep into center, a ball that rose and slowly sailed over everyone's head. Ralph took off after it, ran straight toward the cattails and then disappeared. After a moment, we could see his glove above the cottony fiber, the cattails parting and bending as he waded through; that glove seemed to sail on a predestined line of intersection for the place where the ball was always meant to come down and then the ball, in fact, landed in the glove. Ralph came out of the weeds covered with pollen and cattail dust, a dazed look on his face, the ball clutched in his glove like a baby bird he had just saved from the sky. I think we quit then and went home. And though Ralph never spoke anyway, because his harelip scar had made him quiet, he sat in the backseat of the car stunned, like someone slowly reentering the world after a time away in another land.

In my memories of my childhood, the only thing that was never bad, the only thing consistent, to be trusted, always, was baseball.

On that same Little League field that my grandfather put on his hitting exhibition, I sometimes got to be a star, too. Sometimes, not often. When I was nine and playing Little League I was often overmatched by a big twelve-year-old with a good fastball. I'd sometimes go hitless, maybe strike out a couple of times. When I'd come home after a game like that, even if I'd managed one hit, my father would ask how I'd done, and if I'd say that I struck out twice he would grow, not quite angry, but in a way that I now think unnecessarily cruel, rather disgusted. Why can't you hit? Why aren't you any good, he seemed to be saying. This reaction from a man that I now know wasn't particularly interested in or good at any sport. Someone who had *not* taught me to play baseball. He was a man who didn't have a childhood of games. He worked as soon as he was old enough to deliver papers, milk, anything. Maybe he shunned baseball because his father liked it so much. When my grandfather spoke of the men in town that he coached, my father wasn't one of them. I asked about that once, and I remember Grandpa saying that Dad could have been a good ballplayer, if he had wanted to be. But I think it was just a grandfather wanting to say something good about his grandson's father.

I saw my father play once and he had the look of someone who didn't play baseball very often or very well. It was at a company picnic, and I was watching the men and older boys play softball. It was mill hunks at play, their one game of the year and they were going to hit hard, throw hard, and run hard until they got too tired, too drunk, or hurt themselves. Usually some combination of the above ended a game. My father played his one game of the year, too. He was powerful but awkward. Fast, but out of control. He swung too hard and rarely hit the ball square. This time he nailed one and drove it into the gap; it seemed to shock him and the outfielders as it bolted across the dirty grass and rolled toward a picnic shelter. My father took off toward first but he was never really under control; he never recovered from the force of his swing. After he turned second everything seemed to give way, he began to lean like a wheelbarrow when the load shifts and then his barrel chest and big belly sent him toppling into the dirt where he rolled over a few times and finally lay sprawled about twenty feet from third base. He was down on his face, sweat-soaked T-shirt streaked with dirt, when the ball finally came in from right and someone tagged him out.

For a couple of years I spent a lot of time trying to justify my strike-outs and not getting credit for my hits. He never came to a game and I suppose I was secretly thankful for that; I wasn't subjected to on-the-spot humiliation and many times he would forget or not know that I had a game. When I was twelve my turn came to be the oldest player and get some hits. We won almost every game. We had a great team; many of us, myself included, hit .500 or better. Suddenly, near the middle of the season, there was my father in the stands. I don't know why he came. I was playing third so I could see him sitting across from me every time I looked at first base. I think I was angry that he had intruded into the good part of my life.

He almost ruined that game. I was nervous the first two times I came to bat and didn't get a hit. My third at bat was one of those fantasy situations: *last inning, tie score, two outs, runner on second*, and I'm up. But there was my father in the stands. Our coach came down the line, called me to him and put his arm around my shoulder: you can do it, he said, or something else encouraging and mindless. Something any good coach or father should say. I lined a shot into left center, a low line drive that never got more than four feet off the ground but shot out to the fence and drove home the winning run. I was the hero. I got my hugs or punches, whatever sufficed in the world before high fives, and we all ran to the concession stand for our free ice cream sandwiches. Then my dad came over and offered to give me a ride home and I said no I'm walking with Billy. So he offered us both a ride home and I said we always walk. We walked and it was a great walk. Billy and I replayed our victory and my status as hero was cemented, at least for that day. Billy probably never knew that it was just as important to me to be walking in the woods and not riding in my father's car as it was to get the hit that won the game.

During the summer I turned fifteen I lived in Florida but I was back in Pennsylvania, supposedly visiting my father, according to the terms of the legal separation. Really I was there to see my friends and play baseball. In the mornings, right after breakfast, I would meet those coming down from the other end of town and we would walk to the American Legion field in Tevebaugh Hollow. We had outgrown the Little League field's meager fences, but the Legion field's fences seemed miles away. Our games were full of triples and inside the park home runs. We would play until late afternoon, until it was time to begin the trek home for dinner. After dinner three of us, Bob, Gary and I, would wait on the corner by the dairy store for a ride back to the ball field we would play on that night. We were the only kids allowed to play with older boys and men who played their sandlot games after their mill shifts were over. Tom would pick us up and drive us to whatever field, in Ambridge, Conway, Freedom, Rochester, we could find for that night. I played shortstop with these guys and I knew then that I was a baseball player because the guys who rolled into the dirt parking lots in their cars were like heroes to me. Good players, most of them, who treated me as if I was one of them.

One day, when Bob and I both hit home runs over the left-field fence, 325-foot shots that we liked to tell ourselves would have cleared Forbes Field in right (except for that screen), we were initiated into the club reserved for Tom, our third baseman and best hitter, and Don, a good-looking, long, blond guy whose father owned a car lot so he always got to drive fancy cars. Don was smooth and graceful. He played shortstop for one side and I for the other. He looked better than I did out there, but with Tom covering my backhand, together we got everything Don did and then some. Now I was like them. I didn't know that that was as good as I would get.

That summer my father, baseball, and I crashed together. He was angry that I spent so much time, especially evenings, playing ball. I hardly saw him. On the weekends when he and his girlfriend went to our camp on Lake Pymatuning, I said I was staying home to play ball. That was true, but mostly I didn't want to be with him and the girlfriend. I didn't want to acknowledge their lives, to lend some tacit unspoken approval to the relationship that had driven my mother to a nervous breakdown and us to Florida.

Finally, on the last weekend before I was to go back to Florida, we had our fight. Usually, maybe every time before this, it had been his fight, his anger, his outburst. I told him I didn't want to go to the lake, that I was going to play baseball, and he exploded. He didn't pay for me to come up and play baseball, he yelled. Maybe because I had been accepted that summer so wholeheartedly by the older guys, maybe because I knew for sure, without a doubt, that I was a good baseball player, maybe for just a moment, a glimmer of emotional time, which in the history of my father and me is a long, slow, sad, procession, I was stronger—I stood up and said, "You'll never have to pay to get me up here again," and walked out of the room. It was as good as that first homerun. It's still one of the few moments with my father in which I was not afraid, not intimidated.

Baseball reminds me of how lucky we have to be, good timing is required, that it takes a fortuitous combination of faith and desire to make us happy, to live good lives, to be good to those we love in the lives we live.

29. Trading Heroes

Jeffrey Higa

The only baseball card I ever coveted was of a first baseman for the Atlanta Braves named Mike Lum. This was in 1976, the prime of my baseball card trading years, when I was at the top of my game both in experience and skills. I was a veteran trader from as far back as second grade and had amassed an awesome collection that spanned three decades and almost as many shoe boxes. Although I was consulted a lot on other people's trades—What do you think about being offered a Whitey Ford in his declining years for a 1973 Vida Blue and Rollie Fingers?—like an experienced criminal attorney, I was approached in the most serious trades, by someone wanting to trade up for my rookie Mantle or prewar Williams, for example. I often used my reputation of fear and intimidation to negotiate my exchanges.

At W. O. Gladden Elementary in Kansas City, the only person in the fifth grade who could barter as an equal was my friend Jimmy, who initiated me into the world of baseball card commerce. He was the middle brother from a family of three boys, and the only one in a family of Sicilian descent whose hair was not dark brown but firecracker red, a trait that had last surfaced from the genetic drift in a nearly forgotten aunt from the old country. I've always thought it was this red hair that accounted for the bravado in his personality that I admired. Outside of my peers, I was a quiet kid, but Jimmy was a ribber among kids, grown-ups, friends, and strangers. He could not let a situation pass without comment, and he often ventured into the good, bad, and inappropriate for a laugh. He was fearless about making fun of everyone to their faces, even his parents, an action in my family that would have been akin to condemning myself to death.

He was one of my oldest friends more by happenstance than by devotion, since both our fathers were officers in the air force and worked in the same unit. As a result, our families were sometimes stationed together at the same base, moving in tandem at the will of the air force. He joked that I had to remain his friend because my dad worked for his dad, and "You gotta suck up to the boss's son." But in reality, he was the only friend I had known longer than two years, the typical duration of my father's postings.

Perhaps because Jimmy was my baseball card mentor, he was also my fiercest opponent. He had a completely dispassionate attitude about baseball cards. In his hands, the cards were mere commodities, the players just value indicators like the designs on a bill, for the part that really interested him, the transaction. He was a consummate capitalist with a robber-baron mentality that even grown-ups could recognize. Once, sitting in the back of my family's station wagon, we were trying to complete our fifth grade homework. We were discussing a problem that had stumped us for miles: "$\frac{1}{4}+\frac{1}{4}+\frac{1}{10}=?$" when from the driver's seat my dad asked, "If I gave you two quarters and one dime, how much money would you have?"

"Sixty cents," Jimmy said instantly.

My dad, raised in a generation that taught that sons could learn all they needed by silence rather than explication, paused to let this lesson sink in.

"Six-tenths," I said finally in amazement at my dad's creativity. "That's our answer, Jimmy, six-tenths."

But I could tell Jimmy didn't get it. He was still looking at my dad, thinking about the sixty cents that might be coming to him.

If I had one liability as a trader, it was a touch of sentimentality, a penchant that drove me occasionally to make irrational trades—like a 1954 Bob Feller for a Vince DiMaggio—just so I could complete the DiMaggio brothers trio: Vince, Dom, and Joe. Jimmy knew this about me and exploited my weakness to the fullest. Rather than deal with specific trades of such-and-such player for his Mike Lum, he instead dealt in options: Since it was obvious that he was the only one I knew who owned—what was his name again? Ah, yes, card #208 Mike Lum—he would be willing to trade said card #208, for two . . . no, better make it *three* cards of his choosing from my entire collection. Such was the brutality of his methods.

I never told Jimmy directly that I wanted the card, but with the instincts of a used car salesman, he had surmised my desire from the feigned disinterest I tried to show the card every time I thumbed through his collection. If I didn't pause to look at it, he would wait until I was well past the card before he fished it out of the stack again, parading it in front of me, wondering aloud why I wanted that card so much. And who wouldn't wonder? As a baseball card, it was nothing special, it wasn't an action shot from an actual game like the 1976 Johnny Bench, just up from his crouch, mask off, rising from the dust after making a play at the plate. The Mike Lum card was a staged figure card in the most generic of poses: Standing in the field, not even at the plate, the bat resting on his shoulder, with an indifferent grin aimed at the camera. It exuded none of the fierce competitiveness I associated with professional baseball. Even in Lum's best year of 1973, when he batted .294, with 82 RBIs and 16 home runs, that card in mint condition commands only a humble fifty cents. Not exactly an investment-grade instrument.

As a player, Mike Lum wasn't any great shakes either. He wasn't The Hammer. He never held a batting title in the league or even on the team. Mike Lum was solid and dependable, a journeyman player who had come up through the ranks to earn his starting spot on the roster. He had none of the flashy pizzazz of a Mays or even the sex appeal of the young George Brett. Mike Lum was the kind of guy you hired to plug a hole in your defense, not the kind of guy you created your game plan around.

Aspiring to the Major Leagues myself, I practiced my fielding in the backyard regularly, throwing the baseball as hard as I could against the concrete foundation of the house, then running down the grounders that came barreling back at me. I was the starting shortstop for my team, a position for which I was always picked even though I did not have the feline quickness required for the spot. Even at that age, I knew I wouldn't be able to improve my reflexes, so I worked at the only things I knew I could improve: my fielding and my stupidity. What I couldn't stop with my practiced glove, I would stop with my body, and this willingness to step into the path of the ball was considered a rare ability in the jittery Little League.

On Sundays, my father also joined me in the backyard, ostensibly to do yard work, but little by little drawing closer to me and offering me advice in his usual father-as-coach manner: "Are you an old lady? Bend your back and get that glove all the way down to the ground. . . . What kind of move was that? This is baseball, not ballet—don't anticipate, just move toward the ball. . . . Jesus H. Christ! The job of an infielder is to stop the ball before it gets past you, not to watch the ball go by and then try and stop it!" This continued as it always did until he was throwing me the grounders himself, spicing up the fare with an occasional line drive ("You just dropped the easiest out in baseball!") or pop fly ("You should be thinking of the infield fly rule right now. Explain it to me!"), leaving the lawn mower idling in the corner of the yard, snuffling like an abandoned child.

Eventually his keen eye picked up on my throwing motion, a gruesome sight that caused him, I believe, real physical pain not unlike an ulcer. Although he had been the person who taught me how to throw a baseball, I threw, in his words, "worse than a girl, like a duck almost." The textbook throwing method he had tried to instill in me—three-quarters over the top, upper arm parallel to the ground, hand pointing at ten o'clock, and cranking the whole assembly forward—never felt natural, so I had developed a kind of throwing shorthand: not throwing the ball so much as propelling it with an ungainly push. A push, I might add, that had speed and accuracy and could, from shortstop or third base, nail a runner down going to first. Nevertheless, every time my father noticed it, he would speculate on the physics of my motion and wonder aloud how I managed to get the ball moving at all.

Eventually he would try and reteach me how to throw, winding his arm back and snapping it forward in an exaggerated, heuristic motion that sent the ball rocketing to me, where it slammed into my glove with a bone-splitting crack. This day, perhaps because I was tired out by the fielding practice earlier, I did not even attempt to follow his example, and he became increasingly agitated. His throws came harder and harder at me, and I threw the ball back more and more limply, hoping that by association he would also start throwing weakly. I allowed my concentration to stray just a bit, indulging in nostalgic remembrance of my carefree practices with the wall, when an explosion jarred me from my reveries. When I came to, I was flat on my back with the taste of blood in my mouth, staring up into the blue summer sky. My mother hovered over me, berating my father for his carelessness.

We all moved inside, where my father went in the kitchen to suffer more abuse from my mother and get his usual post–yard work beer. I retreated to the family room where I could tend to my wounds in front of the television.

A few minutes later, my dad came in and watched me nurse my bloody nose. "Use your glove next time," he said as he handed me a box of tissues. "That's what it's for."

"Okay," I said, accepting the tissues and the apology.

That being done, he directed me to turn the channel. I dialed through *Gilligan's Island* and the PGA until I got to something we both could watch, a live game between the Braves and the Reds.

"The Reds will win," I said, having unquestioningly swallowed the marketing of the Big Red Machine.

"We can watch anyway, can't we," snapped Dad.

I shrugged and purposefully made elaborate ministrations to my nose.

My father preferred an equitable, nonverbal approach to watching ball games on television, grunting up in appreciation when either team made a good play or hit, and grunting down in chastisement when someone performed poorly. Watching in this manner turned a baseball game from a competition between good and evil into a study of the game itself, and as such, a burden to those of us who liked to cheer undeservedly for our team and boo mercilessly at the enemy. At the time, the only benefit I could see from watching games his way was the calm *c'est la vie* attitude he exuded at the end of the game, having sided with neither the victor nor the victim in the contest.

So I knew something unusual was happening when in the midst of the third inning, my dad said, "Ahh, there he is."

"Who?" I asked, scanning the screen.

"There, the first baseman," my father said, pointing to the screen. "Mike Lum."

"Who's Mike Lum?"

My dad was struck mute by my ignorance. The look on his face at that moment must have mirrored the one he had earlier when he realized that I had done nothing to prevent a baseball from hitting me in the face.

"He's our favorite player," he finally answered.

"He is?" My dad had never mentioned having a favorite player before, preferring to praise individual performances or special talents, like Aaron's run for the record or Seaver's concentration on the mound.

"Of course," he said. "He's the first Major Leaguer from home."

Home was Hawaii, the place where all my relatives and grandparents lived, the place where both my parents were born and raised, and the only mooring post, in our nomadic military life, that we ever meant when we talked about "going home."

Suddenly, I felt I knew Mike Ken-Wai Lum personally, as if he had been a friend of the family for years. I could envision the scene at his parents' house right now, aunties and uncles and cousins who, well, looked like my aunties and uncles and cousins sitting down to watch the game of their boy who had "made it." From the dining table, I could smell the food I missed so much: sushi, poi, kalua pig. I could even see his old baseball coach from Roosevelt High School in Honolulu, sitting back on the sofa watching the game, telling his wife for the thousandth time, "See, I told you. I always knew that boy would make it." At that moment, the entire gallery of my baseball heroes—Gehrig for guts, Mantle for bat, Robinson for fielding—dropped away in an instant for this Atlanta Brave who, I was sure, had still retained the lilting rhythms and peculiar slang of the Hawaiian pidgin English that I loved to listen to every time we phoned home to Grandma.

"At first base, huh?"

"Umm," he said. But instead of settling back into his silence, he leaned slightly forward as if to see the television better. "I wanted to go professional once."

I froze. This kind of talk during a game was unprecedented and I didn't know what to expect next. I remained quiet for fear of breaking the spell.

"And I think I would have made a pretty good first baseman."

I didn't doubt it. I had watched him play for the air force teams and had seen the intensity he brought to the games. He was solid, focused, and consistent, always waiting for the umpire to call a runner out before rising from his stretch. Even his teammates recognized his reliability and had taken to calling him Mr. Responsibility. Ask any Major League manager, they'll tell you that someone named Mr. Responsibility is the person they would want to guard their right corner.

"First base is the kind of position everyone thinks they can play," he said staring at the screen, "but it's a thinking man's position. Your head always has to be in the game. A first baseman is involved with probably 90 percent of the plays in the game. Few can play it well."

I nodded my head in agreement. I had never thought of first base in that way, having always reserved the position as the last stop for the overweight and over-the-hill players whose bats were too big to retire.

"I could have gone semipro. I had some offers. But I had just finished college and the war was on and I didn't want to get drafted into the infantry, so I went and volunteered with the air force. By the time that was over, why, I was married and you were coming along and the air force seemed like a pretty good place to have a career, and well . . ." His voiced trailed off. In the wake of silence that followed, I could think of nothing to say that would console him.

"God," he said, "I loved the game so much, I used to sleep with that mitt."

My younger sister entered the room at that point and Dad and I said nothing more the rest of the afternoon. But for the rest of that game, I spent as much time watching him as I did the television.

More changed for me that day than my newborn desire to own a Mike Lum baseball card. By the next season, I began to spurn the vainglorious position of shortstop as all quickness and light and became enamored with first base. My father and I abandoned our peppery fielding drills for close exercises in subtlety and concentration so that I could become, in his words, "a perfect first baseman, a player of composure." He trained me in the arcane lore of the position: how to plant my foot on the corner of the bag so a runner could not dislodge it, how to open myself up as a target for the infielders, how to stretch that extra little bit to shave down the lead of a quick runner. At the end of my first season as the team's starting first baseman, they awarded me a new nickname, Jr. Responsibility, and Dad awarded me a new first baseman's mitt. An ugly contraption, it looked like the bastard offspring of an illicit union between a worn-out catcher's mitt and a desperate oven mitt. But like a good first baseman, it was completely utilitarian.

The day I turned "one day short," a military term for one's last day on base, I took my final trip to Jimmy's house. The next morning we would be flying out to my dad's new assignment at Yongsan Post in Seoul, Korea, and Jimmy's dad would be transferring to Mississippi a few weeks later. I was armed with a shoe box of my top-shelf cards, the premium material: Lou Gehrig, Sandy Koufax, Willie Mays (true, in his twilight years in a Mets uniform), and the entire set of both the championship 1972 Oakland A's and Cincinnati Reds cards, whole team sets that I had laboriously collected. I was even prepared to break one of our unwritten rules: I had brought my Bart Starr and Gale Sayers football cards, willing to trade cross-sport and risk introducing, at the very last minute, a whole new calculus. We sat down on his younger brother's bed, the bottom mattress on a set of bunks, which Jimmy commandeered as his office during the day, and I prepared to deal. I dove into Jimmy's pile of baseball cards and with no pretense, for there was no time, pulled out card #208. No words were spoken; we both knew what I wanted. I opened my shoe box and waited for him to make the first move. I was a warrior primed my whole life for this battle and I was prepared to throw myself upon my sword and fight down to my last card if I had to.

He picked up the Mike Lum card and studied it slowly, once again, from front to back. This was something he did only with this card, usually preferring to divine the fear of his opponent to discern the value of the cards being traded. He always inspected the Mike Lum card with the same quizzical look on his face; perhaps he had missed something, something he would be able to read from the stats on the back of the card at the last minute. Finally he shook his head, sighed, and put the card into his shirt pocket. "Let's go outside," he said.

The day was very cold, winter tapering off to a wicked tail that blew knives through us and froze the hard-packed snow onto the earth. We crossed his backyard and climbed to the top of the hill behind his house, neighborhood common property that we nevertheless considered "ours." Over the winter we had terraced the hill with mounds of snow and spent our weekends carving out a sledding course with teeth-rattling, gut-impaling moguls along one side, and along the other side, a death-defying speed course that twisted sinuously through a stand of trees. However, our proudest construction, and the one that we reserved for our-selves, was a monstrous ramp that lay in the middle of the steepest part of the hill, which we had watered until it was as slick as a ski jump. One of us would add a new feature to the ramp, a left-hand twist to the exit or a greater curl to the end so that our launches would land us on our backs, and then dare the other to try it. The ramp had grown into an amalga-mation of perverse stunts, a record of our sadistic imaginations over the long winter. We stood at the top of the hill for a long time, neither of us saying anything, he with Mike Lum safely ensconced within his jacket, and I with my shoe box under my arm, surveying our creation.

Although it was not yet dinnertime, the evening had surrendered quick-ly to night and darkness poured like ink over the land. Soon we would hardly be able to see. Finally, Jimmy turned to me and said, "Do you think we'll still be best friends next year?"

I was stunned by the question. Neither of us had ever mentioned any-thing about being best friends. We never felt the need for confessions of that sort. Yet, as soon as he said it, I knew he was correct. It dawned on me that this must be the way of true best friends, neither needing to speak about it. "I don't know," I answered.

He didn't say anything, and we both knew my answer had been inade-quate. We could see our mothers through the windows in his house, get-ting the dishes ready for the last big feast between our two families. Both our mothers had prepared their specialties: Jimmy's mom had made her Italian sausage and apple pies, and my mom had made her wontons and sweet-and-sour spareribs. "Probably not," I decided.

Jimmy just nodded, and I felt a sudden relief as it became clear to me that he had been thinking the same thing. We watched as Jimmy's moth-er walked out the back door looking for us, soon joined by my mother, both of them retreating back inside when they could not find us in the darkness at the top of the hill. Jimmy fished around in his jacket and then flipped me Mike Lum. "Here," he said, "you can have this."

I looked at Jimmy. I looked at the card in my hand. I repeated these movements one more time before I could think of something to say. "I can trade you for it," I said, motioning to the box.

"Nah," he said, "let's go." He started walking down the hill toward his house, but I was still too dazed to move.

"What do you want for it?" I called after him. He didn't say anything. I wanted to trade him for it. I had been prepared for a long, grueling night of negotiations, angry words, betrayals, and last-minute desperation tactics. Haggling had always been part of our relationship. I ran up alongside him. "How about this? Or these?"

I even pulled out my Babe Ruth Batting Champion card, not a real Babe Ruth player card, but the only baseball card we had ever seen that had the Babe's picture on it. I had traded with someone's father to get it and we both considered the card one of my better deals. Jimmy didn't even look at me and continued his silent walk toward the house.

We were almost to the back door and I was getting desperate. "Here, take this," I said and handed him the whole box.

But Jimmy just ignored me and walked through the back door, where I followed. We located our spots at the kids' table and sat down for our families' final meal together.

We moved the next day, and a couple of months later in Korea, I gave away my entire sports card collection to my sister, who was just then entering the prime of her trading card years. I had lost interest since I couldn't find a sparring partner as good as Jimmy. His sleight of hand and cold calculations had always kept me teetering at the razor's edge of trading exhilaration or failure. I kept the really good cards for myself—the Hall of Famers and, of course, Mike Lum. But my sister never approached the cards as I did. Her temperament was more like that of a private collector: organizing the cards first by year and then by team, instead of by value as Jimmy and I had preferred, noting which ones she was missing and trying to find those by buying packs of cards. She never really traded because she couldn't bear to part with something that she owned.

I saw Jimmy again, when I moved to St. Louis for graduate school and he lived a few hours away in rural Illinois. He is now a mortgage broker with his own 800 number. He still trades as a hobby, but instead of cards, he now trades cars. His most recent trade involved exchanging his early 1980s dandelion-yellow Corvette for a worn-around-the-edges, 1960s model steel-blue convertible Mercedes, a much less common car and hence, a greater value. He traded the car with a professor at the university I attended. "Someone you might know," he told me, as if we all belonged to the same secret club. He seemed to delight in the fact that he had gotten the upper hand over this economics scholar.

Once, I even cautiously brought up our final baseball card trade, at the wedding of Jimmy's younger (no longer littler) brother. Jimmy, though, seemed to have forgotten all about Mike Lum, talking instead about other cards he had taken at a steal, and what those cards are now worth and how those people must be kicking themselves. Neither of us has ever mentioned our conversation at the top of the hill on that cold winter evening, but with best friends, sometimes you don't need to.

30. Work-ups
Baseball in the Fifties
Christopher Buckley

By the time I was two years old, that is, as soon as I could tell a baseball from a beach ball, my father had trained me in the proper batting stance and often would show me off to adults who came over to visit in the evenings. I have a clear memory of standing in the living room in pajamas—white ones with red and blue baseballs and bats printed all over them, the kind with feet built in—and stiffly assuming the batting stance before heading off to bed. This was 1950, and by then the country, and baseball, had moved into modern times—stadiums in the major cities of the East, kids playing sandlot or city league, grammar school, high school, and college. Actually going to a Major League game was a real event, and it seemed almost everyone listened on the radio, shared a lineup of heroes and a jargon.

For decades baseball was big news spring and summer, and the 1950s, to a great extent, were a carryover of the 1940s. My social studies textbook still had scenes of men in hats and baggy coats and trousers, women in suits with squared shoulders and wide lapels; the "metropolis" was crawling with Hudsons, Nash Ramblers, and checkered cabs. In the auditorium for a geography film, the same four-prop "modern" plane landed each year on a strip of dust in South America. We'd seen *The Babe Ruth Story*, starring William Bendix. Joe DiMaggio was married to Marilyn Monroe. It was traditional, even reasonable, that a pennant race was a major topic of discussion every fall. There was the big black-and-white cover of *Life* magazine with a shot from a late inning of the Series. To us, as to many, not much was more important than baseball. Not bikes or grades, not a dime for the soda fountain after school. Baseball was social tonic, a counterpoint of common joy set against routine. It was one thing most everyone understood together.

Eighth grade began in the 1960s, and like a batter looking for the off-speed pitch and getting the heater, we just weren't ready for what was coming. TVs were in most every living room, and the whole technological and commercial space-wired juggernaut was gearing up just over the horizon, yet it was not obvious to us then. Standing in the rush of 1960–61, fresh from the 1950s, the bat was still on our shoulders. Our mindset was a content and dreamy one. Everyone liked Ike, but no one really paid attention to his parting speech about a military industrial complex. We didn't for a moment think we'd be some of the last kids riding bikes to school or around town with baseball mitts always threaded over our handlebars. We had no idea that many of our generation would become "long-haired hippie radicals" marching in the streets of Berkeley and Chicago, opposing the government and another war before the decade was over. We couldn't see that we were slipping calmly over the edge of a world with our inherited small-town values of camaraderie and plain dealing, values that seemed a part of baseball whether it was played in Ebbets Field in Brooklyn or a school yard in Santa Barbara.

Although Los Angeles was only two hours away on the three-lane Pacific Coast Highway, we were pretty much off the map. The tourist industry was almost nonexistent; the saying we knew even as kids was, "Santa Barbara—for the newly wed and nearly dead!" Few movie stars lived in Montecito then, and all the president's men were twenty years away. Rock stars were far off, too. Elvis, or, from the camera angle, half of him, had been on the *Ed Sullivan Show*, and I remember that in 1959 or 1960 Tuck Schneider's older brother Joe had been suspended from Santa Barbara High School for combing his hair in a "ducktail." That was as close as we got to any rock 'n' roll fallout in those years. A couple minor leaguers assigned to the Dodgers' Single A farm club that played at Laguna Park were still years away from the big leagues. And baseball thrived. We had semipro, Little League, pony league, CYO school league, and the neighborhood games, and when not enough kids could be rounded up for teams or work-ups, a few of us would play hit-the-bat, three-flys-up, or over-the-line. Baseball was a portable ritual, where a hit or home run allowed you to momentarily run the bases like any one of the known pantheon of Major Leaguers—and almost everyone could play.

The World Series was played every September, so fall found us arriving at school with mitts hanging from our handlebars and bats balanced on top, found us playing catch or "burn-out" before class, then coming in and hanging our gloves up on the coat hooks in the back of the room. Ball gloves could contribute to your status. Some had them and some did not. Many had only hand-me-downs, gloves from older brothers or sisters. It was always an event when someone got a new glove—it happened rarely enough that the new owner was the center of attention for a week or two at least. We did not know many brand names then, but it meant a little to have a Wilson or a Rawlings. I had an inexpensive second baseman's mitt. Having, when I was seven, lost my father's "professional" fielder's glove—the one preserved emblem of his youth—I had to make do with a glove that was too small for a number of years. But at the beginning of seventh grade, I embarked on a campaign of complaint so relentless that after a month or so my father, much to my surprise, gave in. I was sure my ability to perform was hampered by the old glove— pocket too small, no good in the outfield. I was going to be a starter on the school team, and the other starters all had decent gloves. I wanted to be admired, wanted to make a move up in that society, though at the time I thought my reasoning was only practical.

One evening then, after work, my father presented me with a new fielder's glove—a Wilson Bob Feller model—and the requisite lecture about responsibility. He'd picked it up at Otts, our town's only department store, for about thirteen dollars on sale, a fair sum of money in those days, but with the best gloves selling for twenty-five or thirty, it was a bargain, and he knew it. It was large, perfectly shaped, and made of supple yellow leather. The next day I took my week's allowance and went to Jedlicas, the western supply store, and bought a piece of rawhide to restring the top of the fingers, pulling them tighter together with the thicker, stronger string. I rubbed Neetsfoot Oil into it and left it with the fingers tied around a softball overnight for a week to form a pocket large and permanent, soft and responsive, one that would close like a Venus flytrap over any ball it touched. It was easily the best glove I ever owned, the best I ever saw.

But this was still 1960 and we trusted people. One day toward the end of eighth grade, heading home with my mind on Linda Underwood or Virginia Cortez, I let a friend's younger brother borrow the glove. A work-ups game was still going on, and he promised to return it to the classroom and hang it on a hook in the back of the room. He didn't. Timmy Armour—I still remember his name—just tossed it on the walkway next to the classroom where we often threw our lunches or sweaters. He honestly expected it to be there the next day. It wasn't and was never seen again. My father was not about to buy me another one. I'd given my old mitt to my friend Sozzi, a kid who had four older sisters and had never had a glove of his own. There was no way to ask for it back.

I would get by borrowing. We still left our gloves in the field just behind our positions when we came to bat, so if we were playing teams, it was easy to come up with a glove. Everyone, however, wanted to use Harry Fowler's glove. It was the biggest glove anyone had ever seen, bigger than any I've seen since. Harry's father was a contractor doing well and obviously decided to get his son the biggest-ticket item on the rack. It was a Nokona, and its fingers were so long and stiff that the mitt really didn't have a pocket like most but operated on the hinge principle, one half collapsing toward the other over anything in range. It was not nearly as quick or as sure as the wonderful glove I had lost, but it was *the* item on the field. Everyone wanted to use "the vacuum cleaner." Harry knew its worth, its prestige; at the same time, he was generous and allowed lots of kids to use it. With few things to be jealous about in those days, ball gloves could be a point of contention, but playing work-ups, switching positions often, and borrowing gear, there were no real problems. The game was the thing—just running the bases, taking your chances on a steal, accelerating steadily around third and sliding into home, never caring if you ripped the knees out of your uniform corduroy pants.

Baseball—softball as we played it in the Catholic school league—was not just for the boys. In spring, the boys fielded a team to play the other schools in the league, and the girls had a team playing on the same schedule, and often we traveled across town in station wagons together. Although there were two or three guys known for hitting homers, I always remember Peggy Dormier, a tall, dark, sinewy girl who could hit the ball as far as anyone. Playing center field on the lower diamond while the girls practiced on the upper, I turned from my position when I heard that blunt reverberation of the bat when a softball was really being tagged, and would look up to see one sailing high against the blue, off the grass onto the asphalt where the smaller kids were playing four-square. I'd see Peggy then slowing down as she rounded second base, realizing it had cleared everything. She was quiet and modest, mostly because her popularity on the ball field did not carry over to the classroom or cliques. She was poor, and though we all wore uniforms, hers showed wear while the girls who were better-off, more blond or more popular, wore blouses starched and ironed, white as March clouds. We knew baseball, but not much else. Later in the 1960s, most of us would become aware of the fact that because of class, money, or race alone, and despite all religious protestations to the contrary, participation in and access to our society and its rewards had been, and would be, denied to many.

But baseball was an equalizer of sorts. Some girls, like Peggy, were great hitters, some could play the infield well, and I recall Maggie Tappinier being one of the best pitchers, boy or girl. Playing work-ups eliminated any favoritism of position or batting order; it eliminated being chosen for one side or the other. In work-ups boys and girls raced together out of the classroom after school and tagged up on home plate; the first three or four were batters, and the rest called out the positions they wanted in order of their arrival. When a batter grounded out or was tagged out, he or she went to right field, and everyone else moved up one position: the catcher becoming the fourth batter, the pitcher moving to catcher, first base to pitcher, and so on. The only exception was when someone caught a fly ball—he or she took the batter's place and the batter took that person's position in the field. So even if you were one of several stuck in the outfield, you had a chance of getting your "ups" before the bell rang to go in or the last bus pulled out of the yard. Everyone was in it together.

The lower grades fairly idolized seventh and eighth graders who were the star athletes on the team. At the beginning of the year you could approach them, actually talk to these heroes by asking what position they were "going out for." There was no coach until spring and no official tryout process. Each player just declared his intention and somehow a lineup evolved. Positions on the team were a main topic of conversation; it was almost like a political caucus. Myths developed, too, and in the insular world of our small parochial school, they perpetuated themselves; repeating stories was our way to prove that we knew what was happening. And things happened that, to us, seemed wonderful, grand. One of my first memories of being a second grader at Mt. Carmel School was a baseball game across town in old Pershing Park. A nun took me and a couple of other kids. Sitting there on weathered wood-slat bleachers, the green paint peeling off in the sun, I wasn't quite sure what was going on. I do remember that the eighth graders playing in the game seemed huge, about the size, in present-day comparison, of starting forwards in the NBA. I think we were behind until one of the Sosa brothers hit a line drive into left-center, which must have won the game, because everyone jumped up off their splintery seats and went happily out to the cars. Years later, kids still talked about the Sosas pulling it out in the late innings, and we felt good that we all knew the same tales, had seen or said we had seen that game.

It was said that Tote Borgatello, the pitcher for our school team, could make the ball drop. Now this was a thirteen-inch softball, underhand pitching, and the pitcher's rubber could not have been more than thirty or thirty-five feet from the plate, so the laws of physics did not provide much room for a ball to break sharply in any direction. Nevertheless, watching a game, seeing an opposing batter whiff at a third strike, we all concurred that Tote was putting something on the pitch, making it dip somehow at the last instant. Tote had dark hair and eyes, and when asked how he managed the trick pitch, he would just smile and say nothing, his dark eyes sparkling. Perhaps all pitchers have that in common, school league or majors? I still remember the day after one of the games between the fifth and sixth grades when Tote volunteered that a backhand stop he'd seen me make at shortstop was pretty good and I should think about going out for the team next year. I was beaming for days. That was a signal that I'd almost made it, and it meant everything in the limited context of school, sports, and those few years.

We played baseball almost all year long out there alongside the acacias, eucalyptus, and pines that bordered the blue sky and the edges of our field.

The grass grew steadily and green, and we were playing work-ups before and after school, jumping the fence into the Vogels' yard to retrieve foul balls. There were no league championship games then, only the National and American Leagues and the World Series in September. One girl in our class had a portable TV. Those who owned TVs had large Philcos or Sylvanias, housed in mahogany or blond wood cabinets, that they were paying off on time. A portable in 1958 was a second set, and hardly anyone owned one of those. The nun blackmailed our class into promised good comportment through Christmas if we were allowed to see the Series. So one morning, right after the salute to the flag and after each grade filed back into their rooms from the yard, the girl's father drove his big Buick across the asphalt and right up to the door. He got out, opened the trunk, lugged the set in, and put it up on the nun's desk, adjusting the rabbit ear antennas until the snowy black and white came clear and there was only the smallest hint of "ghosts" behind the players. We knew we were lucky—no other class got to watch—and with the exception of two or three students, we all followed every pitch, even staying inside to eat our lunches at our desks. Undoubtedly that year it was the Yankees beating some National League club—the World Series script did not vary much in the late 1950s—nevertheless, we were enthralled. Our biggest year for the Series was 1960, when the Pirates won on Bill Mazeroski's homer. Santa Barbara was a long way, in every way, from Pittsburgh— east to west, industrial to pastoral, large to small. Nevertheless, most of us supported the National League, so we backed the Pirates; everyone was tired of the Yankees winning the Series almost every year. Everyone except Tuck Schneider, that is; he was a die-hard Yankee fan who bet all takers and to whom a bunch of us had to pay up every September when the Yankees won. The bet was a quarter, and a quarter then was a week's spending for Big Hunks or Milky Ways. At the end of each Series, everyone grudgingly paid off in pennies, and Schneider always had a heavy bag to lug home. Our collective revenge arrived while Bolduc, Wesley, Witucki, and I were moving tables and chairs in the rectory under direction of the monsignor, who, fortunately for us, had his transistor radio tuned in and positioned in the window for the best reception. When Mazeroski connected for the game-winning homer, we let out a subdued cheer but could hear a roar rise from our homeroom two buildings away where they were watching. Schneider made himself scarce, and we did not have to hear about the Yankees for a while.

The Dodgers and Giants set up on the West Coast while they were waiting for their stadiums to rise. The Giants played in old Seal Stadium waiting for Candlestick Park, and the Dodgers made do with the L.A. Coliseum while the city council forced the last poor families out of Chavez Ravine. The coliseum rigged a high netlike fence in the short left field. I went to a couple of games there with my father, whose favorite team was the St. Louis Cardinals. The Dodgers had just made a trade with the Cardinals for outfielder Wally Moon, who, though his power and career were running out of gas, was made to order for that short porch in left. He hit a patented high fly ball to left that cleared the fence for a home run, a ball that in any other park would have been an easy out. I remember Stan Musial, Red Schoendienst, Enos Slaughter, as much from listening to my father and trading baseball cards as from anything I actually saw them do at games; even in those days, it was hard to get seats close to the field in L.A. It was especially exciting in 1959 when I raced home after school to watch the playoff between the Milwaukee Braves and the Dodgers at the end of the season. I remember Warren Spahn, who always looked lost inside his baggy uniform, and I had once seen Lew Burdette turn a triple play to get out of a jam. Playing catch, kids would imitate Burdette's tics, his routine of straightening his cap, his jersey, his throwing hand going to his mouth, his belt, before he threw each pitch. Eddie Matthews, the Braves' third baseman, was from Santa Barbara, but along with Aaron and Adcock he could not overcome the Dodgers that year. Duke Snider, Gil Hodges, Drysdale, Koufax, Carl Furillo, and Charlie Neal became household names. We all knew pretty much what there was to know about the sport at the time—who led the league in homers, Sandy Koufax's ERA, how many times Hank Aaron had repeated on the fifteen-minute TV show *Home Run Derby*. And, when trading cards were only worth trading, we knew the value of a Cookie Rojas versus a Cookie Lavagetto, a Charlie Neal versus a Jimmie Foxx, or a Musial versus a Mantle. It all meant something to us, and we were content; the times still seemed to run on such intangibles.

By our last season in eighth grade, we were sure our league was going to change to ten-inch, a game somewhere between softball and hardball. A ten-inch ball was only one inch larger than a regular baseball, but rubber coated and lighter. It was, however, pitched overhand, though not from a mound, and the catcher needed all the usual gear. I had a live arm and some control, but I had no game experience pitching and also had to bring all my imagination to bear to actually *see* my curve ball curve. My friend Cameron Carlson, who was catching, assured me that, yes, my pitch had curved, a little. We didn't know what we were doing, but we'd seen pitching and catching overhand plenty of times—on TV—and were still young enough to believe that we could do it, or at least manage a version of it that would play in our league.

I was in a bit of a pressure cooker as we headed for our first game with archrival Dolores School—we didn't really have a backup pitcher if I lost it out there. I knew from previous years how hostile the parents of Dolores players could be, how vicious the little kids were along the sidelines. We arrived at the school feeling confident nonetheless, knowing we had been practicing ten-inch while other schools had been playing softball. I fully expected to burn it by the batters, hear Cameron's official hardball catcher's mitt pop as strikes were called out. As we began to stretch out along the first base line and I loosened up my arm, a Dolores nun ran from the distant white classroom building and descended on home plate like a dark rain cloud. She announced that she had a telegram from the archdiocese forbidding ten-inch games and overhand pitching. No use now for Cameron to squat down and give me a different signal each time for the same pitch; we were back to softball and I was out in right field with little action. Schneider came in to pitch and Sozzi covered second. I did get one memorable hit that day using a thirty-five-ounce Louisville Slugger I had brought. I sent a fly deep to center field. The kid playing there turned clumsily and took off, running out of grass and onto the hardtop of the schoolyard. Without looking, and with his back completely turned to the diamond, he stuck out his glove and the ball fell directly into it from over his right shoulder. He was as surprised as I was stunned. I'd broken into a trot rounding second, sure it was gone, and just couldn't believe it when he held it up above his head; the ball and mitt wiggling in the air, the fielder looked like some kid holding up the first fish he'd ever caught. Longest ball of the day, and this kid pulls off a catch like that, a real *sapo*—a local Mexican term we used for unconsciously, unbelievably lucky. For what little consolation it was, I even heard one of the Dolores mothers saying it was a real sapo catch.

There were other games that spring of 1961, but nothing stands out in memory. As a class we had pretty much quit playing work-ups the spring before. Now our interests were more focused on records, radio, and who had the new 45 by Dion and the Belmonts, the Fleetwoods, the Ventures. Who was having a party, who was going for a walk with whom behind the buildings after the nuns and teachers had left. When we stayed after school now, it wasn't to run across the grass and tag up for positions on the diamond. There was no one skipping the first bus home and waiting for the next one an hour later so he or she could get their "ups." The dust of the ball field had settled and faded away with the 1950s.

Our world had changed as all do, but the new times had a pronounced spin to them as well. Baseball became less important, less relevant. It no longer defined a collective experience, and as a topic it became, in an ironic way, one of many that produced friction, signaling the much publicized "generation gap." Vietnam took over the TV. Staying in college—not going to Vietnam—became important. Staying alive once you found yourself in a jungle became more important. The game was rigged by LBJ, Westmoreland, and the Pentagon, but diving into a sandbag shelter to escape a mortar attack, ducking your head in a firefight, was no game. No one in Vietnam was wondering how the Dodgers were doing. We lost a lot of kids there while folks here went to the ballpark, while dividend checks were sent out to shareholders of Shell Oil and Colt Manufacturing. In four years of college, I watched only two games of the World Series, and those were during my freshman year. One friend, a first baseman who could really dig out the low throws, went down in a gunship; he survived, but it took seven operations to make his glove hand 20 percent useful. Among others who came back, some felt edgy, out of touch with past and present. For others, the aftereffect snuck up on them years later— a little like what happened to that pitcher for the Pirates in the late 1970s who, after a solid career and a championship season, just couldn't get the ball over the plate anymore, who had something snap in his nerve, in his radar on that sixty-six-foot path to the plate, and who ended up selling college rings. But by the late 1970s, I'd come back to baseball, Teaching part-time at community colleges and universities, I became one of the "freeway faculty." Driving forty-five minutes between various campuses and home, I started to listen to Dodger pregame and postgame shows, interviews, and baseball talk shows on one of the few stations my AM radio could pull in. I listened to what part of the games I could, and often would turn on the set for the late innings when I got home. Facing weekends with seventy-five compositions to respond to, I started sitting down in a big chair with an armful of papers and working Saturday and Sunday from one game to another—network games, ESPN, TBS, and anything else I could tune in. It was a way to break up the mind-numbing repetitiveness of seven or eight hours of grading. The games were slow enough that you could divide your attention between a men-at-the-corners, two down, hit-and-run situation and a lack of coherence and the comma splice. The background patter of a broadcast became a mental liniment for the cramping muscles of the part-time teacher trying to pick up a living. Time passed and I landed a good full-time position, but I kept up with the games—by then a habit, an unconscious comfort that connected with my youth, something I was becoming more conscious of losing having lurched into my thirties.

At this point in time, with a sizable portion of seriousness and loss behind me, politics and change looked to have come and gone almost seasonally, and all we finally got was older. Headlong into the 1990s, things less certain, living far from my friends and home, I begin to doubt the worth of a great deal that has had to do with career, getting ahead, the hundred additional concerns taking up time, energy, and spirit. On TV, I much prefer games on natural grass. Years ago, I never thought I'd use, automatically, a term like "natural grass"—by definition, there was no other kind. It doesn't matter much who is playing, but if the game is played on a real field and not Astroturf, I'll watch.

Now and then I see a 1957 Chevy with its swanlike fins, or a two-tone 1956 Chevy Nomad wagon with those thin chrome strips on the fold-down tailgate, and it brings things back. All that time ago, there was something sustaining in expecting less. You got along. A lot less was conspicuously consumed—fewer models and styles—there were fewer pressures, and fewer of us. More time to play ball. Of course, the choices then were easier, but maybe that's a point in favor of the past? Even a constant pastime like baseball now faces problems of "smaller market" teams being unable to compete and possibly survive. As a result of smaller shares of TV revenue, the teams can't afford the high-priced free agents, and a losing year means even less revenue. But baseball made a comeback in the 1980s, and attendance has climbed yearly since then.

I know it's simplistic, but nine out of ten days, all I want I to do is drive an old Chevy again, lean back against the wide bench seat, switch the AM radio to a game, shift that three-speed on the column, and cruise with the windows down. I'd like to drive it home, up Cabrillo Boulevard or down East Valley Road toward my old grammar school and get a bunch together for work-ups. I want to pull up to the field and open the four doors or the tailgate and let folks out to tag up for positions—happy to be there, alive among people who recognize the same trees and grass and clouds I do. I'd be happy to just stand there a while worrying about nothing more than whether I'll be able to bend down far enough to field a hot grounder hit my way. I'd like to be positioned in that center-field grass, sun holding on in the west over the blue line of the eucalyptus, and see Peggy Dormier at the plate—see her connect and send one flying deep, see that moon-white softball almost breaking into orbit before spinning down in the direction of my glove, and then hear my old friend Sozzi calling, "I got it. I got it," as he cuts in front of me for the running catch and carries it in toward home.

31. Jose Canseco, Hero
Michael Chabon

Before I start arguing that it's muddleheaded, and misses the point, to disparage the greatness of a baseball player for his want of goodness as a man—before I rise to the defense of Jose Canseco—let me begin by offering one example of my own muddleheadedness in this regard. A big part of what I have always admired about the late Roberto Clemente *as a ballplayer* is what a good, strong, thoughtful man he seems to have been, his stoic dignity in the face of ignorance and bigotry, how he died while trying to help the victims of a great disaster, et cetera. I choose to view Clemente's grace on the field as reflecting and reflected by the graceful way in which he conducted his public life (when one has demonstrably nothing to do with the other) and both together as lasting proof of some private gracefulness as a man, when I have no way of ever really knowing what form the true, secret conduct of his life may have taken. I have no idea what Clemente's relationship was to drugs, or what his feelings would have been about performance enhancers like anabolic steroids, but I would like to think that he would have viewed them both with disfavor, and that he was faithful to his wife, temperate in his habits, and modest about his accomplishments. Yes, I would like to think that— because I'm just foolish and mistaken enough to think that great baseball players must also be good men.

There is no question that *sometimes* Jose Canseco was a great baseball player. If you have any doubt about that, you weren't paying attention to Canseco on the days, during the seasons, when he paid attention to the game, and that's hard to imagine since, like Clemente, the man arrested the eye of the spectator, held the attention like a shard of mirror dangling from a wire in the sunshine, even when he was just standing around waiting for something to happen next. But I'm not going to get into that here. The question of Canseco's greatness or lack thereof can be debated endlessly, with statistics and anecdotes to support both sides, and some of us will never understand why Ron Santo, Gil Hodges, and Dick Allen are not in the Baseball Hall of Fame while others, most of whom serve on the Hall's Veterans' Committee, will always vote, as the committee did once again on March 2, to keep them out. And God knows I have no intention of claiming that Jose Canseco qualifies as a good man, according to the conventions of my own garden-variety morality of consistent effort, altruism, and personal integrity defined as the keeping of one's promises to other people. Canseco's want of goodness on those terms is also arguable, I suppose, though not by me. But I will go out on a limb and venture that any list of the one hundred greatest baseball players who ever lived would conform to the pattern for our species, and therefore contain a sizable number of men who spent most of their lives fumbling with an inherent tendency to shirk, ignore the sufferings of others, tell lies, and evade responsibility. Playing baseball well does not make you a better person, any more than writing well does. The illusion that lures us into the error of confounding Clemente's goodness as a man with his greatness as a ballplayer is that when a man is playing baseball well, as when a man is writing well, he seems to himself, in that moment, to be a better person than he really is. He puts it all together, he has all the tools, in a way that is impossible outside the lines of the ball field or the margins of the page. He shines, and we catch the reflected glint of that, and extend the shining one an overall credit for luminosity that almost nobody could merit. Clemente, I think, did; he shone with the grace and integrity of his play even when he was not on the field.

Roberto Clemente was a hero, in other words, and Jose Canseco, by this definition, is not. By his own admission, Canseco has shirked, and hurt people, and lied, and broken a lot of promises, large and small. And used steroids. And therefore, many people seem to feel, he is not to be admired, neither in the past, during his brief heyday, so that we must retroactively rescind our delight in his style and our amazement at his prowess, put an asterisk beside our memory of the pleasure of his company over the course of a few long summers, nor in the present, not even when he steps forward to tell the truth, a big, meaningful, dolorous truth that most of us, measured by our own standards of heroism, would have a hard time bringing ourselves to tell. Canseco can't possibly be a hero to anyone—he laid down that burden many years and arrests and screw-ups ago—and furthermore (goes the rap) there is nothing remotely admirable about Canseco's allegation of widespread, inveterate use of steroids, by himself and by ballplayers like Mark McGwire, who have a readier claim on our admiration and shoulder more naturally its weight.

Canseco, we are informed by sportswriters, by commentators, and by his former teammates, opponents, and coaches, is only out for money. If lying would have paid better than telling the truth, then Canseco would have lied (and indeed, some have suggested, perhaps that is what happened). Canseco is greedy, faithless, selfish, embittered, scornful, and everlastingly a showboat. He is a bad man, and that makes him, retrospectively (except among those who claim always to have felt this way), a bad ballplayer. Not to mention a bad writer.

The question that concerns me in all this is not one of the obvious ones, like what to tell my children, or what to do about the problem of steroids, or how to think about the records that may have been broken by cheaters, or how to protect against perfidy, avarice, taint, and scandal the dear old national game. Like all obvious questions, none of them can really be answered. All human endeavor is subject to cracking. It's the hard, Tex Avery truth of the universe: put your finger over one leak and another one pops up, just beyond your reach. Violence, gambling and game fixing, pestilential racism, overexpansion, competitive imbalance, labor strife, mind-boggling cupidity, and cheating of every variety and school: for most of its history the game of baseball has, like everything we build, been riddled with holes, some cavernous, some of them irreparable. I don't know what is to be done about this latest debacle, and neither do you. No, what I want to know about Jose Canseco is, how come I still like the guy so much?

No, I'll go even further: I admire him. Not in the way I admire Clemente—not even remotely, which says something about what an ambiguous thing admiration can be. Like all showboats, Canseco courts the simpler kind of admiration, starting in the mirror each morning. He is slick, he drives too fast, he is nine feet tall and four feet wide and walks with a roosterish swagger. But there has always been something about him, about his style of play, his sense of self-mocking humor, his way of looking at you looking at him, that goes beyond vanity, self-aggrandizement, or being a world-class jerk-off.

Canseco has been described as a charmer and a clown, but in fact he is a rogue, a genuine one, and genuine rogues are rare, inside baseball and out. It's not enough to flout the law, to be a rogue—break promises, shirk responsibilities, cheat—you must also, at least some of the time, and with the same abandon, do your best, play by the rules, keep faith with your creditors and dependents, obey orders, throw out the runner at home plate with a dead strike from deep right field. Above all you must do these things, as you do their opposites, for no particular reason, because you feel like it or do not, because nothing matters, and everything's a joke, and nobody knows anything, and most of all, as Rhett Butler once codified for rogues everywhere, because you do not give a damn. One day you make that breathtaking play at the plate from deep right. Another you decide, for no good reason, to come into the game during the late innings of a laugher and *pitch*, retiring the side (despite allowing three earned runs on three walks and a pair of singles)—and ruining, forever, that cannon of an arm.

I've never seen a man who seems more comfortable than Jose Canseco with who he is—not with who *we* think he is, like our president, or with his best idea of himself, like our president's predecessor, but with himself, charmer and snake, clown and thoroughbred. The man isn't lying—give me a break. He doesn't need to lie: what would be the point? He doesn't care what you think of him; if anything, he derives a hair more pleasure from your scorn and contumely than he does from your useless admiration. By coming forward now to peel back the nasty bandage on baseball's wound, it's not that Canseco has nothing to lose, as some of his critics have claimed. A man like Canseco never has anything to lose, or to gain, but his life and the pleasure he takes from it.

That this also remains exactly true for each of us is a thought that makes no impression on me in my daily intercourse with all of the things I give a damn about, and it probably makes none on you. We aren't wired to see things that way, and we can never be blockade runners, or Casablanca casino owners, or fatally gifted ballplayers who sometimes, as Canseco once did, permit a baseball to bounce off the top of our heads before its departure from the ballpark. We have no style, you and I; only people who don't give a damn have style.

There was a time, though, when men like Canseco, without taking anything from the luster of men like Roberto Clemente, could also be accounted as heroes. They were the ones, the Ulysses and Sinbads and Raleighs, who sailed to places we couldn't imagine and returned, after a career of wonder and calamity and chagrin, not one whit better than they were when they left. And no better, surely, than we—possibly worse. And yet, in the end, they were the only ones fit to make the voyage, and when they came back they carried a truth in their baggage that no one else would be clown enough, and rogue enough, and hero enough to speak.

32. Babe Ruth's Ghost

Louis D. Rubin Jr.

When in 1960 Jim Brosnan, then a pitcher for the Cincinnati Reds and before that for the Cardinals and Cubs, published his first book, *The Long Season*, there was incredulity in press boxes from Fenway in Boston to Candlestick in San Francisco. For Brosnan had *written* the book, not collaborated with a ghostwriter; that is, a sportswriter had not been employed to chat with him for a couple of hours and produce a book "by" or "with" Brosnan.

What was more, those who read *The Long Season* discovered that Brosnan's taste in literature and music was clearly of the highbrow variety. On one occasion his teammates had been startled to discover a copy of the two-volume boxed Random House Proust atop his locker. Such aberrant conduct had so intimidated at least one of his managers, Solly Hemus of the St. Louis Cardinals, that their professional relationship grew permanently sour, with Brosnan eventually being traded to Cincinnati, where he helped pitch the 1961 Reds to the pennant.

Hiring professional writers to ghostwrite books by ballplayers is a custom that goes back into the dark abysm of professional baseball history. The need to do so is obvious. Patrons of the game are eager to read about how their heroes play it, and who better to tell of that than the hero himself? Yet almost by definition most professional athletes are ungifted at literary composition; the words "literary athlete" are, if not a contradiction in terms, then by all odds an unlikely combination, on the order of a nonviolent terrorist or a taciturn disc jockey. Someone else who is gifted at manipulating words rather than throwing or hitting a baseball must therefore come to the rescue, customarily a professional sports journalist who is reasonably familiar with the working principles and personalities of the national game.

The genre, to be sure, is not confined to books about athletes. Military heroes are frequently in need of literary aid; for every U. S. Grant, who wrote his own memoirs with the editorial help of Samuel L. Clemens, there have been dozens of illustrious generals and admirals for whom the pen was more cumbersome than the sword, and who sought help from less martially renowned but verbally fluent aides-de-camp. Politicians, industrialists—these, too, have employed spectral assistance. But with ballplayers it is almost mandatory to do so; the time in the limelight is so brief, the opportunity so obvious.

The roles of athlete and professional wordsmith in such a joint literary endeavor can range from fairly extensive collaboration over a period of months, with much interaction, to no more than a session or two with a notebook or cassette tape recorder, in which case the ghostwriter will depend largely on record books and newspaper files for his material, with the athlete being consulted mainly to corroborate an occasional reference.

I read somewhere of a telephone conversation between Willie Mays, a gifted ballplayer but not renowned for his literary interests, and Charles Einstein, who assisted Dr. Mays in writing his memoirs, which reportedly went along these lines:

"Hello, Willie? This is Charlie."

"Charlie who?"

"Charlie Einstein. You know, the one who wrote the book."

"What book?"

Whether it actually happened I cannot say. The point is that depending on the concerned parties, the actual role of athletes in the research and writing of books of which they are nominal authors can be slight indeed.

The degree of involvement may also, though not necessarily, be indicated by the manner in which the collaboration is described on the title page of the book. The book in question can be written "by A *and* B," or "by A *with* B," or "by A *as told to* B," depending on the wishes of the participants and the rectitude of the book's publisher. Or it can even be listed as having been written "by" A alone, with the fact of B's collaboration nowhere displayed.

I have to say that the standards for volunteering such information have improved in recent years. Rare is the ghostwritten sports book today that omits all mention on the title page of the presence of a professional collaborator in its preparation. In this respect the production of such books is considerably more honest and straightforward than in the instance of ghostwritten books by celebrities in other fields of human endeavor.

Mainly this is because, unlike politicians, business executives, generals of the army, and the like, most professional athletes feel in no way demeaned by public knowledge that a literary work appearing under their name was not in fact written by them. In the circles they frequent, no disgrace is attached to such an arrangement.

To repeat, it is nothing new; the practice has been going on for generations. To cite an example: *Pitching in a Pinch* by Christy Mathewson, which came out in 1912 and remains one of the best baseball books, was penned not by the renowned Big Six of the old Giants but by John Wheeler, founder of North American Newspaper Alliance. This fact appears nowhere in the original edition but was revealed only in 1977, when the late Red Smith prepared an introduction for a new printing (*Pitching in a Pinch: or, Baseball from the Inside*).

Nor does it seem likely that Dr. Mathewson had more than a nominal relationship to the juvenile novels issued under his name during the years of his pitching renown, though he may have checked the baseball material to see that no obvious improbabilities were included. I suspect, however, that *Pitching in a Pinch* does contain information that was actually furnished by Dr. Mathewson himself. (Frank DeFord believes Matty wrote much of it. Well, maybe. . . .)

It was in the 1920s that the ghostwritten sports book entered upon its full splendor. The audience for sports underwent a vast expansion during the Prohibition decade, and the demand for "as told to" books intensified accordingly. It was not the custom then, however, to let it be known to the public that literary assistance may have been given to the athlete-author in the writing. As with Mathewson's book of the previous decade, such books were normally presented as having been penned solely by the sports hero whose name appeared on the jacket and title page.

I recently came upon a gem of the ghostwriting genre: *Babe Ruth's Own Book of Baseball* by George Herman Ruth. The Babe, of course, was the supreme baseball figure of his era; his fame surpassed even that of

U.S. presidents and movie stars. A book written by him could be counted on to sell numerous copies, and in 1928, the year in which his book appeared and which immediately followed the season in which he hit a then unparalleled sixty Major League home runs, Ruth's renown was at perihelion.

As was and is well-known, the Bambino was no litterateur. He possessed only a reform school education, and as a reader it is doubtful that he ever during his lifetime willingly sweated his way through the contents of an entire book, much less composed one himself. To assist him with his literary endeavors, therefore, G. P. Putnam's Sons secured the services of a ghostwriter, who, as Jerome Holtzman notes in his introduction to the University of Nebraska Press's Bison Books reprint edition (1991), was Ford C. Frick. At the time a sportswriter for the New York *Journal*, Frick later became president of the National League and then commissioner of baseball. During the 1920s, the Christy Walsh Syndicate frequently employed him to assist the Babe in his literary endeavors. Frick took care of the writing, and Ruth provided the byline.

The late Fred Lieb offered a prototypical Bambino story in his book *Baseball As I Have Known It* (1977). On one occasion Dr. Ruth and several of his Yankee teammates, while traveling aboard a Pullman car, were discussing his collaborator, who had been working with him for several years. The Babe called over to Lieb, who was seated across the aisle: "What's the name of the guy who writes for me? It rhymes with 'quick,' 'thick,' 'Dick.'"

"The name is Frick," Lieb told him. "Ford Frick."

Exactly how the Ruth-Frick collaboration worked is not recorded, but it is possible to make certain assumptions based on the published text itself as well as on all that we know of the Babe's way of doing things. Here, for example, is a passage in Dr. Ruth's book, appearing in a chapter titled "Batters and Batteries," during which he takes as his exemplars several performers on the New York Giants of the era previous to that in which the Babe played for the Yankees.

> *So far as a pitcher is concerned, good catching means everything to him and poor catching means his ruination. That's true even of veteran pitchers. No matter how much natural stuff a pitcher*

*may have he can't pitch well unless he has absolute confidence
in his catcher. And certain pitchers and catchers work together so
long that the pitcher is lost pitching to any other man. Mathewson
and Myers were such a team. Matty always pitched to Myers and
despite the fact that Bresnahan was a great catcher, he and Matty
never were able to team up successfully. Roger on the other hand
could handle Bugs Raymond like a whiz, while Myers was lost
with Bugs' pitching.*

Now there are several things wrong with Dr. Ruth's published historical note as processed through Frick. In the first place, the tenures of Roger Bresnahan and Chief Meyers—Frick had the name spelled incorrectly—on the Giants did not overlap. Dr. Bresnahan left the club after the 1908 season, whereas Dr. Meyers, although joining the Giants late in 1908, got into no games until the season following. Moreover, when Dr. Bresnahan departed it was to go to St. Louis as catcher-manager, in the trade that brought Bugs Raymond to the Giants for the first time. So Dr. Raymond could not possibly have worked with Dr. Bresnahan. And as for Matty's alleged inability to pitch well when Dr. Bresnahan was his catcher, the latter was in place behind home plate for the Giants during each of the three World Series shutouts that Matty tossed against the Philadelphia Athletics in 1905.

It was, however, apparently true that Chief Meyers did have trouble working with Bugs Raymond, and vice versa. What probably happened was that Bresnahan's role was being confused with that of yet another Giant catcher of the era, Art Wilson, who is cited in Matty's book as having caught Dr. Raymond "almost perfectly."

The Bambino's information on the history of Major League pitcher-catcher relationships, therefore, was considerably skewed. Was it, however, Dr. Ruth's information at all?

I doubt it. Very likely Frick, who knew the Babe's milieu well and had ghostwritten newspaper columns for him in the past, chatted with him a few times, took some notes (this was long before the day of the cassette recorder), and composed *Babe Ruth's Own Book of Baseball* pretty much by himself.

My guess is that when Frick interviewed Dr. Ruth on the topic of pitcher-catcher relationships—if indeed he ever actually did so—the conversation proceeded along something like the following lines.

> Frick: *"How about the catcher, Babe? Is he important to the pitcher?"*
>
> Ruth: *"Sure. Somebody's got to catch the [expletive deleted] ball."*
>
> Frick: *"Yes, but what I mean is, when you were a pitcher did it matter to you which particular catcher was behind the plate? Did you have one catcher that you preferred to throw to?"*
>
> Ruth: *"Nah, just so they could catch the [expletive deleted] ball and throw through, I didn't give a [expletive deleted] who was back there."*
>
> Frick: *"Still, some pitchers do have favorite catchers, don't they?"*
>
> Ruth: *"Oh, I guess so. Maybe a few of them."*
>
> Frick: *"Somebody told me once that Matty—you know, Christy Mathewson, on the Giants—liked to pitch to Chief Meyers, but not to Roger Bresnahan."*
>
> Ruth: *"Oh yeah?"*
>
> Frick: *"So I understand. On the other hand, they say that Bugs Raymond couldn't work with Meyers. He had to have Bresnahan."*
>
> Ruth: *"Could be. I never seen either one of the [expletive deleted]s pitch, myself."*

To all but the most uncritical of readers, the prose style of the book's opening sentence reveals quite clearly who will be doing most of the ensuing writing and thinking: "My earliest recollections center about the dirty, traffic-filled streets of Baltimore's river front." The pronoun is that of the Bambino, but the nouns, adjectives, and verb are assuredly the idiom of Ford Frick.

At times Frick did attempt to adapt his style to the Ruthian vernacular: "Old Jack Quinn of the Athletics is another man who has a delivery that's a pippin"; "And control! Say, that Collins had better control of his slow one than most fellows have of their fast ones"; etc. For the most part, however, Dr. Ruth's ghostwriter stuck to a more formal mode and made little effort to make his prose mirror the Babe's way of talking— which, since Ruth is known to have used four-letter words reflexively, was just as well.

In ghostwriting the Babe's book, Frick faced a daunting task. From all accounts Ruth had little gift for recall and none whatever for reflection. He lived almost totally in the present, was largely unconcerned for anything but his own personal doings, took almost no interest in the lives and activities of his teammates except as affecting him, and was without awareness of or curiosity about the complexities of human personality. The retelling of amusing anecdotes, the accumulation of colorful diamond lore—these were not his forte. For the most part he couldn't even remember the names of most of those who played with and against him; habitually he addressed each and all as "kid."

Dr. Ruth knew the game of baseball itself extremely well but as a trade, in much the same way that a plumber can be master of the art of plumbing without having psychological insight into other pipefitters or thoughts about the decor of bathrooms. The Babe could discourse on hitting, but not the mannerisms of individual hitters; he could describe the technique of the hook slide, but convey little of the competitiveness and ferocity of those who utilized it well.

Frick was also up against the problem that his collaborator was a public figure, a busy man, and there must have been a severe time limit within which the project had to be completed. Written with the impact of the fabulous 1927 season to give it vogue and topicality, it was designed to come out the following year. All Frick could do was to set his book's overall design, sketch out his chapters, arrange for a session or two with the Babe, perhaps ask for explanations of techniques and procedures, seek to prompt comment on people and events, and then sit down at his typewriter and begin writing. As Jerome Holtzman notes in his introduction to the 1991 reprint, "From my experience as a ghostwriter, I know that eventually the writer must fly solo."

There are several passages in which Dr. Ruth is made to hold forth on the virtues of Tyrus Raymond Cobb, the Georgia Peach who dominated pre-Ruthian Major League Baseball. As might be expected, Dr. Cobb's skill at stealing bases evokes a lengthy tribute.

Now Tyrus Raymond Cobb, who by inner nature and style of play came close to being an outright psychopath, detested George Herman Ruth and the long-ball game into which baseball had been transformed by the latter's slugging prowess, and it is known that he took bitter umbrage over having been supplanted by the Babe as the game's prime luminary.

The Bambino, by contrast, was not the hating type—he liked little kids, good-looking women, and almost everybody else. But that he had been stung by the Georgia Peach's often-voiced contempt for himself and what he exemplified, and quite justifiably resented the older player, is certain. On several occasions the two of them almost came to fisticuffs.

It seems unlikely, therefore, that, recognizing though he did the extraordinary skill with which Cobb hit and ran the bases, the Babe would on his own initiative have opted to devote several thousand words in praise of Dr. Cobb's intelligence, judgment, technique, and pluck.

Dr. Ruth's reported discourse on base stealing even includes an anecdote, "one of the funniest lines I ever heard," in which a noted catcher of the early 1920s, Wally Schang, was asked by Connie Mack to tell what he would do if Detroit trailed by one run, Cobb was on second base, and Schang knew that he was about to steal. "I'd fake a throw to third then hold the ball and tag him as he slid into the plate," Schang replied.

It is barely possible that the Babe actually volunteered the anecdote, which was well-known among players and sportswriters and had seen print before, but far more likely Ford Frick himself had heard and remembered it, thought it appropriate to the matter under discussion, and inserted it in the book. In all probability the conversation that resulted in Ruth's lengthy eulogy of Ty Cobb's skills went something like this.

> Frick: *"How about base runners, Babe? Who would you say was the best? Cobb?"*
> Ruth: *"Yeah, I guess you gotta give the [expletive deleted] credit."*

From there Frick, in Jerome Holtzman's words, flew solo.

Yet it should be understood that Dr. Ruth would almost certainly have had no objections to Frick's extended tributes to Dr. Cobb's skill at playing the game. What appeared in a book, whether allegedly written by him or anyone else, was of small concern to him. That he even bothered to read the book he supposedly wrote seems quite dubious to me.

It is unfortunate that Ford Frick did not check his facts and avoid having Babe Ruth utter historical impossibilities such as the Bresnahan-Meyers comment. In 1927–28 a baseball writer struggling to complete a book on a deadline did not have readily available to him such reference works as Reichler's *Baseball Encyclopedia*, Thorn's and Palmer's *Total Baseball*, or Neft's and Cohen's *Sports Encyclopedia: Baseball*. To make certain of his historical facts, Frick's almost sole recourse would have been to comb through the successive yearly volumes of the Spalding and Reach guidebooks, and if the book was to be ready for the 1928 season there was little time to spare for research.

Besides, did it really matter very much? Then as now the principal audience for "as told to" sports books, whether so labeled as such or not, consisted of teenagers and young adults—but far less informed in sports history and versed in statistics than their present-day counterparts. To be sure, doubtless there were certain knowledgeable New York fans—by Ruth's heyday they were coming to be called that, rather than "cranks" or "bugs" as in the earliest years of the century—who at once recognized that Roger Bresnahan could not possibly have caught the games that Bugs Raymond pitched for John McGraw's Giants, and who remembered very well that he had been Mathewson's battery mate throughout the famous all-shutout World Series of 1905. But nobody expected Dr. Ruth to get all his facts right, anyway. What the Babe knew how to do was to hit a baseball.

Today's "as told to" ghostwriter has it much rougher. In 1928 there was no Society for American Baseball Research in existence, with a militant multithousand membership dedicated to the compilation and extrapolation of baseball data. Nor were most of the sportswriters of the so-called Golden Age of sport nearly so sophisticated, so alert to the history and minutiae of their professional subject matter as the majority of their counterparts are today.* What could pass without comment or disapproval then would be swiftly spotted and castigated now.

More than that, the likelihood nowadays is that some of the other ballplayers themselves would read the ghostwritten book, with a critical eye not only for personal innuendo but for professional accuracy and soundness. For reading—which the late Rogers Hornsby for one always took care not to do during the playing season, on the theory that his batting eye would be adversely affected (he made an exception for racing forms)—is by no means an unheard-of habit among today's Major Leaguers.

But reading is one thing, and writing quite another. Therefore the sports ghostwriter still actively plies his trade. The tendency in recent decades, in some quarters at least, is to imitate the ballplayer's mode of discourse with uncensored exactitude of idiom. Indeed, one suspects that to add piquancy and photo-realism to the presentation, the vernacular voice is even given intensification. Thus Peter Golenbock as alter ego of Sparky Lyle in *The Bronx Zoo* (1979).

> *After what Reggie [Jackson] did tonight, all the mustard in the world couldn't cover him. He hit a single to right, and as he rounded first, he gave one of his stares at [Lyman] Bostock in right as if to say, "Go ahead, challenge me, you motherfucker." Bang. Bostock fired the ball in and picked him off first base. Challenge me, my ass. It made me so sick because there is absolutely no reason for that. And what I thought was interesting was that nobody said a word. It used to be "Look at that crap." Everyone would bitch and moan to each other about it. Billy [Martin] would go crazy. Now everyone goes "Oh." Ellie [Hendricks] said, "Did you see that?" I said, "Yep," and that was all there was to it. I went back to the john and fed my black widow another moth.*

This may have been Sparky Lyle's actual, cassette-recorded language. The conventions for reproducing the spoken word in books have been considerably liberalized since the Golden Age of sport in the 1920s. It was obviously of no concern to Dr. Lyle that his musings be presented in such fashion by his collaborator, and without any important recognition of a possible distinction between spoken and written language. Clearly Golenbock and his publisher thought it literarily desirable to make the young adult readers of *The Bronx Zoo* believe that they were being given the authentic, unbowdlerized discourse of playing field and locker room. All things considered, however, I believe I prefer Ford Frick.

Though by no means all of them, however. Two years ago appeared *When Boston Won the World Series: A Chronicle of Boston's Remarkable Victory in the First Modern World Series of* 1903 by Bob Ryan, who in company with other sports authorities appears frequently on ESPN. There was no Series played the following year, 1904, Ryan declares, because John McGraw, the New York Giants manager, disdained to take on the winner of the upstart American League pennant. For his pains, when in 1905 McGraw's Giants played the Philadelphia Athletics, Ryan goes on to say, they were shut out in every game. Anyone presuming to write about early twentieth-century baseball history might be expected to know that in the famous "shutout series" of 1905 the Giants defeated the Athletics four games to one, with the losing team being shut out each game, three times by Christy Mathewson. Mr. Ryan is, however, a prose stylist of rare virtuosity. I offer a sample; he is referring to old-time baseball: "Illiterates almost undoubtedly out-numbered college men." And, "Almost undoubtedly, someone was going to lose Game 3 because of the absurd playing conditions."

33. Throw Like a Girl, or What Baseball Taught Me about Men and Life

Rachael Perry

I loved baseball long before I loved boys, so I think it's fair to say that during the summer of 1984, with all the boldness and courage of a girl too young for a training bra, I didn't really want to marry Lance Parrish. Even if the thought had crossed my mind—which it *hadn't*—there were too many obstacles. I was nine, for example, and he was twenty-eight, married and a father of two boys with another baby on the way (a girl, it turned out, born between games 2 and 3 of the World Series that year). And there were other things: he was a giant, I'd barely crossed the five-foot mark; he was from Pennsylvania, way on the other side of Lake Erie, and I was from a small town in Michigan where no one locked their doors; and, finally, Lance Parrish was famous and I was not. The only stranger who might have recognized me on sight was probably the librarian behind the desk at Brandon Public.

We lived in the kind of town that seemed generic heartland America: if we were an item at the grocery store—say a group of condiments or a staple of sugar—there's no doubt we would've been wrapped up in a wholesome flour-bag white, set at the bottom of the aisle, yards from any displays or in-store advertisements. "I'm sorry," we might say politely to an unsuspecting customer who picked us up to read about our contents. "Did you really mean to choose us?" We were auto workers and farmers, carpenters and homemakers, salesmen and fishermen. We went to church on Sundays and we shoveled our driveways; we cleaned our bathrooms and our floors every week; we tried to put away a little from every paycheck so we could take our families canoeing on the Au Sable River in July or to Cedar Point during the off-season; we gathered around each other's kitchen tables every Saturday night, drank beer, told ghost stories, and talked about the Tigers.

So this is where baseball and I met each other: barefoot in the backyard, the sun pale and warm on my shoulders, the grass a bit cold and damp under my toes. When other girls played with Barbie and Rainbow Brite and Care Bear and My Little Pony, I oiled up my mitt, tied a ball in it, slipped it under my mattress, and dreamed about baseball. When other girls pulled on gymnastics leotards or strapped dance slippers across their shoulders, I fingered the laces of the ball, traced each stitch like it was a clue to the secrets of life. Baseball was my ballet—in it I found grace, poise, strength. I started to observe life around me in terms of baseball: the forward progress of extra bases, how some people threw fastballs and some people threw curve balls and some people threw off-speed pitches, the hope of the next at bat.

I played baseball. I listened to baseball on the radio. I watched baseball on television. And I noticed him right away, Lance Parrish. There was something magnetic about the way he played, the way he swung the bat, the way he commanded his pitchers, the way he anchored his team and stomped around the field. He was built like a hero—muscled, thick, sturdy—but there was something else, something that was obvious to me and that I could thoroughly understand: his absolute joy for the game.

It's said that in the locker room Sparky Anderson (Hall of Famer and forever Tiger to Detroiters, regardless of the logo on his cap in Cooperstown) often described baseball as war: "I want you guys to look to your right. I want you to look to your left. I want you to gaze across the room. Is there any guy here in this locker room that you wouldn't want to be in a foxhole with?"

Oh, how I admire Sparky's baseball genius. I'm convinced he knows more about the game than anybody else alive. But baseball and war? Dugouts as foxholes? In the heat of a game, I can see it—competitors, challenges, heroes—especially because victory demands the excellence of individual efforts woven into the singular purpose of the team. But when the lights over the field click off, when the ground crews have raked the infield and covered it, when the players have signed their last autographs and are heading home to tend wounds or wounded egos, I think baseball isn't war. Sit in the stands and smell the fresh air. Wait and wait and wait while a batter fights off lousy pitches, protecting the plate. Suck in some breath when it looks like the runner at third is bolting toward home and the guy at the plate shows bunt. The richness of that kind of anticipation isn't like war at all. Think about it. It's like love.

"You've got to step and throw, Rach. Step and throw. Like this."

My grandfather in the front yard, wearing tan slacks, loafers, and a beige pullover in spite of or to spite the heat. He was strong and square, short. A boxer back in the day, not a ballplayer—he claimed to have been one fight away from a few rounds with Joe Louis during a tournament in Detroit in the 1930s. Later, when my grandfather was sick and thin and too frail to change out of his maroon terrycloth housecoat, it was this image I would choose to see: an athlete in a robe, fighting for his life.

"I know," I said, and of course I did.

"'Course you do," he said; caught the ball, stepped, tossed. "You don't want to throw like a girl, do you?"

My grandfather's words swerved and curved like the goofiest pitch; he always said what he meant, but he never seemed to mean what he said. He was subtle about it: a twitch of the mouth, a hand scratching his gray-ish buzz, his fingernails clacking against the table: dat-dat-dat-dat-dat (shave-and-a-hair-cut), dat-dat-dat-dat-dat. What's worse, he lured unsus-pecting children into his treachery. He'd give my cousins and me carrots and instruct us to hunt for rabbits by walking softly along the path in the backyard and whispering, "Here, Hassenpfeffer. Heeeeeerrrrreeeee, Hassenpfeffer." As a toddler, when he disapproved of where my parents were living, he taught me to recite, "My name is Rachael Jean Perry, I'm two years old, and I live in the ghetto." In the third grade, he assured me that the ladies behind the counter at the cafeteria would be delighted to hear how I thought Salisbury steak was good for my bowels.

I forgave my grandfather his trickery, though, because it was impossi-ble not to—he was the only person in the world who shared with me my two favorite things: books and baseball. We watched the Tigers together; he bought me books by authors called Perry so that I would know what it was like to see my name in print. And, when I got older, my grandfa-ther hardly ever missed any of my high school softball home games— even when, I found out later, his guts must've been twitching and ach-

ing at the cancer that was starting to eat at him from the inside out. My
freshman year of softball at South Lyon High School was not exactly the
glory days, but I got to play shortstop and I got to bat cleanup and I most
certainly did not throw like a girl. It went like this: my grandfather would
drive his red pickup to the edge of the parking lot, which faced both the
back of the high school and the backstop of the softball field. He never
sat with the other parents, raised a ruckus, honked his horn, or waved.
In between games (we almost always played doubleheaders), I'd trot out
to his truck and peel back the wrapper of a cheeseburger he picked up
for me in the fifth inning (or, on a Saturday morning, it would be an Egg
McNuthin), as he told me what he thought of the opposing team's pitcher,
if I needed to adjust my swing, whether I was running the bases aggres-
sively enough. Then he'd grab my shoulder as if to shove me back onto
the field and say, "Don't forget to step and throw."

The year my grandfather died the Tigers went 65-97. His illness worked
at him with the patience of a long pitcher's duel; we were all worn out by
the expectations of death. Still, he and I watched some ball games together that summer. I brought him nacho cheese and sat on the edge of my
mom's old sofa. He was uncharacteristically quiet. I didn't pry. Really,
the games did the talking for us, as we passed the chips and cheese back
and forth and watched the Tigers play.

In the mid-1980s in little Ortonville, Michigan, Brian Spanke was the
closest thing to Lance Parrish I could find.

Naturally, he was a catcher. He wore the number 13, and had this way
of flipping back his mask to rest on his forehead that made him seem an
adventurer or a ship's captain, a man in charge of his surroundings. He
frequently talked and joked with the home plate ump; I could see them
both nodding when Spanke threw the ball back to the pitcher, or those
few seconds of down time when the next batter approached from the
on-deck circle. Sometimes I watched him from behind the backstop,
sometimes the far side of the field where parents set up lawn chairs and
spread out blankets.

Ortonville, at the time, was too far from Detroit to be considered a
suburb. It had a couple of restaurants, a hardware store, a library, and a

pizza place; on the outskirts, there was a tire store, a liquor store—where we were allowed to ride bikes, exchange empty pop bottles, and buy base-ball cards and candy—and an ice cream shack that twirled up soft serve cones: sprinkles on them if you won your ball game, no sprinkles if you didn't. But the heart of Ortonville, almost as if it had been purposeful-ly designed this way, almost as if the flow of traffic deliberately pointed drivers down and around a bend, could be found under the bright yel-low lights of the Little League fields.

There were games on every night. The girls played Tuesdays and Thursdays, the boys Mondays, Wednesdays, and Fridays. We wore bright jewel and pastel T-shirts stamped with the names of local sponsors: A&W, Metro 25, Frosty Boy, Regina's Home for the Elderly. Some of us wore white or gray baseball pants; some just a pair of old sweats or torn-up blue jeans. And when we weren't playing, we were watching. If my child-hood memories were a film, the opening scenes would be these: my father reading our lineup that he'd sketched out with a fat, orange pencil from the back of a lumberyard receipt; the smells of little girls—aerosol hair-spray and cheap fruity perfume and baby powder mosquito lotion—floating over the dirt of the baseball field; how right it felt to hit a pitch in the bat's sweet spot, regardless of whether I got on base; Spanke behind the backstop, the flash of his gold chain necklace and silver braces, his hands stuffed in his pockets.

Brian Spanke, like Lance Parrish, eventually broke my heart. Brian would do it sooner, with a girl from my very own softball team who was lovely and charming and had the creamiest, softest-looking skin I had ever seen. Lance would wait until the Tigers could've had it all again—there was bickering, the newspapers said, over a pay raise or no pay raise, and though I'm pretty sure he made more in a week of playing ball games than my father did in an entire year of building and fixing houses, I some-how couldn't hold it against him. Lance would split to Philadelphia, of all places, and play for a National League team that I couldn't watch on television—then he would spend the next several years moving from city to city, team to team, as penance, I'm sure, for my heartache.

Today, I have a thirteen-month-old daughter who is just learning how to throw: sippy cups from her highchair, foam blocks from a box, stuffed toys to the ground. Often, I'm amazed at her ferocity, her power. She doesn't get much distance—she releases each object at random points in her windup—but the look on her face is such a mixture of determination, frustration, and utter happiness that I can't help but wonder at her potential. Though it's tough for me to picture her as an adult or even an older child, I already imagine what she would look like in a baseball uniform: baby gut hanging over her belt, a little thick through the biceps and thighs, wispy hair feathered back like a blond Darrell Evans. Maybe she'll even wear a catcher's mask.

"You sure had it for Lance Parrish," my father says now. "I don't know why. Most kids, they pick guys who play their positions."

"Not you," he laughs. "You and Lance."

As an adult, I realize the resemblance between my father and Lance Parrish is uncanny. The same sturdy jaw, thick moustache, long nose; the same kind of mythic physical strength. My search for a hero should have started at the front of the dinner table rather than behind the plate, but perhaps I knew that all along. And, as luck would have it, I got my Lance Parrishes—three of them, in fact: a grandfather of a Lance Parrish, a father of a Lance Parrish, and a husband of a Lance Parrish (who—I am not making this up—is also 6´3˝ and 220 pounds, but who makes a much better first baseman than catcher).

Yes, in the spring, when the ground thaws and we can go outside without jackets, I'll wake my daughter up one morning—perhaps, if the timing is right, on opening day—by whispering this into her crib:

> For, lo, the winter is past,
> The rain is over and gone;
> The flowers appear on the earth;
> The time of the singing of birds is come,
> And the voice of the turtle is heard in our land.

Eventually—maybe not that first day we go outside to play catch, because that will be just for the two of us—I will teach her about a Tiger legend named Lance Parrish and the glory of a championship baseball team, about the wave, about how beach balls aren't only for beaches and the echoes of an abandoned place don't always fall silent. Over time I will teach her how to step and throw—I *will* teach her to throw like a girl—and finally, hopefully, I will teach her how baseball is beautiful and irresistible and as irreversible as a first kiss: if it is a part of her childhood, it will be a part of her forever.

34. Sunday Morning Ball at the J
David Carkeet

When I was a boy, I played ball for the 49ers, a Little League team in Sonora, California. I labored under the patient tutelage of my Methodist Sunday school teacher, who always whistled soft tunes to himself and let our catcher, his son, drive the pickup around in the outfield after practice. Our uniforms were made of wool. We would swim all day at the Sonora Pool, then, eyes blurry with chlorine, we would sweat and scratch our way through the game. Then it was off to the brand-new A&W Root Beer stand, which seemed to have plunked into our little town directly from paradise, as a sample.

I read somewhere that everyone has one sharp memory from childhood of a brilliant moment in sports. My moment, which is really only half brilliant, happened at one of those summer evening games. I patrolled at shortstop. The batter was a quick grower with a big head, and big teeth, too: Mike Recek. He was from an even smaller town higher up in the Sierras, and he was known to us from days of yore for single-handedly conquering our elementary school in every sport there was. Recek. We called him "Reject" and "Paycheck" because we were hilarious.

Naturally, Recek hit the ball to me. I had fervently wished that he not do so, and such a wish is a magnet to the ball. It was a mean one-hopper, and somehow it ended up wedged between my forearms. The amazed ump said under his breath, "Nice stop!" (Our trucker-catcher told me this later.) I gunned the ball to first—or rather, toward first, or rather, more toward first than any other base, though not by much. After all, it was Mike Recek, Foothill Olympian, and who was I to throw him out? Some fundamental failure of self-esteem prevented me from completing the play successfully. Recek's big head ended up at second, where it dwarfed me. But I thought then, and later that day, and later still—in fact, just last night in the shower—*Damn, that was a nice stop.*

I left California to see the world but got only as far as Bloomington, Indiana, where I took up the game again. The Indiana University English Department fielded an intramural team initially named the Wily Porkers after William Riley Parker, who was department chair when the team was first organized. Like literary criticism itself, the team name grew more obscure in the years I played on it: the Wily Swine, the Gray Swine, and, in our championship season, Naked Came the Swine.

I got traded to St. Louis and ended up playing ball in the JCCA Sunday morning men's softball league. I walked onto the field for the first time some twenty years ago, a tentative gentile, quiet but willing to let his bat do the schmoozing. Now, on the second Sunday in April, it gives me seasonal comfort to pull into the rear lot at the J and hike down the grassy hill to the four-diamond field. I scout for familiar faces. Yes, there's the guy who ran into me at second last year. There's the guy with the annoying chatter. There's the guy who always legs a double out of what would be a single for anyone else—*always.*

I know them as one knows specialized friends. I know mostly first names, not last. I know where each one hits the ball and how fast he runs—and therefore how much time I'll have to make the throw to first. I know who gets mad on the field and who makes a mockery of anger. I know who praises and who carps.

I know them by occupation from overheard dugout chat: lawyers, dentists, accountants (their hitting improves after April 15), retailers, a pawnbroker, a social worker (after failed at bats, he hurls his bat in anger at the backstop), a high school math teacher (he likes to call out to opposing pitchers who have given up a run without making an out, "You have an incalculable ERA"), and a veterinarian, who prompted the oddest line I've ever heard on the field, called to him between pitches by a fellow outfielder: "Just how *do* you fix a broken nose on a dog?"

Many of them are closely linked by blood, by marriage, by year-round friendship, or by active participation in the J. Others are outsiders like me, but none *quite* like me. I'm the only one who showed up on an obscure Jewish holiday, puzzled by the empty field. And when a teammate once described an opposing player as "meshugah," he felt obliged to ask if I knew what that meant. Though it was intended as a courtesy, I felt singled out.

But I *am* an outsider. So I observe. I hear things and wonder about them. A small, peculiar jogging track lies below the ball field, where our foul balls and overthrows sometimes end up. "An Israeli track," someone once called it. Why? What does that mean? When a player's wife was due to deliver a child in a few weeks, on the last day of the season a teammate wished him "lots of mazels." Did the speaker make up this variant of "mazel tov," or is it common? I wondered about this and still wonder. And when they look at me, do they ever think *non-Jew*? I hope they don't, but they must.

Sonora, home of the 49ers, was not blessed with ethnic richness. Its population broke down as follows:

Hispanic	80
Jewish	8
African American	1
Asian	0
Other	0
People Like Me	2,411
Total	2,500

If Clinton's cabinet looked like America, Ike's looked like Sonora. The one black man in town was blessed daily with the dubious praise, "Why, I don't even think of him as a Negro." The two Jewish families escaped comment, at least within my hearing. I entered college in giddy ignorance of other peoples. Trying to impress a freshman girl I had just met, I made a guess at her religion. "Catholic?" I said. I had left her name out of my calculations: Leah Silberstein.

Some years later and a little less ignorant, I married into the tribe, which ultimately brought me to the J. Coming out of a yoga class there, my wife saw a poster for the men's softball league. She knew I pined for a return to the diamond. She knew of my longing for another chance to throw out Mike Recek, whose name I mutter in fitful sleep. She signed me up.

It has turned out to be a perfect league for me. The quality of play is good, but it's frequently bad enough to give one comfort in one's own naked shame. The intensity is high but not fanatical. There are arguments, occasionally loud ones, but nothing worse. At the end of one testy game, a dentist began to menace the opposing captain, who stopped him with the words, "I'm a lawyer—touch me and I'll sue your ass." That was the closest thing to a fight that I've ever seen.

As ballplayers, they *care*. They want to be good, much better than they are. When they pop up, they cry out in anguish. An infield bobble can become a crisis of introspection. Most of them are Cardinals-raised, and they know the lingo. They call the ump "Blue" without self-consciousness. They know a skillful play from a lucky one; "look what I found!" is the standard jeer for the latter. "Pick me up" is the way they own up to an error. "Shake it off" signals their forgiveness of yours.

Of course there are days when the league is less than idyllic. The fields are pebbly and erratically graded, and a ground ball can be punim-threatening. Diamond number four lacks a water fountain, and, as Casey Stengel said of the old Busch Stadium, "It holds the heat well." Sometimes the jokes are tiresome, especially the ones about aging ("You would have beaten that throw last year!"). Jokes about aging are never funny, especially to one who, to avoid being felled by the rifle shot of a pulled hamstring, must arrive early every Sunday for extra stretching.

Over the years, players perhaps wiser than I have retired, and I miss many of them. What happened to Handelman? Where is the third Brodsky brother? Where is Ronnie? Where is pesky Harold? Fleet-footed Rick? Witty Shawn? I have come close to hanging up my rubber cleats. I know that I could get hurt. I know I need to grow up and stop throwing out Mike Recek. Summer commitments have taken me away for a year here and there. A new baby made me shelve my glove for three years. Each time I quit, I thought it would be for good. But such an ache! It sent me back, nervous at first, but then I was immediately heartened by the welcome, the warmth, the foolish communal joy.

I see things simply now. To quit this league is to die. To quit playing ball is to accept the end. So I will keep showing up on Sunday morning until they carry me off. When this happens, when the ballplayers watch me being borne up the grassy hill on a stretcher, I hope at least one of them turns to another and says, "Was he Jewish?"

35. Good-byes

Tom Stanton

On the drive to Tiger Stadium Sunday morning, I turned off the interstate onto Van Dyke Avenue, one of several major roads that head out of Detroit like spokes from a hub.

Streetcars once ran here, past bright stores and sidewalks bustling with activity. It wasn't a wealthy neighborhood but it was lively and safe. Now boarded buildings line Van Dyke, interrupted by beauty salons, pawnshops, and missionary churches with barred windows. It's the kind of place where visitors check the locks on their car doors and time the traffic signals to avoid stops.

Yesterday, after I passed the railroad tracks, the streetscape became familiar. Lyford was on the right, bordering the hilly field where Dad played as a boy and where Uncle Teddy choked a kid until he turned blue and where Johnny Castiglione searched for chunks of coal that fell from trains. Up further on the left was Georgia Park, the site of Dad's success against Hal Newhouser. I passed Elgin, Wisner, and Montlieu streets. Along the stretch would have been Temrowski's Drug Store, C. F. Smith Grocer, and Forest Lawn Bar, where Uncle Tom played war flipping bottle caps as his oldest brothers fought the real thing overseas. Talenda's Bowling, once a Club Crusader hangout, had become a liquor store, and next to the former Maurie's Candy Store were the skeletal remains of the greenhouse where the Stankiewicz kids pooled their money for Grandma's Easter corsages. Nature had reclaimed the spot, twines and trees consuming the framework.

I turned right onto Nuernberg at Holy Name Church, now St. James Baptist. A security guard stood outside the wooden doors, watching parishioners' cars. Behind the church was Holy Name School, where Dad listened to the final game of the 1935 World Series, and behind it was the auditorium, now occupied by the Police Athletic League. Somewhere pinched between these buildings there had been a ball field where Uncle Bucky challenged the unspoken church-league color barrier. In 1934, long before Jackie Robinson became a Dodger, Bucky recruited Jack George, a black teen, for Dad's squad. "Bucky was trying to get people riled up," Dad said recently. "But nobody said nothing because Jack George was a hell of a pitcher. He didn't stay on our team long. He was too good." (Incidentally, it would take another couple decades for the Tigers to put a black player on their roster.)

At Gilbo I turned and headed back toward Montlieu. There were fields where homes once stood and a hungry dog sniffing for food. There was a car on blocks and another with its hood up and a man working on the engine. There were houses, as well, one with a potted mum in a front window.

In the late 1970s Uncle Teddy moved from the neighborhood. Within days the home was stripped of bricks and siding, then set afire, the Babe Ruth cards still in the wall. Eventually its charred bones crumbled.

Uncle Clem visited at Christmas in 1985 and he asked to be driven to Montlieu Street. He needed to see for himself. As we approached, his lips tightened around a Newport cigarette and he blew smoke into rings.

"Oh, for chrissakes," he said, looking at the lot.

Fresh snow, like a coroner's white sheet, covered the land. He turned away.

"It's as if we were never here," he said.

It is discourteous—and perhaps wrong and conceited—to say that this neighborhood died when it deteriorated, when it became something different from our memory of it. Half of the houses have disappeared since my father's boyhood but families still live here. Children still walk to church in their dress clothes, though contrasted by a backdrop of vacated buildings. A colorful, molded-plastic play set accents one yard and kids probably play ball on sunny afternoons. By my eyes this area hasn't changed much in fifteen to twenty years. It wasn't the kind of place I would have chosen to live then, it's not the kind of place I would choose to live now. But I keep coming back, like the Canada geese that land each autumn near my house at a driving range that used to be a wide-open field.

Some architects say we cannot ignore the history of a property. There is memory associated with it. They compare it to a palimpsest, parchments that in Roman times were scraped and reused but retained shadows of earlier markings. Land is like that, etched by its past.

As kids we write our names on walls and carve them into trees and onto park benches. As adults we buy video cameras and commission family portraits. If we're rich, we may give money to be honored with a hospital wing, a library, or a park. Ultimately, our names are marked in stone and cemented into the ground amid trees and grass. All of this for a little immortality.

It's for the same reason that we want the terrains of our youth to remain forever as we remember them. For as long as they do, a part of us also remains.

Twenty-four weeks ago on a chilly day in April, I began this journey. Today, Monday, September 27, I will complete it, having seen all eighty-one home games, including this one, the last at Michigan and Trumbull. It's almost 10:00 a.m. and already Howard Stone has been in his parking lot for five hours. He arrived before the sun cast its first long shadows of morning, before the TV trucks had pulled up. This afternoon, after the cars have been parked, he will do what he hasn't done all year: see a game.

"I'm going with my son-in-law," he says. "We're going to bond."

Though the gates won't open until 1:30, a few fans have begun circling the stadium, looking protectively at the dull, blue-tiled wall as if to say, "We'll get through this together. We're right beside you."

Inside, Amzie Griffin cleans his glass shelves and sets out merchandise.

"Thirty-nine years," he says. "All in all it's been a good run. It's going to be sad for me tonight. I like it here. As a matter of fact, I love it. I'll never say good-bye. I'll always drive by and say, 'See you later.' As you can tell I'm getting a little emotional about it. I raised three of my children here, my two oldest boys and my youngest daughter. They worked with me and now my granddaughter does."

A busy day lies ahead for Amzie. Crowds will be enormous, lines congested, emotions high.

For the moment, though, I walk in solitude along the concourse with shafts of light sliding through slats and fences. I climb the ramps that lead to the center-field bleachers, to the top row under the scoreboard where my rose-gardening grandpa sat in the late 1930s, and then back down to the lower bleachers where I met architect John Lee Davids and Pete Munoz, who never did get Ken Griffey's autograph, through the narrow gate that separates the cheap seats from all others and up the tunnel near the visitors' bullpen, dodging the worker who hoses the cement walkway; past one dugout and up the cracked steps to where Zack saw his first game and up further to the top level, passing Mary Pletta, who readies her hotdog grill, and over a catwalk into Al the Usher's area—he's not around yet—as team president John McHale Jr., in red bow tie, strolls by alone and acknowledges pitcher Dave Mlicki, who pans the park with a video camera. I notice the front-row seats where Dad, Uncle Teddy, and I sat and from which I called down to Willie Horton as a game played on the field. He was on the dugout steps and he waved back. It was my first exchange with someone whose skin was a color different from my own and it shaped me in a subtle way.

Downstairs, relief pitcher Todd Jones, in shorts and T-shirt, poses for photos with the servers who work the boxed seats. Ushers have begun to arrive, a few wearing their retired orange uniforms.

"Get your butt to the gate," Joe Falls yells at one of them. They laugh and hug in the aisle.

In section 217 in the cool shade in my usual seat, I rest my eyes on the field, most of it washed in sunlight. Near third base a worker softens the dirt with a rake. In center a sprinkler sprays the grass, the water glistening like diamonds on green felt. Through the mist, I see the white number 440 on the farthest part of the outfield wall, proclaiming the exaggerated distance from home plate, daring hitters to swing for it. Soon the lines will be chalked, the bases anchored, and the plate painted white. The sight is serene and sublime and comforting, too, for in all my years of coming here the field has looked the same. The wooden seats were removed in the 1970s, the walls painted blue. The Tiger Plaza, a food court, was added in the 1990s. The park has changed some. But the grass has always been green and the flagpole has always stood in fair territory in center field.

This ballpark challenges the notion that you can never go home. For no matter how my life has evolved and how many years have passed and how far my hairline has shifted, I feel like a kid when I come here. This place awakens those spirits and allows me to reclaim parts of myself that otherwise might be lost. Here my life echoes with those of the men and boys who have meant the most to me.

We all need places like this.

I meet Mike Varney in the Tiger Plaza before the game. He drove in from Milwaukee after waking at 3:20 this morning to a wrong-number phone call from Thailand. He had not set an alarm and the call came minutes before he was due out of bed.

"I think it was my dad," he says.

"Your dad passed away in the 1980s, Mike."

"Yeah, but I think he put that call in to make sure I woke up and got here on time. He wouldn't want me to miss this."

We head to our seats and find my father and brother.

The grandstand is a collage of banners, testaments of faith and friendship.

So long, old girl, one says.

This will always be home, states another.

Baseball cries today on a third.

As the 4:05 start approaches, Ernie Harwell introduces Al Kaline, the greatest living Tiger, and the crowd rises for number 6, who is wearing his uniform. Kaline tips his cap and backs away from the microphone, biting his lip. The ovation continues for more than a minute. He steps forward again. The applause builds once more. Kaline bows his head and swallows hard. In the visitors' dugout Kansas City players stand and watch, joined by former third baseman George Brett, the Hall of Famer, who was a rookie in 1974 when the right fielder ended his career.

Kaline recalls his first day at the park.

"I was awestruck," he says. "As a kid fresh out of high school, I suppose that was only natural. Yet today, forty-six years later, I stand before you a grown man, a veteran of thousands of games in this park, and again I find myself humbled and somewhat overwhelmed by the events unfolding in front of us."

A quiet has settled on the stadium.

"While common materials may have been used to build this place—concrete, steel, and bricks—the memories are the cement that has held it together for eighty-eight wonderful seasons. . . . Is it a specific game that you will remember most about Tiger Stadium? Maybe Ty Cobb sliding hard into third. George Kell diving to his left. Norm Cash or Kirk Gibson blasting one into the lights in right field. Or will it be a memory of your family and friends, sharing a story with your best buddy or listening closely as your dad tells you of the first time he came to the ballpark years ago?"

At game time Brian Moehler carries out his ritual on the pitching mound, drawing his deceased father's initials into the dirt. Moehler is wearing Jack Morris's 47. Like all of our starters, he is honoring a member of the all-time team. Tony Clark wears 5 for Hank Greenberg and Damion Easley 2 for Charlie Gehringer. Gabe Kapler has Cobb's numberless back—and socks that show.

In the left-field grandstand Uncle Tom wonders about Billy Rogell, who threw out the first pitch. "That man has got to be old," he says. "I used to play in the Billy Rogell Baseball League and he was old then." (Rogell, ninety-four, debuted in the majors in 1925.)

My uncle had such a grand time here in August that he insisted on coming back. He's with his son-in-law and grandson on this Monday. Clogged aisles will keep him from joining my dad today. But they ask about each other and that makes me proud.

Of all the gifts this year has brought, the best has been seeing Dad and Uncle Tom together after decades apart and hearing them talk about Grandpa Stankiewicz, life on Montlieu Street, and baseball. Their rolling conversation transported me to a time when Uncle Teddy and Uncle Clem traded stories in a way that illuminated my life and made me feel part of something bigger than myself.

There is a talent to telling stories and my old uncles possessed it, though their styles differed. An actor by nature, Clem would unwind his tales like taut kite string and they would soar. Teddy did it in such a way that you had to nudge him along with questions. At story's end he would seem as surprised as you by the outcome. Sixty years on, he still would have shock on his face as he remembered waking from surgery on the kitchen table and discovering that the family doctor had not only removed his tonsils but also his foreskin. "I knew my tonsils weren't down there," he said.

Something sad happens to memories as our loved ones die off. Our pool of stories evaporates like salted water on a stove. We remember many, of course, and we add our own. But others are lost forever. When Uncle Teddy and Uncle Clem and Mom passed on, they took a share with them and those can't be reclaimed. But to have Uncle Tom reenter our lives now allows us to replenish the supply. It also makes Dad's life a little more complete.

I've always found that places rouse memories better than songs, smells, or snapshots. A grove of birch trees in northern Michigan recalls my mom, with her easel at the riverbank and her brush moving furiously before the paper dries. The playground at Robert Frost School conjures rivalries and friendships and the time I accidentally split open Ron-Ron Mancini's head with a baseball bat during a game of 500.

Perhaps it's the same with you.

All season I've heard players and fans say that what they will take from this park are memories. I will also. But while I've been blessed with many things in my life, a good memory is not one of them. With the ballpark closed, how long will it be before I forget to remember the sight of William in the front row getting Lance Parrish's autograph? Or Taylor filling every square on his score sheet? Or Zack counting the fans in the bleachers? How long, absent the view from our seats, before my sons forget our times here together?

This final game rolls into the eighth inning, the Tigers ahead 4–2.

Detroit loads the bases for Gabe Kapler. Cameras flash throughout the park in anticipation. But he grounds to the pitcher for a force at home, which brings up Rob Fick, another rookie. On the first pitch Fick smacks a ball onto the roof in right field, assuring the win and earning himself a spot in Detroit baseball history.

As the crowd celebrates, Fick rounds the bases and thanks his father, Charles, who died ten months ago. "I looked up in the sky and thought of my dad," he said later. "I just know he had something to do with all of this."

For the last out Todd Jones fans Carlos Beltran on a ball that bounces to the plate.

Brian Moehler gets the victory. No one leaves the park.

In the ceremony that follows, Tigers of all eras emerge in uniform one by one from the gate in center to serene orchestral music. They head out to the positions they played, unannounced, each one cheered as fans recognize a face on the scoreboard or a name on a uniform.

First Mark Fidyrch, who falls to his knees on the pitcher's mound. Then Bill Freehan, the eleven-time All-Star, as resolute as a palace guard. And Dave Bergman and Dick McAuliffe and Tom Brookens and a parade of dozens more, men in their thirties and forties and on up into their eighties and nineties, some jogging, some walking, some limping, a few riding in carts.

"There's Mickey Stanley," I whisper to Dad.

He nods.

Dan Petry follows. Then a guy name Eisenstadt, whom I don't know.

Dad scrunches his face for three seconds. "Pitched in the thirties."

We name the players as they emerge as if it were a test of our worth as fans.

John Hiller, Steve Gromek, Billy Pierce . . .

This is a forgiving audience. No one stares when your eyes get wet as Willie Horton takes left field. Horton locks his hands behind his head and pulls his elbows forward trying futilely to keep his emotions from escaping. He came here as a boy, played high school ball on this field, and as a star wore his uniform in the streets during the 1967 riots to appeal for calm. His heart is in this city and in this park.

It's the players I worshiped as a kid who draw my tears: Hiller, Horton, and Lolich heading out one last time.

The championship teams of 1968 and 1984 are well represented under these lights. But the men who played on the 1935 team when Dad was a boy are mostly gone now. Greenberg, Gehringer, Goslin, Cochrane, Tommy Bridges, "Schoolboy" Rowe, Pete Fox, Marv Owen, Gee Walker, even Jo-Jo White.

"That looks like Gates Brown," Dad says.

In fact it's Ron LeFlore who has put on a lot of weight.

The man in front of me turns to his friend and shakes his head in amused embarrassment as tears trickle toward his beard.

Jack Morris, Charlie Maxwell, Gates Brown . . .

This final procession is so solemn that even the drunks have quieted.

Al Kaline. Trammell and Whitaker together.

On the field ballplayers pass the folded Tiger Stadium flag from center to home plate, player to player, until, to my surprise, it ends up in the hands of the submarine pitcher, Elden Auker.

When men reach a certain age—seventy-seven, let's say—a difference of a year or five is no longer discernable. It's difficult to tell an eighty-one-year-old man from an eighty-four-year-old if both are healthy. Similarly it's hard to imagine that Dad was thirteen when Auker made it to the Tigers in 1933. There is a ten-year difference in age, yet they look like peers.

"Each of us has touched this flag today as Tiger Stadium has touched each of us. Take this flag to Comerica Park, your new home," Auker says to catcher Brad Ausmus, pausing for Comerica's boos to subside, "and take with it the boyhood dreams, the perseverance and the competitive desire it takes to become a Detroit Tiger. Never forget us, for we live on by those who carry on the Tiger tradition and who so proudly wear the Olde English D."

My dad is beside me in his Tiger ball cap.

Over this half year I've struggled to make sense of this season, to understand my need to be here and my attachment to this field where men play a child's game. I am beginning to understand and oddly I owe some of that understanding to Elden Auker. I would never have guessed it in April.

Auker was a fair pitcher, not the best on the team. He played ten years in the big leagues, never won twenty games, and his earned run average was often near five. Back in late June, appearing on the mound before a game, he provided an epiphany. I saw my father in him and I started to realize and have come to confirm, with Auker before me and Dad beside me, why I've been drawn to this mission. It's almost as if twenty-seven years ago, by mimicking Auker's underhand delivery when we played catch in our yard, Dad set this year in motion, that he was preparing me for the final season.

I've noticed something today. It's not the seventy- and eighty-year-old men who are wiping their eyes. It's the generations that came after them and we're hurting not only for the loss of this beautiful place but for the loss of our fathers and grandfathers—belatedly or prematurely. The closing of this park forces us to confront their mortality and when we confront their mortality we must confront our own. If the park is here, part of my dad will always be here, as will a part of me. A little bit of us dies when something like this, something so tied to our lives, disappears. This season has helped me realize that my life is becoming more like the stories of my father and my uncles, set in places that exist only in memory. In my perfect world Tiger Stadium would be as I've always remembered it and it would remain long after I'm gone to help my boys remember me.

After his friend Johnny Castiglione passed away, Dad delivered another in a lifetime of lessons: We live on through our attachments to people, through our relationships with the ones we love.

The ballpark has nearly cleared as we take a slow walk to gate nine, looking at the overhang and at Newhouser's number 16 and at the green of the field.

"Are you all right, Dad?" I ask, rubbing his shoulders.

"Oh, yeah," he says. "How about you?"

"I think so."

I lay a red rose near the dugout for Grandpa, and we head off into the night.

Contributors

Lee K. Abbott is the author of six collections of stories, most recently *Wet Places at Noon*. His new book, *All Things, All at Once: New & Selected Stories*, is forthcoming from W. W. Norton in 2006. He teaches at The Ohio State University in Columbus.

Jocelyn Bartkevicius teaches creative writing at the University of Central Florida. Her work has appeared in anthologies and such journals as *Hudson Review, Missouri Review, Fourth Genre, Iowa Woman, Gulf Coast,* and *Bellingham Review*. Bartkevicius's essays have received *Iowa Woman* and *Missouri Review* awards as well as the Annie Dillard Award and citations in *The Best American Essays*. She is completing a memoir, *The Emerald Room*.

Rick Bass is the author of eighteen books of fiction and nonfiction, including, most recently, *The Hermit's Story* (2003), a collection of fiction, and *The Roadless Yaak* (2002), an anthology of nonfiction about the last roadless areas of northwestern Montana's Yaak Valley, where there is still not a single acre of designated wilderness. He lives in Montana with his wife and daughters.

Larry Blakely lives in Portland, Oregon, and teaches at Clark College. He's published over a dozen baseball stories in a variety of literary magazines and is the author of a collection of stories, *Dust and Dreams* (Bear Creek Press, 2006). Although he's over fifty, he still keeps his glove oiled, just in case.

Earl S. Braggs is UC Foundation Professor of English at the University of Tennessee at Chattanooga. His collections of poetry include *In Which*

Language Do I Keep Silent (Anhinga Press, 2006), *Crossing Tecumseh Street* (Anhinga Press, 2003), *House on Fontanka* (Anhinga Press, 2000), *Walking Back from Woodstock* (Anhinga Press, 1997), *Hat Dancer Blue* (Anhinga Press, 1993), and a chapbook, *Hats* (Linprint Press, 1989). His novel in progress won the Jack Kerouac Literary Prize. He is a recent winner of a Tennessee Arts Commission Individual Artist fellowship and a Chattanooga Allied Arts grant.

Christopher Buckley is the author of fourteen books of poetry, most recently *And the Sea* (Sheep Meadow Press, 2006). Among his awards are two NEA grants in poetry (1984 and 2001) and a Fulbright Award in Creative Writing to the former Yugoslavia. He has published two books of creative nonfiction, *Cruising State* (1994) and *Sleep Walk* (Eastern Washington University Press, 2006). He teaches in the Creative Writing Department at the University of California–Riverside.

Rick Campbell's most recent book is *The Traveler's Companion* (Black Bay Books, 2004). His first full-length book, *Setting the World in Order* (Texas Tech, 2001), won the Walt McDonald Prize. His poems and essays have appeared in *Georgia Review, Missouri Review, Tampa Review, Southern Poetry Review, Puerto Del Sol, Prairie Schooner,* and other journals. Campbell has won an NEA Fellowship, a Pushcart Prize, and two fellowships from the Florida Arts Council. He is the director of Anhinga Press and the Anhinga Prize for Poetry, and he teaches English at Florida A&M University in Tallahassee. He lives with his wife and daughter in Gadsden County, Florida.

David Carkeet has written several novels, among them *The Greatest Slump of All Time* (Harper and Row, 1984). His memoir, *Campus Sexpot* (University of Georgia Press, 2005), won the Creative Nonfiction Award given by the Association of Writers and Writing Programs. For many years he taught linguistics and writing at the University of Missouri–St. Louis. He lives in Vermont.

Ron Carlson's most recent book is his selected stories, *A Kind of Flying*

(W. W. Norton, 2003). His novel *Five Skies* will be published by Viking in 2007. He is a professor of English and the director of the Graduate Program in Fiction at the University of California–Irvine.

Michael Chabon is the celebrated, prize-winning author of stories and novels, some of which refer to a deceased Pittsburgh Pirates catcher by the name of Eli Drinkwater.

Mick Cochrane is the author of two novels, *Flesh Wounds* (Nan Talese/ Doubleday, 1997) and *Sport* (St. Martin's Press, 2001). His work has appeared in *Minnesota Monthly, Northwest Review, Kansas Quarterly*, and *Cincinnati Review*. He is a professor of English and writer-in-residence at Canisius College in Buffalo, New York.

Hal Crowther is a critic, essayist, and syndicated columnist who lives in Hillsborough, North Carolina. "Dealer's Choice," his column on Southern letters and manners, has appeared in the *Oxford American* since 1994. His fourth collection of essays, *Gather at the River: Notes on the Post-Millennial South* (Louisiana State University Press, 2006), was a finalist for the National Book Critics Circle prize for criticism. His previous collection, *Cathedrals of Kudzu: A Personal Landscape of the South* (Louisiana State University Press, 2000), won the Lillian Smith Book Award, the Fellowship Prize for Non-Fiction from the Fellowship of Southern Writers, and the Book of the Year prize for essays from *Foreword Magazine*. For his first book, *Unarmed But Dangerous* (Longstreet, 1995), Crowther was cited by Kirkpatrick Sale as "the best essayist working in American journalism today." A former newsmagazine editor, screenwriter, and film and drama critic, he won the *Baltimore Sun*'s H. L. Mencken Writing Award in 1992, the American Association of Newsweeklies' first prize for commentary in 1998, and a career prize, the Russell J. Jandoli Award for Excellence, in 2001. A work in progress, "Babe in the Woods," is a book-length essay on innocence. His wife is the novelist Lee Smith.

Philip F. Deaver attended his first professional baseball game when he was eleven, in the company of his father. It was the Cardinals versus the Pirates, summer of 1957. Wally Moon was the Cardinals' left fielder, Al Dark was at short, Eddie Kasko was at third. Back in the day, Deaver played shortstop and third, though in his one summer at Culver Military Academy he played catcher. In all his baseball days he was never allowed to pitch. This doesn't still bother him. Deaver is the thirteenth winner of the Flannery O'Connor Award for Short Fiction for the book *Silent Retreats* (University of Georgia Press, 1988). His most recent book is a collection of poetry, *How Men Pray* (Anhinga Press, 2005).

Andre Dubus was one of our best short story writers. After the accident that crippled him, he became one of our best memoirists. Although he did write one novel, *The Lieutenant* (1967), Dubus was dedicated to the short story and novella genres and published most of his work in small but distinguished literary journals such as *Ploughshares* and *Sewanee Review*. His last collections were *Dancing after Hours* (1996) and *Meditations from a Movable Chair* (1998). His writing awards include the PEN/Malamud, the Rea Award for Excellence in Short Fiction, and the Jean Stein Award from the American Academy of Arts and Letters. He received fellowships from the Guggenheim and MacArthur foundations, and several writing awards are named after him.

Leslie Epstein was born in Los Angeles to a family of filmmakers. Not surprisingly, films have made up a good part of the subject matter of his fiction. He has published nine books of fiction, most recently *San Remo Drive* (2003). His best-known novel, *King of the Jews* (1979), has become a classic of Holocaust literature. In addition to a Rhodes Scholarship, Epstein has received many fellowships and awards, including a Fulbright grant, a Guggenheim fellowship, an award for Distinction in Literature from the American Academy and Institute of Arts and Letters, a residency at the Rockefeller Institute at Bellagio, and grants from the Ingram Merrill Foundation and the National Endowment for the Arts. He has been the director of the Creative Writing Program at Boston University for more than twenty years. His newest novel, *The Eighth Wonder of the World*, will be released in fall 2006.

Gary Forrester, who with his family recently relocated to New Zealand, played center field for the Williamstown Wolves, a baseball club established in 1896 in the Australian state of Victoria. His first novel, *House-boating in the Ozarks*, was published by Dufour Editions (2006); among other things, it recounts the St. Louis Cardinals' bittersweet season of 2003. The piece included here, "Begotten, Not Made," is an excerpt from his second novel of the same title. In the 1990s Forrester composed and performed the music on three bluegrass albums under the nom-de-guitar Eddie Rambeaux.

Lee Gutkind is founder and editor of the popular journal *Creative Nonfiction*, the first and largest literary journal to publish nonfiction exclusively, and the author of a dozen books of fiction and nonfiction. Gutkind's memoir, *Forever Fat: Essays by the Godfather* (University of Nebraska Press, 2003), was partially inspired by an article by James Wolcott in *Vanity Fair* which pinpointed Gutkind as the "godfather behind creative nonfiction." His upcoming book, *Almost Human: Making Robots Think*, will be published by W. W. Norton in 2007.

Jeffrey Hammond, the George B. and Willma Reeves Distinguished Professor in the Liberal Arts at St. Mary's College of Maryland, teaches English and American literature, classical and biblical literature, and nonfiction writing. His creative nonfiction has won a Pushcart Prize, *Shenandoah*'s Carter Prize for Essay, and the *Missouri Review* Editors' Prize. His most recent books include *The American Puritan Elegy: A Literary and Cultural Study* (Cambridge University Press, 2000); and *Ohio States: A Twentieth-Century Midwestern* (Kent State University Press, 2002), which was a finalist for an Independent Publisher Book Award in the essays/creative nonfiction category.

Jeffrey Higa grew up an air force brat; he was always starting over in new schools, new neighborhoods, new teams. He thought that when he grew up he would settle in one place and live there the rest of his life. When wanderlust hits you early, however, it leaves a permanent mark. He has spent the majority of his life roaming around the country, stopping at several writing programs before he graduated with a master's degree from the University of Missouri–St. Louis. Since then he has published humor and fiction in *Honolulu*, *Bamboo Ridge*, *Zyzzyva*, and *Sonora Review*, and won the 2003 *Kumu Kahua* Playwriting Contest. He currently lives in Honolulu with his wife and daughter.

Peter Ives directs the Writing Center at Rollins College in Winter Park, Florida, and was a creative writing teacher at Trinity Preparatory School. His work has appeared in a number of anthologies and literary journals, including *Gettysburg Review*, *Laurel Review*, *Florida Review*, and *Fourth Genre*. He is completing a collection of essays.

Richard Jackson is the author of nine books of poetry, most recently *Heartwall* (winner of the University of Massachusetts Juniper Prize, 2000) and *Unauthorized Autobiography: New and Selected Poems* (Ashland, 2003). The editor of two journals, two anthologies, and a couple dozen chapbooks of translations, Jackson is the winner of Guggenheim, NEA, NEH, and Witter Bynner fellowships as well as the author of five Pushcart selections. He was a Fulbright Exchange Poet to the former Yugoslavia and is the author of two prize-winning critical books. His poems have been translated into a dozen languages. Jackson teaches at the University of Tennessee–Chattanooga, where he directs the Meacham Writers' Conference, and at Vermont College, where he coordinates the Slovene residency; he has won teaching awards at both schools.

William Least Heat-Moon was born of English-Irish-Osage ancestry in Kansas City, Missouri. He holds a doctorate in English and a bachelor's degree in photojournalism from the University of Missouri. In addition to his breakthrough book *Blue Highways*, he is also the author of *PrairyErth* (Houghton Mifflin, 1991) and *River-Horse* (Houghton Mifflin, 1998).

Lee Martin is the author of two novels, *The Bright Forever* (Shaye Areheart Books, 2005), a finalist for the Pulitzer Prize in Fiction, and *Quakertown* (Dutton, 2001); two memoirs, *Turning Bones* (University of

Nebraska Press, 2003) and *From Our House* (Dutton, 2000); and a story collection, *The Least You Need to Know* (Sarabande, 1996). His stories and essays have appeared in places such as *Harper's, Georgia Review, Creative Nonfiction, Fourth Genre, River Teeth, Prairie Schooner, Kenyon Review,* and *Southern Review.* Martin has won fellowships from the National Endowment for the Arts and the Ohio Arts Council. He directs the Creative Writing Program at The Ohio State University.

Michael Martone's new book, *Michael Martone*, a memoir in contributor's notes, was published by FC2 in 2005. *Unconventions*, a collection of essays on writing, also appeared in 2005, published by the University of Georgia Press.

Cris Mazza is the author of a dozen novels and collections of fiction. Her most recent books are the novels *Disability* (FC2, 2005) and *Homeland* (Red Hen Press, 2004), and a memoir titled *Indigenous: Growing Up Californian* (City Lights, 2003). Among her other notable titles are *Dog People* (Coffee House Press, 1995 and 1997) and *Your Name Here:___* (Coffee House Press, 1997), plus the critically acclaimed *Is It Sexual Harassment Yet?* (FC2, 1992). She was coeditor of *Chick-Lit: Postfeminist Fiction* (FC2, 1995), *Chick-Lit 2 (No Chick Vics)* (FC2, 1996), and other anthologies of women's fiction, and was a recipient of an NEA fellowship. In spring 1996 Mazza was the cover feature in *Poets & Writers Magazine*, and in December 2004 *Poets & Writers* published her essay "Chick-Lit and the Perversion of a Genre."

Kyle Minor was born in West Palm Beach, Florida, and lives in Columbus, Ohio. His work has appeared widely in literary magazines including *Quarterly West, Carolina Quarterly, River Teeth, Antioch Review,* and *Mid American Review.* Minor's stories and essays have won several literary awards, most recently from *Atlantic Monthly.* He is a regular book reviewer for the *Columbus Dispatch* and editor of the *Frostproof Review.* He teaches fiction writing and composition at The Ohio State University.

Dan O'Neill was born January 31, 1953. He was named by dedicated St.

Louis Browns fan Larry O'Neill after former Browns manager Daniel Phillip Howley (1927–29). Having graduated with a bachelor of journalism in 1981, O'Neill initially worked as sports editor of the *Tri-County Journal* in Pacific, Missouri, where he wrote, photographed, designed, pasted, and prayed over a weekly sports section. O'Neill was hired by the *St. Louis Post-Dispatch* in February 1985 after a successful tryout covering a dirt track auto race. His career highlights include lunch with Stan Musial, spring training chat sessions with Whitey Herzog, and being one of only two people he's aware of to witness the 62nd homer of both Mark McGwire and Sammy Sosa.

Susan Perabo is writer in residence and associate professor of English at Dickinson College in Carlisle, Pennsylvania. Her story collection, *Who I Was Supposed to Be* (1999), was named a Book of the Year by the *Los Angeles Times*, *Miami Herald*, and *St. Louis Post-Dispatch*. Perabo's first novel, *The Broken Places*, was published in 2001. Her nonfiction has recently appeared in several magazines and anthologies, and she is currently at work on a new collection of short stories. She holds a master of fine arts degree from the University of Arkansas–Fayetteville.

Rachael Perry's first collection of stories, *How to Fly* (Carnegie Mellon University Press, 2004), doesn't have any pop flies, sacrifice flies, infield flies, or fly-outs, but she hopes you'll like it anyway. She lives and writes in South Lyon, Michigan, where she tirelessly cheers on the Tigers and holds her breath for another pennant.

Kurt Rheinheimer's short story collection, *Little Criminals* (Eastern Washington University Press, 2005), includes two baseball stories. His fiction and essays have appeared in many magazines and newspapers, including *Redbook*, *Glimmer Train*, the *Baltimore Sun*, and others. He lives with his wife, Gail, in Roanoke, Virginia, where he is editor-in-chief of the glossy regional *Blue Ridge Country*.

Louis D. Rubin Jr., a native of Charleston, South Carolina, is University Distinguished Professor of English Emeritus of the University of North

Carolina–Chapel Hill. He retired from teaching in 1989 and as editorial director and publisher of Algonquin Books in 1991. Among his books is *The Quotable Baseball Fanatic* (2000).

Luke Salisbury is a professor of English at Bunker Hill Community College in Boston. He is the author of *The Answer Is Baseball* (Times Books), which the *Chicago Tribune* called the best baseball book of 1989, and a novel, *The Cleveland Indian* (Smith), which was nominated for the Casey Award in 1992, and *Blue Eden* (Smith, 1994), a novel in three stories. Mr. Salisbury contributed to *Red Sox Century: One Hundred Years of Red Sox Baseball*, *Baseball & the Game of Life*, *Ted Williams: A Portrait in Words and Pictures*, *DiMaggio: An Illustrated Life*, and *Jackie Robinson: Between the Baselines*. His work has appeared in the *Boston Globe*, *Ploughshares*, *Stories Magazine*, *Pulpsmith*, *Confrontation*, *Fan*, *Elysian Fields*, *Spitball*, and *Nine*. Mr. Salisbury attended the Hun School, New College, and received an MA in creative writing from Boston University. His novel *Hollywood and Sunset* (Shambling Gate Press, 2005) was a finalist for a Ben Franklin, a *Foreword Magazine*, and an IPPY award.

Floyd Skloot's memoir, *In the Shadow of Memory*, won the 2004 PEN Center U.S.A. Literary Award. The sequel, *A World of Light*, appeared in 2005. Skloot's essays have been included in *The Best American Essays*, *The Pushcart Prize* anthology, *The Best American Science Writing*, and *The Art of the Essay*. He lives in Portland, Oregon.

Tom Stanton has been a journalist for twenty-seven years and a Detroit Tigers fan for ten more. He has authored three baseball books: *Hank Aaron and the Home Run That Changed America* (HarperCollins, 2004), *The Road to Cooperstown* (St. Martin's Press, 2003), and *The Final Season* (St. Martin's Press, 2001), which won the Casey Award for the best baseball book of the year. A fourth book, *Ty & Babe*, will be released in 2007 by St. Martin's Press. He is also editor of *The Detroit Tigers Reader* (University of Michigan Press, 2005). He can be reached at http://www.tomstanton.com.

Michael Steinberg has written, cowritten, and edited five books and a stage play. In addition, his essays and memoirs have appeared in many literary journals and anthologies. Steinberg's last book, *Still Pitching*, was chosen by *Foreword Magazine* as the 2003 Independent Press Memoir of the Year. He is also the founding editor of the journal *Fourth Genre: Explorations in Nonfiction*. The fourth edition of his coedited anthology, *The Fourth Genre: Contemporary Writers of/on Creative Nonfiction* (with Robert Root), is forthcoming in 2006.

Tim D. Stone's articles on business, baseball, or German unification have appeared in the *New York Times*, *Wall Street Journal*, *Economist*, *Baltimore Sun*, and *San Francisco Chronicle*. He is writing a novel set in Berlin between German unification and the first Gulf War. He lives in San Rafael, California, with his wife and son.

Robert Vivian's first book was *Cold Snap as Yearning* (University of Nebraska Press, 2001). His first novel, *The Mover of Bones*, will be published in fall 2006 (University of Nebraska Press). His poems, essays, stories, and plays have been published in over fifty journals, and many of his plays have been produced in New York City. A long time ago he was an All-State center fielder in Nebraska. He teaches creative writing at Alma College in Michigan.

Source Acknowledgments

Thanks to the original publishers of these stories:

Dan O'Neill's "The Heat Is On for Cards" appeared in the sports section of the Sunday, July 11, 2004, issue of the *St. Louis Post-Dispatch*.

"The Softball Memo" by Ron Carlson is excerpted from "Mine," *Gentleman's Quarterly* (April 1995).

"Reaching Home" by Susan Perabo first appeared in *Ninth Letter* vol. 1, no. 2 (Fall-Winter 2004).

Robert Vivian's "Death of a Shortstop" originally appeared in the *Mid-American Review* vol. 24, no. 2 (Spring 2004).

River Teeth kindly granted permission for this appearance of "Opening Ceremonies" by Kyle Minor (from vol. 7, no. 1 [Fall 2005]).

"Brothers" by Andre Dubus first appeared in *Salon*, and was included in his *Meditations from a Movable Chair* (Vintage Contemporary Editions, 1999).

"Jimbo" by Rick Bass is an excerpt from *Oil Notes*, which was first published by Houghton Mifflin/Seymour Lawrence in 1989 and re-published by Southern Methodist University Press in 2004.

A portion of Cris Mazza's "My Life in the Big Leagues" appeared in a different form under the title "Diamonds Are a Girl's Best Friend" in *North American Review* vol. 287, no. 6 (November–December 2002).

Kurt Rheinheimer first published "The Bad Case: A 50th Birthday Love Letter" in *Elysian Fields Quarterly: The Baseball Review* vol. 21, no. 2 (Spring 2004), under the guiding hand of St. Paul publisher-editor Tom Goldstein.

"Billy Gardner's Ground Out" by Floyd Skloot appeared in *Antioch Review* vol. 61, no. 2 (Spring 2003): 198–207.

"The Roar of the Crowd" by Leslie Epstein was published in *American Prospect* magazine, May 8, 2000.

"Trading Off: A Memoir" by Michael Steinberg won the 1994 *Missouri Review* Editor's Prize and appeared in vol. 17, no. 1 (Spring 1994).

Lee Martin's "Fielder's Choice" first appeared in his memoir, *From Our House* (Dutton, 2000).

"A Fan Letter to Lefty Gomez" by Jeffrey Hammond first appeared in *Sport Literate: Honest Reflections on Life's Leisurely Pursuits* vol. 4, no. 1 (Fall 2001): 8–22.

"In April, Anything Could Happen" by Mick Cochrane first appeared in an April 1987 issue of the *St. Paul Pioneer Press* under the headline "Unrepentant Twins Fan Retrieves Faith of His Childhood for Opening Day."

"Willie Rooks's Shirt" by Lee Gutkind is an excerpt from his book, *The Best Seat in Baseball, But You Have to Stand!* which was initially published by Dial Press (1975) but has since been published in paperback by Southern Illinois University Press (1999).

Hal Crowther's essay, "Death in the Afternoon," originally appeared in *Spectator Magazine* on April 1, 1988.

"Meat" by Michael Martone originally appeared as part of a chapbook of stories called "Four Men in Uniform" published by *Indiana Review* vol. 10, nos. 1 and 2 (1987): 73–83.

William Least Heat-Moon's short riff on the fastball and TV was excerpted from his book *Blue Highways: A Journey into America* (Little, Brown, 1983), pp. 278–81. Used by permission of the author.

"A Dispatch from Tucson" by Larry Blakely originally appeared in *Sport Literate: Honest Reflections on Life's Leisurely Pursuits* vol. 2, no. 4 (1999): 6.

Sonora Review 40 (Spring 2001) first published "Trading Heroes" by Jeffrey Higa.

"Work-ups: Baseball in the Fifties" is drawn from Christopher Buckley's *Cruising State: Growing Up in Southern California* (University of Nevada Press, 1994).

"Jose Canseco, Hero" by Michael Chabon first appeared in the spring of 2005 in the *New York Times* opinion page following the appearance of several ballplayers before a U.S. Senate subcommittee looking into you-know-what. © 2005 by Michael Chabon. All rights reserved. Reprinted by arrangement with Mary Evans, Inc.

Louis D. Rubin Jr.'s "Babe Ruth's Ghost" was first published in *Sewanee Review* vol. 101, no. 2 (Spring 1993): 240–47.

David Carkeet's "Sunday Morning Ball at the J" first appeared as "Diamonds Are Forever" in the magazine *St. Louis* (March–April 1996): 78–79.

"Good-byes" by Tom Stanton is excerpted from his book *The Final Season* (St. Martin's, 2001).